Psychology Revivals

The Cognitive Neuropsychology of Language

Damage to the brain can impair language in many different ways, severely harming some linguistic functions whilst sparing others. To achieve some understanding of the apparently bewildering diversity of language disorders, it is necessary to interpret impaired linguistic performance by relating it to a model of normal linguistic performance. Originally published in 1987, this book describes the application of such models of normal language processing to the interpretation of a wide variety of linguistic disorders. It deals with both the production and the comprehension of language, with language at both the sentence and the single-word level, with written as well as with spoken language and with acquired as well as with developmental disorders.

The Cognitive Neuropsychology of Language

Edited by
Max Coltheart
Giuseppe Sartori
Remo Job

Psychology Press
Taylor & Francis Group

LONDON AND NEW YORK

First published in 1987
by Lawrence Erlbaum Associates, Ltd

This edition first published in 2014 by Psychology Press
27 Church Road, Hove, BN3 2FA

Simultaneously published in the USA and Canada
by Psychology Press
711 Third Avenue, New York, NY 10017

Psychology Press is an imprint of the Taylor & Francis Group, an informa business

Publisher's Note
The publisher has gone to great lengths to ensure the quality of this reprint but points
out that some imperfections in the original copies may be apparent.

Disclaimer
The publisher has made every effort to trace copyright holders and welcomes
correspondence from those they have been unable to contact.

ISBN: 978-1-84872-309-2 (hbk)
ISBN: 978-1-315-83280-7 (ebk)
ISBN: 978-1-84872-310-8 (pbk)

THE COGNITIVE NEUROPSYCHOLOGY OF LANGUAGE

Edited by
Max Coltheart
Giuseppe Sartori
Remo Job

LAWRENCE ERLBAUM ASSOCIATES, PUBLISHERS
London
Hillsdale, New Jersey

Lawrence Erlbaum Associates Ltd., Publishers
27 Palmeira Mansions
Church Road
Hove
East Sussex BN3 2FA

Reprinted 1989

British Library Cataloguing in Publication Data

The Cognitive neuropsychology of language.
1. Neurolinguistics
I. Coltheart, M.
612′.8   QP399
ISBN 0-86377-036-3

Typeset by Latimer Trend & Company Ltd., Plymouth
Printed and bound by A. Wheaton & Co. Ltd., Exeter

Contents

List of Contributors

Sandra Balliello
Clinica Neurologica dell'Università di Padova, Via Giustinia 5, 35128
Padova, Italy

Rita Sloan Berndt
Department of Neurology, University of Maryland School of Medicine,
22 S. Green Street, Baltimore, Maryland 21201, USA.

Sandra Black
Department of Psychology, University of Toronto, Toronto, Ontario M55
1A1, Canada

Daniel Bub
Montreal Neurological Institute, 3801 University Street, Montreal, Quebec
H3A 2B4, Canada

David Caplan
Montreal Neurological Institute, 3801 University Street, Montreal, Quebec
H3A 2B4, Canada

Alfonso Caramazza
Department of Psychology, The Johns Hopkins University, Baltimore,
Maryland 21218, USA

CNL–A *

Max Coltheart
Department of Psychology, Birkbeck College, University of London, Malet Street, London WC1E 7HX

Gianfranco Denes
Clinica Neurologica dell'Università di Padova, Via Giustinia 5, 35128 Padova, Italy

Andrew W. Ellis
Department of Psychology, University of Lancaster, Lancaster LA1 4YF, England

David Howard
Psychology Department, University College, University of London, Gower Street, London WC1 6BT

Janice Howell
Neurology Department, University of Western Ontario, London, Ontario N6A 5C2, Canada

Remo Job
Dipartimento di Psicologia dello Sviluppo e della Socializzazione, Università di Padova, Via B. Pellegrino 26, 35137 Padova, Italy

Andrew Kertesz
Neurology Department, University of Western Ontario, London, Ontario N6A 5C2, Canada

Helgard Kremin
Unité III de l'I.N.S.E.R.M., E.R.A. 274 du C.N.R.S., 2ter rue d'Alésia, 75014 Paris, France

Jacqueline Masterson
Department of Psychology, City of London Polytechnic, Old Castle Street, London E1 7NT, England

Gabriele Miceli
Servizio di Neuropsicologia, Università Cattolica, Roma, Italy

Diane Miller
Department of Psychology, University of Lancaster, Lancaster LA1 4YF, England

Domenico Parisi
Istituto di Psicologia, C.N.R., Reparto Processi Cognitivi e Intelligenza
Artificiale, Via dei Monti Tiburtini 509, 00157 Roma, Italy

Karalyn Patterson
MRC Applied Psychology Unit, 15 Chaucer Road, Cambridge CB2 2EF,
England

Andrea Pellegrini
Clinica Neurologica dell'Università di Padova, Via Giustinia 5, 35128
Padova, Italy

Giuseppe Sartori
Instituto di Psicologia, Università di Padova, Piazza Capitaniato 3, 35100
Padova, Italy

Myrna F. Schwartz
Moss Rehabilitation Hospital, 12th Street and Tabor Road, Philadelphia,
Pennsylvania 19141, USA

Philip H. K. Seymour
Department of Psychology, The University, Dundee DD1 4HN, Scotland

Tim Shallice
MRC Applied Psychology Unit, 15 Chaucer Road, Cambridge CB2 2EF,
England

Christina Shewell
Department of Speech Therapy, Addenbrooke's Hospital, Cambridge CB2
2QQ, England

Maria Caterina Silveri
Servizio di Neuropsicologia, Università Cattolica, Roma, Italy

Lorraine K. Tyler
MRC Applied Psychology Unit, 15 Chaucer Road, Cambridge CB2 2EF,
England

Virginia Volterra
Istituto di Psicologia del C.N.R., Via dei Monti Tibertini 509, 00100 Roma,
Italy

Preface

This volume is the result of a discussion meeting on "The Cognitive Neuropsychology of Language," held at the Ateneo Veneto, Venice. The meeting could not have been held without the support of the following institutions, to whom we offer our gratitude: Consiglio Nazionale delle Richerche; Comune di Venezia; Università degli Studi di Padova; Istituto di Psicologia dell' Università di Padova; Ateneo Veneto; Cassa di Risparmio della Marca Trivigiana.

In addition, we are deeply indebted to the Assessorato alla Sicurezza Sociale del Comune di Venezia; to the Assessorato alla Sanità del Comune di Venezia; and to Professor G. Vicario, Direttore dell' Istituto di Psicologia dell' Università di Padova, for their helpful support in organising the Conference.

Max Coltheart
Giuseppe Sartori
Remo Job

1 Functional Architecture of the Language-Processing System

Max Coltheart
Department of Psychology, Birkbeck College, University of London, Malet Street, London WC1E 7HX

The contributors to this book share a core set of assumptions about human linguistic behaviour and how it may be studied. The first of these assumptions is that language performance—the perception and the production of written and spoken language—is mediated by an internal information-processing system, the language-processing system, which acts to form and to transform various types of linguistic representations. The second assumption is that this language-processing system is modular in character. The term "modular" is meant to indicate that the system is made up of relatively independent sub-systems—that is, individual information processing components—each responsible for a particular circumscribed linguistic processing task, such as identifying letters, producing spoken words, or accessing semantic representations. The third assumption is that there are two different but equally valid and equally valuable methods for investigating the nature of a modularly organised language-processing system. One way is to carry out laboratory investigations of some language-processing task with normal subjects. Alternatively, one can study people in whom brain damage has impaired the ability to perform certain language-processing tasks. This is "the cognitive neuropsychology of language," a sphere of investigation in which theories about the language-processing system are used to interpret data from patients with linguistic impairments, and data from such patients are used to test and to refine such theories. All of the work reported in this book adopts this approach to the study of language.

Our book is not intended as a basic introductory text. Nevertheless, it does aspire to a degree of comprehensiveness; the book includes material on all the major aspects of language processing. We see the book as providing something like a state-of-the-art review, an attempt to capture what is currently going on in a new and rapidly-expanding field.

This first chapter is not meant as an introduction to cognitive neuropsychology, either; it is meant instead as a guide to the sixteen chapters which follow. Some readers may wish to begin with it, to provide an idea of where they will be going. Others may prefer to read it last, to find out where they have been. General introductions to the subject are available elsewhere: some examples are Coltheart (1985), relevant chapters in Harris and Coltheart (1986), Ellis (1984) and Ellis and Young (1986).

The study of the cognitive neuropsychology of language received a considerable impetus in 1973, when Marshall and Newcombe published their paper "Patterns of paralexia." In this paper, they defined three different varieties of acquired dyslexia (reading disorder caused by brain damage), which they referred to as visual dyslexia, surface dyslexia, and deep dyslexia. What was of particular significance was that a model of normal reading was proposed in this paper, and the three different acquired dyslexias were interpreted as three different patterns of impairment to this multicomponent model.

The impetus provided by this paper was two-fold. Firstly, a considerable amount of research in the decade following the paper was devoted to learning more about the characteristics of two of these dyslexic syndromes: deep dyslexia (e.g., Coltheart, Patterson, & Marshall, 1980), and surface dyslexia (e.g., Patterson, Marshall, & Coltheart, 1985). Secondly, additional acquired-dyslexic syndromes were defined and interpreted in relation to models of normal reading (phonological dyslexia, for example—see Beauvois and Derouesné, 1979, and Shallice and Warrington, 1980); and subsequently syndromes of impaired *spelling* were also defined and related to models of normal spelling (e.g., Beauvois & Derouesné, 1981; Bub & Kertesz, 1982; Ellis, 1982, 1984; Hatfield & Patterson, 1983; Shallice, 1981).

There can be no doubt that the fractionation of "acquired dyslexia" and of "acquired dysgraphia" into specific syndromes, and the efforts to interpret these syndromes in relation to models of normal reading and spelling, have allowed considerable progress to be made in our understanding of normal and abnormal processes in reading and spelling. But it has also become clear that the syndrome approach is basically a ground-clearing exercise that needs to be supplanted once initial progress has been made.

The reasons for this are perhaps easiest to illustrate with respect to the basic syndromes of acquired dyslexia—deep, surface, and phonological dyslexia. A central symptom of deep dyslexia is the semantic error—the patient, in a single-word reading task, reads *admiral* as "colonel," *forest* as "trees," or *turtle* as "crocodile." How are we to explain such errors? One possibility is semantic damage: perhaps the semantic component of the language-processing system is degraded in such a way that relatively specific semantic details such as those which distinguish *admiral* from *colonel*, or *turtle* from *crocodile*, can no longer be used. An alternative possibility is a difficulty of access to names: the patient cannot produce the name "turtle," so, instead of simply not responding, chooses something semantically close to the name he cannot find.

Picture-word matching tasks allow us to distinguish between these two possibilities. The deep dyslexic patient is given the word *turtle*, with pictures of a turtle, a crocodile, and some unrelated object such as a table, and is asked to point to the picture that matches the word. If there is semantic damage in deep dyslexia, errors in picture choice will occur. The patient will never point to *table*, but will sometimes choose *crocodile*, since he will not always know whether the word he is looking at is *turtle* or *crocodile*. If the reading-aloud problem is instead one of name retrieval, the picture-word matching task will *not* yield errors. So, do deep dyslexics make errors in this kind of picture-word matching task?

Some (e.g., G.R.—Newcombe & Marshall, 1980) do. Others (e.g., P.W. and D.E.—Patterson & Besner, 1985) do not. The conclusion seems inescapable: for some deep dyslexics the semantic errors are caused by semantic impairment whereas for others they are not. So, is there no single answer to the question "What is the cause of semantic errors in deep dyslexia?" More generally, is there no justification for using one deep dyslexic patient to study an entity, a syndrome known as "deep dyslexia," since there is no guarantee that any one patient will be representative of all?

Surface dyslexia provides the same kind of example. Suppose we find a patient who in oral reading of single words makes frequent regularisation errors such as reading *broad* as "brode," *pint* to rhyme with "mint," or *quay* as "kway." How are we to explain such errors? It seems obvious that the words are not being processed lexically—i.e., word-specific information is not being accessed—so the patients have to read aloud non-lexically, by rules relating orthographic units to phonological units. But at what stage is lexical processing defective? One possibility is that these irregular words are not being recognised as words and so not gaining access to the lexical system at all. Another possibility is that the *pronunciations* of the words are inaccessible at an output stage (even though the words have been recognised correctly at a lexical input stage), so if a pronunciation is required it can only be produced by non-lexical rules.

Tests of comprehension allow us to distinguish between these two possibilities. If the problem is at a lexical input stage, the surface dyslexic will fail to comprehend a word like *quay* as well as failing to read it aloud correctly. If the problem is at a lexical output stage, the patient will understand the word even though misreading it. The question is thus: when surface dyslexics misread an irregular word, do they always also misunderstand it?

Some (e.g., C.D.—Coltheart, Masterson, Byng, Prior, & Riddoch, 1983) do. Others (e.g., E.S.T.—Kay & Patterson, 1985) do not. The conclusion seems inescapable: for some surface dyslexics, the failure of lexical processing always arises at a lexical input stage, whereas for others the failure can be at a lexical output stage. So there is no single answer to the question "Where is the lexical-processing deficit in surface dyslexia?" More generally, there is no justification for treating surface dyslexia as a homogeneous syndrome.

Phonological dyslexia—an impairment in the reading aloud of non-words—provides the same kind of example. Firstly, there may be at least three different sources of the non-word reading impairment. For some patients it is at an orthographic analysis stage of the non-word reading process (e.g., M.S.—Newcombe & Marshall, 1985). For others it is at the stage of assigning phonemes to graphemes (e.g., W.B.—Funnell, 1983a). For yet others it is at a phonological assembly stage (e.g., M.V.—Bub, Black, Howell, & Kertesz, this volume). Secondly, the lexical processing system, whilst functioning well enough in phonological dyslexia to permit words to be read aloud well, may nevertheless be damaged in various ways in various patients (e.g., W.B.'s semantic system was impaired) or may be intact. Thus phonological dyslexia is a heterogeneous condition even though all patients assigned this label have in common poor non-word reading and good word reading.

Other examples of syndrome dissolution are provided in this book's final chapter by Ellis, who argues that the cognitive neuropsychology of language is now at a stage where the syndrome approach is no longer a useful one. His arguments have to do with acquired language disorders. In contrast, it may well be the case that the study of developmental disorders of language has not yet reached the stage where it would be profitable to abandon the syndrome approach. Indeed, Seymour in Chapter 16 shows that progress can be made in understanding developmental dyslexia by distinguishing sub-types—that is, syndromes—of developmental dyslexia, such as developmental phonological dyslexia. Future work may reveal that developmental phonological dyslexia is itself a heterogeneous condition, and eventually it may become clear that a policy of assigning individual cases to syndrome categories is no longer paying off. But before this stage could be reached we will need to know more about the syndrome of developmental dyslexia, and further progress will need to be made in developing a model of learning to read that is sufficiently detailed and explicit that it can conveniently be used for interpreting individual cases of developmental dyslexia.

Sufficiently detailed and explicit models of *skilled* language processing, of course, do now exist—at least for processing at the single-word level—and it is because of their availability that cognitive neuropsychology can move beyond the syndrome approach in the study of acquired language disorders. Figure 1 (reproduced from Chapter 13 in this book) illustrates one such model, which is intended to describe a functional architecture for the language-processing system, i.e. to describe the processes involved in the production and the reception of written and spoken single words and non-words. This model is sufficiently general that most of the contributors to this book would be willing to adopt, or at least to countenance, something like it; yet it is specific enough to provide a useful framework within which to discuss all of the chapters of the book—at least those chapters which are mainly concerned with processing at the single-word level. Each of these chapters can thus be thought of as providing information about particular regions of the model as it is set out in Fig. 1.1.

PROCESSING SINGLE WORDS AND NON-WORDS

Visual and Auditory Input Processing

In any model of the kind represented by Fig. 1.1, initial lexical processing of speech or print is mediated by word-recognition devices, one for spoken words and one for printed words. These are labelled "Auditory Input Lexicon" and "Orthographic Input Lexicon" for generality. Different people have proposed different specific ideas about the nature of these devices, such as the logogen model (e.g., Morton & Patterson, 1980) or the cohort model of auditory word recognition, summarised in Chapter 7.

The nature of the *input* to these word-recognition devices (that is, what the components of Fig. 1.1 labelled "Orthographic Analysis" and "Acoustic Analysis" actually do) has been a somewhat neglected theoretical topic. As far as visual word recognition is concerned, the most explicit proposal concerning input to this device is that it takes the form of *abstract letter identities* (Coltheart, 1981; Johnston & McClelland, 1980). On this view, a printed word is first processed by a feature analysis system, and the output of this system is passed on to a system of letter identifiers, which are abstract in the sense that a single identifer responds to all fonts and cases of a particular letter—the same detector, for example, is used to identify *A* and *a*. An alternative arrangement which would have the same effect would be to have separate *A* and *a* detectors which generate identical output.

Once abstract identities have been assigned to all the letters in the input string, these identities are transmitted to the Orthographic Input Lexicon system to permit the word to be identified. Figure 2.1 in Chapter 2 illustrates precisely this approach to the question of what the input is to the Orthographic Input Lexicon. Chapter 2 also provides some evidence that this approach cannot be correct—or, rather, that it is at best only part of the story.

Patient T.M., described by Howard in Chapter 2, was unlike most patients with acquired dyslexia in that he was very poor at one of the most elementary

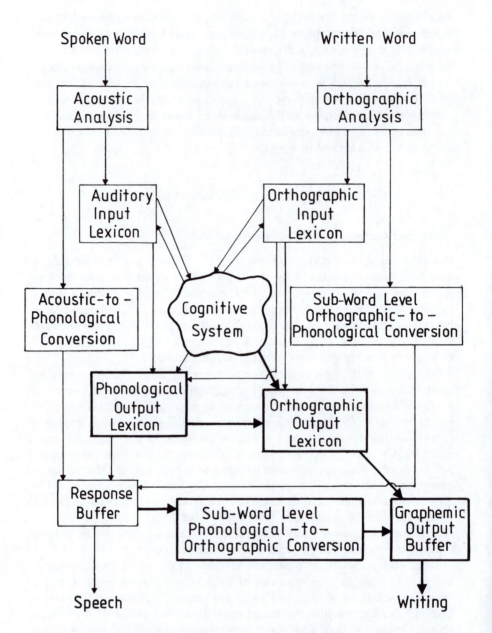

FIG. 1.1 A simple process model for the recognition, comprehension and production of spoken and written words and non-words. (Reproduced from Chapter 13 of this volume.)

reading tasks, cross-case matching. He was at chance, for example, in tasks such as selecting which of the printed letters B, K, D, P corresponds to the printed target *b*. This task is normally used to assess whether the abstract letter identifiers are functioning normally, and so T.M.'s inability to perform the task at all implies that he could not carry out abstract letter identification at all. However, his ability to read words was by no means entirely abolished: he generally read correctly between 30% and 40% of words given to him in tests of single-word reading. Howard suggests that this is because there is not one but two sources of input to the Orthographic Input Lexicon. The first source is abstract letter identities as discussed above: this source is abolished in T.M. The second source is not easily characterised, but must make use of such features of words as idiosyncratic shapes, or must treat words globally in some fashion. This source of input will not permit word identification to be very precise, but will allow at least some degree of correct identification even when the precise system, the one based on abstract letter identification, cannot be used.

Howard also suggests that the global or feature-based input may well be precise enough to be useful when there are strong contextual constraints—as in reading continuous text, where word identification may often simply be a matter of confirming expectations. Seymour, in Chapter 16, proposes a similar two-component theory of input to the Orthographic Input Lexicon in the context of a discussion of the earliest stages of learning to read. His view is that the global or feature-based input system is what is used when children have just learned to read a few words.

The Orthographic Analysis component of Fig. 1.1 is used not only when the input is a printed word, but also when it is a printed non-word. It would seem that the normal reader's ability to read non-words aloud correctly depends upon a sequence of processing stages which begins with the Abstract Letter Identification procedure described above (since the global or feature-based procedure for processing print could not yield sufficiently accurate orthographic information to guarantee correct non-word reading). One view of how non-words are read, expressed in Fig. 1.1, is that, after letters are identified, the letter string is parsed into orthographic segments, the phonological segments corresponding to these orthographic segments are retrieved (by accessing a system of orthographic-to-phonological conversion rules), and then the string of phonological segments is held in a phonological output buffer so that these segments can be blended into a unified phonological representation which is the non-word's pronunciation. As discussed earlier in this chapter, a disruption at any point in this sequence of processing stages will produce a dyslexia in which non-word reading is impaired—that is, a phonological dyslexia.

One such case is described by Bub and colleagues in Chapter 4. This patient, M.V., was poor at reading non-words, but, since she was almost perfect at giving the syllabic sound for single letters, it would seem that abstract letter identification, and also the assignment of phonological to orthographic segments, were both intact in this patient. Orthographic segmentation appears to have been operating too, because her performance on a lexical decision task was sensitive to a variable related to orthographic segmentation. Hence it appears that the main contributor to the non-word reading difficulty in M.V. must be the final stage, the (phonological) Response Buffer: M.V. can obtain the right phonological segments for the non-word, but has difficulties in holding these long enough to blend them into a unified phonological whole.

If this interpretation of the non-word reading deficit is correct, it follows from Fig. 1.1 that M.V. must also have problems in repeating words and non-words and in spontaneous speech, since these tasks too require the Response Buffer. Bub and his colleagues showed that this was so, and indeed showed that reading non-words and repeating non-words yielded exactly the same patterns of error, suggesting that the two tasks were impaired for a common reason. Given Fig. 1.1, the only processing component common to the two tasks is the Response Buffer.

This patient, M.V., contrasts with the patient Lisa, described in Chapter 3. Both patients had a severe impairment in the ability to read non-words aloud, but whilst M.V.'s impairment arises primarily at the response buffer stage of the procedure for reading non-words, Lisa's must arise earlier in the procedure, since her ability to repeat non-words was perfect, unlike M.V.'s. Other cases of acquired dyslexia in which the pattern of impairments include specific difficulty in reading non-words are described in Chapters 13 and 14.

In Chapter 16, Seymour describes a *developmental* case of phonological dyslexia, and proposes that this represents an instance in which the system for orthographic-to-phonological conversion (in Seymour's terms, the grapheme-phoneme translation channel) has not been adequately acquired. When more is known about exactly what this system is like in children who are in the process of learning to read, it will be possible to analyse developmental phonological dyslexia in still more detail (for example, to identify which component of the grapheme-phoneme translation channel is imperfect in individual cases).

We have been considering the nature of the input to the Orthographic Input Lexicon of Fig. 1.1. Much less is known about the nature of the input to the Auditory Input Lexicon. A well-worked-out theory of auditory word recognition, the cohort model (summarised in Chapter 7), proposes that auditory word recognition is carried out on-line, moment-by-moment, as information from a spoken word flows into the system; but the proponents of this theory have not committed themselves as to what the nature of this information is. It might be refined (e.g., the product or a rather thorough phonological analysis of auditory input) or it might be crude (being purely acoustic information as proposed in Fig. 1.1). This distinction between refined and crude input to the Auditory Input Lexicon is analogous to the distinction drawn in Chapter 2 by Howard between two different types of input to the Visual Input Lexicon (abstract letter identities versus a global or feature-based representation). Therefore it is perhaps worth pursuing the idea that both these kinds of input can be used by the Auditory Input Lexicon, since Howard's chapter provides evidence suggesting that this is true for orthographic input (although of course, one could not simply assume that the two systems *must* operate in analogous ways). These are uncharted waters. Detailed studies of patients with impaired ability to repeat auditory input (particularly comparisons between repetition of speech and repetition of such non-speech stimuli as environmental sounds) may inform us here. Some relevant aspects of repetition deficits are described in Chapters 4, 13 and 14.

The analogue to repetition of speech is copying of print. Just as one *could* repeat by mere mimickry of any auditory input, speech or non-speech, so one *could* copy by "drawing," a procedure applicable to any visual input, not just something printed. Is there any evidence that copying of print is more than this; that there is some special procedure for copying print over and above drawing it, just as there is a special procedure for repeating auditory input when it is speech? The answer seems to be yes. Patients who have normal vision but impaired orthographic analysis, or impaired output from the orthographic analysis system, copy print "slavishly," as if a printed word or non-word were an entirely novel visual input made up of entirely novel elements. This was true of T.M. (see Chapter 2) and is frequently reported of patients with "letter-by-letter reading" or "pure alexia" (e.g., Patterson & Kay, 1982), a disorder in which writing can be intact whilst reading is impaired by a defect which appears to be prior to the Orthographic Input Lexicon component of Fig. 1.1. Indeed, one such patient once explained to me that the reason why he copied print poorly and non-fluently was because he was not really copying, he was "drawing." Such observations imply that a direct pathway from Orthographic Analysis to Graphemic Output Buffer (not drawn in Fig. 1.1) needs to be intact if copying of print is to be normal (rather than slow and slavish). This reasoning is used by Miceli, Silveri and Caramazza in Chapter 11: their patient, who had a spelling/writing disorder, could copy well (indeed, he could copy words and non-words extremely well even when the copying was delayed and was in script and the stimulus was in upper-case type). This was taken to imply that the Graphemic Output Buffer was functioning normally in this patient, and hence that the source of his dysgraphia must be damage to some component other than the Graphemic Output Buffer.

In general, then, it appears that the apparently simple tasks of repeating speech and of copying print are not so simple, but depend on several different information-processing stages if they are to be accomplished with normal accuracy and speed. Try copying a word written in the Chinese script, or even a word written in an unfamiliar alphabet such as that used for writing Thai, and you will see that this is so.

Visual and Auditory Word-recognition

Models of the kind set out in Fig. 1.1 assert that the language-processing system includes components specialised for the recognition of familiar written or spoken stimuli, components separate from the system containing semantic information. For any such view, certain "non-semantic" properties of words (such as word frequency, for instance, or structural complexity) would exert their effects at the word recognition stages, whilst semantic properties of words (such as concreteness/abstractness) would affect the system containing semantic information, referred to in Fig. 1.1 by the term Cognitive System.

Observations reported in Chapter 3 are relevant here. In this chapter, Sartori and colleagues describe a patient, Lisa, whose comprehension at the single word level was extremely poor. For example, she was at chance on the task of sorting single printed words into the categories ANIMAL versus NON-ANIMAL. This was not, however, because of failures at the level of the Orthographic Input Lexicon, because the patient could perform reasonably well when asked to judge whether printed letter strings were real words or non-words. A natural inference is, then, that the reading comprehension impairment is due to damage to the Cognitive System. If so, Fig. 1.1 requires that the patient should be just as impaired at comprehending *spoken* words, since according to the model this task uses the Cognitive System too. This implication was confirmed: spoken word comprehension was impaired as well as written word comprehension.

However, the patient could perform well on one task which arguably involves the Cognitive System: sorting words into the categories ABSTRACT versus CONCRETE. Sartori and colleagues propose that this finding implies that an ostensibly semantic distinction (abstract/concrete) is represented within the Orthographic Input Lexicon. One could avoid taking this theoretical step by adopting the view (e.g., Morton & Patterson, 1980; Warrington, 1981) that a fundamental distinction within the Cognitive System is that between abstract and concrete concepts. If the nature of Lisa's impairment of the Cognitive System was that the most general and basic semantic information could be accessed, whilst more specific and detailed information could not, this would account for her ability to perform the ABSTRACT versus CONCRETE classification and not the ANIMAL versus NON-ANIMAL classification. This pattern of performance ought to be the same regardless of whether the input is a spoken word or a printed word, and such equivalence across input modality was in fact observed in this patient.

Similar issues arise in connection with data reported by Patterson and Shewell in Chapter 13. Their patient, G.A., when given an auditory lexical decision task, was decidedly superior with content words compared to function words. Whether this effect is due to grammatical class or to concreteness/abstractness, it is not what would be expected if one performs the lexical decision task at the level of word-recognition systems and if these systems are sensitive only to non-semantic variables such as word frequency. One could retain the latter view by rejecting the former, that is, by arguing that the lexical decision task depends upon access to the semantic level (and so is performed less well with function words because their semantic representations are less rich or less salient). It would follow from this argument that G.A. should show the same effect with *visual* lexical decision, if visual and auditory words contact a common semantic system. But G.A. did not: her lexical decision accuracy with *printed* words was essentially the same for content as for function words. The simplest interpretation of these results is that G.A. had a selective loss of function words within the auditory word recognition system. This interpretation is, of course, inconsistent with the idea that syntactic or semantic distinctions are not represented at the word-recognition level, but is consistent with the proposals of Sartori et al. in Chapter 3, who argue that such distinctions *are* represented at this level. The interpretation is also consistent with the finding that G.A. was remarkably good at a function-word comprehension task with *written* function words (13/14 correct) but not significantly above chance when the function words were *spoken* (8/14 correct; chance 7/14), although, as Patterson and Shewell emphasise, the number of trials here was very small.

I do not mean to argue here that one *cannot* reconcile the data from G.A. with the view that semantic and syntactic distinctions are not represented at the Input Lexicon level. It is a question of constraining, rather than refuting, theories. For example, suppose one argued that G.A.'s difficulties with spoken words arose because it was the *route* linking Auditory Input Lexicon to Cognitive System which was impaired (impaired in such a way that content words were transmitted more effectively than function words). This would account for all the findings mentioned in the previous paragraph, whilst permitting one to retain the view that semantic and syntactic distinctions are not represented at the Input Lexicon level. But this constrains one's future theorising: one is debarred from adopting certain views of the nature of the arrows in diagrams such as Fig. 1.1. Specifically, any view adopted must be one in which it is possible for impairments of these arrows to be word-class-specific; and there are interpretations of the arrows in such diagrams which do not permit such effects.

Let me give another illustration of the way in which the data from G.A.

can be used to constrain theorising. A feature of Fig. 1.1 is that it distinguishes input lexicons from output lexicons. Some theorists do not make this distinction: for example Allport and Funnell (1981) and Funnell (1983b) have discussed the alternative idea that there is a single Phonological Lexicon (used both for recognising and producing spoken words) and a single Orthographic Lexicon (used both for recognising and producing written words: see also Coltheart & Funnell, in press). Adherents of views of this kind would need to consider how any patient could show a selective deficit with function words in one orthographic task (writing to dictation) but not another (visual lexical decision), and also how any patient could show a function-word inferiority in one phonological task (auditory lexical decision) whilst showing a function-word superiority in another phonological task (repetition). All of these effects were observed with G.A., and it is clear that any attempt to reconcile them with a model rejecting the distinction between input and output lexicons is going to compel adherents of such models to adopt particular views on issues (e.g., the nature of arrows in box-and-arrow diagrams) about which they might previously have been able to be agnostic.

Semantics and Semantic Access

Some theories of the kind exemplified by Fig. 1.1 make the strong claim that a single common semantic system is used for understanding spoken words, understanding written words, and understanding pictures or seen objects. Not all theorists accept this view. The concept of a common semantic system for comprehending words whether they be spoken or written is generally accepted. What is *not* generally accepted is the view that words and pictures are comprehended via a single semantic system. Amongst those who challenge the view that there is a single semantic system used both for word and for picture comprehension are Warrington and Shallice (e.g., Warrington & Shallice, 1984; Shallice, this volume). They wish to distinguish between a *verbal semantic system* (used for comprehending printed or spoken words) and a *visual semantic system* (used for comprehending pictures or seen objects) and in Chapter 5 Shallice discusses three lines of neuropsychological evidence which have been used to support the view that there are separate verbal and visual semantic systems. This issue is currently a matter of discussion with Humphreys and Riddoch (1984) and Riddoch, Humphreys, Coltheart and Funnell (in press) arguing that it is possible to explain these neuropsychological findings within the framework of a model which postulates only a single semantic system for all modalities of input.

A distinction central to much of the argument here is between impaired access to semantic representations and degradation or abolition of the representations themselves. If, let us say, words can be understood but pictures or seen objects cannot, even when their visual processing is adequate, the one-semantic-system approach has to interpret this as a difficulty in *access* from pictures or objects to semantics, not damage within the semantic system itself (since such damage would impair comprehension of words too). In contrast, a multiple-semantic-system approach can interpret this pattern as an impairment within one semantic system (visual semantics) with another semantic system (verbal semantics) intact. So if one can ever rule out the possibility that the picture comprehension difficulty is an *access* difficulty in cases like this, then such cases would provide evidence for the multiple-semantic-systems view. Hence Shallice has suggested in Chapter 5 certain criteria which might be used in attempts to determine whether comprehension difficulties are access difficulties or are due to impairments of representations within a semantic system. His suggestion is that if a patient's difficulties arise at an *access* stage then (1) there will be no consistency from occasion to occasion in which stimuli can be understood and which cannot; (2) priming may overcome difficulties in comprehension; (3) it should not be the case that specific information about semantic attributes is more difficult to access than general semantic information such as the superordinate class to which a stimulus belongs; (4) there should be little or no effect of stimulus frequency upon the ability to comprehend the stimulus; (5) slowing down the rate of presentation of stimuli may improve performance.

In contrast, a comprehension difficulty produced by impaired semantic representations should be manifested by consistency across occasions, no improvement due to priming, relative preservation of general semantic information, strong frequency effects and no effect of rate of presentation.

One difficulty in applying these criteria is that they are to some extent model-specific. For example, suppose access from, let us say, picture recognition to semantics does not use a single pathway but involves item-specific links from individual representations in the picture recognition system to the corresponding individual representations in the semantic system. If some of these links are destroyed this would constitute an *access* difficulty for comprehending pictures—but there would be consistency across occasions in which items are not comprehended (those items whose links from picture recognition to semantics have been destroyed). Yet such consistency is taken, according to Shallice's criteria, as evidence that the problem is *not* one of access.

Nevertheless, it is reasonable to expect any model to offer criteria for distinguishing access deficits from representation deficits, even if different models offer different criteria. Adjudication between models is sometimes possible only if such criteria are provided. For example, suppose a patient shows impaired comprehension of spoken and written words, and one then investigates the comprehension of pictures. Any model which proposes that words and pictures are comprehended via a single common semantic system must predict that picture comprehension will also be impaired—but only if the word comprehension impairment is a representation deficit. If it is an access deficit (a difficulty in getting to semantics from words) the semantic system itself might be spared and so picture comprehension could be intact.

It remains to be seen how work along these lines in the future will affect the tenability of the view that there is a single semantic system used for comprehending all modalities of input. If it turns out that the semantic system for comprehending pictures and seen objects is separate from the semantic system for comprehending words, the model of Fig. 1.1 would have to be supplemented by the addition of a separate system of visual semantics, with procedures for communicating between the two semantic systems (to enable picture-word matching to be performed, for example).

Whichever of these views is eventually adopted, it already seems clear that the verbal semantic system itself needs to be divided along the abstract/ concrete dimension, since it is frequently found (for review see, e.g., Coltheart, 1980) that patients can comprehend concrete words but not abstract words (and the reverse pattern has also been reported by Warrington, 1975, 1981; see also Warrington & Shallice, 1984). One such patient is described by Patterson and Shewell in Chapter 13: this patient, for example, was very good at judging whether word pairs were synonymous provided they were concrete words (e.g., *sack—bag*) but completely unable to perform this task with abstract words (e.g., *irony—sarcasm*). This difference in comprehension between the two types of words held equally for spoken and for printed words so that the most economical interpretation of the patient's comprehension impairment is that it arises within the semantic system itself. If so, it must be possible for an impairment of representations within the semantic system to affect the representations of concrete and abstract words differentially, perhaps because concrete semantics and abstract semantics are distinct sub-systems within the semantic system (Morton & Patterson, 1980).

Lexical Input-output Connections

There must be connections from each of the two input systems of Fig. 1.1 to the semantic system (to allow us to comprehend spoken words and printed forms). And there must be connections from the semantic system to each of the two output systems (to allow us to speak and to write spontaneously). Is this sufficient as an account of communications between the input systems and the output systems, or are there any forms of lexical input-output connections which bypass the semantic system?

It is clear that there are. The most strongly implied of these lexical non-semantic pathways is the connection between the Orthographic Input Lexicon and the Phonological Output Lexicon (e.g., Funnell, 1983a, 1983b). Chapter 3 reviews various lines of evidence in support of the view that there are direct connections between these two systems and provides additional evidence from the patient Lisa. She could read aloud many words which she could not comprehend. Her reading aloud could not have been mediated by the system of sub-word level orthographic-to-phonological conversion in Fig. 1.1 (because she was extremely poor at reading non-words) nor by semantic mediation between Orthographic Input Lexicon and Phonological Output Lexicon (because access to semantics from print was not possible for her). Hence her reading aloud must rely on direct connections from the Orthographic Input Lexicon component of Fig. 1.1 to the Phonological Output Lexicon.

The existence of this direct pathway is also implied, in a quite different way, by data from the patient Michel, described in Chapter 14. The (somewhat lengthy) argument here runs as follows. This patient had essentially no spontaneous speech at all. His absence of spontaneous speech could not be ascribed to damage to the semantic system, since his ability to comprehend words was quite good. Hence, within the framework of Fig. 1.1, the abolition of spontaneous speech must be due to impairment somewhere within the route from the Cognitive System to the Phonological Output Lexicon to the Response Buffer. The impairment of spontaneous speech could not be due to damage to the Response Buffer itself, because this would affect repetition and reading aloud too, and the patient could read and repeat single words rather well.

How did this patient accomplish single-word reading? Not solely by using the orthographic-phonological conversion system, because his non-word reading was much worse than his word reading; and not solely by semantic mediation, because, as we have seen, access to the Phonological Output Lexicon from semantics was practically non-existent. This implies that the patient was reading principally by the route Orthographic Input Lexicon to Phonological Output Lexicon to Response Buffer, which not only provides further evidence for the existence of this direct route, but also tells us precisely the location of the defect which abolished his spontaneous speech. It can only be a defect of the *pathway* between the Cognitive System and the Phonological Output Lexicon because these two systems themselves are relatively intact (shown by his good word comprehension, and his good oral reading of words with bad oral reading of non-words).

We have seen, then, that there are various lines of evidence in support of the existence of one form of lexical non-semantic input-output pathway, the so-called "direct route for reading aloud." Is there a means for spelling lexically that is non-semantic—that is, can one proceed from Auditory Input Lexicon to Orthographic Output Lexicon without using the semantic system? It is clear what kinds of results would provide evidence for the existence of such a pathway. One pattern would be where words which were not understood could still be written to dictation, whilst writing of non-words to dictation was impossible. Now, for the patient G.A. described by Patterson and Shewell in Chapter 13, writing of non-words to dictation *was* impossible, whilst writing of words to dictation was possible to some degree. However, there was evidence that the limited degree of writing to dictation accomplished by G.A. depended upon access to semantics from spoken words. So G.A. could *not* use a direct lexical–non-semantic route for writing to dictation. This could be because no such route exists; or it could be because there is such a route but it is abolished in G.A.

Evidence for the existence of this route is, however, provided in Chapter 14. Firstly, the patient described there himself reported that he often could write to dictation words which he did not understand, and indeed that sometimes only after he saw what he had written could he understand what had been said to him in writing-to-dictation tasks, a phenomenon first noted by Bramwell (1897, reprinted 1984). This writing must have been done lexically (since he could not write non-words to dictation at all) but, according to the patient's introspections, it was not done semantically. Secondly, this patient had an impairment of auditory comprehension at the single word level, as illustrated by his difficulties in selecting which of two spoken words (e.g., "obstacle" and "difficulty") was closest in meaning to a target word (e.g., "hindrance"), and his writing to dictation seemed more successful than would be predicted if it had always to be mediated by correct auditory comprehension. Here is some evidence that there is a lexical but not semantic pathway for spelling. Whether this pathway is *direct* (as the analogous pathway for reading is considered to be) is another question, since the patient may be using an indirect though non-semantic lexical pathway (Auditory Input Lexicon to Phonological Output Lexicon to Orthographic Output Lexicon). For further consideration of this point, see Patterson (1986).

Writing to dictation and reading aloud are input-output tasks which involve *transcoding*—that is, the input code differs from the output code in these tasks. Such transcoding is not involved in the input-output tasks of repetition and copying; since the output in these tasks is in the same code as the input, one might expect repetition and copying to involve very little in the way of complicated information-processing. However, as is discussed earlier in this chapter, this expectation turns out to be incorrect. The fact that some patients are much better at repeating words than non-words (e.g., G.A. in Chapter 13) shows that there is a lexical procedure for repeating; and that there must be a non-lexical procedure too, since normal subjects can repeat non-words. In Chapter 14 Kremin argues that there are in fact two lexical procedures for repeating, one which proceeds via semantics and one which uses direct connections from auditory word recognition to spoken word production. Less is known about the processing procedures involved in copying print. As already pointed out, patients with intact vision but impaired access from print to lexicon copy print in an abnormal way—slowly and slavishly. So in normal copying there must be a contribution from lexical processing; but we know little about the nature of this contribution. If one were to find a patient who could copy words but not non-words, and if this hypothetical patient in addition could copy words that could not be comprehended, this would imply that there is a lexical but non-semantic pathway for copying print. Such ideas must remain speculative until much more information about patterns of copying impairment is available. However, it is worth noting here a finding by Nolan and Caramazza (1983); their patient, when copying mixed-case words and non-words into lower-case script, was about twice as accurate with words (86%) as with non-words (42%), suggesting that the Orthographic Input Lexicon has some role to play in copying.

Visual and Auditory Word Production

The model in Fig. 1.1 includes two components for producing words—one for production of spoken words and another for the production of written words. As the model is laid out, these two systems are separate and independent of each other. Not every theorist accepts this claim of independence. No one has proposed that spoken word production is normally in any way dependent upon written word production; but a dependency in the opposite direction, a reliance of spelling upon speech, has been claimed, perhaps most extremely by Luria (1970, pp. 323–324).

> Psychologically, the writing process involves several steps. The flow of speech is broken into individual sounds. The phonemic significance of these sounds is identified and the phonemes represented by letters. Finally, the individual letters are integrated to produce the written word.

This theory of the processes involved in normal spelling is tenable only for languages such as Italian, in which each phoneme has only a single possible spelling. The theory must be wrong for languages for which this does not hold—languages such as English, French, and Spanish, for example. In such languages a particular phoneme can have more than one possible spelling, so a process of mapping phonemes onto letters by rule would yield extremely inaccurate spelling. With the words *dome* and *comb*, for example, the Luria system would have to choose the same spelling for the terminal phoneme /m/, so could not spell both words correctly; yet normals can do so. This could only be achieved by retrieving lexical orthographic information—that is, by making use of entries in an Orthographic Output Lexicon.

Thus spelling cannot be completely parasitic upon spoken word production. However, it remains possible that spelling is in some way *assisted* by speech even if speech production is not assisted by spelling. A model of this kind has been proposed by Nolan and Caramazza (1983) and is discussed further by Miceli, Silveri and Caramazza in Chapter 11. According to this model, when words or non-words are being written their orthographic representations have to be held in a Graphemic Output Buffer, but the contents of this buffer are subject to rapid decay, and so spelling is liable to be inaccurate even in the normal person—except that this decay is counter-acted by a process of refreshment of the contents of the Graphemic Output Buffer. The source of this refreshment is a phonological output buffer (the Response Buffer of Fig. 1.1). When words are being written spontaneously or to dictation this theory proposes that their representations are accessed not only in the Orthographic Output Lexicon but also in the Phonological Output Lexicon, and from the latter system they are transmitted to the Response Buffer. Non-words being written to dictation go directly to the Response Buffer. It is postulated that the Response Buffer is not subject to the kind of rapid decay that characterises the Graphemic Output Buffer. Thus, when some piece of information in the graphemic buffer is decaying it can be boosted by input from the phonological buffer.

As I have already pointed out, and as Nolan and Caramazza (1983) discuss, this theory must be supplemented in some way if it is to apply to the spelling of languages where particular phonemes can be spelled in more than one way. If the vowel digraph in *beef* is threatened with decay, and so the vowel phoneme in /bi:f/ is (via phoneme-to-grapheme rules) the source of the needed refreshment of the orthographic representations, how could a de-cision be made between the possible spellings *beef*, *beaf* and *befe*? The solution to this problem offered by Nolan and Caramazza (1983) is as follows. Suppose one or more letters in the Graphemic Output Buffer have decayed so refreshment is needed. Various legal spellings of the contents of the Response Buffer are generated by a phoneme-grapheme rule system. These are matched to the fragmentary spelling present in the Graphemic Output Buffer. So, for example, if only the first *e* in *beef* has decayed, the candidate *beef* will be preferred to such candidates as *beaf* or *befe*, since the closest match is offered by *beef*.

Miceli et al. point out in Chapter 11 that this theory as it stands also cannot explain "phonological dysgraphia"—very poor writing of non-words with very good writing of words (Shallice, 1981)—since difficulty in using phoneme-grapheme rules (indicated by the poor non-word spelling) would impair the refreshing procedure and so ought to harm word spelling too. So they propose that there are also other ways of refreshing the contents of the Grapheme Output Buffer. One of these proceeds directly from the Ortho-graphic Output Lexicon to the Graphemic Output Buffer. This refreshment procedure is of course available only for words. Miceli et al. suggest that its intactness in the phonological dysgraphic P.R. (Shallice, 1981) is the reason for his almost normal spelling of words.

Evidence which might pose problems for the refreshment theory of normal spelling is provided by Miller and Ellis in Chapter 12. As Miceli et al. acknowledge, if the contents of the Graphemic Output Buffer decay, any patient in whom the refreshment mechanism is inadequate should show a serial position effect in spelling—the later a letter is in a word, the more likely it is that it will have decayed before it can be produced. Miller and Ellis's patient showed no serial position effect of this kind, even though his spelling errors were largely of the visual kind attributable to errors at the Grapheme Output Buffer stage.

In Chapter 15, Denes, Balliello, Volterra and Pellegrino describe the case of a child with no spoken output who nevertheless had achieved a considerable competence in spelling. Since phonological support of spelling could not be occurring in this child, his spelling performance is evidence against the view that such support has to be an important part of the spelling process. However, the fact that a language-impaired child can develop a system for spelling in the absence of phonological support does not necessarily refute the view that, in people who acquired language normally, the spelling system acquired is one which depends on phonological support.

The patterns of spelling error exhibited by F.V., the patient studied by Miceli et al. and discussed in Chapter 11, are also not easy to interpret within the framework of any refreshment-decay theory of spelling. This patient could copy words and non-words from memory virtually flawlessly, even when copying from upper case stimuli into cursive writing. This suggests that the Grapheme Output Buffer itself was not damaged. So the patient's dysgraphia was attributed to an impairment of the phoneme-grapheme conversion system. But if so, why should he have been almost as bad at spelling words as at spelling non-words, given that the authors have acknowledged that word spelling, but not non-word spelling, is supported by lexical refreshment from the Written Word Production system? They use the latter idea to explain why words are spelled well and non-words badly in phonological dysgraphia (Shallice, 1981). To fit F.V. in here, they propose that he did not use the lexical refreshment procedure whereas P.R. (Shallice, 1981) did, and they note that this might be attributed to language-dependent differences in the normal spelling system. If refreshment is in fact needed for normal spelling, it must be substantially lexical when it is English that is being spelled (as in the case of P.R.) but could be entirely non-lexical when, as in the case of F.V., it is Italian that is being spelled. If this is so, then one would expect never to find phonological dysgraphia in Italian, since damage to the phoneme-grapheme system must affect words and non-words equally, rather than harming non-word spelling and leaving word spelling intact.

A rather different approach to theorising about the nature of lexical output systems is adopted by Miller and Ellis in Chapter 12. In relation to spelling, they distinguish between a word level (the Orthographic Output

Lexicon of Fig. 1.1) and a letter level, but propose that the way in which the Orthographic Output Lexicon controls graphemic output is by a system of inhibition and activation of individual letter representations: the activation of a specific entry in the Orthographic Output Lexicon leads to activation of the appropriate letter units at the letter level and inhibition of the inappropriate letter units at this level. On this model, visual spelling errors involving deletions, substitutions and transpositions, such as those produced by F.V. (Chapter 11) and R.D. (Chapter 12) are attributed to weak activation of the letter level from the lexical level.

Miller and Ellis propose that inhibition and activation also characterise the process of producing speech, the idea here being that the Phonological Output Lexicon controls a system of individual phoneme representations. When an entry for an individual word is activated in this output lexicon the appropriate phonemes at the phonemic level are activated and the inappropriate ones inhibited. Neologistic jargon, as shown for example by Miller and Ellis's patient R.D., and as described by Schwartz in Chapter 8, is interpreted as arising because activation from the lexical level (Phonological Output Lexicon) to the phoneme level is abnormally weak. This will cause both activation and inhibition to be inadequate and so incorrect phonemes will sometimes be produced in attempts to speak. It is not clear on this analysis why neologisms would occur in reading, at least not on reading regular words (since the use of the Subword-Level Orthographic-to-Phonological Conversion system allows the reader to avoid using the route from Phonological Output Lexicon to the phonemic level, the route whose damage is postulated to be the source of neologisms). But R.D did produce neologisms in reading regular words (e.g., *public*—"/pʌbək/", *feeling*—"/swɪtiŋ/", and *help*—"/hɛpt/"; Ellis, Miller, & Sin, 1983, p. 129). If, instead, one postulates that it is noise *within* the phonemic level or Phonological Output Buffer, then the observed neologisms in reading regular words and non-words, and also repeating, would be expected. The trouble here (Ellis, personal communication) is that this explanation provides no account of why R.D.'s ability to produce phonological output was greatly affected by word frequency, nor any account of why accuracy of picture naming was not affected by phonemic length of the response required.

This brings to an end our journey through the region charted by Fig. 1.1. We have seen that some parts of this region have been rather thoroughly explored, whilst others—the Graphemic Output Buffer, for example—have not; and there are even disputes about the extent to which Fig. 1.1 can be applied to picture processing. Nevertheless, the contents of this book reveal that a very great deal has been learned over the past five years about the architecture of the language-processing system we use when we do things with words and non-words.

Of course, there is more to language processing than doing things with single words and non-words, invaluable though our knowledge of processing at the single-item level is and will continue to be, and several of the chapters in this book are concerned with language processing above this level—with questions about the comprehension and production of phrases, clauses and sentences, and about disorders which occur at these levels.

SENTENCE PRODUCTION AND COMPREHENSION

In aphasic patients, the ability to produce sentences is often impaired in ways that appear closely related to specifically *syntactic* processing. For example, in spontaneous speech sentences may be abnormally short, or abnormally simple syntactically (e.g., embedded clauses may appear only rarely or not at all). It may sometimes even be impossible for the patient to produce syntactically structured output at all. Impairments of morphological process-ing are also seen: difficulties in producing prefixes and suffixes. Chapter 8 reviews these kinds of difficulties and considers their implications for theories of normal sentence processing.

These are all impairments in sentence production. Analogous deficits in sentence comprehension can be observed, and are also discussed in Chapter 8. When pragmatic cues to sentence comprehension are eliminated, various patterns of sentence comprehension can be observed. Some patients cannot comprehend reversible sentences such as "The girl hits the boy" in sentence-picture matching tasks, provided the pictures include one of a boy hitting a girl as well as one of a girl hitting a boy. Only a picture containing a girl, a boy, and hitting will be chosen: but the patient will not know who is hitting whom. Other patients can perform well with reversible sentences in the active voice, but not those in the passive voice. Patient S.P., described by Caplan in Chapter 6, showed this pattern of performance. Here it may be concluded that the patient, unable to process morphological markers indicating that a sentence is in the passive, adopts the strategy of assuming that the first noun in the sentence is the agent of the action described. This strategy will produce perfect performance with active sentences and zero correct responses with passive sentences. However, this precise pattern is not usually seen: more commonly, the patient achieves some intermediate level of performance (say, around 50%) with passives whilst approaching 100% with actives. Caplan discusses two possible explanations for this pattern—either the patient sometimes succeeds and sometimes fails to comprehend the passive, or else the patient always creates an ambiguous structure from a passive sentence and so has to guess between two possible interpretations of the sentence.

In relation to patients with grammatical disturbances of sentence produc-tion, a distinction has traditionally been made between *paragrammatism* and *agrammatism*. The paragrammatic patient is one who produces grammatical morphemes (function words and affixes) incorrectly, whilst the agrammatic patient is one who simply omits such morphemes. The analyses of 15 samples of spontaneous speech provided by Parisi in Chapter 9 lend no support to this distinction. Although clinical testing led to the classification of some of his patients as paragrammatic and others as agrammatic, analyses of grammatical morpheme omissions and of incorrect use of grammatical morphemes revealed that the patients lay at various points along a continuum and did not fall into one or other of two clearly defined categories (paragrammatism and agrammatism).

As Berndt discusses in Chapter 10, it was originally considered that agrammatism was a homogeneous disorder with a single explanation, although different theorists had different views about what this explanation should be. A common proposal was that agrammatism is produced when a central syntactic processing mechanism, used both in the production and in the comprehension of sentences, is damaged. Chapters 9 and 10 show that this theory—and indeed *any* theory which proposes that agrammatism has a single cause—is wrong. This is shown by the fact that the various symptoms constituting the syndrome of agrammatism dissociate in a large number of different ways, so that they cannot have a common cause.

Consider the data provided in Table 1 of Chapter 9, by Parisi. These show that, in the spontaneous speech of aphasic patients classified clinically as agrammatic, the following different patterns can be seen in different patients:

1. Abnormally short and syntactically simplified sentences, but no tendency to omit or wrongly produce grammatical morphemes.
2. Difficulties with function words but not with noun suffixes or verb suffixes.
3. Difficulties with suffixes but not function words.
4. Difficulties with verb suffixes but not noun suffixes.
5. As the patient improves, problems with grammatical morphemes diminish, but syntactic structure remains abnormally simple.

Important dissociations are also described by Berndt in Chapter 10 including:

1. Dysfluent and effortful spontaneous speech with comparatively short and syntactically simple sentences, but no difficulties with grammatical morphemes, and perfect comprehension of reversible sentences.
2. Poor comprehension of reversible sentences, with short and syntactically simple sentences in spontaneous speech, but no difficulties with grammatical morphemes in spontaneous speech.

Dissociations between receptive and productive agrammatism are also revealed by the results discussed by Tyler in Chapter 7. Five patients whose production of spontaneous speech was characterised as agrammatic showed effects in an on-line sentence perception task suggesting that they were capable of progressively constructing a full syntactic representation of a sentence as they listened to it.

There seems no alternative to abandoning all attempts to explain agrammatism, since there is no single thing to explain. Instead, it would seem wiser to follow the advice proffered by Ellis in Chapter 17. In his view, once a particular patient has been described in sufficient detail, the next step is to try to explain these observations with reference to an explicit model describing the normal processes of sentence production and comprehension. For this patient, which components of the model are impaired and which are still intact?

Even if every "agrammatic" patient is different in some ways from every other one, this would not be an obstacle. The mental system we use for producing and comprehending sentences must be extremely complex, so there must be an enormous variety of different patterns of sentence processing deficit which can occur. Therefore it would not be at all surprising if one found that each agrammatic patient is unique in some way. Such uniqueness would be irrelevant for the task in hand, which is to determine whether some particular model of sentence production and comprehension can or cannot explain the impaired and retained sentence-processing capabilities of some particular agrammatic patient. Chapters 4, 6, 7, 8, and 9 provide a variety of examples of exactly this approach.

CONCLUSIONS

As the preceding survey of the contents of this book shows, cognitive-neuropsychological research is now dealing actively with all the major aspects of language processing—with both written and spoken language, with language input as well as language output, and with the sentence level as well as the single word level. Controversies between investigators abound, and I have mentioned some (should one postulate separate input and output lexicons for phonology, or is there a single phonological lexicon? Is there one, or are there two, orthographic lexicons? Must we distinguish visual from verbal semantics, or is there a single common semantic system?) But the value of the general approach defined in the first paragraph of this chapter has not yet been much challenged. There may be people who would wish to criticise the conception of human language behaviour as depending upon the use of a modularly-organised information-processing system. Others might wish to argue that we cannot learn about how linguistic tasks are normally accomplished by studying people whose language has been impaired by neurological damage. One of the functions of this book is to provide a focus for such challenges.

REFERENCES

Allport, D. A., & Funnell, E. (1981) Components of the mental lexicon. *Philosophical Transactions of the Royal Society of London, B295*, 397–410.

Beauvois, M. F., & Derouesné, J. (1979) Phonological alexia: Three dissociations. *Journal of Neurology, Neurosurgery and Psychiatry, 42*, 1115–1124.

Beauvois, M. F., & Derouené, J. (1981) Lexical or orthographic agraphia? *Brain, 104*, 21–49.

Bramwell, B. (1985) Illustrative cases of aphasia. *Cognitive Neuropsychology, 1*, 245–258. (Reprinted from *The Lancet*, 1897, *1*, 1256–1259).

Bub, D., & Kertesz, A. (1982) Deep agraphia. *Brain and Language, 17*, 146–165.

Coltheart, M. (1981) Disorders of reading and their implications for models of normal reading. *Visible Language, 15*, 245–286.

Coltheart, M. (1980) Deep dyslexia: A review of the syndrome. In M. Coltheart, K. Patterson, & J. C. Marshall (Eds.), *Deep dyslexia*. London: Routledge & Kegan Paul.

Coltheart, M. (1985) Cognitive neuropsychology and the study of reading. In M. I. Posner, & G. S. M. Marin (Eds.), *Attention and performance XI*. Hillsdale, New Jersey: Lawrence Erlbaum Associates.

Coltheart, M., & Funnell, E. (in press) Reading and writing: One lexicon or two? In D. A. Allport, D. G. MacKay, W. Prinz, & E. Scheerer (Eds.), *Language perception and production: shared mechanisms in listening, reading, and writing*. London: Academic Press.

Coltheart, M., Masterson, J., Byng, S., Prior, M., & Riddoch, J. (1983) Surface dyslexia. *Quarterly Journal of Experimental Psychology, 35A*, 469–496.

Coltheart, M., Patterson, K., & Marshall, J. C. (Eds.) (1980) *Deep dyslexia*. London: Routledge & Kegan Paul.

Ellis, A. W. (1982) Spelling and writing (and reading and speaking). In A. W. Ellis (Ed.), *Normality and pathology in cognitive functions*. London: Academic Press.

Ellis, A. W. (1984) *Reading, writing and dyslexia*. London: Lawrence Erlbaum Associates.

Ellis, A. W., Miller, D., & Sin, G. (1983) Wernicke's aphasia and normal language processing: A case study in cognitive neuropsychology. *Cognition, 15*, 111–144.

Ellis, A. W., & Young, A. (1986) *Human cognitive neuropsychology*. London: Lawrence Erlbaum Associates.

Funnell, E. (1983a) Phonological processing in reading: New evidence from acquired dyslexia. *British Journal of Psychology, 74*, 159–180.

Funnell, E. (1983b) *Ideographic communication and word-class differences in aphasia*. Unpublished Ph.D. thesis, University of Reading.

Harris, M., & Coltheart, M. (1986) *Language processing in adults and children: An introduction*. London: Routledge & Kegan Paul.

Hatfield, M., & Patterson, K. E. (1983) Phonological spelling. *Quarterly Journal of Experimental Psychology, 35A*, 451–468.

Humphreys, G. W., & Riddoch, M. J. (1984) Routes to object constancy: Implications from neurological impairments of object constancy. *Quarterly Journal of Experimental Psychology, 36A*, 385–416.

Johnston, J., & McClelland, J. L. (1980) Experimental tests of a hierarchical model of word identification. *Journal of Verbal Learning and Verbal Behavior, 19*, 503–524.

Kay, J., & Patterson, K. E. (1985) Routes to meaning in surface dyslexia. In K. E. Patterson, J. C. Marshall & M. Coltheart (Eds.), *Surface dyslexia: cognitive and neuropsychological studies of phonological reading*. London: Lawrence Erlbaum Associates.

Luria, A. R. (1970) *Traumatic aphasia*. The Hague: Mouton.

Marshall, J. C., & Newcombe, F. (1973) Patterns of paralexia. *Journal of Psycholinguistic Research, 2*, 175–199.

Morton, J., & Patterson, K. E. (1980) A new attempt at an interpretation, or an attempt at a new interpretation. In M. Coltheart, K. Patterson & J. C. Marshall (Eds.), *Deep dyslexia*. London: Routledge & Kegan Paul.

Newcombe, F., & Marshall, J. C. (1980) Response monitoring and response blocking in deep dyslexia. In M. Coltheart, K. Patterson, & J. C. Marshall (Eds.), *Deep dyslexia*. London: Routledge & Kegan Paul.

Newcombe, F., & Marshall, J. C. (1985) Reading and writing by letter-sounds. In K. E. Patterson, J. C. Marshall, & M. Coltheart (Eds.), *Surface dyslexia: Cognitive and neuropsychological studies of phonological reading*. London: Lawrence Erlbaum Associates.

Nolan, K., & Caramazza, A. (1983) An analysis of writing in a case of deep dyslexia. *Brain and Language, 20*, 305–328.

Patterson, K. E. (1986) Lexical but nonsemantic spelling? *Cognitive Neuropsychology, 3*, 341–367.

Patterson, K. E., & Kay, J. (1982) Letter-by-letter reading: psychological descriptions of a neurolgical syndrome. *Quarterly Journal of Experimental Psychology, 34A*, 411–441.

Patterson, K. E., & Besner, D. (1985) Is the right hemisphere literate? *Cognitive Neuropsychology, 1*, 315–342.

Patterson, K. E., Marshall, J. C., & Coltheart, M. (Eds.) (1985) *Surface dyslexia: Cognitive and neuropsychological studies of phonological reading*. London: Lawrence Erlbaum Associates.

Riddoch, M. J., Humphreys, G. W. Coltheart, M., & Funnell, E. (in press) Semantic systems or system? Neuropsychological evidence re-evaluated. *Cognitive Neuropsychology*.

Shallice, T. (1981) Phonological agraphia and the lexical route in writing. *Brain, 104*, 413–429.

Shallice, T., & Warrington, E. K. (1980) Single and multiple component central dyslexic syndromes. In M. Coltheart, K. Patterson, & J. C. Marshall (Eds.), *Deep dyslexia*. London: Routledge & Kegan Paul.

Warrington, E. K. (1975) The selective impairment of semantic memory. *Quarterly Journal of Experimental Psychology, 27*, 635–657.

Warrington, E. K. (1981) Concrete word dyslexia. *British Journal of Psychology, 72*, 175–196.

Warrington, E. K., & Shallice, T. (1984) Category-specific semantic impairments. *Brain, 107*, 829–854.

2 Reading Without Letters?

David Howard

Psychology Department, University College, University of London, Gower Street, London WC1E 6BT

and

Speech Therapy Department, Regional Neurological Unit, Homerton Hospital, London E9 6BY

INTRODUCTION

How are written words recognised? One currently popular view is that the only information used in addressing word recognition units is derived from prior identification of the component letters: "Word recognition depends on preliminary letter identification" (Henderson, 1982, p. 275). See also Besner et al., 1984; McLelland and Rummelhart, 1981.

This view asserts that in order to recognise a word the component letters must first be identified and that word recognition units are accessed by information that specifies the letter string, and no other information. In addition to a level of letter identities, such theories normally suppose that there are a set of visual analysers that extract visual features from the visual pattern that is the written word, and that letters are recognised on the basis of simultaneous activation of sets of such features. In a similar way, words are then identified on the basis of the recognition of their component letters.

This is, therefore, a straightforward hierarchical linear theory of word recognition (see Fig. 2.1). Levels of coding start with visual features, and become progressively more abstract and of larger scope as word recognition proceeds. Thus it is proposed that a very large number of different words appearing in any of a variety of different typefaces can be recognised by a system that initially extracts a relatively small number of visual features from

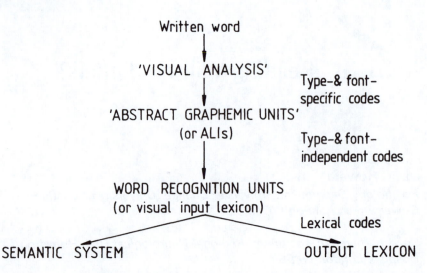

Written word

'VISUAL ANALYSIS'

Type-& font-
specific codes

'ABSTRACT GRAPHEMIC UNITS'
(or ALIs)

Type-& font-
independent codes

WORD RECOGNITION UNITS
(or visual input lexicon)

Lexical codes

SEMANTIC SYSTEM   OUTPUT LEXICON

FIG. 2.1   A single route to word recognition: word recognition depends on letter identification alone.

the stimulus. It is a strong theory in that it asserts that the *only* evidence used in word recognition is the ordered identities of the component letters; other sources of evidence that have the potential of distinguishing between words (for example, word shape) are *not* available for use in word recognition.

McLelland (1976) summarises the empirical consequences of this position thus: "If word perception is mediated by preliminary letter identification, accurate word perception should depend on the familiarity of the arrangement of the letters in a word and not on the familiarity of the visual configuration of the word (p. 81)." On what sorts of evidence is this position based? A number of experiments have been taken to show that any disruption of the global form of words affects the recognition of pronounceable pseudowords (e.g. NORK), as much as it affects the recognition of real words (e.g. PORK), at least as long as the component letters remain in a linear left-to-right order—that is, the "word–pseudoword advantage" is unaffected. So, for example, McLelland (1976) found that the word-pseudoword advantage was unaffected when subjects had to report as many letters as possible from briefly presented stimuli, where letters were presented in aLtErNaTiNg cAsE, compared to a condition where all the letters were in the same case; however, letters were reported less accurately from both words and pseudowords in the case alternated condition. It was harder for subjects to report the letters of a word in its novel, case-alternated form; but, since this was equally true for real words and pseudowords, case alternation was not interfering with any process specific to the recognition of real, known words.

This general finding—that visual format distortions affect the recognition of pseudowords as much as they affect the recognition of words—has been reported in a number of different experiments. For example Besner (1983) found that naming latency for words and pseudowords was equally affected by case alternation; Adams (1979) found that the word-pseudoword advantage was unaffected when each letter in the stimulus was in a different size and typeface from each of the others; and Smith (1969) found that the reading time for text was unaffected by size alternation of the letters.

Evett and Humphreys (1981) demonstrate that brief, masked, presentation of a word in lower case will facilitate recognition of its upper case form even when the subjects were completely unaware of the existence of the lower case prime. This effect also applied when the lower case prime shared only some of the letters of the target, and this did not depend on whether the prime was a real word or a pseudoword; in other words, *while* facilitated the recognition of *WHITE*, as much as *stafe* facilitated *STATE*. Evett and Humphreys use this evidence to argue that there is a level of abstract letter identification units (ALIs) that accumulate information about the identity of letters, irrespective of the case in which they are presented. Thus, for example, G, g, *G* and *g* will all activate the same ALI unit. The ALIs, then, accept visual information that is specific to the type, case and font of the letters and produce an output that is coded independently of the specific visual form in which the letter is presented.

Why, then, should there be any effect of format distortions on word and pseudoword recognition? One possible account is in terms of interfacilitation at the level of the ALIs. Suppose, for example, that the first letter of a word is identified as lower case, it is then a reasonable supposition that the other letters in the word will also be lower case (as well as in the same typeface and of approximately the same size); interfacilitation at the ALI level would then result in preferential accumulation of those visual features that distinguish between letters in the expected case. Expectation that words (and pseudowords) will have a consistent format, would result in slowed recognition of all format distorted stimuli. However, such expectations would not prevent the accumulation of correct letter information by the ALIs; if they produce any output at all, it will be the same irrespective of the stimulus format, and therefore under conditions where the letters remain clearly visible in the correct linear string word recognition *accuracy* should be unaffected by format distortions, although the recognition latencies might, as pointed out above, be slowed.

Neuropsychological evidence appears to support the ALI model of word recognition. Deep dyslexic patients (e.g., Coltheart, Patterson, & Marshall, 1980) are, typically, very severely disturbed in tasks that require knowledge of either the sounds or the names of single letters; there is only one task involving letters that deep dyslexic patients typically perform promptly and accurately—matching single letters across case (for example, choosing from a lower case alphabet which letter corresponds to H; or judging whether pairs such as gG or gP are the same). Despite having no other knowledge of letters, deep dyslexic patients seem to know about the letters' abstract identities, independent of case and format.

In addition, deep dyslexic patients are normally able to read words in a variety of unfamiliar formats as accurately as they read normally written versions. Saffran and Marin (1977) showed that their deep dyslexic, V.S., 30 could easily read words that were case alternated (cAbInEt),

           D   t r
written vertically O , vertically displaced le e ,
           G   t s

or had + signs between the letters $(n + i + g + h + t)$.[1] Deep dyslexic patients can read words presented as a sequence of isolated letters on single cards, and P.W. has even acquired the (renowned) ability to read John Morton's handwriting (Patterson, 1979). These results, together with near normal lexical decision performance, even with abstract or function words that they cannot read, has been taken to imply that, for most deep dyslexics, all the processes involved in word recognition are intact; their problems lie in what they do with the output from word recognition units (Patterson, 1979).

In spite of the existence of the various lines of evidence which have just been discussed, the ALI theory of word reading has not received universal support. Evidence has been found that is consistent with the view that word recognition units may be able to use information other than the linear letter string in order to differentiate between words. Two other information sources have been proposed—*word shape* and *transletter features*. The general scheme of such a position where word recognition units accept information from multiple sources is shown in Fig. 2.2.

Word shape is used to refer to information from the overall contour of the word—for example *yellow* starts with a descender and has a matching pair of ascending letters in the middle.[2] Such information is presumably only available from lower case and hand-written words; where words are written in BLOCK CAPITALS there is no distinctive contour. "Transletter features"[3] are features that transcend single letters and specify the visual

---

[1] This evidence is weak. Saffran and Marin took a set of 75 words that had been read correctly in undistorted form, and then presented these words in distorted formats; 67/75 were read correctly. It is perfectly possible that real effects of format distortion were masked by ceiling effects.

[2] Seymour and Elder (1986) report that children, in their first year of reading, specifically offer such information. One child given the word "smaller" to read, said: "It's 'yellow' because it has two sticks," while drawing the two vertical strokes in the air with her finger.

[3] Transletter features are also (rather inappropriately) called "transgraphemic features," or (more sensibly) "supraletter features."

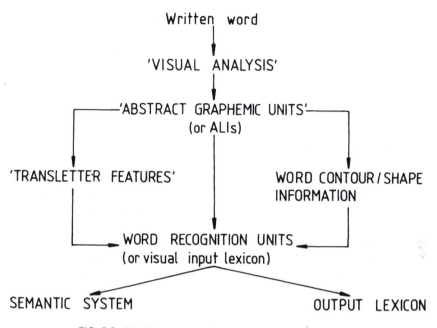

FIG. 2.2   Multiple sources of information in word recognition.

relations between adjacent letters or letter groups. Those theorists that have employed this category have not been precise as to what exactly transletter features are. One way of describing them is as units that specifically accumlate information to identify common letter groups—particularly those that might act as graphemic units—e.g., *th, ght, sh.*

How, in the face of the McLelland and Adams' findings that the word-pseudoword superiority effect is unaffected by case alternation of the stimuli, can one sustain a position that information other than that from ALIs is used in word recognition? The simple answer is that there are a number of results that show format effects in tasks that appear to involve word recognition, even where the letters remain clearly visible in the correct linear order.

For example, Besner (1983) found that case alternation affects words more than pseudowords in a lexical decision task, although there is no such effect when measured in terms of oral reading latency. In order to maintain the theory that word recognition depends only on the ALI route, Besner (1983; see also Besner et al., 1984) is forced to take up the novel position that lexical decision does not necessarily involve lexical access, and can, when required, be performed simply on the basis of a judgement of the visual "familiarity" of the stimulus. This judgement is affected by format distortions, but the mechanism responsible for it (whose nature is unspecified) is not involved in word recognition. This is a serious weakening of the ALI theory; global word information *can* be retrieved and used by the human cognitive system, but only to make metalinguistic judgements on words. One might wonder why such a system should exist if it is not used in word recognition; in what tasks other than lexical decision may this "familiarity discrimination mechanism" play a part?

A number of other results appear to show effects of global word features in word recognition. There is some evidence to suggest that word shape cues may play a role. Underwood and Bargh (1982) found that naming time was reduced by a context sentence with upper case more than lower case words; they suggest that where word envelope information is available, subjects rely less on the context sentence to aid word recognition. Baron and Strawson (1976) found that reading times were marginally slower for upper case than lower case words; this might be taken as evidence for the use of word shape information in the recognition of lower case words. Monk and Hulme (1983) found that in a proofreading task spelling errors were more easily detected when the errors involved deletion of an ascender (which contributes to the overall word shape) than when the letter deleted was "square" (i.e., neither an ascender nor a descender); when the text was presented with the component letters randomly in upper or lower case these word shape effects were abolished.

Evidence for a role of transletter features in word recognition is more elusive. The essential problem is that case alternation, which inevitably disrupts all transletter features, has remarkably little effect on word recognition. Baron and Strawson (1976) found that subjects were slower at reading case alternated words than upper case ones; and Coltheart and Freeman (1974) found more errors for case alternated words. Neither of these results is particularly compelling; if subjects generate "expectations" about the case of letters in a word that would normally aid recognition, but that are not fulfilled in case alternated words, we would expect more errors with brief exposures as well as slowed reading times. There is one class of rather exceptional stimuli whose recognition reliably depends on their case of presentation; recognition of sets of initials that normally only occur in upper case form (e.g. BBC, GPO) is much better when they are presented in their familiar (upper) case than when they are in lower case—bbc, gpo (Henderson & Chard, 1976). But, as Henderson (1982) observes, these abbreviations are a peculiar set, which may be recognised by processes somewhat different from those responsible for the recognition of more conventional words.

Theoretical positions that claim that word recognition units can accept information about word shape or transletter features, as well as the output of ALIs, would predict that those dyslexic patients whose ALI system is in some way defective will be forced to rely to an unusual extent on other features; they will, therefore, be worse at reading words whose visual form is distorted.

Theories that suppose that word recognition depends on the ALI route alone are forced to make the prediction that in no acquired dyslexic patient will the accuracy of word reading be affected by format distortions such as case alternation with clearly visible word stimuli; where the ALI system *is* impaired, recognition of normal and format-distorted words should be equally affected. Indeed, after proposing a format-sensitive familiarity discrimination mechanism to account for case alternation effects in lexical decision, this is almost the only strong prediction that such a theory makes.

In this paper I shall present a case report of a deep dyslexic patient who finds distorted words hard to read, and whose ability to match letters across case is almost entirely abolished. I shall argue that the existence of such a patient presents problems for the theories of word recognition that suppose that word recognition units are addressed by abstract letter codes alone.

CASE REPORT

T.M. is a 46-year-old, left-handed, ex-bill poster. In September 1976 he was admitted to hospital for investigation of weakness and tingling in the right calf on walking that had lasted for six months, weakness of the left hand, and difficulty in expressing himself that had been increasingly apparent for four months. On examination he was found to have a "mild nominal dysphasia," a left visual inattention, and weakness and brisk reflexes in the left arm. An isotope scan showed increased activity in the right posterior parietal and right fronto-parietal regions. It was finally decided that these signs were due to cerebral ischaemia.

Three weeks after admission, T.M. developed a complete left hemiplegia and global aphasia overnight. A second isotope scan two weeks later showed slightly increased activity in the right posterior parietal region, which was judged consistent with a cerebrovascular accident.

Six weeks after his CVA, T.M. was admitted to the Regional Neurological Unit at the Eastern Hospital, London, for rehabilitation. On admission he was found to have normal fundi and visual fields, severe weakness and mild spasticity of the left arm, moderate weakness and mild spasticity of the left leg, and brisk tendon reflexes in all limbs, but more so on the left; he was globally aphasic. Five months later T.M. was discharged, having made some improvement. He was walking but still had weakness of the left leg, almost no movement in his left arm, and a severe Broca's aphasia. Since then he has lived at home, and until January 1983 he attended a day centre three days a week, as well as a weekly speech club. The data reported in this paper were collected between March 1981 and November 1983.

T.M. left school at 14. During his National Service he was a storeman, which apparently involved a considerable amount of record-keeping.

According to his family (and himself) he used to be good at reading and writing; reading was one of his main pleasures. Before his CVA he read the *Daily Mirror* every day.

Language

T.M. is now a severe Broca's aphasic. His spontaneous speech is limited and consists principally of content words, with little grammatical structure, but normal articulation. His description of a picture, in which a group of people are having a picnic in front of a church, ran:

> er er er dog a dog oh no horse an horse an horse man man woman er er er man woman er er women man dogs er Our Father which art in heaven er dark dark clouds church church church churches gate a gate er er f— f— dog oh er a tower a tower a tower dog man er dog oh er man man clouds.

On formal assessment T.M. has limited but fairly accurate auditory comprehension: he points to named objects (14/18), and follows one-stage commands, but cannot cope with more complex ones. His main activity is watching television (he particularly enjoys old films, and is very knowledge-able about horse-racing); he claims to have no difficulty in understanding the speech in the programmes. He can repeat single words (32/32), and three word phrases (18/20), but not longer sentences. His forwards digit span is three. His speech is limited, but fairly effective in terms of communication, with intelligent use of one or two word utterances, and free use of mime. He is very poor at picture and object naming, producing many semantic errors (e.g., *chair* → "bed").

Reading

1. *Reading Errors.* In oral reading of single written words T.M. makes semantic, visual, derivational, and inflectional errors; in addition he pro-duces a variety of compound errors, multi-word responses, and responses which bear no obvious relationship to the stimulus (see Table 2.1 for examples).

The relative proportions of these errors are not especially meaningful, as this depends on the nature of the stimulus set used to elicit them. But to give some idea, in the first 1002 single lower case words that I gave him to read, which were, as a set, heavily biased towards concrete words, T.M. read 324 (32%) correctly. The 678 errors were distributed as follows: 7% were derivational or inflectional errors; 22% semantic errors; 3% visual or semantic errors; 15% visual errors; 3% visual then semantic errors; 18% multi-word responses; 16% unrelated responses and 15% omissions.

TABLE 2.1
Examples of T.M.'s Errors in Oral Word Reading

Semantic Errors			Derivational and Inflectional Errors		
average	→	bad	wheel	→	wheels
battery	→	poultry	fire	→	bonfire
husband	→	father	wash	→	washing
missile	→	America	door	→	outdoors
shilling	→	money	wife	→	housewife
smile	→	happy	bake	→	baker
whisky	→	scotch	light	→	candlelight
soldier	→	army	animal	→	animals
cat	→	dog	fence	→	fencing

Visual Errors			Visual or Semantic Errors		
office	→	police	brother	→	father
library	→	birthday	roof	→	loft
truth	→	teeth	tomato	→	potato
moon	→	saloon	lorry	→	trolley
river	→	driver	lemon	→	melon
work	→	walk	foot	→	hoof
watch	→	witch	train	→	tram

Derivational Then Semantic Errors			Unrelated Responses		
discord	→	a plane	street	→	book
			umbrella	→	marshmallow
Visual Then Derivational Errors			shut	→	doctor
			catch	→	wallpaper
			find	→	walk
knife	→	housewife	come	→	now
winter	→	typewriter	pedal	→	bible
night	→	fighting	trousers	→	fencing
logs	→	hedgehog			

Multi–word Responses		
intellect	→	reading, writing, and arithmetic
hint	→	sweets hot
hat	→	cat, cat window
student	→	doctors, doctors but not yet
guitar	→	octave piano Vera Lynn
sequel	→	saw after
shelf	→	horse er camel
island	→	lots, lots far away land land ho!

TABLE 2.1 continued
Examples of T.M.'s Errors in Oral Word Reading

Visual Then Semantic Errors

river	→	motor	[via DRIVER]
noise	→	cold	[via NOSE]
witch	→	clock	[via WATCH]
clay	→	skipping	[via PLAY]
pile	→	beer	[via PALE ALE]
simile	→	laugh	[via SMILE]
hawk	→	hatchet	[via TOMAHAWK]

(Responses are counted as visual errors if at least half the letters in the response are in the stimulus in approximately the same order.)

The examples of visual errors in Table 2.1 seem to show a tendency for visual errors to preserve the letters at the end of the word, while the mistakes affect particularly the letters at the beginning. An analysis of all 92 visual errors remaining after all the repeated stimulus-response pairs had been eliminated confirmed that the probability that a letter from the stimulus word would be present in the visual error response did, indeed, depend on its position in the word. Only 32% of the first letters and 57% of the second letters of the stimulus words were present in the response, whereas for the penultimate and final letters these figures were 89% and 93% respectively. With T.M., therefore, visual errors were most likely to involve the beginnings of words. It is tempting to suggest that, although his visual fields are full on clinical testing, this might be a consequence of his *right* hemisphere lesion. Other deep dyslexic patients, such as P.W. and D.E. (Morton & Patterson, 1980) and K.F. (Shallice & Warrington, 1975), who have *left* hemisphere lesions, make visual errors that most often involve the final, rightmost letters of the word.

It is possible that some, at least, of T.M.'s derivational errors are attributable to these same visual factors. Of 40 derivational errors (those remaining after repeated stimulus-response pairs are eliminated), 13 involve addition of a free morpheme as a prefix to make a compound word (e.g., *ball*→"football"; *chair*→"armchair"; *fly*→"butterfly"). Such errors appear to be rare in other deep dyslexic patients—there are no examples of this in the error corpora for P.W., D.E., or K.F. (Patterson, 1980; Shallice & Warrington, 1980). The opposite process—addition of an extraneous free morpheme after the stimulus word to make a compound—does occur both with these patients (e.g., K.F.: *gentle*→"gentleman"; P.W.: *break*→"breakfast") as well as T.M. (*screw*→"screwdriver"). So just as T.M.'s visual errors seem to involve, preferentially, the beginnings of words, so too his derivational errors are more likely to involve the addition of prefixes than is the case with other deep dyslexic patients.

2. *Reading Abstract Words.* T.M is very poor at oral reading of abstract words. On Coltheart's (1980) matched lists of high and low imageability words, he was correct with 10/28 high imageability words and 2/28 low imageability words. On a set of eighty words which cross high and low frequency and high and low imageability (i.e., the high frequency words are matched to the low frequency words in imageability and length, and the high imageability words are matched to the low imageability words in frequency and length), T.M.'s scores were as follows:

High imageability, high frequency e.g., road, doctor, window 9/20
High imageability, low frequency e.g., hawk, infant, bubble 5/20
Low imageability, high frequency e.g., idea, answer, theory 2/20
Low imageability, low frequency e.g., span, pardon, custom 0/20

T.M.'s accuracy of word reading is evidently affected by both the stimulus imageability and its frequency.

3. *The Relationship Between Stimulus Word Frequency and Imageability and Reading Errors.* To investigate the relationship between stimulus characteristics and types of reading error, an analysis was performed on all the words from the sample of 1002 reading responses for which the stimulus word has a known imageability value. Where a word had been presented more than once within the corpus, one of the reading responses to it was randomly selected. This yielded a total corpus of 454 reading responses; the characteristics (in terms of imageability and word frequency) of the words leading to responses in each of the major categories are shown in Table 2.2. Considering only content word stimuli, words that are correctly read are significantly more imageable than those that result in an error of any category ($t(437) = 3.42$; $p < 0.001$), but they do not differ in log word frequency ($t(437) = 0.49$; ns). Considering the distinction between words that

TABLE 2.2
The Characteristics of Words Giving Rise to Reading Responses of Different Categories

Reading response	Number in sample	Imageability		Log word frequency	
		mean	s.d.	mean	s.d.
Correct	114	583	81	1.46	.70
Derivational errors	18	591	41	1.47	.76
Semantic errors	67	577	64	1.51	.68
Visual errors	51	564	57	1.35	.63
Unrelated responses	55	543	91	1.38	.67
No response	50	551	79	1.27	.67

must have accessed the correct visual input lexicon entries (correct + derivational errors + semantic errors) and those that show no evidence of having
done so (visual errors + unrelated responses + omissions), these two groups
differ both in imageability (t(353) = 4.25; p < 0.001) and in log word frequency (t(353) = 1.94; p < 0.05).

4. *Reading Function Words.* T.M. has never, in my experience, read an
isolated function word correctly. On a list of 10 short, frequent function
words his errors were 6 omissions and: *are*→"dog"; *him*→"baby"; *across*
→"stop"; *when*→"window".

5. *Reading Non-Words.* On a list of 20 pronounceable non-words, half of
which were pseudo-homophones, T.M. read none correctly. For 13 he made
no response; his overt errors were: *mun*→"suck"; *foo*→"noose"; *wabe*→
"table"; *slar*→"coffee"; *fale*→"armchair"; *rool*→"stool"; *nork*→
"woodwork". All his responses are real words, and in several cases they are
visually similar to the non-word stimuli.

6. *Word Length and Reading.* T.M. was presented, on a VDU screen,
with randomly ordered concrete words of 3, 5, 7 and 9 letters matched for
word frequency and imageability. There were 20 words of each letter length.
The results (Table 2.3) show that T.M.'s accuracy of word reading and the
latency of correct responses are unrelated to word length (comparison of
length of words read correctly and those not t(78) = 0.73, n.s.; correlation of
correct RT with letter length, r(25) = −0.27, n.s.).

7. *Lexical Decision.* On Coltheart's (1980) "easy lexical decision," which
involves only short, frequent, concrete words (e.g., car, school) and pronounceable non-words derived from them (e.g., cag, schoom), T.M. made 2/25
misses and 6/25 false positives; this yields a d' of 2.11.

TABLE 2.3
The Effect of Word Length on Reading Accuracy
and Latency of Correct Readings
(20 words of each length)

Word length (letters)	Proportion read correctly	Mean latency of correct responses (secs)
9	.35	2.77
7	.15	2.78
5	.50	3.40
3	.35	4.73
Mean	.34	3.51

8. *Written Word Comprehension.* On the written version of the Peabody Picture Vocabulary Test (PPVT: Dunn, 1965) T.M. had a raw score of 34 (mental age equivalent 3.4 yrs); on the auditory version he scored 93 (mental age = 13.4 yrs). In matching a written word to one of four pictures he scored 21/25 when the foils were semantically unrelated to the target; this fell to 16/25 with related foils (difference $p < 0.02$; McNemar's test).

9. *Letters.* Asked, on an auditory request, to point to a letter out of a set of four, T.M. scored 7/20 correct. In naming letters he managed only 1/20; all his errors were other letters.

10. *Reading and Naming Compared.* In naming a set of 300 pictures T.M. was correct on 0.30; in oral reading of the written picture names he scored 0.32. The contingency coefficient between reading and naming (0.396), was as high as the contingency between two sets of different pictures of the same objects (0.392). In reading these picture names neither log word frequency nor word phoneme length had any effect on his performance (log frequency $t(298) = 1.18$; phoneme length $t(298) = 0.44$) (see Howard, Patterson, Franklin, Orchard-Lisle & Morton, 1984). However the varieties of error T.M. makes in reading and naming are rather different; he occasionally makes the same semantic errors in the two tasks (e.g., *kennel*→"dog"), but, obviously enough, he does not make visual reading errors in picture naming.

Writing

T.M. is effectively agraphic. He can, laboriously, copy his name or other words with his right, non-preferred hand; he cannot write anything spontaneously or to dictation.

Summary

T.M. is clearly a deep dyslexic. He makes semantic, visual, and derivational/inflectional errors in oral word reading; he is very poor at reading abstract words, and unable to read function words or non-words. Nevertheless T.M. is unlike most cases of deep dyslexia that have so far been published in a number of ways. Specifically:

1. He is very bad at reading. On concrete words he makes many fewer correct responses than most deep dyslexics; on reading the set of 300 picture names referred to above, two other deep dyslexics, P.W. and B.B.,[4] both

---

[4]Further details of the other deep dyslexic patients can be found in the following sources. P.W. and D.E. are described by Patterson (1979) and elsewhere, and B.B. by Patterson (1981). N.T. and H.R.M. are briefly described by Howard (1982).

scored 0.90; T.M. got only 0.32 correct. He makes visual errors on stimuli that are far more concrete than is typical of other patients.

2. He makes an unusual number of errors on lexical decision. P.W. and D.E. are essentially normal on lexical decision with concrete words (Patterson, 1979); H.R.M. made no errors on Coltheart's "easy lexical decision"; and another deep dyslexic, N.T., made two. T.M. made eight errors.

3. While some deep dyslexics have been reported to make semantic errors in comprehension of concrete written words (e.g., G.R.—Newcombe & Marshall, 1980), T.M. seems to make them at an unusually high rate. In matching written words to pictures, P.W. and D.E. made no errors whether the foils were related or not; B.B. made no errors with unrelated foils and two when they were related to the target.[5] T.M. made four errors with unrelated foils and nine with related foils. On the written version of the PPVT, N.T., H.R.M., P.W., B.B., and D.E. all score in excess of 100; T.M. manages only 34.

4. Deep dyslexics typically produce many function words as incorrect responses to function word stimuli. Within the small number of function words that he has attempted, T.M. has only done this once (was→"is").

While T.M. shares the qualitative features of deep dyslexia (apart from function word errors), he is quantitatively rather worse than the "classic" cases. In some of the tests that follow "control" data will be reported from another deep dyslexic, V.I.S., who is also "bad" at oral word reading.

V.I.S. became aphasic as a result of an embolic left hemisphere CVA following coronary surgery in November 1978.[6] Assessment on the Boston Diagnostic Aphasia Examination (Goodglass & Kaplan, 1972) shows that she is a severe Broca's aphasic, with distorted articulation. In oral word reading she makes semantic errors (e.g. crowd→"people"; cash→"money"; average→"half"; bulb→"plants"), visual errors (boat→"boots"; badge→ "badger"; clock→"cloth") and derivational and inflectional errors (snake →"snakes"; tree→"trees"). She is worse at reading abstract words than concrete ones (high imageability 10/28; low imageability 0/28). She is very poor at reading non-words; on 15 pseudo-homophones she read two correctly (doo, hoo), and none of 15 non-homophonic pseudowords. On the written version of the PPVT she scored 69. V.I.S. does make some semantic errors in comprehension of written words; on the written version of Funnell's test she scored 13/16 with related foils (match the written word "tangerine"

---

[5] Karalyn Patterson kindly collected these data.

[6] I am grateful to Liz Clark, Chief Speech Therapist at Queen Mary's Hospital, Sidcup for permission to see V.I.S.; and to Sally Byng for allowing me to quote some of the results from her testing of V.I.S.

to written "orange" or "lemon"); and 16/16 with unrelated foils (match "tangerine" to "orange" or "lake") (Funnell, 1983).

V.I.S. is similar to T.M. in a number of ways; she shows a similar level of success (or lack of it) in reading high and low imageability words. Both are deep dyslexics and severe Broca's aphasics. There are two rather obvious differences: V.I.S. scores better on written word comprehension on the PPVT than T.M.; and, whereas T.M. is a left-hander who became aphasic after a right hemisphere CVA, V.I.S. is a right-hander who had a left hemisphere CVA.

CROSS CASE MATCHING

T.M. has great difficulty in cross case matching of letters. In matching single written letters to one of a choice of four of the opposite case he scores at chance (Table 2.4: 1), even though in a set of 20 different letters some have visually similar upper and lower case forms. In identity matching with the same stimuli, he manages only 14/20; he succeeded with 8/10 upper case and 6/10 lower case letters. While this is very much better than chance, it is very poor performance.

In Patterson's test, where the patient has to judge whether a 4–6 letter word (or non-word) in upper case is the same as a lower case word (non-matching pairs differ in one letter), T.M.'s scores are no better than chance in either condition (Table 2.4: 2).

With a four letter word to match to one of four in the opposite case, where the three foils differ in only one letter from the target, T.M. scores 9/20. This is better than chance (binomial, $p < 0.04$) but scarcely a brilliant performance. With the equivalent test with non-words (derived by rearranging the word stimuli) he scores only 6/20 (Table 2.4: 3).

In these three tests the "control" deep dyslexic, V.I.S., is consistently very much better than chance; in no task is her error rate above 10%.

To establish whether T.M. simply has a problem with the process of matching itself, he was given a test where he had to match a picture of an object to a different picture of the same name when the foils were semantically and visually related to the target. Thus one item consisted of a picture of a *horse* to match to either a different picture of a *horse*, or a *cow*, a *sheep* or a *goat*. On this T.M. was correct 24/25 (96%); matching of pictures presents him with no problem.

In order to establish whether this problem was specific to cross case matching, T.M. was then given a matching task in which two different typefaces were used in upper and lower case, and stimulus and response sets were systematically varied between these four categories. For each of the 16 cells the same 20 matchings were constructed; the order on the card of the

TABLE 2.4
Cross Case Matching of Letters and Words

1. Single letters (written). (Chance = .25).		
	Cross case	Identity
	d	d
	B K D P	b k d p
T.M.	5/20	14/20
	ns	p < 0.001
V.I.S.	20/20	—

2. Judging if pairs of words or non–words are the same across case.
(Words 4–6 letters long; typed in elite).

	Words	Non–words
	deer	larn
	DEER	LERN
T.M.	25/40	25/40
	ns	ns
V.I.S.	39/40	37/40

3. Matching 4 letter words and non–words across case. (Written).

	Words				Non–words			
		hand				hdan		
	LAND	HAND	HANK	HARD	LDAN	HDAN	HKAN	HDAR
T.M.				9/20			6/20	
				p < 0.05			ns	
V.I.S.				20/20			19/20	

five letters in the response set was randomly varied, although the items making up the set remained constant. The 16 cells were then randomly ordered: the first item from set A, the second from set B, the third from set C and so on made up the first 20 items; the next 20 consisted of the first from set B, the second from set C and so on. Each particular matching of a letter was therefore separated from the next by 20 items; each occurrence of a particular stimulus-response set pair was separated from the next by 15 items. The first 160 matchings were presented in one session, preceded by five practice items; the second half was done a week later. The elite is standard 12 point elite; the Olivetti typeface is one designed specially for literacy students with large type.

The results are shown in Table 2.5. On the four tests involving identity matching the mean score was 0.85; on each of the four performance was much better than chance (p < 0.001). The four matchings across type (i.e. match an elite letter to an Olivetti letter of the same case) are at a mean of 0.73; again all are much better than chance (p < 0.001). In the four matchings across case but not across type mean correct is 0.45; only one of these tests is better than chance. In the remaining four sets of matching across case and type the mean score is 0.51; one score is better than chance at p < 0.05 and

TABLE 2.5
Proportion of Correct Responses in Matching One Letter to a Choice of Five
(n=20 in Each Cell)

| Stimulus | | Response set (5) | | | | |
| | | Olivetti | | Elite | | |
		UC	LC	UC	LC	Mean
Olivetti	UC	.90*	.40ns	.85*	.50+	.66
	LC	.60*	.85*	.65*	.70*	.70
Elite	UC	.75*	.45ns	.85*	.35ns	.60
	LC	.45ns	.60*	.45ns	.80*	.58
Mean		.68	.58	.70	.59	.64

(UC = upper case; LC = lower case; * = $p < .001$; + = < p.05; chance = .20)

one at $p < 0.001$. These four groups of scores differ significantly (Kruskal-Wallis, $chi^2(3) = 11.66$; $p < 0.01$). Pairwise comparisons show that the scores on identity and cross type matching do not differ, but are both significantly better than matching across case or across case and type; the latter two do not differ.

Comment

V.I.S.'s excellent performance in cross case matching tasks shows that difficulty here is not a general feature of "severe" deep dyslexia. In contrast, T.M. is very poor at cross case matching; he is very much better at identity matching, but even so he makes a substantial number of errors. In a set of 20 different letters to match across case some must be very similar in their upper case and lower case presentations; although the set was biased to include the most visually dissimilar matches (e.g., Aa; Gg), it also includes pairs such as Zz and Kk which could easily be matched on the basis of visual similarity alone. Therefore, scores that are marginally above chance on cross case matching should not be taken as evidence that T.M. has any case- and type-independent knowledge of the identity of letters.

The only cross case matching task in which he achieves a score marginally above chance is matching of real words; given some knowledge of the meanings of the words involved this task could be done on the basis of a comparison between *semantic* codes—no information about letter identities is necessarily involved. Good performance in matching pictures demonstrates that T.M. does not have a problem with matching *per se*.

To match letters across case efficiently a subject needs to have access to knowledge of the abstract identities of the letters (i.e., the output of the ALIs), and, probably, a "graphemic buffer" in which to store the outputs of the ALIs for comparison. T.M.'s performance in this task, which is no better than one would expect if he were doing it on the basis of visual similarity alone, is not evidence that he does not have functioning ALIs; he may have an ALI deficit, or he may have a "graphemic buffer" deficit, or he may have both. However the graphemic buffer should not be involved in reading case alternated words; difficulty there will indicate that there is a problem with the ALI reading route.

THE EFFECTS OF VISUAL MANIPULATIONS ON ORAL WORD READING

I argued in the introduction that, if access to the word recognition units is achieved only on the basis of the output of the ALIs, then reading *accuracy* should be unaffected by any manipulations of the visual form of words that leaves the component letters in a linear left-to-right order with the individual letters clearly recognisable. In this section I shall describe the effects of various manipulations of this sort on T.M.'s oral word reading.

1. The Effects of p+l+u+s Signs Between Letters

Fifty words were presented singly on cards either typed in lower case elite or typed with plus signs between letters. Each word was presented twice, once in each mode of presentation in separate sessions. There were alternating blocks of five words in each mode; the words came in the same order in two tests a week apart. The results (Table 2.6) show that T.M. is very much worse at

TABLE 2.6
Effects of Visual Manipulations on Oral Word Reading. The Effect of p+l+u+s
s+i+g+n+s (Typed Elite; n=50)

	T.M.		V.I.S.	
	Lower case	Plus signs	Lower case	Plus signs
Proportion correct	.34	.04	.50	.38
Errors:				
Derivational	0	1	0	2
Semantic	6	3	3	9
Visual	6	5	1	2
Visual/semantic	0	0	1	1
Visual then semantic	0	0	1	0
Multi–word	5	1	3	3
Neologisms	0	0	3	1
Unrelated	9	26	0	1
Omissions	7	12	13	12

reading words with plus signs (McNemar, $p < 0.001$). His errors on these words are mostly omissions or unrelated responses. In contrast, V.I.S. is only marginally worse at reading the mutilated words and this difference is not quite significant (McNemar $p = 0.07$, one tailed).

Words with plus signs between the letters differ from normal words both in the presence of the plus signs and the greater distance between the component letters. The experiment was therefore repeated using a different word set and typeface, including an additional condition in which letters were separated by single spaces.

The results (Table 2.7) show that the conditions differ significantly (Cochran, $Q(2) = 15.76$; $p < 0.001$). Performance on normal lower case words is equivalent to those with spaces between the letters; plus signs are significantly worse than either.

TABLE 2.7
Effects of Visual Manipulations on Oral Word Reading. The Effect of p+l+u+s
s+i+g+n+s and s p a c e s (Typed Olivetti; n=72)

	Lower case	Plus signs	Spaces
Proportion correct	.36	.17	.42
Errors:			
Derivational	5	2	4
Semantic	16	7	8
Visual	3	1	5
Visual/semantic	2	0	3
Visual→semantic	1	0	1
Multi–word	14	4	13
Unrelated	3	43	6
Omissions	2	3	2

2. The Effects of Case Alternation

A set of 100 cards was prepared; there were 50 words typed either in lower case elite, or case alternated with the second letter the first capital. The size of the upper and lower case letters was not matched. They were presented in alternating blocks of five words in each mode, in the same order in two separate sessions a week apart.

The results (Table 2.8) show that T.M. is significantly worse at reading case alternated words than their lower case equivalents (McNemar, $p < 0.025$, one tailed). Again the extra errors on the case alternated words are mostly unrelated responses. V.I.S. is entirely unaffected by case alternation; she is, if anything, rather better on the case alternated words. Problems with these words are therefore not a feature of "severe" deep dyslexia.

Are problems with these case alternated words a consequence of the

TABLE 2.8
Effects of Visual Manipulations on Oral Word Reading. The Effect of cAsE aLtErNaTiOn
(Typed Elite, Not Size Matched; n=50)

	T.M.		V.I.S.	
	Lower case	Case alternated	Lower case	Case alternated
Proportion correct	.34	.14	.44	.50
Errors:				
Derivational	3	1	8	5
Semantic	5	7	1	3
Visual	5	9	1	2
Visual/semantic	0	0	1	1
Multi–word	8	3	4	2
Neologisms	0	0	2	2
Unrelated	9	16	3	1
Omissions	3	7	8	9

alternating case of the letters, or of their alternating size? To investigate this, words were presented on a VDU by a BBC computer in normal mode 4 lower case, in alternating case with the lower case letters enlarged to the same height as the upper case (apart, of course, from ascenders and descenders which were larger), and in lower case size alternated letters. The words occurred in the same order of presentation in each of the three tests 24 hours

TABLE 2.9
Effects of Visual Manipulations on Oral Word Reading. The Effect of Size Alternated Lower
Case Letters Compared to Case Alternation Holding Size Constant and Small Lower Case
Letters (BBC Computer Mode 4; n=75)

	Small lower case	Size alternated	Case alternated
Proportion correct	.59	.35	.47
Mean RT correct (secs)	3.49	3.11	3.35
Standard error	.36	.37	.39
Errors:			
Derivational	1	5	5
Semantic	8	16	11
Visual	9	10	6
Visual/semantic	2	1	0
Visual→semantic	0	1	0
Multi–word	4	6	2
Unrelated	4	7	13
Omissions	3	3	3

apart. Each word occurred once in each mode of presentation, the order of which was randomly assigned.

The results (Table 2.9) show that the three presentation conditions have significant effects on T.M.'s success rate in reading ($Q(2) = 13.89$, $p < 0.001$). Pairwise comparisons using McNemar's test show that performance with normal, lower case presentation is better than case alternation ($p < 0.05$) or size alternation ($p < 0.001$); the difference between size alternation and case alternation fails to reach significance ($p = 0.12$, two tailed), although the absolute size of the difference is as large as that between lower case and case alternation.

3. The Effect of Diagonal Word Presentation

T.M. was given words either typed normally in lower case, or typed diagonally with each letter a half line lower than the one before, in alternating blocks of four in two sessions.

He is very much worse at reading the diagonal words (see Table 2.10; McNemar, $p < 0.02$). Again his errors on these are mainly unrelated responses.

4. B.B.C. or b.b.c.?

If T.M. *can* read aloud or understand sets of initials in their unusual, lower case of presentation then this will be evidence that he has functioning ALIs. The reason for this is that there is evidence that normal people have lexical representations for these abbreviations that are case specific (Henderson &

TABLE 2.10
Effects of Visual Manipulation on Oral Word Reading. The Effect of Writing Words Diagonally (Lower Case Elite Type; n=50)

	Lower case	Diagonal
Proportion correct	.27	.08
Errors:		
Derivational	3	1
Semantic	10	7
Visual	6	3
Visual/semantic	2	0
Unrelated	13	29
Omissions	1	4

Chard, 1976). To access these representations T.M. must be able to convert the lower case letters into upper case forms.[7]

T.M. was given 30 such abbreviations to read in their upper and lower case forms (typed Olivetti). The items were presented in the same random order in two separate sessions; the order of conditions for each abbreviation was random, with equal numbers of items in each condition in each session. He read none of them correctly. He made a variety of errors, for example:

T.U.C.→trade unions	*t.u.c.*→farming
I.R.A.→army	*i.r.a.*→seaside
R.S.P.C.A.→animals	*r.s.p.c.a.*→Corsica
O.A.P.→meals	*o.a.p.*→washing
F.B.I.→America	*f.b.i.*→SOS
G.E.C.→Conservative moneywise	*g.e.c.*→SSSR[8]

His responses were rated on a four point scale for semantic relatedness to the stimulus by three sophisticated judges, blind as to the case of presentation or the source or purpose of the data. The median ratings were taken; with upper case presentation 14/30 were rated moderately or closely related compared to only 1/30 of the lower case initials. The only set of initials for which he produced a semantically related response with lower case presentation was *m.i.5*→"national security"—this was the only stimulus that involved any non-letters.

T.M. is clearly severely impaired in his comprehension of these sets of initials when they are presented in lower case. Performance in this provides no evidence that he has functioning ALIs. However, other deep dyslexics who are unimpaired in cross case matching and reading mutilated words have some difficulty with reading t.u.c. or f.b.i. (Patterson, personal communication). It is T.M.'s almost total failure to show evidence of comprehension of lower case abbreviations that is striking.

Comment

Unlike most deep dyslexics, and unlike his "control," V.I.S., T.M. has great difficulty when asked to read words whose usual visual form has been mutilated, even though their component letters remain clearly visible and in linear order and T.M. has unlimited time to respond. He must, therefore, have additional sources of information available from words presented in

---

[7] I am grateful to Derek Besner for suggesting this.

[8] T.U.C. is Trades Union Congress; I.R.A. is the Irish Republican Army; R.S.P.C.A. is an animal protection society; O.A.P. stands for old age pensioner; the F.B.I. is an American "security" organisation; and G.E.C. is a British-based multinational company.

their familiar lower case form. Where the normal form is severely mutilated, as in words where either case or size are alternated, or there are plus signs between the letters, his reading is very poor.

SCRIPT EFFECTS IN ORAL WORD READING

If T.M. is using information from the shape of the word in addressing word recognition units, then his performance should be better for lower case words than their upper case equivalents, as upper case words have no distinctive contour. Hand-written words might be easier still, as it is possible that they emphasise overall contour, even at the expense of the legibility of individual letters.

T.M. was therefore given 75 words in upper case or lower case elite, or in my (moderately careful) handwriting; the test was in three sessions with each mode of presentation in blocks of five.

The results (Table 2.11) show a significant difference between conditions $(Q(2) = 8.00, p < 0.025)$; he is significantly more successful with written words than upper case $(p < 0.001)$, but none of the other differences are significant.

I, therefore, attempted to replicate the result using a different word set, a different type face and different (and worse) handwriting. The results (Table 2.12) show no significant differences between conditions $(Q(2) = 1.74, p > 0.3)$. The advantage, such as it is, is with upper case words.

I then attempted to replicate the result of the first experiment using the original procedure and stimuli. The results (Table 2.13) show no difference between conditions $(Q(2) = 1.39, p = 0.5)$.

Finally, a comparison was made of T.M.'s reading of words in three typefaces, two of which, while conventional, are relatively rarely seen. 20

TABLE 2.11
Script Effects in Oral Reading 1. A Comparison of Script, Elite Lower Case and Elite Upper Case (n=75)

	Written	*Lower case*	*Upper case*
Proportion correct	.47	.39	.31
Errors:			
Derivational	2	4	5
Semantic	18	16	18
Visual	5	8	13
Visual/semantic	0	3	4
Visual→semantic	2	1	0
Multi–word	3	5	5
Unrelated	7	7	⁊ 7
Omissions	3	2	0

TABLE 2.12
Script Effects in Oral Reading 2. A Comparison of Script, Olivetti Lower Case and Olivetti Upper Case (n=72)

	Written	Lower case	Upper case
Proportion correct	.35	.39	.43
Errors:			
Derivational	0	7	2
Semantic	10	12	13
Visual	8	3	2
Visual/semantic	3	6	5
Multi–word	6	4	8
Unrelated	16	7	7
Omissions	4	4	4

point Times was chosen as a familiar and conventional typeface, and compared with a gothic script (Letraset 20pt Old English) and a computer script (Letraset 20pt Data 70). Sixty words were presented three times in the same order in separate sessions; each word occurred once in each typeface, and the order of typefaces for each word was randomly assigned with the constraint that one third of the words in each session had each typeface.

The results (Table 2.14) show that T.M. is equally successful at reading words in each typeface (Q(2) = 1.04; n.s.). Although the gothic and computer typefaces are not very frequently encountered, T.M. does not find them hard to read.

Comment

There are no reliable script effects on the accuracy of T.M.'s reading. Upper case words, despite their lack of word shape information, are as likely to be

TABLE 2.13
Script Effects in Oral Reading 3. A Comparison of Script, Elite Lower Case and Elite Upper Case—a Replication of Script Effects 1 (n=75)

	Written	Lower case	Upper case
Proportion correct	.35	.35	.29
Errors:			
Derivational	4	6	5
Semantic	18	17	22
Visual	9	7	8
Visual/semantic	2	4	3
Visual→semantic	1	1	2
Multi–word	4	4	2
Unrelated	10	10	8
Omissions	1	0	3

TABLE 2.14
Script Effects in Oral Reading 4. A Comparison of Reading Single Words Written in Times,
Gothic and Computer Typefaces (n=75)

	Times	Gothic	Computer
Proportion correct	.42	.37	.43
Errors:			
Derivational	4	7	4
Semantic	12	9	17
Visual	7	4	7
Visual/semantic	0	1	0
Visual→semantic	1	3	0
Multi–word	6	3	2
Unrelated	4	8	2
Omissions	1	3	2

read correctly as lower case or hand-written words. Words in unusual typefaces are read as accurately as those in a familiar typeface.

WORD SHAPE AND LEXICAL DECISION

The set of experiments on the effects of different scripts seem to indicate that T.M. does not rely on information from the word contour in word recognition. Another way of approaching this same question is through lexical decision. Use of word contour might mislead T.M. into misclassifying non-words such as *womaw* or *salab*, that preserve the contour of real words, more often than non-words whose final letter creates an impossible shape in the context of the other letters (e.g. *womah*, *salam*).

Eighty word triads were prepared, each consisting of one real high imageability word, and two non-words derived from it by substitution of the final letter. One of these preserved the shape of the original word (shape preserved non-word), and the other made a shape which was impossible in the context of the other letters (shape changed non-word). With 40 triads the shape change involved the substitution of a square letter by an ascender or a descender, 20 involved substitution of an ascender by a square letter or a descender, and 20 involved substitution of a descender by a square letter or an ascender. The stimuli were presented by a BBC microcomputer in lower case mode 7 double height letters in three separate sessions in random order, with the following constraints: (1) only one member of each triad occurred in any session; (2) there were no sequences of more than three words or non-words; (3) equal numbers of stimuli of each sort occurred in each session.

The results (Table 2.15) are straightforward: there is no trace of a difference in either accuracy or latency of response between the two classes of

TABLE 2.15

Word Shape and Lexical Decision; Accuracy and Mean Reaction Times of Responses to Real Words and Two Types of Non–word (n=80 of Each Type; the Standard Errors of the Mean Reaction Times Are in Brackets)

	Real words	*Non–words*	
		Shape Preserved	*Shape changed*
Examples	money	moneg	monem
	tiger	tigen	tigel
	girl	girk	gire
Response			
Yes	68	28	28
No	12	52	52
Reaction times (secs)			
Yes responses	2.72 (.12)	3.29 (.24)	3.38 (.18)
No responses	2.32 (.15)	2.45 (.18)	2.46 (.16)

non-word. Thus, in lexical decision, T.M. is not mislead by the similarity in shape between *womaw* and *woman*. It seems unlikely that there are any real differences that are masked by either floor or ceiling effects; T.M.'s performance, while better than chance, is fairly poor (overall d' = 1.42). He makes substantial numbers of false positives—but whether he does so is not affected by a non-word's contour resemblance to a real word.

This experiment, therefore, confirms and extends the results reported in the previous section; neither lexical decision nor oral word reading yields any evidence that T.M. relies particularly on contour information in word recognition.

DISCUSSION

To summarise the important results, T.M. is:

1. Very poor at cross case matching of letters.
2. Unable to understand abbreviations written in the inappropriate case.
3. Very much worse than normal at oral word reading if letters are separated by + signs; if letters are case alternated or size alternated; or if they are written diagonally.
4. Unaffected in oral word reading accuracy by whether words are in upper or lower case, or are hand-written; whether they are in common or uncommon typefaces; or by whether the letters are separated by spaces.

These problems are not, in any simple way, related to T.M.'s deep dyslexia. Other deep dyslexic patients, and the "severe" deep dyslexic control, V.I.S., do not show these difficulties. In any case, all current accounts of the deep dyslexic symptomcomplex agree that the problems of such patients arise *after* word recognition units have been accessed.

There is at least one case of a patient who had difficulty in cross case and cross script matching (A.R.—Warrington & Shallice, 1979); but the effects of format distortion on A.R.'s reading are not reported. As far as I am aware, there are no reports of acquired dyslexic patients who can read (at least to some extent) and who have specific difficulty in reading mutilated words.[9]

T.M. and the ALI Theory of Word Recognition

Is it possible to provide an account of T.M.'s problems that remains compatible with the theory that word recognition depends on preliminary letter identification alone?

On the face of it this is a difficult task; T.M. behaves in exactly the way one would expect of a patient who has *no* knowledge of the abstract identity of letters. He shows no ability to use their output either in a task requiring *explicit* knowledge of letter identities (letter cross case matching), or in a task that requires *tacit* use of this knowledge (understanding b.b.c.). The ALI theory makes a very specific prediction here: a patient who has no access to the output of ALIs will be unable to recognise any words. T.M. undoubtedly can do so, even if rather poorly.

The ALI theory was constructed to explain why format distortions have so little effect on word recognition. It predicts specifically that these distortions do not affect the accuracy of word recognition. Yet case alternation, size alternation, diagonal word presentation, and + signs between letters all reduce the accuracy of T.M.'s oral word reading by significant and substantial amounts.

Despite this, can one generate an argument that will reconcile the existence of T.M.'s symptomcomplex with the ALI theory? It is possible to identify the level of the problem responsible for T.M.'s difficulty with format distorted words with some precision. It is clear that his difficulties cannot be accounted for by a deficit at a level more peripheral than the ALIs; if T.M. has a problem with visual analysis, all words, mutilated or not, should be equally affected. Processes at a level more central than that of the ALIs are supposed to have no access to information specifying the format of the word. As other deep dyslexics do not show format effects, the remainder of his dyslexic symptoms are unrelated to this problem; his problems with reading

---

[9]Children in their first year of school are much less accurate at reading case alternated words compared to those in lower case (Seymour & Elder, 1986).

distorted words cannot be due to a deficit more central than the word recognition system.

One possible account is in terms of the "expectations" of the case of the letters within a word which are supposed to allow the preferential accumulation of visual features appropriate to words with a consistent format. Suppose that T.M. generates "overexpectations" such that a detection of an initial lower case letter will *prevent* the accumulation of information to identify a letter in an inconsistent (upper) case that follows. This predicts that T.M. will be poor at recognising case alternated words. To account for the difficulty in reading size alternated words, the expectations must specify the size as well as the case of the other letters. To explain the effects of diagonal word presentation, we must suppose that T.M. generates expectations about the position of the letter as well. But, s p a c i n g of the letters does not affect T.M.'s reading, so we are now forced to claim that these expectations specify only *some* information about the position of the letters that follow. Clearly an account in these terms would have to explain why T.M. should be so disabled by expectations that have so small an effect on normal subjects, and why these expectations specify certain features and not others.[10]

T.M. and the Theory of Multiple Sources of Information in Word Recognition

A simpler explanation is that words in a normal format have additional information that T.M. can use in accessing word recognition units; that is, that multiple sources of information are used in word recognition. The amount of information that he can receive from an ALI route must be fairly low to account for his very poor performance with the mutilated words. What, then, is the additional information that T.M. uses?

Does T.M. use word shape/contour information in reading? Upper case words lack any distinctive contour, but T.M. is as good at reading them as lower case words. T.M. does not appear to rely on contour information in reading; nor does he appear to use contour information in lexical decision.

Does T.M. use transletter features in reading? Since it is never clearly specified exactly what transletter features are, this question is not easy to answer. They will, clearly, be severely disrupted by case alternations, size

---

[10]Can T.M.'s difficulties be accounted for by the ALI theory in terms of the theoretical position put forward by Norman and Bobrow (1975)? An account in these terms might take a form somewhat as follows: the lack of an effect of format distortion on normal word recognition is due to the fact that in normal conditions word recognition is a data-limited process. For T.M., who has limited resources available, distorted words will present a particular problem, as he will be unable to allocate the additional resources needed. The trouble with such an account is that the ALI theory is put forward to explain why recognition of distorted words appears *not* to require more resources than the recognition of normal words.

alternation or + signs, all of which disrupt T.M.'s reading. But one must expect that s p a c e s between letters would also disrupt them to some extent; this manipulation does not affect T.M.'s reading.

This leads to the interesting position that there is no convincing evidence that T.M. relies on any of the three sources of information that the "normal" literature suggests to access his word recognition units. One possibility is that T.M. is using all of these routes (or a combination of two of them), but all are operating inefficiently; a disruption of any one will lead to a reduction in accuracy in oral word reading. This account, vague as it is, might account for much of the data; but, there is a problem. Spaces between letters should interfere with information from both word shape and transletter features, yet this leaves reading accuracy unaffected.

A Two Route Account of Word Recognition

Is there another possibility? If T.M. does not use an analytic approach that identifies the sequence of letters in a word, could it be that he uses a "global" method for identifying words, treating them not as letter strings but more as if they were pictures, where the parts of which they are composed are meaningless on their own? Words in a familiar form will then be readable, but once distorted by case or size alternation they will become uninterpretable. Simple, and familiar, distortion, by, for example, spaces between letters, will leave the words recognisable in much the same way as an elongated picture of a tiger, or a stylised picture of a tiger, are still clearly tigers.

If a global route to word recognition is proposed, why is there no evidence that disruption of global features of words affects word recognition by normal subjects?

Experiments with normal subjects do, however, yield two contradictory sets of empirical results. Some, like Adams (1979) and McLelland (1976) purport to show no effects of format distortion on word recognition. Others show the importance of global features (Besner, 1983 expt 1; Monk & Hulme, 1983; Underwood & Bargh, 1982). Is a resolution of this contradiction possible?

Evidence for an ALI route is found in experiments that require identification of *letters* in lists of mixed words and pseudowords presented in brief tachistoscopic flashes divorced from any linguistic or communicative context.

Evidence for the importance of global word features comes from experiments where real words are clearly visible in comprehensible text.

This is clearly compatible with the suggestion that normal subjects have two different methods available to them that can be used in word recognition.[11] Any one experiment will find evidence for the use of the route whose characteristics best fit the demands of the task. The ALI route appears to provide the most detailed analysis of limited sensory information when the possibilities of using additional information from outside the stimulus are severely limited. The ALI route is then best equipped to extract each last piece of information from the visual form; it can be likened to an archaeologist studying an exotic culture. A view about the nature of the culture is painstakingly built up by making the best inferences about various components—its pottery, housing, agriculture etc.—that the limited evidence will permit.

The "global" word recognition route is used in situations where abundant information is available from the context. One could conceive of it as operating fairly indiscriminatingly in text reading where "top down" processing can be maximised, acting more as a way of confirming a reader's expectations about a word than as a way of uniquely identifying it. It is, then, the tourist's view; with plenty of prejudice and guide-book information, the tourist makes a quick (and often inaccurate) judgement of a culture on a brief assessment of a few superficial features, while knowing nothing of its component parts.

If T.M. has lost his ALIs, he will be forced to rely on the "global" route for word recognition even in reading isolated words, where its use is normally inappropriate. The use of this "inefficient" route accounts for a number of other features of T.M.'s dyslexia. It explains why he makes visual errors on concrete words, why he makes so many errors in lexical decision, and why he makes comprehension errors on concrete words even where the foils are semantically unrelated to the target. The "global" route to word recognition appears to work preferentially for high frequency words; T.M.'s errors in recognition occur particularly on low frequency words (cf. Monk & Hulme, 1983). On the other hand, in both T.M.'s reading and in word recognition in text there is no word length effect (Monk & Hulme, 1983).

Seymour, in Fig. 15.4 of Chapter 15, outlines a developmentally-oriented model of reading which incorporates two routes for visual word recognition, one based on abstract letter identities and the other based on logographic recognition, and provides evidence that very young normal readers resemble T.M. in that their reading is mediated by the logographic route.

All the evidence is that T.M. has no abstract knowledge of the component parts of words, but he can recognise whole words when they are not subjected to any unfamiliar format distortion. Within the range of normal distortions, his performance is unaffected. As far as it is possible to be an

---

[11] A two route theory of word recognition is not new; Newcombe and Marshall (1980), for example, imply something similar.

ideographic reader of an alphabetic script, T.M. is one; it appears that he recognises words with no knowledge of their component letters.

ACKNOWLEDGEMENTS

I am grateful to T.M. and his family for their co-operation, to Dr M. I. P. Wilkinson and Dr N. E. Gilchrist for their support, and for allowing me to study T.M. who was under their care. I thank Ginnie Orchard-Lisle for her help in collecting some of these data. Ruth Campbell made useful criticisms of a draft of the paper. This work was partly supported by a grant from the North East Thames Regional Health Authority and partly by a grant from the Medical Research Council; travel expenses were met by a grant from the Tregaskis Fund of the University of London.

REFERENCES

Adams, M. J. (1979) Models of word recognition. *Cognitive Psychology, 11,* 133–176.

Baron, J., & Strawson, C. (1976) Use of orthographic and word-specific knowledge in reading words aloud. *Journal of Experimental Psychology: Human Perception and Performance, 2,* 386–393.

Besner, D. (1983) Basic decoding components in reading: Two dissociable feature extraction processes. *Canadian Journal of Psychology, 37,* 429–438.

Besner, D., Davelaar, B., Alcott, D., & Parry, P. (1984) Wholistic reading of alphabetic print: Evidence from the FDM and the FBI. In L. Henderson (Ed.), *Orthographies and Reading: Perspectives from Cognitive Psychology, Neuropsychology and Linguistics,* pp. 121–135. Hillsdale, New Jersey: Lawrence Erlbaum Associates.

Coltheart, M., & Freeman, R. (1974) Case alternation impairs word identification. *Bulletin of the Psychonomic Society, 3,* 102–104.

Coltheart, M. (1980) Analysing acquired disorders of reading. Unpublished manuscript.

Coltheart, M., Patterson, K., & Marshall, J. C. (Eds.) (1980) *Deep dyslexia.* London: Routledge & Kegan Paul.

Dunn, M. (1965) *The Peabody Picture Vocabulary Test.* Minneapolis: American Guidance Service.

Evett, L., & Humphreys, G. W. (1981) The use of abstract graphemic information in lexical access. *Quarterly Journal of Experimental Psychology, 33A,* 325–350.

Funnell, E. (1983) Phonological processes in reading: New evidence from acquired dyslexia. *British Journal of Psychology, 74,* 159–180.

Goodglass, H., & Kaplan, E. (1972) *The assessment of aphasia and related disorders.* Philadelphia: Lea and Febiger.

Henderson, L. (1982) *Orthography and word recognition in reading.* London: Academic Press.

Henderson, L., & Chard, M. J. (1976) On the nature of the facilitation of physical comparisons by lexical membership. *Bulletin of the Psychonomic Society, 7,* 432–434.

Howard, D. (1982) Different ways of being "agrammatic": sentence processing by deep dyslexics. *Working Papers of the London Psycholinguistics Research Group, 4,* 58–69.

Howard, D., Patterson, K. E., Franklin, S., Orchard-Lisle, V. M., & Morton, J. (1984) Variability and consistency in picture naming by aphasic patients. In F. C. Rose (Ed.), *Progress in aphasiology*, pp. 263–276. New York: Raven Press.

McLelland, J. L. (1976). Preliminary letter identification in the perception of words and non-words. *Journal of Experimental Psychology: Human Perception and Performance, 2*, 80–91.

McLelland, J. L., & Rummelhart, D. E. (1981) An interactive activation model of context effects in letter perception: Part one. An account of basic findings. *Psychological Review, 88*, 375–407.

Monk, A. F., & Hulme, C. (1983) Errors in proofreading: Evidence for the use of word shape in word recognition. *Memory and Cognition, 11*, 16–23.

Morton, J., & Patterson, K. E. (1980) A new attempt at an interpretation, or an attempt at a new interpretation. In M. Coltheart, K. E. Patterson, & J. C. Marshall (Eds.), *Deep dyslexia*. London: Routledge & Kegan Paul.

Newcombe, F., & Marshall, J. C. (1980) Transcoding and lexical stabilisation in deep dyslexia. In M. Coltheart, K. E. Patterson, & J. C. Marshall (Eds.), *Deep dyslexia*. London: Routledge & Kegan Paul.

Norman, D. A., & Bobrow, D. G. (1975) On data-limited and resource-limited processes. *Cognitive Psychology, 7*, 44–64.

Patterson, K. E. (1979) What is right with "deep" dyslexic patients? *Brain and Language, 8*, 111–129.

Patterson, K. E. (1980) Reading errors of P.W. and D.E. In M. Coltheart, K. E. Patterson, & J. C. Marshall (Eds.), *Deep dyslexia*. London: Routledge & Kegan Paul.

Patterson, K. E. (1981) Neuropsychological approaches to the study of reading. *British Journal of Psychology, 72*, 151–174.

Saffran, E. M., & Marin, O. S. M. (1977) Reading without phonology: Evidence from aphasia. *Quarterly Journal of Experimental Psychology, 29*, 307–318.

Seymour, P. H. K., & Elder, L. (1986) Beginning reading without phonology. *Cognitive Neuropsychology, 3*, 1–26.

Shallice, T., & Warrington, E. K. (1975) Word recognition in a phonemic dyslexic patient. *Quarterly Journal of Experimental Psychology, 27*, 187–200.

Shallice, T, & Warrington, E. K. (1980) Reading responses of K.F. In M. Coltheart, K. E. Patterson, & J. C. Marshall (Eds.), *Deep dyslexia*. London: Routledge & Kegan Paul.

Smith, F. (1969) Familiarity of configuration vs. discriminability of features in the visual identification of words. *Psychonomic Science, 14*, 261–263.

Underwood, G., & Bargh, K. (1982) Word shape, orthographic regularity, and contextual interactions in a reading task. *Cognition, 12*, 197–209.

Warrington, E. K., & Shallice, T. (1979) Semantic access dyslexia. *Brain, 102*, 43–63.

3 Direct-Route Reading and the Locus of Lexical Decision

Giuseppe Sartori
Istituto di Psicologia, Università di Padova, Padova, Italy

Jacqueline Masterson
Psychology Department, City of London Polytechnic, London, England

Remo Job
Dipartimento di Psicologia dello Sviluppo e della Socializzazione, Università di Padova, Padova, Italy

INTRODUCTION

The Logogen model of word recognition (Morton & Patterson, 1980), which is outlined in Fig. 3.1, postulates that the pronunciation for printed letter strings can be obtained in one of three ways. One of these ways involves treating the stimulus as a sequence of graphemes which are converted by rule into a phonological code. A second way involves categorisation of the stimulus in the visual input logogen system and the subsequent transmission of information to the cognitive system. Here the appropriate semantics can be found and sent to the output logogen system where the phonological code is obtained. The third way again involves the categorisation of the stimulus in the visual input logogen system, but instead of information being subsequently sent to the cognitive system, it is sent directly to the output logogen system where the appropriate phonological code is produced.

This research has been carried out while Jacqueline Masterson was a recipient of a Royal Society postdoctoral fellowship. The work has been partially supported by a grant from Ministero della Pubblica Istruzione (fondi 60%).

CNL–C*

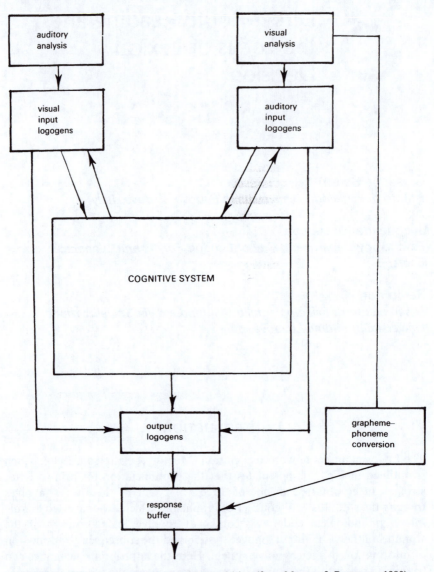

FIG. 3.1   The Logogen model of word recognition (from Morton & Patterson, 1980).

The focus of the present paper is on the third of the three ways for obtaining the pronunciation for printed letter strings, which involves the direct connection between the input logogen system and the output logogen system, and a single case study is presented of a neurological patient whose reading aloud appears to be mediated by this route alone. Whereas empirical evidence for reading aloud mediated by the cognitive system or by grapheme-phoneme conversion is based on a combination of studies conducted with normal skilled readers and neurological patients (see, among others, Coltheart, 1978, 1980; Morton, 1979; Morton & Patterson, 1980), evidence concerning a direct connection between the input and output logogen systems derives solely from studies of neurological patients. The first of these is a report by Schwartz, Saffran and Marin (1980) who describe a case of presenile dementia in a patient suffering from progressive memory loss. The patient was able to correctly read aloud words that she was unable to match to pictured referents. She was also unable to make simple categorical judgements (for example, deciding whether the word represented an animal name) about printed words that she read aloud correctly. The patient's reading aloud performance could not have been mediated by grapheme-phoneme conversion, because words that form exceptions to grapheme-phoneme correspondence rules (e.g., *tortoise*, *leopard*) were read aloud correctly. Schwartz et al. argue that since the patient's reading was not mediated by either access to the cognitive system and thence to output logogens (since she showed no evidence of understanding words she could read aloud), nor by grapheme-phoneme conversion (because she could read aloud correctly many exception words) then the only way to account for the data was to postulate a direct connection between input and output logogens that was not mediated by the cognitive system.

Further evidence for the existence of such a direct connection is provided by Funnell (1983) who reports a patient who had suffered from a cerebrovascular accident that left him with difficulties with expressive speech, auditory comprehension, and reading and writing. The patient was severely impaired in reading aloud non-words (he scored 0/20 correct when reading aloud non-homophonic non-words four and five letters long), but read aloud correctly 85% of words given in a variety of reading tests. A series of word matching experiments showed, however, that reading aloud was not dependent on semantic mediation. In the first of the experiments pairs of semantically related printed words were presented (e.g., *lemon-orange*, *sock-glove*, *twig-branch*) and an additional printed word was presented that was more closely related to one of the words in the pair than the other (e.g., *lemon-orange | tangerine*). The patient was required to select from the pair of words the one which was most closely related to the probe word. The test was repeated using unrelated word pairs (e.g., *plate-glove | mitten*). The patient's matching performance with related printed words was significantly worse than his performance with unrelated word pairs. This pattern of results was also obtained when the probe word was presented auditorily rather than visually. Funnell (1983) argues that the semantic processing deficit shown by the patient is not compatible with his reading aloud ability, since he was able to read aloud correctly all of the words used in the word matching experiments. As the patient had lost the ability to read aloud non-words, and therefore could not be reading aloud by means of grapheme-phoneme conversion, and as reading aloud could not have been mediated by the impaired semantic system, Funnell concludes that the patient's reading is mediated by the direct connections between orthographic and phonological lexical representations.

A third line of evidence for this direct connection is provided by investigations of printed word comprehension in two cases of surface dyslexia (Coltheart, Masterson, Byng, Prior, & Riddoch, 1983). The two subjects, one a neurological patient and the other a developmental dyslexic, when required to provide definitions of printed words, demonstrated a tendency to confuse homophones (for example, defining *steak* as "a fencing post" and *stake* as "a piece of meat"). Coltheart et al. interpret homophone confusions with regularly-spelled printed homophones in terms of the derivation of a phonological code for the word by means of grapheme-phoneme conversion and the subsequent use of this code to gain access to the cognitive system. As the code is phonological rather than visual, then the meaning appropriate to the homophonous partner of the target may be accessed. Homophone confusions with irregularly-spelled homophones cannot be explained in this way, however, because if grapheme-phoneme conversion was used to derive the phonological code for the irregularly-spelled homophones this would result in "regularisation" errors (for example, *steak*→/stik/) and such a phonological representation would not access the meaning of the homophonous partner of the target in the cognitive system. Coltheart et al. argue that homophone confusions with irregularly-spelled homophones must be the result of accessing the phonological representation for the target via the direct connection between input and output logogens and the subsequent use of this phonological representation to gain access to the cognitive system.

The crucial property of this third reading route is that it is lexical but not semantic. It is lexical in the sense that it cannot be used for processing non-words, and it is nonsemantic in the sense that it does not utilise the semantic component of the language-processing system. One can define analogous lexical-nonsemantic procedures for other language tasks. These have as yet received very little attention, but some of the possibilities are discussed in the chapters by Patterson and Shewell (Chapter 13) and by Kremin (Chapter 14). For example, Kremin argues that the patient she studied was performing two language tasks by lexical-nonsemantic procedures, namely, writing to dictation and repeating single words.

The subject of the present report is an Italian neurological patient who shows good reading aloud performance but little evidence of understanding the words she reads aloud. The patient described here is virtually unable to read aloud non-words. Since reading aloud for this patient cannot be mediated by grapheme-phoneme conversion, given that she is unable to read non-words aloud, and since it cannot be mediated by the cognitive system, given that she shows no evidence of understanding some of the words that she reads aloud, it is concluded that her reading is mediated by direct input-output logogen connections. Experimental investigation of the reading ability of such patients is of theoretical importance because a number of predictions can be made about reading performance according to the Logogen model. The first issue that is addressed in connection with the patient described here concerns the locus of the processing involved in the lexical decision task (in which subjects are required to judge whether printed letter strings are words or non-words). Morton (1982) has argued that lexical decisions are based primarily on the operation of processes in the cognitive system. If this is the case then patients who rely for reading aloud on the direct connection between input logogens and output logogens should be incapable of making accurate lexical decisions since they are unable to gain access to the cognitive system when processing printed letter strings. If, however, such patients are capable of good performance in the lexical decision task, then we must conclude that the locus for lexical decisions is at some point other than in the cognitive system.

The logogen system has been described as a passive system containing information-collecting units but no semantic information (Morton & Patterson, 1980; Morton, 1982). This description leads to the prediction that the semantic features of words (such as grammatical class or concreteness) should not have an effect on the reading aloud performance of patients who read aloud by direct input-output logogen connections. The second characteristic of the reading performance of the patient described here that was investigated was the effect of semantic features of printed words that have been described as being represented in the cognitive system only.

CASE REPORT

Lisa, the patient, was a 68-year-old housewife with eight years of formal education. She suffered a transient ischaemic attack in August 1981 and an echo-doppler performed at that time revealed a stenosis of the right internal carotid. On 17 November 1982 she suddenly developed a right hemiparesis with aphasia. On 25 November angiography showed a subocclusion of the right internal carotid 12mm from the origin. On 26 November a CT scan without contrast revealed a large ischaemic area involving the left frontal lobe. A lateral reconstruction showing this ischaemic area is represented in Fig. 3.2.

Neuropsychological examination carried out at the patient's bedside on 22 November 1982 revealed fluent speech, which was without content, and echolalia. The patient was unable to name common objects (a key, a pen, a watch, etc.) although repetition was good for both single words and

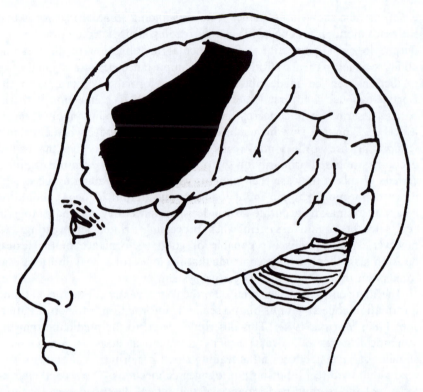

FIG. 3.2   Lateral reconstruction showing ischaemic area (shaded) for LISA.

sentences. One week later a formal examination was carried out using the Milan Aphasia Screening Test. The patient was able to name only 2/20 of the pictures in the test, her errors consisting mainly of perseverations. Automatic sequences (such as days of the week) were correctly recited and repetition was found to be perfect for words, non-words, and short and long (up to 13 word) sentences. However, comprehension of auditorily and visually presented words was found to be severely impaired. The patient scored 1/20 correct on a test of comprehension of auditorily presented words and was able to carry out correctly only 1/10 spoken commands. In tests of reading comprehension she scored 1/20 correct with single words and 0/5 correct with sentences. In writing the names of pictures the patient produced a series of neologisms and spontaneous writing was limited to her signature.

EXPERIMENTAL INVESTIGATION

Given Lisa's comprehension problems, it is crucial to be sure of her understanding of the experimental instructions. Several methods were employed to achieve this. First of all, verbal instructions were accompanied by appropriate gestures; second, a long practice session was carried out, in which plenty of examples were shown to the patient; third, when the task was a visual one, an auditory analog was first performed since her auditory comprehension was somewhat better; finally, her husband was asked to model the tasks to her, and to explain them to her when necessary.

Reading Aloud and Lexical Decision

Lisa was presented with a total of 364 words and 364 non-words for reading aloud and lexical decision. The words presented to the patient were selected taking into account the main psycholinguistic variables that are thought to affect reading performance. As for non-words, they varied with respect to their visual similarity to real words. Non-words high in visual similarity to words were derived by changing one letter of a real word, and non-words low in visual similarity to words were derived from the anagrams of real words.

First consider Lisa's performance in reading aloud. In Table 3.1 the patient's accuracy in reading the three different types of stimuli is reported.

As can be seen, a great discrepancy exists between performance in reading words and non-words. This pattern may be interpreted as reflecting an impairment of the phonological route. Lisa's erroneous responses to both words and non-words usually consisted of visually similar words. Semantic errors and omissions never occurred, and very few derivational errors were observed. A breakdown of the types of errors made by Lisa in reading aloud is given in Table 3.2.

The Effect of Word-Class, Length, Concreteness, and Frequency on Reading Aloud and Lexical Decision

None of the above-mentioned variables seemed to have an affect on Lisa's performance either in reading aloud or in lexical decision. Table 3.3 summarises Lisa's performance on a test involving reading aloud and lexical decision for 40 nouns, 40 adjectives and 40 verbs with orthogonal rotation of

TABLE 3.1
Reading Aloud Performance With Words and Non–Words (% Correct)

Words (N = 364)	Non–words (N = 364)	
	Visually similar (N = 292)	Visually dissimilar (N = 72)
79.6	16.2	6.9

TABLE 3.2
Types of Error in Reading Aloud

Response	Stimulus	
	Words (N = 364)	Non–words (N = 364)
Visually similar word	68%	58%
Visually similar non–word	24%	29%
Visually dissimilar word	4%	4.4%
Visually dissimilar non–word	1%	1%
Other	3%	7.5%
Omissions	0%	0%

the factors of length (4, 5, 6, and 7 letters) and frequency; and 20 function words (five of each of the lengths 4, 5, 6, and 7 letters) all of which were highly frequent. Non-words were constructed by changing one letter in each of the words and were presented randomly intermixed with the words in both the reading aloud test and in lexical decision. The latter test was presented on one occasion visually and on another occasion auditorily.

Table 3.4 represents Lisa's performance in reading aloud and lexical decision for 80 nouns with orthogonal rotation of the factors of concreteness

TABLE 3.3
Reading Aloud and Lexical Decision Performance for Words of Different Length, Frequency, and Grammatical Class

	Reading (% correct)		Lexical decision					
			Visual			Auditory		
	Words	Non-words	Hits %	False alarms %	d'	Hits	False alarms %	d'
Nouns (N = 40)	78	3	92.5	65	1.05	90	5	2.94
Verbs (N = 40)	65	11	87.5	70	0.61	52.5	22.5	0.82
Adjectives (N = 40)	68	20	87.5	62.5	0.83	67.5	10	1.72
Function words (N = 20)	85	20	85	60	0.79	75	10	1.96
High frequency words	81	18	90	66.3	0.86	83.8	10	2.27
Low frequency words	62	15	86.6	63.3	0.76	55	15	1.17
4 letter words	83	23	91.4	60	1.12	62.9	8.57	1.7
7 letter words	74	6	88.6	71.4	0.64	82.9	11.4	2.16

TABLE 3.4
Reading Aloud and Lexical Decision Performance for Nouns of Different Concreteness and
Frequency

	Reading (% correct)		Visual lexical decision		
	Words	Non–words	Hits %	False alarms (%)	d'
Concrete (N = 40)	83	20	90	43	1.46
Abstract (N = 40)	78	7.5	70	40	1.1
High frequency (N = 40)	75	10	83	53	0.88
Low frequency (N = 40)	85	18	78	30	1.32

and frequency. Non-words were again constructed by changing one letter in each of the words and were presented randomly intermixed with words in both tests. Lexical decision was only presented visually.

The lack of influence of any of the psycholinguistic variables manipulated will be considered in the discussion section. However, we should mention here that Gernsbacher (1984) has recently suggested that variability in word recognition latencies in lexical decision tasks with normal subjects is due to experiential familiarity rather than variables such as concreteness, frequency or polysemy. In a series of lexical decision experiments the author manipulated familiarity, bigram frequency, concreteness, and number of meanings. Of these variables it was found that only experiential familiarity affected word recognition latencies. Effects as large as 250 msec. differences in reaction times and an 18% difference in accuracy were found for high versus low familiarity words, suggesting that the variable is a potent predictor of word recognition. Experiential familiarity was not controlled for in the lists presented to the patient, but, as we have seen, variables such as concreteness, frequency, and so on, did not affect her lexical decision performance.

From Table 3.3 it can be seen that auditory lexical decision was carried out accurately for most categories of words. Performance in visual lexical decision (Tables 3.3 and 3.4), while poorer than performance in the auditory modality, is above chance level. In fact, the differences between the hit rate and the false alarm rate were all significant (all Bulmer (1967) tests were at least p. < 05). This poor performance appears, at first, to be discrepant with Lisa's good performance in reading aloud words (79.6% correct). However, if we examine separately hits and false alarms in lexical decision with visual presentation we can see that errors in the task mostly consist of wrongly classifying a non-word as a word. The seemingly discrepant results for reading aloud and visual lexical decision accuracy can therefore be accommodated if we consider at the same time Lisa's performance in reading aloud words and hit rate in lexical decision. According to the theoretical frame-work presented in the introduction, reading aloud performance should be compatible with the hit rate in visual lexical decision but not the false alarm rate. This is because if a patient who is shown to be incapable of using the phonological route has intact input logogens which allow him/her to read aloud words, he/she should be able to use these same input logogens for recognition of the words in the visual lexical decision. Lisa's hit rate in this task is compatible with such a proposal (74.5% words correctly read and 88.6% hit rate; from Table 3.3).

Since Lisa's errors in reading aloud non-words usually consist of visually similar words, and since non-words used in the lexical decision tasks were all visually similar to words, we decided to investigate the effect of using visually dissimilar non-words on Lisa's lexical decision performance.

The Effect of the Similarity of Non-Words to Words on Lexical Decision Performance

Three sets of concrete nouns were used for lexical decision with auditory and visual presentation. Visually similar non-words were constructed by chang-ing one letter in the words and visually dissimilar non-words were con-structed from the anagrams of words. The results are presented in Table 3.5.

From Table 3.5 it can be seen that the similarity of the non-word to a word leads to a decrease in performance in lexical decision, most notably for visual presentation, the pattern of results being due to an increase in false positive responses. It is important to note that, in spite of this, visual lexical decision accuracy with visually similar distractors ranges between a d' of 2.07 and a d' of 1.78. This level of accuracy is generally higher than that obtained in the previously reported lexical decision tasks (see Tables 3.3 and 3.4), and can be regarded as good. The better performance on the set of items containing visually dissimilar non-words can be explained by assuming that visually similar non-words activate the logogens to a greater extent than visually dissimilar words do, thus increasing the likelihood of accepting a non-word as a word.

Tests of Reading Comprehension

Lisa's ability to comprehend printed words was tested using a synonym matching task, a category discrimination task, an odd-word-out test, and a word-picture matching task.

The synonym matching task was constructed using 20 short, concrete nouns that Lisa had read aloud correctly at a previous testing session, and involved ten pairs of synonyms and ten pairs of non-synonyms (obtained by rearranging the synonym pairs) that were printed on cards. Lisa was asked to

TABLE 3.5
Lexical Decision With Visual and Auditory Presentation

	List 1	*List 2*	*List 3*
Visual lexical decision with dissimilar non–words			
d′	2.57	2.72	3.37
Hits %	100	100	100
False alarms %	40.6	35	15
Visual lexical decision with similar non–words			
d′	1.78	2.07	1.94
Hits %	96.8	100	100
False alarms %	53.1	60	65
Auditory lexical decision with dissimilar non–words			
d′	3.34	3.3	3.98
Hits %	100	95	95
False alarms %	15.6	5	0
Auditory lexical decision with similar non–words			
d′	2.85	2.93	3.17
Hits %	90.6	95	100
False alarms %	6.3	10	20

sort the word pairs into synonyms and non-synonyms and the task was preceded by a training session involving both auditory and visual presentation (although experimental trials involved visual presentation only). Testing did not begin until the experimenter was certain that Lisa had understood the task. Her performance was at chance level ($d′ < 0$).

In a second task of comprehension Lisa was required to sort 40 short nouns into "animal" and "not animal" categories. The hit rate in this task was 15/20 and the false alarm rate was 13/20, yielding a d′ of 0.29. When the same words were presented for reading aloud Lisa correctly read 19/20 of the nouns referring to animals and 15/20 of the non-animal nouns. Of the 34 words read correctly 18 were correctly categorised and 16 were not. This result shows that the correct reading aloud does not predict classification performance, giving further evidence of independence of the ability to read aloud and comprehend written words. This task was also presented auditorily and Lisa made 95% hits and 55% false alarms ($d′ = 1.15$).

For the odd-word-out test Lisa was presented with 20 sets of four nouns. In each set three of the words belonged to a particular semantic category (e.g. animals, kitchen utensils) and one did not. Lisa was required to indicate the word which did not belong to the same semantic category as the others for each of the 20 quadruplets. The test was presented visually and Lisa scored 6/20 correct (chance performance on the test would be equal to 5/20).

The word-picture matching task was carried out on the same words used for the three lexical decision tests reported in Table 3.5. Words were presented either visually or auditorily, and the patient was asked to choose the corresponding picture either among the pictures of all the items in the list (for list 2 and 3) or among a sub-set of four of them (list 1). Lisa's performance is reported in Table 3.6.

Tests of Ability to Discriminate Semantic Variables

Lisa was presented with 40 nouns and was required to sort the 20 concrete nouns from the 20 abstract ones (for a list of the words used, see Appendix 1). The two sets of nouns were matched for frequency. Testing was preceded by a training session involving examples presented both visually and auditorily and the experimental trials were not begun until the tester was certain that Lisa had understood the instructions. With visual presentation she made 17 hits and five false alarms ($d' = 1.71$), and with auditory presentation she made 16 hits and two false alarms ($d' = 2.12$).

She was next presented with 20 nouns and 20 function words (for a list of stimulus items used, see Appendix 2) and was required to sort the nouns from the function words. Testing was again preceded by a training session. Presentation in this test was visual only, and she made 17 hits and six false alarms ($d' = 1.57$). Performance on this test is also relatively good. However, its interpretation may not be unequivocal, as nouns tend to be of higher concreteness value than function words.

It could be argued that the patient's poor performance on certain tasks is the result of her failure to understand task instruction. If poor comprehension of the instructions was responsible for poor performance, then we would

TABLE 3.6
Accuracy on the Word–Picture Matching Task

	Visual	Auditory	Number of alternatives in the pictures set	Chance level
List 1 (N = 32)	9/32	8/32	4	8/32
List 2 (N = 20)	1/20	1/20	20	1/20
List 3 (N = 20)	1/20	4/20	20	1/20

expect performance to be worse on tests that were more difficult to explain. This does not appear to be the case, however, since Lisa is impaired at word-picture matching, which would seem to be an easy test to describe to her, and has good performance in concrete-abstract noun discrimination, a task which would appear to be much more difficult to grasp for a patient with impaired oral comprehension. In addition, the result of the task in which she was required to discriminate auditorily presented words on the basis of the feature animal/not-animal confirms our clinical impression that she was able to understand the task.

DISCUSSION

Lisa was able to read on average 80% of the words presented to her for reading aloud but performed at chance level on tests of printed word comprehension. She showed poor performance in reading aloud non-words (16% correct) but as she was able to repeat non-words correctly then her problem with reading them cannot lie at the output stage and is interpreted within the Logogen model as an impairment of the route based on grapheme-phoneme conversion. In addition, Lisa was found to be capable of making accurate discrimination about words in the lexical decision tasks that were presented to her. This was especially true if the stimuli were presented visually with dissimilar distractors, or auditorily.

On the basis of the Logogen model presented in the introduction, the presence of the two impairments of access to the cognitive system from print and of grapheme-phoneme conversion means that Lisa's good reading aloud performance with words must be mediated by the direct connections between input and output logogens. Recently, Shallice, Warrington, and McCarthy (1983) have hypothesised a phonological route which parses the printed string in units of variable size (e.g., phonemes, syllables, morphemes, etc.) and a visual semantic route. Therefore, their theory does not predict the existence of a phonological dyslexic who cannot understand those printed words which he/she can read successfully. It seems to us that Lisa is an example of this, and the data collected on her reading ability seem to us strong evidence in favour of the existence of a direct link between visual word recognition and word production. However, it is possible to think of this connection as not being completely separated from the route going through the cognitive system, as classically assumed, and in the last part of the discussion we will present a single-visual-route model which accounts for the data collected on Lisa.

With reference to the first issue we addressed in the present research, i.e., the locus of lexical decision, two alternative hypotheses may be put forward on the basis of Lisa's pattern of performance. Both assume that in order to judge whether or not a letter string is a word, full access to semantic information is not required. However, they make different claims as to where this less-than-full semantic information is stored, and how it is used in lexical decision. According to the first hypothesis, Lisa's performance is not compatible with the suggestion that the task is carried out on the basis of processes in the cognitive system. If this were the case, Lisa should not have shown good performance in the task, since she shows impairment in access to the cognitive system from print. Her result for lexical decision can therefore be interpreted as showing that it is possible to perform the task on the basis of the logogen system itself. Some experimental data recently reported by Jacoby and Dallas (1981) and by Kroll and Potter (1984) seem to be compatible with this suggestion, since both studies present evidence for two loci for lexical decision, one based on perceptual recognition, and one based on meaning. Since Lisa showed no evidence of being able to access words' meaning, it seems plausible to assume that her good performance in lexical decision is based on perceptual information available at the logogen system. The second, alternative, explanation assumes, following Morton (1982), that lexical decision is performed in the cognitive system. According to this hypothesis, Lisa's ability to discriminate between concrete and abstract words, and between nouns and function words, is evidence that she achieves minimal semantic access from print, and this allows her to perform the lexical decision task. Warrington and McCarthy (1983) and Warrington and Shallice (1984) have reported patients who are able to recognise, e.g., inanimate objects but not animate ones. These authors interpret these data as evidence that the semantic system is hierarchically organised, and that there may be a selective loss of semantic features differing for their specificity. On this interpretation, it could be hypothesised that Lisa's performance in lexical decision is based on access to partial semantic information. We cannot rule out this explanation, as evidence for minimal access in our patient is unclear: she was, in fact, able to discriminate concrete from abstract words but not animals from non-animals. However, the findings of superior lexical decision performance with dissimilar distractors, as well as the high rate of false alarms in the same task, seem to us to be more compatible with the first hypothesis, i.e., that lexical decision is based on operations in the logogen system.

A second feature of Lisa's reading that was investigated concerns the effect of variables that have been considered to be represented in the cognitive system only on her reading aloud performance. While information about grammatical class and concreteness have traditionally been considered to be represented in the cognitive system, Morton (1982) has argued that frequency information is also located here. None of these variables were found to have an effect on Lisa's reading aloud performance. However, Sartori, Job and Barry (1983) have reported a patient who, like Lisa, showed an impairment in comprehension of printed words in the presence of intact ability to read them aloud, together with a non-word reading impairment. The variables of grammatical class, concreteness, and frequency were all found to have a significant effect on the reading aloud performance of the patient. This finding, as pointed out in the introduction, is at variance with the prediction from the Logogen model that patients who show an impairment in access to the cognitive system from print should also not show the effects of variables associated with the cognitive system in their reading aloud performance. Sartori et al. (1983) interpreted the result as indicating that information about such variables is represented at the level of the input logogen system. Tests conducted with Lisa of her ability to make judgements about the grammatical class and concreteness of printed words may be interpreted in this framework. Since Lisa shows no effect of psycholinguistic variables in reading aloud, and has a demonstrated impairment in access to the cognitive system from print then—if these variables are represented in the cognitive system only—Lisa should not have been able to make accurate judgements about the grammatical class or concreteness of printed words. Her performance, however, was good in these tasks. It seems to us that this result indicates that these variables are represented at the level of the input logogens rather than in the cognitive system only, and also that it is possible to monitor the input logogen system, whereas it has previously been described as a completely passive information-gathering system that could not be monitored (see Morton, 1982).

The results presented here, then, from a patient who seems to be reading aloud via the direct connections between input logogens and output logogens, taken together with results presented by Sartori et al. (1983) for a patient with an equivalent reading disorder, indicate that the input logogen system plays a much more important role in the reading process than that which has previously been ascribed to it. Rather than acting merely as a passive information-gathering device, it would appear that information regarding a word's grammatical class, frequency, and concreteness can be categorised at the level of the input logogens and that it is possible to monitor this information. In Fig. 3.3, a revised version of the Logogen model, that accommodates these results, is outlined.

According to this revised version of the model the separate pathways of access to logogens via the cognitive system and via the direct connection from the input logogens, as described in the most current version of the Logogen model (see Fig. 3.1), have been collapsed into one pathway with a "control system" operating at the input logogen stage. This control system is envisaged as being capable of detecting information concerning grammatical class, frequency, and concreteness that is stored with individual entries for printed word in the input logogen system and that becomes available when the printed word corresponding to an individual entry is presented as a

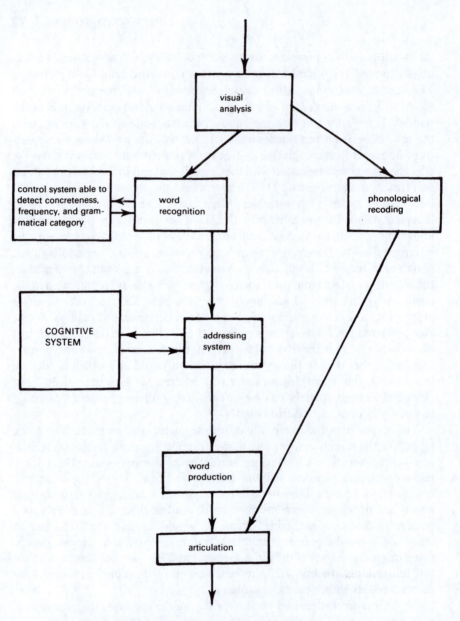

FIG. 3.3 Proposed model of word recognition.

stimulus. An "addressing system" is also proposed, whereby information passing between the input and output logogens may interface with the cognitive system. This addressing system, when disconnected from the cognitive system, may cause visual reading without comprehension. In this way the reading performance of patients such as Lisa, which involves good accuracy but impaired comprehension, is seen as a lack of address to the cognitive system. The effects of word class, frequency, and concreteness on reading aloud (which were reported by Sartori et al.) can be explained as a loss or disruption of certain types of entries at the input logogen stage, and the ability to make concreteness and grammatical class judgements (as reported above for Lisa) can be explained in terms of the operation of the control system.

APPENDIX 1

Stimulus Items Used in Test of the Ability to Discriminate Concrete Nouns From Abstract Nouns

Concrete nouns

uomo (man)	padre (father)
vino (wine)	testa (head)
cosa (thing)	acqua (water)
case (houses)	mondo (world)
pane (bread)	letto (bed)

signora (lady)	macchina (car)
ragazzo (boy)	fratello (brother)
bambina (girl)	domenica (sunday)
mattina (morning)	giornata (day)
dottore (doctor)	finestra (window)

Abstract nouns

pena (punishment)	scopo (aim)
modo (way)	pietà (pity)
pace (peace)	forza (strength)
tipo (type)	pezzo (piece)
arte (art)	posto (place)

fortuna (luck)	bellezza (beauty)
volontà (will)	quantità (quantity)
accordo (agreement)	sorpresa (surprise)
ragione (reason)	fantasia (fantasy)
effetto (effect)	autorità (authority)

APPENDIX 2

Stimulus Items Used in Test of the Ability to Discriminate Nouns From Function Words

Nouns

anno (year)	strada (street)
nonna (grandmother)	lavoro (work)
mese (month)	stanza (room)
roba (thing)	sangue (blood)

donna (woman)	bambino (boy)
posto (place)	persona (person)
testa (feast)	polizia (police)
paesi (countries)	inuerno (winter)
gioco (game)	milioni (millions)

Function words

dopo (after)	allora (now)
ecco (here is)	invece (instead)
meno (less)	appena (just)
ieri (yesterday)	domani (tomorrow)
tale (like)	dietro (inside)

quello (that)	davanti (in front)
altro (other)	lontano (far)
quale (which)	insomma (well)
sopra (above)	intanto (meanwhile)
tardi (late)	davvero (really)

REFERENCES

Bulmer, M. G. (1967) *Principles of statistics*. Edinburgh: Oliver & Boyd.

Coltheart, M. (1978) Lexical access in simple reading tasks. In G. Underwood (Ed.), *Strategies of information processing*. London: Academic Press.

Coltheart, M. (1980) Reading, phonological recoding, and deep dyslexia. In M. Coltheart, K. Patterson, & J. C. Marshall (Eds.), *Deep dyslexia*. London: Routledge & Kegan Paul.

Coltheart, M., Masterton, J., Byng, S., Prior, M. & Riddoch, J. (1983) Surface dyslexia. *Quarterly Journal of Experimental Psychology, 35A*, 469–495.

Funnell, E. (1983) Phonological processes in reading: New evidence from acquired dyslexia. *British Journal of Psychology, 74*, 2, 159–180.

Gernsbacher, M. A. (1984) Resolving 20 years of inconsistent interactions between lexical familiarity and orthography, concreteness, and polysemy. *Journal of Experimental Psychology: General, 113*, 256–281.

Jacoby, L. L., & Dallas, M. (1981) On the relationship between autobiographical memory and perceptual learning. *Journal of Experimental Psychology: General, 110*, 306–340.

Kroll, J. F., & Potter, M. C. (1984) Recognising words, pictures, and concepts: A comparison of lexical, object, and reality decisions. *Journal of Verbal Learning and Verbal Behavior, 23,* 39–66.

Morton, J. (1979) Facilitation in word recognition: Experiments causing change in the logogen model. In P. A. Wrolstad & H. Bouma (Eds.), *Processing of visible language, 1.* New York: Plenum.

Morton, J. (1982) Disintegrating the lexicon: An information-processing approach. In J. Mehler, E. Walker & M. Garrett, *Perspectives on mental representation.* London: Lawrence Erlbaum Associates.

Morton, J., & Patterson, K. (1980) A new attempt at an interpretation, or, an attempt at a new interpretation. In M. Coltheart, K. Patterson, & J. C. Marshall (Eds.), *Deep dyslexia.* London: Routledge & Kegan Paul.

Sartori, G., Job, R., & Barry, C. (1983) An impossible dyslexia. Poster presented at the first workshop on Cognitive Neuropsychology, Bressanone.

Schwartz, M. F., Saffran, E. M., & Marin, O. S. M. (1980) Fractionating the reading process in dementia: Evidence for word-specific print-to-sound associations. In M. Coltheart, K. Patterson, & J. C. Marshall (Eds.), *Deep dyslexia.* London: Routledge & Kegan Paul.

Shallice, T., Warrington, E., & McCarthy, R. (1983) Reading without semantics. *Quarterly Journal of Experimental Psychology, 35A,* 111–138.

Warrington, E., & McCarthy, R. (1983) Category specific access dysphasia. *Brain, 106,* 859–878.

Warrington, E., & Shallice, T. (1984) Category specific semantic impairments. *Brain, 107,* 829–854.

4 Speech Output Processes and Reading

Daniel Bub
Montreal Neurological Institute, 3801 University Street,
Montreal, Quebec H3A 2B4, Canada

Sandra Black
University of Toronto, Toronto, Ontario M5S 2A1, Canada

Janice Howell
Andrew Kertesz
University of Western Ontario, London, Ontario N6A 3K7, Canada

INTRODUCTION

Research with normal as well as with dyslexic readers indicates that recognition and comprehension of single printed words can occur without the prior construction of a phonemic code (for reviews see Coltheart, 1980; Henderson, 1982; McCusker, Hillinger & Bias, 1981). Although lexical access for single printed words may be visually mediated, questions remain about the possible importance of activated phonological codes for other aspects of silent reading. Thus far, unfortunately, the contribution of speech-based information has proved difficult to specify; no definite understanding exists as to the level of phonological representation that may be involved in the processing of written words, nor is there agreement concerning the kinds of tasks that call for the use of such information.

According to current models of reading, a phonological code is obtained via several processing stages as print is converted to sound (e.g., Morton & Patterson, 1980; Newcombe & Marshall, 1980). Once lexical identification is achieved, each word's phonological description is addressed directly in the

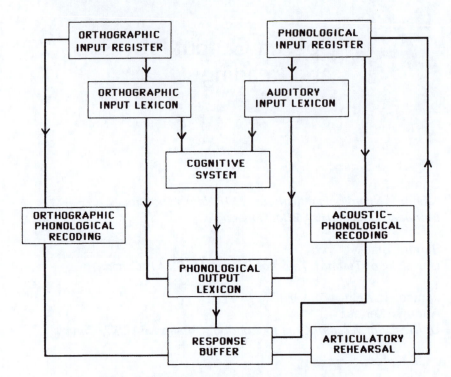

FIG. 4.1   Processing diagram of reading and repetition.

output lexicon (see Fig. 4.1). Subsequently, a pre-articulatory code is made available to a response buffer, which holds information in phonemic form before overt production takes place. If pronunciation is required for an unfamiliar word or nonsense word, the buffer receives a phonemic code via a different procedure—elementary spelling units are assigned phonemic values on the basis of spelling-to-sound correspondences, and phonology is assembled in a piecemeal fashion from these segments.

A substantial number of the attempts to clarify the role of phonology in fluent reading have focussed on the mechanism responsible for the actual programming of motor speech output (i.e. the response buffer and associated processes). The basic assumption of this research is that subjects must subvocalise to activate stored phonological traces. Some insight into the possible function of subvocalisation has been obtained from work on phonemic recoding in short-term memory. There is a great deal of evidence to show that subjects are apt to employ a speech-based code to recall a short list of words, letters or syllables, even when material is presented via the visual modality (e.g., Colle & Welsh, 1976; Conrad, 1967; Levy, 1971). Research indicates, however, that written sequences depend on the mediation of subvocal rehearsal in order to gain access to auditory short-term memory

(Baddeley, Thompson, & Buchanan, 1975; Levy, 1971; Murray, 1968), because if subjects are prevented from rehearsing and stimuli are visually displayed the usual phonemic effects obtained in the memory span task largely disappear. Baddeley (1983) accounts for this result by invoking the concept of an articulatory loop, a component of working memory that temporarily stores phonological information and recirculates it through the process of subvocal rehearsal. This activity (performed by the response buffer and subsequent articulatory programming), is the only means by which printed sequences gain access to phonological short-term storage.

Reading and Subvocal Rehearsal

A problem with the research on speech output processes and reading is that the relevant studies can often be criticised on methodological grounds. Electromyographic work on speech muscle activity (Hardyck & Petrinovitch, 1970) occurring when readers process difficult text has failed to rule out the possibility that muscle tone may increase for any difficult task, and that such an increase need not be limited to the speech musculature. Other investigators have examined the performance of readers who are concurrently engaged in a speech shadowing task (e.g. repetition of random digits) to determine whether articulatory suppression interferes with the ability to process written words and sentences (Kleiman, 1975). This technique, however, also places a substantial processing load on central capacity, so that the source of any adverse effects on reading is ambiguous.

An alternative, and much less demanding, secondary task that is now often used to suppress articulation requires the subject to continuously produce an irrelevant and stereotyped utterance (e.g., successive repetition of the sound "blah"). Several reports have described the effect of such concurrent vocalisation on subjects' ability to recognise slight changes of wording in sentences they had seen or previously heard (Levy 1977; Slowiaczek & Clifton, 1980). While results indicate that articulatory suppression can adversely influence recognition accuracy, particularly for written sentences, these findings do not clarify whether speech recoding serves as a functional component of the reading process. As Baddeley (1979) notes, the fact that testing emphasises memory for the literal wording of sentences makes it difficult to assume that irrelevant articulation disturbs processes directly involved in the active comprehension of written material.

Somewhat better support for the role of subvocalisation in fluent reading has been provided by Baddeley, Eldridge and Lewis (1981). These authors presented subjects with written sentences which occasionally contained a small anomaly, created either by replacing a word in the sentence with a semantically inappropriate one, or by permuting adjacent words to produce an error of word order. Articulatory suppression was found to impair the detection of anomalous sentences, especially when they contained word-

order errors, but did not influence processing speed. Baddeley et al. attempt
to rule out the possibility that the articulatory suppression effect is due to
general secondary task demands on attention; they report that concurrent
tapping does not disturb reading performance. In addition, evidence is
supplied that the detrimental influence of articulatory suppression does not
occur through acoustic interference; the subjects' performance remained
unaffected by irrelevant speech played to them during the reading task.
Baddeley et al. conclude that the articulatory rehearsal loop establishes an
additional source of information (activated in parallel with the execution of
more central components of the reading process) that could be consulted
when the precise wording of text becomes important.

In this chapter we will explore the role of speech output processes in
reading by analysing the performance of a brain-damaged patient (M.V.)
who, we will argue, has sustained specific impairment to the buffer holding
speech codes in pre-articulatory format. Initial assessment of M.V. disclosed
that she was unable to read nonsense words aloud, even though oral reading
of words was relatively intact. This syndrome, termed phonological dyslexia
(Beauvois & Derouesné, 1979), occurs because the mechanism responsible
for nonlexical spelling-sound translation is no longer functional, while direct
lexical access from print is still intact. Potentially, damage to any one of
several processing stages may cause the deficit: (1) graphemic parsing can be
impaired; (2) correspondences between spelling units and sound may be
affected; or (3) phonological information is not adequately processed for
output.

We will demonstrate that M.V.'s impaired ability to pronounce nonsense
words is due neither to a deficit at the level of graphemic parsing, nor to
impairment at the level of abstract correspondences between orthographic
units. Instead, evidence will be put forward suggesting that M.V. has a
specific deficit within the response buffer, which limits her capacity to actively
maintain phonemic information required for nonsense word reading. In the
light of this finding, we assess M.V.'s processing of written sentences.
Assuming that the response buffer represents one essential component of the
articulatory loop, it is reasonable to suspect that performance will be
impaired if the loop is required for accurate reading. Furthermore, if the
activity of the loops is specific to processing written material, no such
impairment should be observed when sentences are orally presented.

The organisation of the chapter is as follows: first we present a general
description of the patient; we document the nature of her difficulty in
translation of spelling into sound, and we show that this problem is a
consequence of a general production deficit. Then we obtain evidence that
the impairment prevents adequate subvocal rehearsal; and the last part of the
paper is devoted to assessing the effect of M.V.'s phonological processing
disturbance on her ability to decode written sentences.

CASE REPORT

M.V. is a 67-year-old, right-handed widow with a Grade 7 education, who once worked as a waitress, but has been a housewife most of her life. She experienced sudden onset of right hemiparesis and aphasia in April 1982. Her hemiparesis recovered well over the next few months. Language assessment on the Western Aphasia Battery (WAB) two weeks post-onset (Kertesz, 1979), revealed hesitant circumlocutory speech with verbal paraphasias and marked word-finding difficulty. Confrontation naming was poor and repetition was impaired if the target contained more than two words (score: 6/10). Auditory verbal comprehension for yes/no questions and word recognition was relatively intact, although she had difficulty with sequential commands (comprehension score: 7/10). Reading comprehension was good for single words and simple sentences, but very poor for complex sentences (reading score: 52/100). She was severely agraphic; she could only write numbers and copy a sentence (writing score: 23/100). She had no apraxia. On the basis of her language scores, which showed repetition more impaired than comprehension, she was classified as a conduction aphasic. Her aphasia quotient (AQ) was 66/100 and had improved in six months to 84/100, at which time she was classified as an anomic aphasic. She showed considerable recovery on naming tasks and in comprehension of sequential commands (comprehension score 9.7/10), and also in her reading and writing (reading score: 78/100; writing scores: 51/100).

By one year her deficit had stabilised. She could reproduce only three digits on immediate recall, but her repetition on the WAB had improved from 6/10 initially, to 8/10. Her AQ was 89. She now scored 90/100 and 69/100 on reading and writing respectively. In spontaneous speech paraphasias were rare, no articulatory difficulties were noted, and she used complete grammatical sentences most of the time. However, she continued to have marked word-finding difficulty and her utterances were halting with frequent long pauses between individual words.

C.T. scanning performed acutely and one year post-onset, revealed a mainly subcortical cerebral infarction involving the post-central and supra-marginal gyri and the white matter deep to them (including the arcuate fasciculus). The infarct extended inferiorly and anteriorly to involve small portions of the superior temporal and precentral gyri, insula, putamen and posterior internal capsule.

Reading comprehension was assessed in more detail at one year by administering the Reading Comprehension Battery for Aphasia (Lapointe & Horner, 1979). She scored perfectly on three subtests of single-word picture matching with visually, phonologically, and semantically confusable foils. She missed a few low frequency items on a synonym choice task (7/10). She performed well on sentence-picture matching (10/10) and was able to answer inferential and factual questions about short paragraphs (9/10). These tasks included material of a Grade 6–7 level of difficulty. Her lowest scores were in functional reading, which included items such as a recipe, weather forecast and bank balance (7/10) and in paragraph-picture interpretation, in which she missed some counterintuitive items (7/10). On a subtest of syntactic complexity involving passives, relative clauses, and derived double objects she achieved 9/10. Her overall score was 88/100, but her reading rate was extremely slow. She would often have to re-read the sentences a number of times in order to arrive at the correct response.

Processing of Printed Input (Single Items)

Single Word Reading.   M.V. was administered 160 nouns which varied in frequency, imageability, and spelling–sound regularity. She read 149/160 (88%) correctly, showing no significant effects of imageability and regularity, but high frequency items were read somewhat more accurately than low frequency items (92% correct versus 80% correct). An additional list of 60 verbs, adjectives, and function words was presented. M.V. correctly read 16/20 verbs, 20/20 adjectives and 18/20 function words. She was given 20 affixed words to read, ten of which were prefixed and ten suffixed. She accurately pronounced 9/10 prefixed words and 6/10 suffixed words. Three responses involved the appropriate stem with an incorrect or omitted affix (e.g., "reform" for *inform*, "work" for *worker*, and "refuse" for *refusal*). She was also administered an untimed lexical decision task, composed of one to two syllable words, which varied in frequency, regularity and imageability, and of non-words created by changing one letter in each word. She achieved a score of 86%, correctly judging 37/40 positive trials and 32/40 negative trials.

Nonsense Word Reading.   Preliminary assessment of M.V.'s ability to read nonsense words was carried out by presenting her with 48 pronounce-able three to four letter, single-syllable nonsense words. Only 11 (23%) responses were correct. Of the errors, 28 (76%) were pronounced as words that appeared to be visually similar to the non-word.

Several of the phonological dyslexics described previously have been found to read non-words homophonic with real words much more accurately than non-homophonic non-words (Derouesné & Beauvois, 1979, 1985; Temple & Marshall, 1983). A further list of 72 monosyllabic non-words was therefore administered, consisting of 36 non-words homophonic with real words, but constructed to minimise visual similarity, and 36 matched non-homophonic nonsense words. The 20 three-to four-letter pseudohomo-phones shared 50% or less of their letters with real words, and the five to six letter pseudohomophones shared 40% or less (e.g., *tuff; phicks*). She correctly read 10/36 homophonic non-words and 16/36 non-homophonic nonwords.

Instructions to use the fact that the pseudohomophones sounded exactly like real words (Derouesné & Beauvois, 1979) did not improve her performance when the homophonic list was presented on a second occasion (12/36 correct).

Orthographic Segmentation.   Further tests were administered to help clarify which processing stage was responsible for M.V.'s impaired nonsense word reading. One interpretation of her poor performance is that she is unable to correctly parse the orthographic string into the appropriate spelling units. To explore this possibility, she was given 20 compound words which could be orthographically segmented into two additional words. For half the stimuli, syllable boundaries corresponded to the lexical segments within the words (e.g., *car-pet*) and for the other half, correct pronunciation did not conform to the pronunciation of the syllables (e.g., *fat-her*) (cf. Funnell, 1983). M.V. was required to pronounce each individual word embedded within the parent word. Results do not suggest that graphemic parsing was impaired (20/20 responses correct).

Correspondence Between Spelling Units.   Since orthographic segmentation appears to be intact, perhaps M.V.'s difficulty arises at a more central processing stage which involves her implicit knowledge of spelling-to-sound correspondence rules? To assess this we administered a speeded lexical decision task based on a procedure described by Taft (1982). Taft examined the effect on lexical decision time of using non-words created by replacing a spelling segment in a real word with a functionally equivalent grapheme. He found that such non-words took longer to reject than a matched control group that shared only visual, and not graphemically equivalent, features with words, so the effect could not be attributed to overall physical similarity. To give some examples, the non-word *steek* is graphemically similar to the real word *steak* because the digraphs *ee* and *ea* can be used to represent the same phoneme (as in *leak* versus *leek*). In this respect, *steek* is graphemically close (GC) to *steak*, whereas the non-word *fleek* is visually close (VC) to such real words as *fleet* and *fleck*, but is not graphemically confusable with them. (In other words, respelling *steek* with matching graphemes can produce a real word, whereas respelling *fleek* in this manner does not.) According to Taft, the GC items yield slower decision latencies than VC items because subjects possess knowledge of correspondences between elementary spelling units which can share the same phonemic values e.g., EA = EE; OU = OW), and apply this knowledge when confronted with novel letter strings. Based on this reasoning, if M.V. no longer activates rule-governed correspondences between spelling units, i.e. if she has lost knowledge of the abstract relationships between graphemes, then her latencies should not differ between VC and GC non-words.

A lexical decision task was therefore administered to M.V., consisting of 36 positive and 36 negative trials. Of the negative trials, half of the non-words were graphemically close to words (e.g., *steek/steak*) and half were visually close only (e.g., *fleek/fleet*). Both reaction time to the nearest millisecond and accuracy scores showed a marked effect of graphemic confusability. Thus, GC words were processed 144 milliseconds slower than VC nonwords (GC = 1514 msec; SD = 293; VC = 1370 msec; SD = 320), While overall accuracy was high (89%), GC trials produced a 30% error rate, while only 16% of VC stimuli yielded incorrect responses. This result suggests that M.V.'s implicit knowledge of the correspondences between graphemic elements is intact and, moreover, supports our earlier contention that orthographic segmentation is functional. Clearly, her sensitivity to the fact that different graphemes are isomorphic, presupposes that she can parse graphemic segments in the first place.

Phonemic Assignment to Graphemes.   If both orthographic segmentation and correspondence rules are functional in M.V., her difficulty may arise because she is unable to assign phonemic values to individual spelling units. Indeed, other cases of phonological dyslexia have exhibited this problem; patients cannot pronounce the sound of individual letters (e.g., "buh" for *b*) even though letters can be accurately named (Patterson, 1982; Funnell, 1983). M.V. was therefore asked to sound out 15 consonants presented on single cards. She experienced little difficulty in producing the sound of individual consonants (14/15 correct).

Our experiments so far have shown that M.V's deficit does not involve orthographic segmentation, abstract correspondence rules or explicit assignment of phonemes to graphemic segments. These findings suggest that impairment in a subsequent processing stage concerned with phonological output is responsible for M.V.'s phonological dyslexia. It may be the case, for example, that her deficit involves a processing stage specific to reading, which mediates the assembly of phonemes once they have been converted from print. Such an explanation has been proposed for some patients (e.g., R.G. and L.B.), partly on the basis of a pseudohomophone effect (Derouesné & Beauvois, 1979; 1986). According to these authors, their patients could produce the phonology of a written non-word by evoking the sound pattern of a homophonic real word. M.V., however, showed no improvement with homophonic non-words, making a specific deficit less plausible. An alternative possibility is that a general deficit exists at a phonemic assembly stage occurring after transcoding from both written and oral input. If this is so, then M.V.'s repetition should be impaired in a similar way to her reading. We therefore undertook a detailed investigation of her repetition skills in order to obtain a comparison with her reading performance.

Repetition

Single Words.   One hundred and thirty monosyllabic words taken from a study by Trost (1970), that sampled singleton consonants and consonant clusters in the initial and final position as well as the full range of vowel sounds, were administered to M.V. for repetition. Performance was near-perfect (96% correct). A further list, published by McCarthy and Warrington (1984), that systematically varied word frequency (Thorndike & Lorge, 1944) and syllable length (one, two and three syllables) was presented. Results showed extremely good performance (see Table 4.1) for high frequency words (97% on A and AA items), and a somewhat lower level of accuracy for low frequency words (78% on items 10/million). There were no consistent effects of syllable length, although repetition of low frequency, three-syllable words was considerably worse than other items (67%).

TABLE 4.1
Percent Correct for Repetition of Words Varying in Frequency and Syllable Length
(Percentages Calculated from 30 Trials per Cell)

	Number of syllables			
	1	*2*	*3*	*Mean % correct*
High frequency	96%	100%	96%	97.3%
Low frequency	83%	83%	67%	78.01%

Nonsense Words.   When M.V. was asked to orally repeat presented non-words, her accuracy declined considerably. She could reproduce 16/20 single CV syllables, but if items were given in pairs, she only retrieved pronunciation of 14/40 syllables and was completely unable to repeat pairs in their correct order. She correctly pronounced 50% of a list of 40 four-letter monosyllabic non-words. Her performance deteriorated as the number of syllables increased (8/12 correct for CVC monosyllables; 6/12 for bisyllables; 2/12 for trisyllabic items).

Phonemic Discrimination

It is clear that M.V.'s repetition of non-words is almost as poor as her reading of them. This result offers some support for the idea that M.V.'s poor oral reading of nonsense words stems from impairment to a component of the speech production system. The possibility arises, however, that M.V. has, in fact, two deficits, one which interferes with non-word repetition and the other with print-to-sound conversion. Her faulty repetition could arise, for example, from a second disturbance involving phonemic perception and/or loss of information from auditory short-term memory. To clarify this issue, we examined M.V.'s ability to encode and briefly retain a meaningless sequence of phonemes. Evidence that information is misperceived or rapidly forgotten would call into question our assumption of a single functional disturbance behind M.V.'s poor transcoding ability.

1. Two Syllables.   A set of consonant-vowel stimuli (PA, BA, TA, CA, DA and GA) were arranged in pairs to produce 20 trials. Half of these syllables differed in place of articulation (e.g., BA, GA) or voicing (e.g., BA, PA), while on remaining trials the items of each pair were phonologically identical. Trials were orally presented in random order, and pair members were separated by an interval of approximately one second. M.V.'s task was to determine whether the two syllables comprising a trial were the same or different. Nineteen of 20 responses were correct, indicating good phonemic discrimination.

2. Delayed Presentation.   We also examined M.V.'s performance on a more difficult version of this test, which demanded some capacity to maintain the internal representation of a syllable for a short period. A five-second delay was inserted between the CV pairs. In addition, we prevented M.V. from subvocally rehearsing during the interstimulus interval by asking her to begin counting softly after hearing the initial syllable until presented with the second one. Discrimination was not adversely affected by a delay introduced between two syllables—M.V.'s same-different judgements were accurate on 19/20 trials.

3. Four Syllables.   When the number of comparison items per trial was doubled, M.V. continued to respond with a high level of accuracy. We administered 20 trials consisting of a pair of syllables (e.g., POO, BA), followed one second later by two additional syllables. On half the trials these were exactly the same as the previous pair, while on remaining trials the consonant of one syllable was altered. (We did not systematically vary voicing and place in these substitutions.) The four CV stimuli were pseudo-randomly presented so that a syllable did not always remain in the same relative position between pairs. Tested in this way, M.V. obtained a score of 17/20 correct.

4. Nonsense Words.   For this test equal numbers of mono-, bi-, and tri-syllabic nonsense words were used as stimuli. M.V. was asked to compare two spoken items per trial that were either identical or different by one phoneme. The discrepant phonemes occurred equally often at initial, medial or final positions within the nonsense string. The items comprising a pair were separated by a delay of five seconds, and during this interval M.V. either remained silent or counted aloud. With an unfilled delay between stimuli M.V. was able to correctly perform on 16/18 trials. When the delay was accompanied by articulatory suppression, 21/24 responses were correct.

The adequate recognition we have just described rules out the possibility that loss of phonemic discrimination or poor auditory short-term memory is the basis for M.V.'s repetition difficulty. Her combined impairment of nonlexical reading and repetition suggests, instead, that damage has occurred to a phonological output process serving as a component of print-to-sound as well as acoustic-phonological translation. To gather further evidence for this, a more detailed analysis of her repetition and reading errors was conducted using additional non-word stimuli. It seemed reasonable to expect that the pattern of errors would not vary with the modality of presentation if her mispronunciations arose from a common output deficit.

Comparison of Reading and Repetition of Non-words

To generate a corpus of errors for comparative analysis, more extensive lists of monosyllabic non-words were presented to M.V. for reading and repetition. Of 266 items given to her to read out loud, she pronounced 42% accurately. Sixty-two per cent of her mispronunciations were lexicalisations. She was also administered another set of 240 non-words to repeat. She correctly pronounced 53%, producing lexicalisations on 49% of her incorrect responses.

An analysis of errors was carried out on all her incorrect attempts at reading or repeating non-words. Errors were classified as consonants or vowel substitutions, omissions, additions or transpositions (if the substituted vowel or consonant was present elsewhere in the target word), and the number of error types for each non-word was noted. Approximately two-thirds of her mispronunciations in both modalities involved only one error type per word (reading 71%; repetition 69%) and in one-third there were two error deviations per word (reading 29%; repetition 31%). As indicated in Table 4.2, substitutions predominated, constituting 80% of her reading errors (49% consonants; 31% vowels) and 62% of her repetition errors (41% consonants; 21% vowels). Single phoneme omissions, the next most common error type, occurred more frequently in the presence of consonant clusters, especially during non-word reading (reading 23%; repetition 12%). Phoneme additions, which comprised approximately 10% of her errors, usually occurred in lexicalisations and were more frequent in the absence of consonant clusters. Transpositions were very uncommon.

TABLE 4.2
Analysis of Error Types

1. *Reading*

	List A	List B No clusters	List C Clusters	Total
No. administered	108	57	101	266
No. correct	48 (44%)	28 (49%)	35 (38%)	111 (42%)
Error type (%):				
Substitutions (cons.)	37	59	38	41
Substitutions (vowel)	24	28	16	21
Total substitutions	61	83	54	62
Omissions	15	5	39	23
Additions	18	12	7	12
Transpositions	6	0	0	3

2. *Repetition*

	List I	List II No clusters	List III Clusters	Total
No. administered	40	88	112	240
No. correct	20 (50%)	53 (60%)	54 (48%)	127 (53%)
Error type (%):				
Substitutions (cons.)	50	49	49	49
Substitutions (vowel)	35	36	26	31
Total substitutions	85	85	75	80
Omissions	9	2	19	12
Additions	6	13	6	8
Transpositions	0	0	0	0

Reading and Repetition—A Subphonemic Analysis. The frequency of lexicalisations, the number of deviations per non-word, the frequency of vowel and consonant substitutions, and the relative proportion of error types were all remarkably similar in the two modalities. Such definite parallels in reading and repetition make a dual deficit extremely unlikely and suggest there is a common phonological factor impairing M.V.'s performance. These findings encouraged us to undertake a more refined phonological comparison between her reading and writing errors. We have indicated that M.V.'s most common error-type is the substitution of one phoneme in the non-word stimulus with another phoneme. This kind of error is also frequently made by aphasics with impaired speech production at the *whole-word* level. Subphonemic analyses of these paraphasic responses have shown that they are by no means randomly determined—in general, consonant substitutions differ from the target phoneme by one (or at most two) distinctive features. (Blumstein, 1973; Burns & Canter, 1977; Monoi, Fukusako, Itoh, & Sasanuma, 1983).

If M.V. has sustained impairment to a phonological output process common to reading and repetition, we might anticipate that her mispronunciations will partially reflect the underlying phonemic form of the nonsense word. Her consonant substitutions should therefore be constrained by the phonological distance between target and error, regardless of the modality of input.

In pursuing this line of enquiry, it is important to remember that approximately half of M.V.'s mispronunciations are lexicalisations (e.g., "monk" for *munt*), which are typically thought to reflect a guessing strategy based on the superficial resemblance between the nonsense item and a real word (e.g. Patterson, 1982). When written nonsense words are presented for oral reading, a lexicalisation may reflect the fact that the patient has located a visually-similar word in the orthographic input lexicon to produce a response. For repetition, pronuncation would occur by retrieving a word in the phonological output lexicon that sounds similar to the nonsense word.

If some of M.V.'s responses occur in this way, a subphonemic analysis of her substitution error may be expected to produce different results for her lexicalisation responses compared to her non-word responses. The latter type of mispronunciation might stem from an attempt to capture the phonological specification of a nonsense word through a deficient output mechanism. This procedure could well yield responses which are close phonemic approximations to the target. M.V.'s lexicalisations, however, might only be expected to yield phonologically principled errors for *repetition* performance, assuming that the closest-*sounding* word to the nonsense stimulus is used for a pronunciation. We would not expect that the lexicalisation of a *written* nonsense word bears phonological resemblance to the target, given a strategy incorporating *visual* overlap between the non-word and an orthographic lexical address. To take this possibility into account, we analysed substitution errors separately for morphemic ("monk" for *munt*) and nonmorphemic ("sive" for *sife*) outcomes.

A four-feature scheme of place, manner, nasality, and voicing, similar to that used by Trost and Canter (1974), was employed to determine the distinctive feature distance between substituted and target consonants. The place category was subdivided into anterior and coronal, and the manner category into vowel, strident, and continuant, according to the matrix of essential distinctive features provided by Chomsky and Halle (1968).[1] Results are shown in Fig. 4.2.

The large majority of M.V.'s consonant substitutions were one feature away from the target for reading (74% of 66 errors) as well as repetition (88% of 56 errors). A distance of two features was found for only 20% of her reading errors and 10% of her repetition errors (see Fig. 4.2). Separate analysis of her lexicalisations and nonlexical errors disclosed the same pattern of results. The vast majority of M.V.'s substitutions differed from the target consonant by one distinctive feature alone, including the substitutions that changed written nonsense words into legitimate words.[2] Our phonological analysis has therefore led to the intriguing discovery that all M.V.'s responses are constrained by phonological factors, even those responses that, on face value, appear to be responses based on lexical guesswork.

A potential artefact, on considering these results, is that M.V.'s substitution errors in reading were phonemically close to the target simply because of a fortuitous correlation between acoustic and visual similarity for letters. For example, the letters N and M are very close phonetically, but they also happen to be visually confusable as well. It is conceivable that the majority of M.V.'s mispronunciations of nonsense words (e.g., "bast" for *dast*, "rome" for *rone*) are actually visual errors, that produce a spurious effect of phonetic distance. To take this into account, the data were reanalysed after excluding all substitutions for letters that were physically close, using criteria from the visual confusion matrix for lower-case letters provided by Bouma (1971). This removed 15 items from the analysis but the overall pattern remained

---

[1] A more fine-grained, four-feature analysis was also carried out using the following distinctive features to further subdivide place and manner: place was categorised as bilabial, labiodental, interdental, alveolar, palatal, velar, and glottal; manner was subdivided into stops, fricatives, affricates, liquids, glides, and vowels. This yielded a different distribution of one and two feature distances within each modality, but the strong parallels between reading and writing were still observed. The results from this analysis are shown in the following table:

Number of features	Modality	
From target	Repetition errors	Reading errors
1	44%	36%
2	44%	48%
3	12%	16%

[2] An interphonemic distance of one feature away from the target predominated in all her consonant substitutions as follows:

	Lexicalisation	Non-lexicalisation
Reading	88%	90%
Repetition	86%	82%

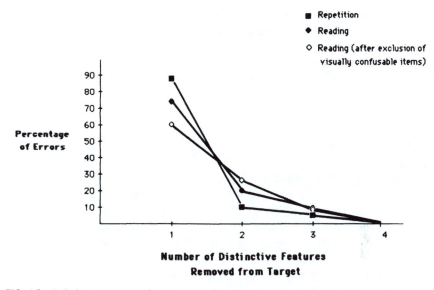

FIG. 4.2   Relative percentage of errors one to four features removed from target in reading and repetition tasks.

unchanged (see Fig. 4.2).[3] Thus, it seemed unlikely that her reading errors could be attributed to orthographic similarity.

A second potential artefact of the kind of analysis represented by Fig. 4.2 is pointed out by Miller and Ellis in Chapter 12. They showed, even if a patient's phoneme substitutions are *not* genuinely constrained by the phonetic structure of the target phoneme, there will be more phoneme substitutions within one or two features of the target phoneme than more than two features away from it—simply by chance. They estimated, for example, that if chance is the only factor operating, 72% of substitutions will differ from one target by one or two features, and 28% by more than two features. They also estimated that errors with feature distance of two will occur considerably more often than those with feature distance of one if chance is the only factor operating. Neither of these properties of the chance levels characterises the data in our Fig. 4.2. The proportion of one-feature and two-feature errors is much higher than .72, and one-feature errors are vastly more

---

[3]The following lower-case letter groupings are listed by Bouma as being visually confusable: short letters—aszx, eoc, nmu, rvw: ascenders—dhkb, tilf; descenders—gjpqy. Consulting the lower-case visual confusion matrices provided by Engel, Dougherty and Jones (1973) and Geyer (1977) eliminated only four more errors and made little difference to the overall graph.

common than two-feature errors. We therefore calculate that the phonetic-distance effects in Fig. 4.2 are genuine ones.

In conclusion, our comparison of overall error type and of phonetic distances in consonant substitutions reveal striking parallels between M.V.'s non-word reading and repetition. These parallels hold even if visually confusable consonant substitutions are eliminated and if lexicalisations are separately scrutinised. The weight of accumulated evidence, therefore, strongly supports our contention that a single deficit, at the level of phonological output processing common to both acoustic-phonological and print-to-sound translation, is responsible for M.V.'s poor performance in non-word speech production. The following considerations allow us to specify further the locus of this phonological impairment within the language system more precisely. First, M.V.'s adequate retrieval of whole-word pronunciation clearly indicates that the deficit arises subsequent to the activation of lexical phonology. Second, the difficulty must originate before the specification of output in articulatory form, since this aspect of speech production also appeared intact. There is no reason to assume, moreover, that an articulatory disturbance *per se* would interfere more with the production of nonsense items than real words.

This line of reasoning points to a phonemic planning impairment, at the level of the response buffer, as the primary cause of the breakdown in M.V's speech production. Several aspects of performance, taken together, indicate that M.V. is unable to organise the requisite number of phonemic segments within the buffer because the capacity of this subsystem has become severely limited and/or because its contents are subject to abnormally rapid decay.

In support of this interpretation, we note that M.V. is less able to pronounce items when the number of target phonemes increase (her repetition of single CV syllables is fairly accurate, for example, but she is almost totally unable to output a tri-syllabic nonsense word or a pair of CV syllables), an outcome consistent with the assumption that the buffer's capacity to maintain activated speech code for response assembly has been compromised. Another factor which strongly influences production, in addition to sequence length, is the lexical status of the material—M.V. experiences much more difficulty in repeating or reading nonsense items than familiar words. A substantial proportion of her mispronunciations, furthermore, are lexicalisations which we have found to be phonologically related to the correct response.

We conclude from these results that M.V. often fails to retain an exact description of a pre-articulatory sequence, especially when the sequence is not supported by a lexical address. Apparently, the presence of word-specific information allows the system to compensate for any deterioration in the quality of speech codes activated for production. M.V.'s lexicalisation responses can be seen as a direct outcome of this whole-word feedback—

incompletely specified traces for a meaningless sequence trigger a higher-level interpretative mechanism which evaluates the response options. Since the potential candidates at this level of representation are morphemes that provide the best possible fit to the description in the response buffer, the output selected will be a word that is a close phonological approximation to the target.

TESTING FOR ADEQUATE SUBVOCAL REHEARSAL

It is generally acknowledged that speech output processes contribute in important ways to short-term memory performance. An earlier model by Baddeley (1979, 1981) (also see Ellis, 1979, 1980) proposed that phonemic retention of a short list of verbal items is accomplished entirely by the response buffer and related articulatory programming, which enables the buffer's contents to be continuously recycled. More recently, however, this account has been modified to include a component of the speech input system as the primary short-term store for phonological codes, while the speech production mechanism is considered to function largely as a rehearsal device controlled by subvocalisation (Baddeley, 1983).

The dual concepts of a phonological input store and an articulatory rehearsal process provide a framework that can be used to interpret a number of phenomena obtained from memory span tasks, including:

1. *The phonological confusability effect*—recall of similar sounding items is poorer relative to dissimilar items (Conrad & Hull, 1964) because the former are considered to lay down confusable traces within the input register.

2. *The word length effect*—memory span decreases as word length increases (Baddeley, Thompson, & Buchanan, 1975), an outcome that has been linked to subvocal rehearsal as a means of refreshing memory traces before they fade. Articulation of long duration items is necessarily slower and, consequently, the number of words that the system can maintain over a given period is reduced.

3. *The influence of articulatory suppression*—this procedure impairs performance and eliminates the word length effect (Baddeley, Thompson, & Buchanan, 1975) because, according to the model, irrelevant vocalisation occupies the motor speech system so that articulatory rehearsal does not occur.

Suppression has also been found to abolish the adverse effect of phonemic confusability when material is visually presented (Levy, 1971). This result can be explained by assuming that subvocal rehearsal provides the only means by which written information is registered in phonological short-term memory.

Auditory presentation, in contrast, allows direct access to the system without articulatory activity.

The above remarks suggest that an assessment of M.V.'s memory span and rehearsal capabilities may prove valuable in substantiating our analysis of the constraints on her speech system. We would expect that any limitations in her ability to organise pre-articulatory sequences in the response buffer will also adversely affect the rate of her subvocal rehearsal, and we may find evidence for disturbed rehearsal by exploring some basic attributes of M.V.'s immediate memory performance.

Phonemic Confusability

Two sets of letters were used, Set I comprising of phonologically similar items (B C D G P V and T) and Set II consisting of dissimilar items (F Q K R X W and Z). Letters were selected at random from each set to generate two blocks of 20 sequences that were either two or three letters in length.[4] No letter occurred more than once per sequence. Half the trials were dictated to M.V. by the examiner at a rate of one letter every second. The remainder were visually displayed as black upper-case letters on white flash cards. M.V. was asked to repeat each list after it was presented[5] and, if possible, to maintain the items in their correct order.

The percentage of sequences or items correctly reproduced for the two input modalities (visual/auditory) are shown in Table 4.3. It is apparent from M.V.'s poor letter span that her short-term memory is impaired. The impairment does not preclude the use of phonological coding for recall, however, since there is a clear effect of phonemic confusability on performance with auditory input. No such influence of confusability can be seen if letters are visually administered though, and we therefore conclude that M.V. does not (or cannot) use subvocal rehearsal as a control process for converting visual codes into phonological short-term memory.

Word Length

Nine bi-syllabic words (*college, puma, kettle, Quebec, measles, London, physics, essay, carbon*) and nine five-syllable words (*hippopotamus, university, physiology, Prince Edward Island, tuberculosis, aluminium, periodical, refrigerator, British Columbia*) were selected. M.V. was thoroughly acquainted

---

[4]Pilot work revealed that M.V. experienced great difficulty in reproducing three-letter sequences and we therefore did not test her beyond this length. Incidentally, her digit span (100% correct for 3 items, 50% for 2 items) was somewhat higher than her span for letters.

[5]M.V.'s performance did not appear to be influenced by response modality—her scores remained unchanged when she responded in writing and when she could select the appropriate response by pointing to a printed version of the memory set after each trial.

TABLE 4.3
Visual and Auditory Memory Span for Phonologically Similar and Dissimilar Letters

Percent correct	Phonologically dissimilar				Phonologically similar			
	Two letters		Three letters		Two letters		Three letters	
	S	I	S	I	S	I	S	I
Auditory items	80	90	20	57	50	70	10	56
Visual items	70	90	30	56	90	100	40	70

S = Sequences correct
I = Items correct

with the memory sets before testing. Her repetition of the individual words was adequate, although she occasionally mispronounced physiology (typical response—"phyology") and refrigerator (often rendered as "refrigiator"). Responses were sufficiently close to the actual targets for us to score them without difficulty.

We generated two blocks of nine trials, comprising of two and three word sequences, respectively, from the bi-syllabic list. No word was duplicated within a trial. Another two blocks were similarly constructed from the five-syllable word list. The examiner dictated the items on each trial at a rate of one per second. Instructions to M.V. were the same as for the previous experiment. All items were available to M.V. on prompt cards during recall. Results are displayed in Table 4.4. Unlike normal subjects, M.V.'s memory span does not deteriorate for longer words. The presence of a length effect usually implies, as we have indicated, that subvocal rehearsal is employed to refresh the contents of the phonological register. Since rehearsal takes place through motor speech programming, it proceeds at a slower rate for material that requires more time to pronounce, and longer words are therefore less easily re-activated before forgetting occurs than shorter words.

TABLE 4.4
Memory Span as a Function of Word Length (auditory Presentation)

	Two syllables				Five syllables			
	Two items		Three items		Two items		Three items	
	S	I	S	I	S	I	S	I
Percent correct	67	92	17	55	83	92	0	50

S = Sequences correct
I = Items correct

The fact that M.V. is insensitive to the length of dictated words, as well as the phonemic confusability of printed letters, allows us to infer that subvocal rehearsal plays no part in her performance. Unfortunately we do not yet have sufficient grounds for making the stronger claim that the failure to rehearse is a direct outcome of her speech disturbance. A case report by Vallar and Baddeley (1984a) indicates that the use of subvocal rehearsal depends on the integrity of phonological short-term memory in addition to the articulatory system. They describe a patient with a severely-reduced memory span but without any apparent speech deficit, who, like M.V., showed no tendency to utilise articulatory recoding for immediate recall of verbal sequences. According to the authors, the patient chose not to rehearse because her short-term memory was too impaired for this strategy to be of any value. It is possible that M.V. abandoned rehearsal for the same reason.

End-Item Recall

We can try to set up a memory span task that might encourage M.V. to subvocally rehearse, if she indeed retains the necessary speech programming skills. Some research with normals has shown that the last items in a sequence are very accurately reported when subjects are told to recall them before attempting the initial portion of the list (Posner, 1964). With standard recall instructions of course (i.e. repetition of the material in the order presented), marked recency effects are found—errors increase linearly over the final three or four serial positions, but the most accurate performance occurs for the last item.

Morton (1970) has argued that a semi-backwards strategy benefits end-item recall through the ability of the subject to maintain information subvocally. The basis for the argument is as follows—the terminal items are the last to have been rehearsed immediately after a sequence has been presented. Thus, their phonological traces are highly accessible, either because they are still maintained within the response buffer, as Morton assumes, or alternatively because rehearsal has enhanced their level of activation within the speech input register. When recall is semi-backwards, the information can be retrieved before it begins to deteriorate but, for serial recall, it decays or is replaced during the reproduction of the initial portion of the list.

M.V. can successfully repeat three isolated digits in their correct order. If she can also rehearse that many items adequately, we would expect her to be capable of maintaining the final three items of a sequence for selective recall. If she is unable to rehearse, however, she will be forced to rely on decaying phonological traces for the three end-items, and the usual effects of serial position will be obtained. To test this possibility, we presented M.V. with 24 digit sequences for repetition. Sequences were 4, 5 or 6 items in length. On half the trials, M.V. was told prior to presentation that she was to recall only the last three items (if possible, in their order of occurrence), while on remaining trials she was asked to recall the entire series of digits.

Results are displayed in Fig. 4.3 below. Overall accuracy for the last three items was slightly higher with end-item recall instructions than serial recall instructions. Nevertheless, serial position effects are clearly present for both modes of recall, suggesting that M.V. must consult a rapidly decaying trace even when given the opportunity to selectively rehearse part of a sequence in short-term memory.

Articulatory Rate

The experiments described above are all indirect procedures for examining M.V.'s ability to subvocally rehearse. Interpretation of the results are less than straightforward, especially in view of the definite limitations on her short-term memory capacity. A much more direct way of assessing the efficiency of M.V.'s articulatory rehearsal is simply to measure the rate at which she can produce a speech sequence. Baddeley, Thompson and Buchanan (1975) have shown that the memory span of normal subjects is well predicted by their articulatory rate, a finding that lends support to the notion that speech motor processes mediate phonemic rehearsal in short-term memory. If M.V. is incapable of sustaining adequate rehearsal because she can only organise a limited quantity of speech code in the response buffer for an utterance, we would expect her rate of articulation to be much slower than average.

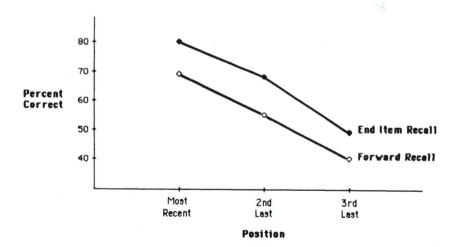

FIG. 4.3   End–item recall compared to recency effect in forward recall sequences consisting of 4–6 digits.

We administered two tests of rehearsal rate. In one test, also used by Vallar and Baddeley (1984a), M.V. was asked to count aloud five times from 1–10 as quickly as she could without pausing. The time taken to complete the entire sequence was measured by a stopwatch. A total of five trials were given in this way to compute an average rate of articulation.

The production of numbers in series is a highly automatic and redundant task. M.V.'s counting rate may certainly be less rapid than a normal subject's, but it would not be too surprising if we found that her performance is only moderately impaired. We have already observed that M.V. is much more capable of achieving correct output when phonemic sequences form words, as opposed to nonsense items. Perhaps if several words together comprise a highly overlearned sequence (such as the numbers 1–10), she may achieve a higher response rate compared to her pronunciation of a random group of words.

A second test of production was therefore conducted that employed three unrelated words per trial as stimuli for rapid serial repetition. Words were all high frequency, high imagery items. M.V. was allowed time to thoroughly familiarise herself with the target set before she began to respond. Furthermore, the three items were printed on flash cards in their order of pronunciation and displayed to her throughout a trial. Words were monosyllables (e.g., *cat*, *boy*, *leg*) on five trials; and an another five trials, tri-syllabic items were used (e.g., *family*, *telephone*, *animal*). M.V. was instructed to repeat each sequence of three words five times in succession without stopping, as quickly and accurately as possible. The mean rate of articulation for counting and word repetition can be seen in the Table 4.5.

M.V. is clearly unable to sustain a normal articulatory rate (AR), even when production is confined to a simple counting task. But the severity of her speech output deficit is most dramatically apparent in the slowness of continuous repetition for a non-redundant sequence. Performance here is grossly deficient—on the average, M.V. can produce no more than one word every two seconds. Production was slower for polysyllables than for mono-

TABLE 4.5
Articulation Rate for Counting, and Continuous Repetition of 3-Word Sequences

Task	Time (Seconds)	
	M.V.	*Controls (N=5)*
Counting		
(1—10) × 5	18.2 (SD = 3.3)	10.8 (SD = 2.1)
Repetition of Word		
sequences (5 × 3 words)	*M.V.*	*Controls (N=3)*
Monosyllables	26 (SD = 2.9)	4.0 (SD = 0.4)
Trisyllables	32 (SD = 6.0)	6.7 (SD = 1)

syllables, of course; syllable length exerted a similar effect on the AR of the control group.

A normal subject presumably achieves a high AR by organising the phonemic representation of several items simultaneously in the response buffer, and repeatedly executing the preplanned utterance. The situation for M.V. is entirely different; consistent with our analysis of her impairment, she appears to be incapable of activating a number of words in pre-articulatory form at the same time, so that every target is retrieved *de novo* for a pronunciation. If the sequence is overlearned, this may be accomplished reasonably quickly from long-term memory, though to be sure M.V. can still not attain the fluency of a person with intact phonemic planning skills. For an unfamiliar sequence, the pronunciation of each word must be re-addressed from lexical representation, a procedure that would be inefficient at the best of times. Given that M.V. has word-finding difficulty over and above her phonemic output problem, the mapping of lexical information to the response buffer will be particularly slow in her case.

Thus, we have good evidence that M.V. encounters great difficulty in reiterating a speech sequence that arises, we argue, because of a restriction on the amount of phonemic information she can adequately prepare within the response buffer for an utterance. Since the buffer is part of the mechanism responsible for subvocal rehearsal, we may infer that any procedure which usually requires this activity will also be compromised.

ABILITY TO DECODE WRITTEN SENTENCES

To what extent does M.V.'s subvocal rehearsal deficit interfere with her sentence reading? Baddeley, Eldridge and Lewis (1981) have presented some data indicating that normal reading performance can be disrupted if the speech output processes mediating rehearsal are occupied by irrelevant articulatory activity. Under suppression, subjects often failed to detect semantic and word-order anomalies in written sentences. Since detection of word-order errors was particularly poor, Baddeley et al. conclude that the most important function of articulatory rehearsal is to provide information about the exact wording of text.

The issue of whether speech output processes contribute to reading needs further investigation. As we have already noted, it is not at all clear that the decrement caused by suppression is specifically due to interference with rehearsal or whether, in fact, suppression is a sufficiently demanding second-ary task to impair performance by occupying general processing resources. Second, we do not know if articulatory rehearsal is necessary for processing written sentence material in particular, since no data is available concerning the possible effect of suppression on sentence acceptability judgements in the auditory modality.

Our investigation of M.V. has disclosed that her ability to rehearse subvocally is severely impaired. Are there any constraints on the kind of information she can extract from written (and spoken) sentences that could be understood in the light of this impairment? We have noted that her reading at the sentence level occurs slowly but accurately. She is capable of understanding material appropriate to a Grade 6 or 7 reader (see case report) but she proceeds hesitantly in doing so, and often re-reads sentences several times before she is satisfied that she has grasped their meaning. Thus, the picture we have is of a reader who is certainly no longer capable of fluent performance, but who, nevertheless, retains some competency to process moderately complex sentences and paragraphs.

In the present section, we examine M.V.'s ability to process the word-order of written and spoken material, using the sentence acceptability task employed by Baddeley, Eldridge and Lewis (1981) (also see Baddeley & Lewis, 1981). If articulatory rehearsal is needed to determine the word-order of text, we should find that M.V.'s judgements are often incorrect for written as opposed to spoken sentences. Furthermore, if articulation is primarily involved in processing order information but not meaning, we should find that her detection of semantic anomaly is far superior to her detection of word-order errors.

Two lists of 16 sentences were constructed, such that half the items on a list were anomalous. For one of the lists, sentences contained semantic errors (e.g. the bacon was eaten by the flower) whereas word-order errors (e.g. they gave me ride a home) occurred in the other list. The location of errors within the test sentences was balanced between lists. M.V. was instructed to work through each list, placing a check next to correct sentences and a cross next to sentences that she thought were incorrect. She was asked to do this as quickly as possible, but was also told to pay close attention to the exact wording in the sentences. Subsequent to the reading task, M.V. carried out acceptability judgements for the same sentences auditorily presented. Results are indicated in Table 4.6.

It is clear that M.V. was readily able to detect semantic errors regardless of

TABLE 4.6
Percent Correct in Detecting Sentence Anomalies

Type of sentence anomaly	Modality of Presentation			
	Spoken		Written	
	Positive	Negative	Positive	Negative
Semantic	100%	87%	100%	87%
Word–order	87%	87%	87%	12%

the modality of presentation. Word-order anomalies were also accurately detected in spoken sentences. In contrast, performance was markedly impaired when sentences were *read* and word-order judgements were required; the majority of M.V.'s errors occurred because she failed to reject sentences that contained word-order anomalies, and indeed her overall performance was exactly at chance. This outcome is just what we would expect if she is sensitive to the semantic information in written sentences without being able to analyse exact details of wording.[6] We conclude that M.V.'s difficulty is modality-specific and that monitoring of word-order is affected independently of her ability to access semantics.

DISCUSSION

We have described a patient who initially came to our attention because of our interest in phonological dyslexia. M.V.'s most striking impairment, on first examination, was her extremely poor oral reading of nonsense words, occurring without a similar breakdown in the pronunciation of real words. It soon became apparent to us, however, that we were dealing with a much more general problem in phonemic assembly that: (1) affected the production of orally presented, as well as written, nonsense words; and (2) also placed definite restrictions on M.V.'s whole-word pronunciation, which could be clearly brought out under appropriate testing conditions.

Analysis of the errors M.V. produces during nonsense word reading and repetition disclosed a number of findings that clarify the nature of her deficit. First, there is a striking similarity in the kind of mispronunciations for the two transcoding tasks, consistent with the hypothesis that a single functional locus is responsible for impairment to both spelling-sound and acoustic-phonological translation. Second, M.V.'s substitution errors for single phonemes in nonsense words are very often one (or at most two) distinctive features away from the target, suggesting that mispronunciations stem from a malfunctioning *phonological* process that can approximate the pronunciation of a nonsense word, but not capture it fully. Interestingly enough, this

---

[6] An interesting observation which emerged during the course of testing illustrates the kind of difficulty that M.V. encountered in attempting to detect word-order errors. On several trials we noted that she would, in fact, strive to articulate the sentences, especially when she was unsure whether or not they contained an error. On arriving at the point in the sentence where the word-order anomaly occurred, M.V. would occasionally utter part of the error aloud. This would immediately cause her to backtrack and re-check the order of the words by articulating them again. This painstaking strategy rarely allowed her to detect an error in the sentence, however M.V. invariably produced the corrected form of an anomalous sentence during an attempt to specify the order of words by articulating them (e.g. They gave me ride a home)—Response: "They gave me ride ... They gave me a ride. ... They gave me a ride home. That looks o.k. to me."

phonetic distance effect was found for both nonlexical responses to nonsense words (e.g., stimulus: SIFE; response: SIVE) and lexicalisation responses (e.g. stimulus: MUNT; response: MONK). Lexicalisations are typically thought to reflect a guessing strategy based on the resemblance between the nonsense word input and the whole word addresses within the lexicon. For a written nonsense word, the patient uses a visually similar word in the orthographic input lexicon to produce a response when grapheme-phoneme conversion is impaired. If repetition is required, a similar-*sounding* word to the nonsense target is selected for a response.

According to this interpretation, we may expect to see a phonological relationship between M.V.'s lexicalisation responses and a nonsense word dictated to her for repetition. Her lexicalisation of written nonsense items, however, should not be linked to the targets phonologically, since a visually-based guessing strategy is generally assumed (cf. Patterson, 1982). The fact that substitution errors in M.V.'s lexicalisations are one feature away from the target phonemes for reading as well as repetition provides strong support for our contention that a common deficit underlies both transcoding processes.

The origin of the mispronunciation errors for nonsense words may be conceptualised as follows. We can assume that the processes operating on nonlexical input require segmental build-up of information before a pronunciation can be achieved (cf. Seymour & MacGregor, 1984). Grapheme-phoneme conversion, for example, is considered to operate on elementary spelling units parsed in left-to-right fashion from the orthographic string. If these segments are assigned phonemes on a piecemeal basis and blended together in the response buffer, then any problem in sustaining the activation of codes at this level will produce distortion in the output.

Consider the nature of the response if the specification of phonemic elements is only partially lost, rather than totally obliterated. M.V. may assemble the deteriorated traces in the buffer directly and will then produce a non-word response that incorporates many of the phonological features of the target. There is another process at work, however, which influences performance—the contents of the response buffer should not be considered as isolated from the rest of the language system. Models of speech production (and constraints on the performance of normal speakers that have motivated such models) allow for the fact that interaction takes place between phonemic output processes and whole word levels of representation. For some models (e.g., Dell & Reich, 1980; Dell, 1985), the interaction occurs via positive feedback from phonemic to nonphonemic levels—activated phonemes in the response buffer spread their influence to whole-words that contain the same or similar elements. For other models (e.g., Baars, Motley, & MacKay, 1975; Motley, 1980) interaction occurs through a lexical editor rather than a positive feedback mechanism; the editor evaluates the potential output that could fit a partially specified pre-articulatory sequence and approves the one that is most consistent with its editing criteria.

We need not choose between these two accounts for the purpose of the present discussion. It is important only to note two points. Firstly, the concept of morphemic influences on the phonemic sequencing process is supported by considerable evidence from normal speech production. For example, Baars, Motley and MacKay (1975) demonstrated that the probability of a spoonerism in laboratory-induced speech errors was much greater when segment exchanges created legitimate words (e.g., "queer old dean" for *dear old queen*) than non-morphemic strings (e.g., "heft lemisphere" for *left hemisphere*). This lexical bias effect implies that activated phonemic sequences are monitored in some way by a mechanism that uses word-specific pronunciation to determine an appropriate response. The second point to note is that lexical feedback or editing has its primary role in compensating for noise or distortion in the phoneme sequencing process. A spreading activation mechanism accomplishes this by reinforcing strings of sounds that are consistent with higher-level information. The lexical editor would theoretically attempt to specify the intended utterance when the choices for output are ambiguous by coming up with a word that conforms as closely as possible to the phonological description of the pre-articulatory sequence.

The idea that an output buffer interacts with or relies upon support from an output lexicon, applied here to speech output, has also been applied to the case of *orthographic* output—i.e. to spelling rather than speaking. This kind of idea is inherent in the model of spelling proposed by Miceli, Silveri and Caramazza in Chapter 11, and also in the lexical activation hypothesis advanced by Miller and Ellis in Chapter 12 and discussed in connection with both spoken *and* written output.

Our analysis of M.V.'s performance has led us to conclude that the contents of her response buffer are: (1) susceptible to an abnormal degree of noise or interference; and (2) that this disturbance is seen in exaggerated form during the production of unfamiliar speech sequences. As we have indicated, the contents of the buffer, comprising a degraded specification of the correct output, can be synthesised for pronunciation immediately and the result will be a *nonsense word* which approximates the target phonologically. Alternatively, lexical levels of representation could be used to compensate for the impoverished quality of the traces in the buffer.[7] Since this mechanism normally attempts to capture a description of the phonemic sequence in the

---

[7]Given that we assume two alternative approaches for producing a nonsense word, the interesting question arises as to when each of these mediates pronunciation. What triggers a lexical strategy as opposed to immediate assembly of the buffer contents? A reasonable suggestion, we think, is that the two approaches simply reflect the amount of time elapsing before a decision is made to respond. Lexical feedback requires some time to operate (Dell, 1985), so the longer M.V. waits before attempting to read or repeat a nonsense word, the greater the likelihood of a lexicalisation. This account leads to the prediction, of course, that lexicalisation responses should be significantly slower than nonlexical responses. We are in the process of evaluating this possibility.

buffer on the basis of the closest phonological (whole-word) match, we should expect the majority of M.V.'s lexicalisation responses to be words that share many distinctive features with the nonsense target.

The impairment which has so drastically affected M.V.'s production of nonsense words has left her with substantial ability to retrieve the pronunciation of lexical items. What property of whole-words allows her to achieve such a high level of performance? One consideration is that all the segments for the pronunciation of a word can be transferred together from the phonological lexicon into the response buffer. This procedure would place less demands on the system than the alternative method of obtaining a pronunciation through analytic build-up of speech segments. More importantly, though, the same principle that forces M.V. to produce lexicalisations in her attempt to convert the deteriorated phonemic traces of a nonsense word into a response, also allows her to correctly retrieve the pronunciation of a word.

Activated speech elements for words tend to deteriorate rapidly within the response buffer, just as do segments for nonsense words. M.V. has sufficient higher-level information about the target word, however, to offset the loss of trace quality at the phonemic level. We assume that the compensatory information includes both lexical and semantic descriptions of the word, as lexical feedback alone would probably be insufficient to always successfully disambiguate the contents of the buffer. The speech output codes for a word like *card*, for example, could not be easily recovered once confusion begins about their exact specification because the lexical entries *cord*, *guard*, *cart*, etc. are so close phonologically that they would often substitute for the intended target. If semantic criteria are also applied to the phonemic sequence (cf. Motley, 1980), only one morpheme will qualify as the most reasonable candidate for output.

There is ample evidence that definite restrictions exist on M.V.'s word production skills, in spite of the ability to compensate for her speech planning deficit. Though production of familiar words was extremely accurate, mispronunciations often occurred for low frequency words, especially if items were greater than two syllables in length. M.V.'s impairment was dramatically apparent when she was required to rapidly and continuously repeat a sequence of three words. Rate of articulation was found to be extremely slow, even for monosyllabic, high-frequency items. These results are consistent with our interpretation of M.V.'s disturbance—she is limited in the quantity and reliability of the phonemic traces that can be activated for an utterance and therefore the efficiency with which she can execute continuous rehearsal of speech code is greatly reduced.

Examination of M.V.'s reading performance has disclosed that she is completely unable to detect slight anomalies of word-order in written sentences. The impairment clearly does not preclude the accurate extraction of meaning—she can readily identify sentences that contain semantic anomalies. We have also shown that the deficit is specific to written input; there is no evidence of a similar problem in the processing of auditorily presented sentences.

The difficulty that M.V. experiences appears very similar to the kind of problem normal subjects encounter when reading under articulatory suppression. Thus, our results provide some support for the notion that speech output processes contribute to certain aspects of reading. We consider that M.V.'s inability to process written word-order is linked to the deficiency in her subvocal rehearsal, which normally acts as a control procedure for transferring written information into phonological short-term memory. Evidence indicates that the storage capabilities of this system are needed to encode the surface structure of sentences; patients with a severely reduced memory span have great difficulty in comprehending sentences (both oral and written) that require temporary retention of verbatim content before meaning can be fully determined (Caramazza, Basili, Koller, & Berndt, 1981; Saffran & Marin, 1975; Vallar & Baddeley, 1984).

M.V.'s impaired ability to monitor the precise wording of written sentences cannot stem directly from a limitation in phonological short-term memory—she retains sufficient storage capacity to easily detect word-order anomalies in spoken sentences. Rather, the breakdown in her performance is caused by severely impaired subvocal rehearsal, which prevents her from converting written information into a phonological representation in short-term memory. It is of interest that M.V. is incapable of accurately judging word-order, even for the relatively simple material presented to her. Normal subjects, if prevented from rehearsing, only show a deficit for fairly complex sentences. Apparently, phonological recoding becomes important when the reading task places considerable demands on the cognitive system. M.V.'s poor processing of word-order for written sentences can be seen as an outcome of a basically inefficient reading system, coupled with a severe disturbance in subvocal rehearsal.

REFERENCES

Baars, G. J., Motley, M. T., & MacKay, D. G. (1975) Output editing for lexical status in artificially elicited slips of the tongue. *Journal of Verbal Learning and Verbal Behaviour, 14*, 382–391.

Baddeley, A. D. (1979) Working memory and reading. In P. A. Kolers, M. E. Wrolstad, & H. Bouma (Eds.), *The processing of visible language*. New York: Plenum Press.

Baddeley, A. D. (1981) The concept of working memory: A view of its current state and probable future development. *Cognition, 10*, 17–23.

Baddeley, A. D. (1983) Working memory. *Philosophical Transactions of the Royal Society of London, B302*, 311–324.

Baddeley, A. D., & Lewis, V. L. (1981) Inner active processes in reading: The inner voice, the inner ear and inner eye. In A. M. Lesgold & C. A. Perfetti (Eds.), *Interactive processes in reading*. Hillsdale, N.J.: Erlbaum.

Baddeley, A. D., Eldridge, M., & Lewis, Y. (1981) The role of subvocalisation in reading. *Quarterly Journal of Experimental Psychology, 33A*, 439–464.

Baddeley, A. D., Thompson, N., & Buchanan, M. (1975) Word length and the structure of short-term memory. *Journal of Verbal Learning and Verbal Behaviour, 14*, 575–589.

Beauvois, M. F., & Derouesné, J. (1979) Phonological alexia: Three dissociations. *Journal of Neurology, Neurosurgery and Psychiatry, 42*, 1115–1124.

Blumstein, S. E. (1973) *A phonological investigation of aphasic speech*. Paris: Mouton.

Bouma, H. (1971) Visual recognition of isolated lower case letters. *Vision Research, 11*, 459–474.

Burns, M. S., & Canter, G. J. (1977) Phonemic behaviour of aphasic patients with posterior cerebral lesions. *Brain and Language, 4*, 492–507.

Caramazza, A., Basili, A. G., Koller, J., & Berndt, R. S. (1981) An investigation of repetition and language processing in a case of conduction aphasia. *Brain and Language, 14*, 235–271.

Chomsky, N., & Halle, M. (1968) *The sound pattern of English*. NY: Harper and Row.

Colle, H. A., & Welsh, A. (1976) Acoustic masking in primary memory. *Journal of Verbal Learning and Verbal Behaviour, 15*, 17–31.

Coltheart, M. (1980) Reading, phonological recoding and deep dyslexia. In M. Coltheart, K. Patterson, & J. C. Marshall (Eds.), *Deep dyslexia*. London: Routledge & Kegan Paul.

Conrad, R. (1967) Interference or decay over short retention intervals? *Journal of Verbal Learning and Verbal Behaviour, 6*, 49–54.

Conrad, R., & Hull, A. J. (1964) Information, acoustic confusion and memory span. *British Journal of Psychology, 55*, 429–432.

Dell, G. S. (1985) Positive feedback in hierarchical connectionist models: Applications to language production. *Cognitive Science, 9*, 75–112.

Dell, G. S., & Reich, P. A. (1980) Toward a unified theory of slips of the tongue. In V. A. Fromkin (Ed.), *Errors in linguistic performance: Slips of the tongue, ear, pen and hand*. New York: Academic Press.

Derouesné, J., & Beauvois, M. F. (1979) Phonological processing in reading: Data from alexia. *Journal of Neurology, Neurosurgery and Psychiatry, 42*, 1125–1132.

Derouesné, J., & Beauvois, M. F. (1986) The phonemic stages in the non-lexical reading process: Evidence from a case of phonological alexia. In K. E. Patterson, J. C. Marshall, & M. Coltheart (Eds.), *Surface dyslexia*. London: Lawrence Erlbaum Associates Limited.

Ellis, A. W. (1979) Speech production and short-term memory. In J. Morton & J. C. Marshall (Eds.), *Psycholinguistic series vol.2.: Structures and processes*. Mass: MIT Press.

Ellis, A. W. (1980) Errors in speech and short-term memory: The effects of phoneme similarity and syllable position. *Journal of Verbal Learning and Verbal Behaviour, 19*, 624–634.

Engel, G. R., Dougherty, W. G., & Jones, G. B. (1973) Correlation and letter recognition. *Canadian Journal of Psychology, 27*, 317–326.

Funnell, E. (1983) Phonological processes in reading: New evidence from acquired dyslexia. *British Journal of Psychology, 74*, 159–180.

Geyer, L. H. (1977) Recognition and confusion of the lower case alphabet. *Perception and Psychophysics, 2*, 487–490.

Hardyk, C. D., & Petrinovitch, L. R. (1970) Subvocal speech and comprehension level as a function of the difficult level of reading material. *Journal of Verbal Learning and Verbal Behaviour, 9*, 647–652.

Henderson, L. (1982) *Orthography and word-recognition in reading*. London: Academic Press.

Kertesz, A. (1979) *Aphasia and associated disorders*. New York: Grune and Stratton.

Kleiman, G. M. (1975) Speech recoding in reading. *Journal of Verbal Learning and Verbal Behaviour, 24*, 323–339.

Lapointe, L. L., & Horner, J. (1979) *Reading comprehension battery for aphasia*. Oregon: CC Publications.

Levy, B. A. (1971) Role of articulation in auditory and visual short-term memory. *Journal of Verbal Learning and Verbal Behaviour, 14*, 304–316.

Levy, B. A. (1977) Reading: Speech and meaning processes. *Journal of Verbal Learning and Verbal Behaviour, 16*, 623–638.

Levy, B. A. (1978) Speech analysis during sentence processing: Reading and listening. *Visible Language, 12*, 81–102.

McCarthy, R., & Warrington, E. K. (1984) A two route model of speech production. *Brain, 107*, 463–485.

McCusker, L. X., Hillinger, M. L., & Bias, R. G. (1981) Phonological recoding and reading. *Psychological Bulletin*, 89, 217–245.

Monoi, H., Fukusako, Y., Itoh, M., & Susanuma, S. (1983) Speech sound errors in patients with Conduction and Broca's aphasia. *Brain and Language, 20*, 175–194.

Morton, J. (1970) A functional model for memory. In D. A. Norman (Ed.), *Models of human memory*. New York: Academic Press.

Morton, J., & Patterson, K. (1980) A new attempt at an interpretation, or, an attempt at a new interpretation. In M. Coltheart, K. Patterson, & J. C. Marshall (Eds.), *Deep dyslexia*, London: Routledge & Kegan Paul.

Motley, M. T. (1980) Verification of "Freudian Slips" and semantic prearticulatory editing via laboratory-induced spoonerisms. In V. A. Fromkin (Ed.), *Errors in linguistic performance: Slips of the tongue, ear, pen and hand*. New York: Academic Press.

Murray, D. J. (1968) Articulation and acoustic confusability in short-term memory. *Journal of Experimental Psychology, 78*, 679–684.

Newcombe, F., & Marshall, J. C. (1980) Transcoding and lexical stabilisation in deep dyslexia. In M. Coltheart, K. Patterson, & J. C. Marshall (Eds.), *Deep dyslexia*. London: Routledge & Kegan Paul.

Patterson, K. (1982) The relation between reading and phonological coding: Further neuropsychological observations. In A. W. Ellis (Ed.), *Normality and pathology in cognitive functioning*. London: Academic Press.

Posner, M. I. (1964) Rate of presentation and order of recall in immediate memory. *British Journal of Psychology, 55*, 303–306.

Saffran, E. M., & Marin, O. S. (1975) Immediate memory for word lists and sentences in a patient with deficient auditory short-term memory. *Brain and Language, 2*, 420–433.

Seymour, P. H. K., & MacGregor, C. J. (1984) Developmental dyslexia: A cognitive experimental analysis of phonological, morphemic and visual impairments. *Cognitive Neuropsychology, 1*, 43–82.

Slowiaczek, M. L., & Clifton, C. (1980) Subvocalisation and reading for meaning. *Journal of Verbal Learning and Verbal Behaviour, 19*, 573–582.

Taft, M. (1982) An alternative to grapheme-phoneme conversion rules? *Memory and Cognition, 10*, 465–474.

Temple, C. M., & Marshall, J. C. (1983) A case study of developmental phonological dyslexia. *British Journal of Psychology, 74*, 517–533.

Thorndike, E. L., & Lorge, I. (1944) *The teacher's word book of 50,000 words*. New York: Teacher's College.

Trost, J. E., & Canter, G. (1974) Apraxia of speech in patients with Broca's aphasia: A study of phoneme production accuracy and error patterns. *Brain and Language, 1*, 63–80.

Trost, J. E. (1970) A descriptive study of verbal apraxia in patients with Broca's aphasia. *Doctoral Dissertation*, Northwestern University.

Vallar, G., & Baddeley, A. D. (1984a) Phonological short-term store, phonological processing and sentence comprehension: A neuropsychological case study. *Cognitive Neuropsychology, 1*, 121–141.

Vallar, G., & Baddeley, A. D. (1984b) Fractionation of working memory: Neuropsychological evidence for a phonological short-term store. *Journal of Verbal Learning and Verbal Behaviour, 23*, 151–161.

5 Impairments of Semantic Processing: Multiple Dissociations

Tim Shallice

MRC Applied Psychology Unit, Cambridge CB2 2EF, England

Within cognitive psychology there has been much debate in recent years on what processes at the semantic level underlie word comprehension and the identification of objects (see e.g., Glucksberg, 1984; Snodgrass, 1984; Te Linde, 1982). This paper will be concerned with the types of disorder that arise from impairments of these processes and the light they can throw on our understanding of normal function. A standard assumption is that to access a semantic representation requires the prior attaining of some form of pre-semantic representation of the input, such as the identification of a word-form or logogen in the perception of words or perceptual classification—the accessing of a "pictogen"—in the recognition of objects (see e.g., Morton, 1970 for words; Warrington & Taylor, 1978 for objects; Seymour, 1979 for review). The present discussion will be concerned with the processes that follow the attainment of these pre-semantic types of representation.

Disorders at the level of attainment of a semantic representation are now widely accepted both for verbal material (see Caramazza & Berndt, 1978; Lesser, 1978 for reviews) and for visual material (see Ratcliff & Newcombe, 1982, for review). However, there is a tendency to view these disorders as of a single type. For instance, Caramazza, Berndt and Brownell (1982) in a sophisticated analysis argue for the existence of five stages in the naming process, using as an example the naming of a cup. These stages are:

1. Low-level perceptual analysis.
2. Modality-specific identification of "semantically interpretable components" (e.g. of a handle shape or the diameter-to-width ratio) by a top-down parser driven from the following stage.

3. Modality-independent identification.
4. Selection of a particular lexical item.
5. Production of the selected word.

A characteristic of this type of model is that objects and words have a single modality-independent semantic representation. In addition there is a tendency to interpret positive correlations between the performance of patients on semantically related tasks as arising from certain of the patients having a "semantic deficit," to use the terminology of Caramazza, Berndt and Brownell (1982). It will be argued in the present paper that this type of position probably requires amending in two ways. It appears necessary to postulate multiple semantic representation systems and also to distinguish disorders of access and ones of "degradation" of the "stored information."

MULTIPLE SEMANTIC REPRESENTATION SYSTEMS

Within cognitive psychology there is a well-known theoretical dispute on whether distinct verbal and visual semantic representation systems exist (see Seymour, 1979 for review). At present evidence on normal subjects appears not to favour one or other of the two positions particularly strongly (see e.g., Snodgrass, 1984; Te Linde, 1982).

Within neuropsychology, at least three types of argument have been put forward for the existence of multiple semantic representation systems. All have arisen from the study of the "modality-specific" aspects of syndromes, where the term is used in this context to differentiate not only visual non-verbal, auditory non-verbal, and tactile non-verbal processes, but also each of these from verbal processes (activated from any form of sensory input). The lines of evidence derive from the characteristics of the modality-specific aphasias (Beauvois, 1982), the existence of modality-specific priming in semantic access dyslexia (Warrington & Shallice, 1979), and modality-specific aspects of semantic memory disorders (Warrington, 1975; Warrington & Shallice, 1984) respectively. Each of these lines of evidence is independent of the other two, so that for a unitary semantic representation system position to be maintained all three arguments must be refuted.

In the modality-specific aphasias, stimuli can be named from all modalities but one, and yet evidence can be obtained that in the impaired modality semantic representation systems can be accessed satisfactorily. For instance, in tactile aphasia objects can be named from visual presentation but not from touch; yet their use can be demonstrated in the blindfolded patient with tactile presentation. Over the last 10 years there have been detailed descriptions of at least four cases: visual (Beauvois, 1982; Lhermitte & Beauvois, 1973); auditory (Denes & Semenza, 1975); and tactile (Beauvois et al., 1978).

The simplest explanation for these syndromes is that multiple semantic systems do exist, but that there is an impairment in the transmission of information from one of the modality-specific semantic systems to verbal systems (including the verbal semantic system) (see e.g., Beauvois, 1982). Thus in the case of tactile aphasia a purely tactile semantic system would be considered to be intact as indicated by the patients' ability to use objects correctly when blindfolded, and yet the naming impairment for tactile input alone would be explained by an impairment in the transmission of information from tactile to verbal semantic systems. Recently, however, two alternative explanations for the modality-specific aphasias have been developed.

Ratcliff and Newcombe (1982) have argued that one of these syndromes could arise as a result of a lesion to a modality-specific naming route analogous to the so-called "third-route" of Schwartz, Saffran and Marin (1980) and Morton and Patterson (1980) for reading. Thus it is argued by Ratcliff and Newcombe that "optic aphasia could be caused by disruption of the non-semantic route in much the same way as deep dyslexia is associated with loss of non-semantic routes for reading." However, to hold this position for any one of the syndromes it is necessary to make two separate assumptions. First it must be assumed that a modality-specific naming route for the naming of objects does exist. In addition it needs to be presupposed that a semantic route operating normally is insufficient to support accurate naming, as a lesion to the non-semantic route would leave the semantic route available for use in naming.

Neither of these assumptions is at all solidly based. For the first, however, certain patients do exist whose impairment is easy to explain on the assumption of a visual non-semantic naming route. Heilman, Tucker and Valenstein (1976) described one such patient having "transcortical aphasia with intact naming" and two further patients have recently been described by Kremin (1984). In all three patients oral naming is virtually entirely intact (> 90%) with performance on a task of comprehension of pictures much inferior (20–56%). However, the comprehension task consisted of a 4-alternative forced choice procedure in which the patient had to point to a picture in the same semantic category as a target picture. To perform this task satisfactorily might well require semantic processing of a considerably more abstract type than that involved in, say, the demonstration of object use—the way that modality-specific semantic processing was assessed in bilateral tactical aphasia. Some indirect support for this suggestion can be obtained from Goodglass and Baker's (1976) study on the organisation of aphasics' semantic fields; judgements of semantic similarity of the co-ordinate type (e.g., *orange→apple*) were considerably slower and less accurate than, say, those based on attributes (e.g., *orange→juicy*) both for normal subjects and for a "high comprehension" aphasic subgroup (although rather strangely not for a "low comprehension" aphasic subgroup). Thus the existence of a naming route which bypasses the visual semantic processes involved in demonstrating object use is not clearly established by the investigations of transcortical aphasia with intact naming carried out to date. Moreover the evidence from normal subjects seems to be rather unfavourable to the idea. It has been found that semantic decisions are faster with pictures but naming faster with written words (e.g., Fraisse, 1960; Potter & Faulconer, 1975; Te Linde, 1982), which has been interpreted in terms of pictures lacking a specific naming route. Evidence on priming has led Carr et al. (1982) to a similar conclusion, although not phrased in information-processing language.

The second assumption that is essential for Ratcliff and Newcombe's (1982) argument is that the semantic route, operating normally, will not suffice for accurate object naming. Its normal operation is held to produce the semantic errors that occur in optic aphasia. No independent evidence is presented for this position. It is supported by analogy with deep dyslexia on the assumption that the semantic errors that occur in that syndrome arise in the course of the normal operation of the semantic route. This was the original assumption of Newcombe and Marshall (1980a) for deep dyslexia, but evidence is now available on the existence of at least two types of impairment in particular deep dyslexia patients in the operation of the semantic route—in the attainment of the semantic representation (Shallice & Coughlan, 1980) and in response selection (Morton & Patterson, 1980; Patterson, 1978). Therefore the assumption that deep dyslexia reflects isolated intact reading by the semantic route appears most implausible. Moreover in certain cases of phonological alexia reading appears to be based on the operation of the semantic route, as meaningfulness affects the patient's reading performance (Beauvois, Derouesné, & Saillant, 1980); yet semantic errors do not occur. The analogy used by Ratcliff and Newcombe therefore appears extremely shaky.

The second alternative explanation put forward by Riddoch and Humphreys (1983) is that the modality-specific aphasias are in essence semantic access disorders. This has an intuitive plausibility for some of the cases reported. For instance, for the auditory aphasic patient of Denes & Semenza (1975), the conclusion of preserved auditory identification of non-verbal sounds was based on the patient's good performance on a forced-choice sound-picture matching test. It could be argued that good performance on this task could be obtained with less semantic processing than that required for intact naming of the sounds. Moreover the patient claimed not to know what the sound was; this has a resemblance to the phenomenology of semantic access disorders (to be discussed later). However, I know of no clear case where a semantic access patient could perform accurately on forced-choice tests when unable to explicitly identify the stimuli. A.R. (Warrington & Shallice, 1979), for instance, could not. Hence this possible counter-explanation has yet to receive concrete support.

For other modality-specific aphasics a semantic access explanation appears less plausible. Thus for the bilateral tactile aphasic patient of Beauvois et al. (1978) tactile-naming produced 30% errors, a much inferior performance to that on tests that do not involve naming; miming use to tactile presentation was 99% correct and tactile-visual matching (where physical properties could not be easily used) was 100% correct. Performance on the second and third of the tests is much higher than would be expected on a semantic access account. Neither the Riddoch and Humphreys' suggestion of the ambiguity of certain mimes (e.g., *boot*, *sock*) or their other suggestion that certain characteristic actions may not be based on semantic representations seem adequate to account for the discrepancy.

A second line of evidence that multiple semantic representation systems exist can be derived from semantic priming experiments performed with the semantic access dyslexic patient A.R. (Warrington & Shallice, 1979). A characteristic of A.R.'s semantic access dyslexia was that his ability to read a word (e.g., *pyramid*) was increased considerably and significantly more by an auditory verbal prompt (e.g., *Egypt*) than by presenting a picture of what the word represented. Moreover, object naming was only marginally increased by an auditory verbal cue. As A.R. performed at a near normal level on Warrington's (1975) test probing detailed knowledge of objects and animals, it is implausible that this pattern of results can be explained by any visual agnosia. The most plausible explanation is that A.R. could not transmit information from a visual semantic system to a verbal one and so could not prime reading by means of a picture or picture naming by a verbal cue. (N.B. I am assuming that reading accesses the verbal semantic store). A.R.'s almost complete inability to name objects presented visually when contrasted with reasonable performance in naming objects from their descriptions—a test from Coughlan and Warrington's (1978) battery—fits with this explanation. However, as these aspects of the impairments of the patient A.R. were investigated less thoroughly than his semantic access difficulty, on its own, this line of evidence is not conclusive.

A third line of evidence comes from the study of patients who appear to have lost information permanently from their semantic memory (see Warrington, 1975). It will be argued in the next section that tests can be developed for whether a representation has indeed been lost from the store or not. One important criterion is consistency in the inability to identify particular items over test sessions. As an illustration E.M., one of Warrington's original semantic memory patients, when describing word meanings had a contingency coefficient of 0.58, very close to the maximum possible of 0.71, when the items that were judged correct were compared over two test sessions seven months apart (see Coughlan & Warrington, 1981).

If this type of operational criterion is accepted, then on a single semantic store position it follows that the same items would be lost whatever modality was used for testing. In fact such patients can show considerable differences between modalities. Thus E.M. was significantly better at identifying a visually-presented object by giving a description of its non-visually apparent properties or its function than she was in giving an account of it from presentation of its name (Warrington, 1975). A related result was obtained in patient W.L.P. (Schwartz, Saffran, & Marin, 1979). This patient, who was similar to E.M. both in terms of aetiology and in the functional time-course of the disease process, made many semantic errors in written word-picture matching at a time when the words could be read aloud virtually perfectly by morphemic correspondences. Yet the use of the objects utilised in the matching task could be mimed perfectly. In this patient, however, no direct test of whether the deficit was a storage one was carried out.

In both patients a possible, if rather implausible, alternative explanation to a dual-store account would be that of transmission failures from word-form *systems* (auditory *and* visual) to a unitary semantic system. However, in two further patients, J.B.R. and S.B.Y., investigated by Warrington and Shallice (1984) this explanation is even less plausible. These patients performed at a comparable level in visual object identification and in name comprehension. Yet they showed very little consistency in object identification assessed by judgements of their descriptions when the comparison was between different modalities—four out of five comparisons were insignificant—but all three comparisons possible within a modality gave significant consistency of responding (see Table 5.1). That their deficit did, in fact, lie at

TABLE 5.1

			J.B.R.		S.B.Y.	
	Stimuli	*No.*	*Within modality*	*Between modality*	*Within modality*	*Between modality*
Exp1	Zinkin Pictures	40	0.61**(V)	0.26	0.48**(V)	(i)0.15
					0.33*(A)	(ii)0.49*
Exp2	Objects	48	—	—	—	0.12
Exp5	Objects	40	—	—	—	0.04

Note: Contingency coefficients between performance in two sessions for J.B.R. and S.B.Y. for both within modality and between modality comparisons (from Warrington & Shallice, 1984). Responses were divided into correct or wrong according to whether the majority of three independent judges considered the description of word/picture to provide "reasonable evidence that the core concept is conveyed." V refers to visual input (i.e. a picture of the object); A to auditory verbal input (i.e. the object's name). Only conditions where both sets of corresponding results lay between 20% and 80% correct were considered. It should be noted that the maximum possible 2×2 contingency coefficient is 0.71. A significant contingency coefficient is marked by an *(.05) **(.01).

the semantic level was shown by a number of arguments. The principal one was that they showed a very large selective loss of knowledge of the properties of items in certain categories (in particular, foods and living things, by comparison with inanimate objects: to document and establish this phenomenon was in fact the main purpose of the analysis of their agnosias).

This type of dissociation between word comprehension and object identification in patients with degraded semantic representations is also most easily explained in terms of there being multiple semantic representation systems. In fact we think that evidence exists for further subdivision within these semantic systems, in particular into subsystems specific for sensory properties and ones specific for functional significance. (The evidence for this further subdivision has been reviewed elsewhere in Warrington, 1981a; see also Warrington & McCarthy, 1983; Warrington & Shallice, 1984).

This therefore leaves two alternatives for an explanation of modality-specific semantic effects. One possibility is that the modality-specific effects are primary and within some or all of the modality-specific semantic systems, subdivisions for different types of semantic operation or property exist. Alternatively, the subdivisions for different types of semantic operation or property, such as sensory properties, functional significance, control of use, the facilitation of selection restrictions, are primary and pre-semantic systems (perceptual categorisation, word-form) differ in their ease of access to these different regions of the overall semantic system. To differentiate between the alternatives neuropsychologically may well prove difficult.

DEGRADED REPRESENTATIONS AND IMPAIRED ACCESS

Whether a particular disorder of semantic processing is best understood in terms of damage to representations in a store itself or in terms of impaired access to a store has been investigated using two different methodologies. In two group studies Milberg and Blumstein (1981) and Blumstein, Milberg and Schrier (1982) found that Wernicke's aphasics show an associative priming effect in a lexical decision task both for latency and for errors. They therefore argue against the idea that the Wernicke's aphasic has an impairment to the semantic system itself of "restricted semantic fields and/or associative capacities." Instead they argue for an access interpretation. In fact their conclusion that automatic activation of semantic information is relatively spared in Wernicke's aphasia, although conscious access to it is not, does not seem justified by their findings. For instance, a decrease in error rate in lexical decision from 40% for unrelated primes to 33% with related primes in the Blumstein et al. study (1982) does indeed show an effect of priming, but even primed performance where access is facilitated is extremely poor. In any case their methodology presupposes that all Wernicke's aphasics have qualitatively the same semantic disorder. In the light of the following analysis of the impairment in individual patients such an assumption may well be inappropriate.

Using the individual case approach, Warrington and I were impressed by the different patterns of semantic difficulties shown by A.R. (Warrington & Shallice, 1979), whom we considered a semantic access patient, and the semantic memory patients mentioned above. The two types of patient had in common a much greater ability to discriminate which superordinate category an item was in than to explicitly identify it. However, to account for the differences between them we argued that a patient who has lost information permanently from the store might be expected to differ from one who has difficulty accessing information in the store in four ways:

1. We argued that in a "degraded store" deficit the ability or inability to identify a given item should be very consistent across test sessions. However, in an access difficulty the ability to access information might be subject to all sorts of temporary local factors; in this case there would be considerable inconsistency between the way the subject responds to the same item on different testing sessions.

2. If an item could not be identified, then on a "degraded store" difficulty it should not be possible to elicit identification by priming. If the representation no longer exists one could not prime it. On an access difficulty an improvement with priming should be possible.

3. For the "degraded store" difficulty Warrington (1975) had argued that there was a relatively invariant order in which information about an item was lost. Superordinate information should be more resistant than attribute information. That a canary was a living thing would be less vulnerable than that it is yellow. For the access difficulty, by contrast, no such invariance would be expected. The eliciting of attribute information *given that superordinate information has been accessed* would be no more difficult than initially eliciting the superordinate.

4. It was argued that item frequency would be expected to be a major factor in determining which items were lost for the "degraded store" difficulty. For an access difficulty frequency would be expected to be a less important factor as the variability produced by specific access/information retrieval problems would tend to flatten any underlying "normal" frequency function.

5. An additional criterion has been added by Warrington and McCarthy (1983). They argued that if performance depended upon rate of presentation where the rates involved were not particularly fast—they used rates varying from one item per 2 second to one item per 30 seconds—then improved performance at the slower rate would support an access interpretation.

Over the past 15 years 11 patients have been studied at the National Hospital because their impairment was of theoretical interest and had a major semantic component. These are:

1. Warrington's (1975) "semantic memory patients" A.B., E.M., C.R. (see also Coughlan & Warrington, 1981).
2. A.R., a "semantic access dyslexic" (Warrington & Shallice, 1979).
3. C.A.V., a "concrete word dyslexic" (Warrington, 1981b).
4. V.E.R., a "category specific access dysphasic" (Warrington & McCarthy, 1983).
5. J.B.R., S.B.Y., B.A.R., I.N.G. with a different category-specific semantic impairment (Warrington & Shallice, 1984).
6. M.L., with a form of letter-by-letter reading markedly different from the standard variety (Shallice & Saffran, 1986).

I will use these case studies as a database to assess whether application of the above criteria suggests that two groups of patients exist. In general the theoretical inferences on the degraded store/access issue will be considered independently of the type of input, auditory–verbal, written or object, being used. The patients will be considered in two groups. The first consists of the patients in categories 1–5 whose impairments fit reasonably well into the "degraded store" and "semantic access" categories. The patients in these categories where there is sufficient relevant data (i.e., all except B.A.R., and I.N.G.) will be considered first. In the following section the impairments of the remaining patient will be considered.

Table 5.2 provides a summary of the relevant characteristics of the eight patients in the first set. If one ignores A.B. and C.R. where insufficient data is available to make the comparison, then the other six patients fall into two sharply distinct groups—E.M., J.B.R. and S.B.Y. on the one hand and A.R., C.A.V. and V.E.R. on the other. The first group all have higher contingency coefficient values than the second group, and considering that 0.71 is the maximum possible value the contrast in consistency of responding is marked for most of the patients. The effects of frequency on the performance of the two groups is also very different: for the first group performance with high frequency stimuli is very good, and with the exception of S.B.Y there is a large frequency effect, but neither of these characteristics holds for the second group. Finally, all the first group are markedly better at retrieving superordinate information about stimuli than attribute information. The second group, though, can retrieve attribute information about stimuli given knowledge of the superordinate. Thus on a 3-alternative forced-choice test of words that he could not read A.R. performed at only 57% on a superordinate choice task (e.g., *cabbage—animal, plant* or *object*) but at 75% on an equivalent test of attributes (e.g., *cabbage—green, brown* or *grey*). By

TABLE 5.2

Procedure	Consistency (Within Modality)	Frequency High [A or AA]	Low [< 50]	Priming (P) Rate (R) Effects	Superordinate Attribute Information
A.B.$_1$ Defining	NT	96	51	NT	NT
E.M.$_1$ Defining	0.58	96	51	NT	Super > > Att
C.R.$_1$ Defining	NT	96	60	NT	NT
J.B.R.$_2$ Defining	0.61	91	68	NT	Super > > Att*
S.B.Y.$_2$ Defining	0.4	84	72	NT	Super > > Att**
A.R.$_3$ Reading	0.31	46	42	Strong P	Equal
C.A.V.$_4$ Reading	0.23	56	36	Strong P	NT
V.E.R.$_5$ Word-picture matching	At chance	61	55	Strong R	NT

Note: Access/degraded store characteristics of National Hospital patients (from 1 Warrington, 1975, and Coughlan & Warrington, 1981; 2 Warrington & Shallice, 1984; 3 Warrington & Shallice, 1979; 4 Warrington, 1981b; 5 Warrington & McCarthy, 1983). The results are based on three different procedures: (1) providing a definition for a presented word (see Table 5.1 legend), (2) reading aloud, and (3) word-picture matching using a 4 or 5 alternative forced–choice procedure. The consistency measures are in general contingency coefficients; frequency results are given in terms of percent correct; superordinate/attribute contrast is based on the ability to perform forced-choice tests or the ability to give superordinates for categories where attribute information could not be provided (*). The consistency measure for J.B.R. is based on identifying objects and for S.B.Y. it is the mean of that and its verbal equivalent. For V.E.R. consistency was measured by a different procedure and the frequency results are based on performance on Peabody 1–25 compared with Peabody 26–100, both performed twice. Some of the frequency data in this table is only approximate; it is based on the average of cells in published tables. NT = not tested.

contrast, E.M. with auditory presentation was 98% correct with the former but only 72% correct with the latter. (One of the second group, V.E.R., was not tested in a comparable fashion; she, however, showed a rate effect.)

It should be noted that the individual patients involved in this comparison had very different characteristics in addition to the ones being considered here. V.E.R., for instance, was a global aphasic while E.M. and J.B.R. were both phonologically and syntactically intact. Moreover, in the comparison being made performance with different types of stimulus material and very different testing procedures is being conflated. Despite these problems the characteristics of the semantic disorder do appear to be similar within a group of patients and there is a marked contrast between the two groups. The analysis therefore appears to provide reasonable, if by no means conclusive, evidence that at least two types of impairment of semantic processing can be identified. A plausible characterisation of the two types of impairment would seem to be in terms of loss of information from within a semantic store and a difficulty in accessing information in the store. The contrast would be orthogonal to the modality-specific and category specific ones discussed earlier.

PROBLEMS AND COMPLICATIONS

There are a number of interconnected theoretical and empirical issues that remain to be resolved:

1. Can an access difficulty be distinguished theoretically and empirically from a partial transmission failure/noisy transmission route between one of the pre-semantic word-form or logogen systems and a semantic system?

2. Can an access account be differentiated theoretically and empirically from the lexical irradiation (Weigl & Bierwisch, 1970), spreading activation (Saffran, Schwartz, & Marin, 1976), or unstable semantic system (Newcombe & Marshall, 1980b) theories that have been put forward to account for semantic errors?

3. Do all semantic access patients have a functionally similar disorder?

4. Can the characteristics of patient M.L. who appeared to combine a word-form dyslexia and a semantic access problem be incorporated into this conceptual framework?

5. Is the account compatible with descriptions of other individual cases in the cognitive neuropsychology literature?

The first of these issues concerns transmission failures. It is fairly easy to distinguish partial transmission failures from access failures conceptually. For instance, consider Rieger's (1978) model of semantic access (see also Rieger & Small, 1979). In this model knowledge about language is distributed across a population of procedural experts, each representing a word of the language and each an expert at diagnosing the word's intended usage in context from among the many possibilities. The experts themselves exist in two forms in the model. In word expert structure form each corresponds to a directed hierarchical graph that represents an ordered set of decisions that converge on a single appropriate sense of the word. When the word expert "runs" as a process it can ask questions of other experts so as to select the appropriate branch of the sense net. (One incidental aspect of the model is that it provides indirect computational support for a relatively heirarchical model of word sense structure which is assumed in criterion three of the previous section.) Within a model of this form an impairment of the directed graphs themselves would correspond to storage damage and an impairment of the word expert process would correspond to an access failure.

This latter type of impairment is clearly conceptually distinct from a partial transmission failure. On the other hand if, as seems quite plausible, the word expert processor contains no internal memory of the input received from lower systems, but instead relies on continuing input from word-form/ logogen systems, then a partial transmission failure could mimic an access disorder empirically. The successful completion of the access process operating *sequentially in real time* would depend upon the reception of an adequate signal from lower systems throughout the whole period the access process took to operate. If an adequate signal was not maintained an access disorder would be mimicked. Thus it seems entirely possible that an access disorder, while being conceptually quite distinct from a partial transmission failure, could be empirically very difficult to distinguish from it. To consider the question adequately much more detailed models than those customary in cognitive neuropsychology at present would be required.

The theoretical relation between the access explanation and the related group of theories put forward to account for semantic errors—lexical irradiation, spreading activation and "unstable" semantic systems—is more complex. If those positions are interpreted in terms of a particular node in a semantic network being completely activated, *after* which processes of irradiation, spreading activation and so on lead to other nodes being activated, these positions differ from the access one. If, however, these processes are seen as occurring *prior* to complete activation of the "correct" node—which is never actually achieved (e.g., Shallice & McGill, 1978)—then such theories become specific versions of the access position. Again, in the present level of theoretical development the two types of theorising are orthogonal rather than compatible or contradictory.

Turning to a related but more concrete issue, it is unclear whether all disorders that have been characterised as "access" ones are qualitatively equivalent. One considerable empirical difference between A.R. and C.A.V's access difficulties exists. One of the major features of A.R.'s dyslexia was that he could categorise words he could not read very much above chance. We viewed this as a cardinal feature of semantic access dyslexia indicating that the impairment was in the semantic realm. (It does not appear in the list of criteria above as degraded store deficits show the same feature.) C.A.V., however, could not categorise words he could not read. Warrington (1981b) has suggested that the much poorer performance of C.A.V. on this task was because a five-choice test was used. C.A.V. when asked to categorise a word he could not read as animal, plant, part of the body, food or object scored only 7/32. A.R. in a comparable situation obtained 22/32 (69%), well above chance. However, most of A.R.'s impressive categorising performance occurred in two-choice situations. Thus when presented with 100 names of authors or politicians he read only 14 correctly, but categorised 80% of the rest correctly. (That A.R.'s good categorisation abilities could not be due to attaining the semantic representation and then having nominal difficulties was shown in a number of different ways; for instance his ability to provide accurate details of authors/politicians was considerably weaker when attempting to read compared with hearing the name.)

Another empirical problem concerns patient M.L. (Shallice & Saffran, 1986). M.L. read words very slowly in the letter-by-letter fashion typical of classical alexia without agraphia. Such disorders have been attributed within an information-processing framework to an impairment of a pre-semantic word-form system (Warrington & Shallice, 1980), or in more classical fashion, to the input to such a system (Patterson & Kay, 1982). Moreover, if a word was displayed too briefly for M.L. to perform the letter-by-letter process, then it could be shown in a number of ways that he was typical of letter-by-letter readers (e.g., Patterson & Kay, 1982) in not being able to identify words. Thus using a two second exposure time he identified only 3/24 words. Moreover his naming times for unlimited exposures were greater than four seconds on 39/40 trials for words of five or more letters—the length used in all further investigations—and for auditory input he had no naming difficulties at all; he was not aphasic. However with two second exposures for a number of pairs of categories, M.L. categorised well words that he could not read (see Table 5.3). (One interesting aspect of the data is that he was unable to categorise concrete categories effectively showing a similar pattern to C.A.V. on the five choice task of assigning the word to one of animals, plants, parts of the body, foods and objects.) How, though, is his intact categorisation performance to be explained given his letter-by-letter reading?

There are a number of possible explanations. One is that a semantic access difficulty can exist in conjunction with relatively preserved letter identification and preserved spelling; in this case it manifests itself as letter-by-letter reading. It would, though, be qualitatively different functionally from "normal" letter-by-letter reading where categorisation of unread words is not possible (Patterson & Kay, 1982).

A second explanation is that in M.L. the visual word-form system, which on the Warrington and Shallice (1980) approach is the pre-semantic system damaged in letter-by-letter reading, is in fact impaired. However the impairment is partial. The output of the visual word-form system is "weak" or "noisy." So the input to the relevant semantic system is similar to that produced by a partial transmission failure. It must then be assumed that such an input is sufficient for the semantic system to perform a categorisation judgement but not for precise identification. In degradation impairments superordinate information is most resistant to the disease process (see also Goodglass & Baker, 1976); it is therefore plausible that in the normal operation of the system less information is required to access the category in which the input item lies than to precisely identify the input.

There is one specific aspect of M.L.'s impairment which fits well with this explanation. M.L. had relatively preserved lexical decision using two second

TABLE 5.3

Performance on Categorisation of Words that Could Not Be Read on Two Occasions by M.L.

		I						II			
	No. presented	No. read		Categorisation of unread words			No. Read		Categorisation of Unread Words		
		Before cat	After cat	Correct	Wrong	Correct by chance	Before cat	After cat	Correct	Wrong	Correct by chance
In/out Europe	50/100	0	14	34	2	(18)	11	9	68	12	(40)
Author v. politician	50	1	6	40	3	(21.5)	6	5	32	6	(19)
Living things v. non-living objects	100	1	10	77	12	(44.5)	0	5	79	16	(47.5)
Pleasant v. unpleasant words	60	0	0	49	11	(30)	2	4	45	9	(27)
Leisure v. work words	60	3	2	37	16	(26.5)	2	2	43	13	(28)
People v. object adjectives	40	0	0	24	16	(20)	—	—	—	—	—
5 choice	40	0	0	12	28	(8)	0	1	14	25	(7.8)

Source: Shallice and Saffran, 1986

exposures, although he did not know what the words were (Shallice & Saffran, 1986). However the distractors in this experiment were either very close to an English word or differed considerably from any English word, although otherwise they were equivalent in their orthographic characteristics. M.L. produced many false positive responses (47%) to distractors which differed by one letter from an English word; those distractors that differed by two letters were only 13% likely to be thought of as words. Thus how close a pseudoword is to an English word affects how likely he is to give a false positive response. This supports the idea that an impairment exists in the output of the visual word-form system. If this were the case, then it would provide some concrete support for the claim that the empirical distinction between a partial transmission impairment and semantic access difficulties is a difficult one to make. It would also indirectly support the proposal that the non-conscious semantic effects which occur with pattern masking (e.g., Marcel, 1983) can be explained as a result of pattern masking interrupting the input to the semantic systems prematurely so that it is effectively weak or noisy (see Shallice & McGill, 1978). However the interpretation of M.L.'s dyslexia remains very speculative (for alternative views see Shallice & Saffran, 1986).

Finally, does the distinction between semantic access and degraded store deficits map on to the comprehension difficulties of other individual patients described in the neuropsychological literature? Quite often in testing comprehension disorders the property common to the two hypothesised types—the ability to provide an approximate semantic response (e.g., a superordinate) in the absence of explicit identification—has been demonstrated (e.g., Deloche, Andreewsky, & Desi, 1981; Newcombe & Marshall, 1980b; Schwartz, Saffran, & Marin, 1979). However as the relative preservation of superordinate discrimination compared with explicit identification is to be expected with both types of disorder it does not help to distinguish between them. In general the more detailed findings which would allow tests of the existence of the subtypes have not been carried out. For instance, few consistency assessments are available in the literature and where they exist they tend to concern the nature of error responses (e.g., Newcombe & Marshall, 1980b) or to involve forced-choice matching (e.g., Schwartz et al., 1979) where guessing makes interpretation difficult. More detailed empirical analyses of comprehension disorders are clearly required.

To conclude, there now seems to be reasonable evidence that a number of different semantic systems exist, each of which may be further subdivided (see Warrington, 1981a) and that, orthogonally, access and degraded store impairments can be distinguished. However, the overall picture with respect to the neuropsychology of semantic systems is by no means clear. Our theoretical tools remain very primitive and a number of empirical anomalies remain to be dissolved.

REFERENCES

Beauvois, M. F. (1982) Optic aphasia: A process of interaction between vision and language. *Philosophical Transactions of the Royal Society of London, B298*, 35–47.

Beauvois, M. F., Derouesné, J., & Saillant, B. (1980) Syndromes neuropsychologiques et psychologie cognitif. Trois exemples: Aphasie tactile, alexie phonologique et agraphie lexicale. *Cahiers de Psychologie, 23*, 211–245.

Beauvois, M. F., Saillant, B., Meininger, V., & Lhermitte, F. (1978) Bilateral tactile aphasia: A tacto-verbal dysfunction. *Brain, 101*, 381–401.

Blumstein, S. E., Milberg, W., & Shrier, R. (1982) Semantic processing in aphasia: Evidence from an auditory lexical decision task. *Brain and Language, 17*, 301–315.

Caramazza, A., & Berndt, R. S. (1978) Semantic and syntactic processes in aphasia: A review of the literature. *Psychological Bulletin, 85*, 898–918.

Caramazza, A., Berndt, R. S., & Brownell, H. H. (1982) The semantic deficit hypothesis: Perceptual parsing and object classification by aphasic patients. *Brain and Language, 15*, 161–189.

Carr, T. H., McCauley, C., Sperber, R. D., & Parmelee, C. M. (1982) Words, pictures and priming on semantic activation, conscious identification and the automaticity of information-processing. *Journal of Experimental Psychology: Human Perception and Performance, 8*, 757–777.

Coughlan, A. K., & Warrington, E. K. (1978) Word–comprehension and word–retrieval in patients with localised cerebral lesions. *Brain, 101*, 163–185.

Coughlan, A. K., & Warrington, E. K. (1981) The impairment of verbal semantic memory: A single case study. *Journal of Neurology, Neurosurgery and Psychiatry, 44*, 1079–1083.

Deloche, G., Andreewsky, E., & Desi, M. (1981) Lexical meaning: A case report, some striking phenomena, theoretical implications. *Cortex, 17*, 147–152.

Denes, G., & Semenza, C. (1975) Auditory modality-specific anomia: Evidence from a case of pure word deafness. *Cortex, 11*, 401–411.

Fraisse, P. (1960) Recognition time measured by verbal reaction to figures and words. *Perceptual and Motor Skills, 11*, 204.

Glucksberg, S. (1984) The functional equivalence of common and multiple codes. *Journal of Verbal Learning and Verbal Behaviour, 23*, 100–104.

Goodglass, H., & Baker, E. (1976) Semantic field, naming and auditory comprehension in aphasia. *Brain and Language, 3*, 359–374.

Heilman, K. M., Tucker, D. M., & Valenstein, E. (1976) A case of mixed transcortical aphasia with intact naming. *Brain, 99*, 415–426.

Kremin, H. (1984) Spared naming without comprehension. Paper presented at the International Neuropsychological Society Conference, Aachen, June 1984.

Lesser, R. (1978) *Linguistic investigations of aphasia*. London: Edward Arnold.

Lhermitte, F., & Beauvois, M. F. (1973) A visual-speech disconnexion syndrome: Report of a case with optic-aphasia, agnostic alexia and colour agnosia. *Brain, 96*, 695–714.

Marcel, A. J. (1983) Conscious and unconscious perception: Experiments on visual masking and word recognition. *Cognitive Psychology, 15*, 197–237.

Milberg, W., & Blumstein, S. E. (1981) Lexical decision and aphasia: Evidence for semantic processing. *Brain and Language, 14*, 371–385.

Morton, J. (1970) A functional model of memory. In D. A. Norman (Ed.), *Models of human memory*. New York: Academic Press.

Morton, J., & Patterson, K. E. (1980) A new attempt at an interpretation, or, an attempt at a new interpretation. In M. Coltheart, K. E. Patterson, & J. C. Marshall (Eds.), *Deep dyslexia*. London: Routledge & Kegan Paul.

Newcombe, F. & Marshall, J. C. (1980a) Response monitoring and response blocking in deep dyslexia. In M. Coltheart, K. E. Patterson, & J. C. Marshall (Eds.), *Deep dyslexia*. London: Routledge & Kegan Paul.

Newcombe, F., & Marshall, J. C. (1980b) Transcoding and lexical stabilisation in deep dyslexia. In M. Coltheart, K. E. Patterson, & J. C. Marshall (Eds.), *Deep dyslexia*. London: Routledge & Kegan Paul.

Patterson, K. E. (1978) Phonemic dyslexia: Errors of meaning and meaning of errors. *Quarterly Journal of Experimental Psychology, 30*, 587–601.

Patterson, K. E., & Kay, J. (1982) Letter-by-letter reading: Psychological descriptions of a neurological syndrome. *Quarterly Journal of Experimental Psychology, 34A*, 411–441.

Potter, M. C., & Faulconer, B. A. (1975) Time to understand pictures and words. *Nature (Lond), 253*, 437–438.

Ratcliff, G., & Newcombe, F. (1982) Object recognition: Some deductions from the clinical evidence. In A. W. Ellis (Ed.), *Normality and pathology in cognitive function*. London: Academic Press.

Riddoch, J. & Humphreys, G. (1983) Optic aphasia and access to semantic information. Paper presented at the Experimental Psychology Society meeting, Oxford, July 1983.

Rieger, C. (1978) Grind—1: First report on the Magic Grinder story comprehension project. *Discourse Processes, 1*, 267–303.

Rieger, C., & Small, J. (1979) Word expert parsing. University of Maryland Computer Science Technical Report No. 734.

Saffran, E. M., Schwartz, M. F., & Marin, O. S. M. (1976) Semantic mechanisms in paralexia. *Brain and Language, 3*, 255–265.

Schwartz, M. F., Saffran, E. M., & Marin, O. S. M. (1979) Language and reference in dementia: A case study. *Brain and Language, 7*, 277–306.

Schwartz, M. F., Saffran, E. M., & Marin, O. S. M. (1980) Fractionating the reading process in dementia: Evidence for word-specific print-to-sound associations. In M. Coltheart, K. E. Patterson, & J. C. Marshall (Eds.), *Deep dyslexia*. London: Routledge & Kegan Paul.

Seymour, P. H. K. (1979) *Human visual cognition*. London: Collier Macmillan.

Shallice, T., & Coughlan, A. K. (1980) Modality specific word comprehension deficits in deep dyslexia. *Journal of Neurology, Neurosurgery and Psychiatry, 43*, 866–872.

Shallice, T., & McGill, J. (1978) The origins of mixed errors. In J. Requin (Ed.), *Attention and performance Vol. 7*. Hillsdale, N.J.: Erlbaum.

Shallice, T., & Saffran, E. M. (1986) Lexical processing in the absence of explicit word identification: Evidence from a letter-by-letter reader. *Cognitive Neuropsychology, 3*, 429–459.

Snodgrass, J. C. (1984) Concepts and their surface representations. *Journal of Verbal Learning and Verbal Behaviour, 23*, 3–22.

Te Linde, J. (1982) Picture-word differences in decision latency: A test of common coding assumptions. *Quarterly Journal of Experimental Psychology, 8*, 584–598.

Warrington, E. K. (1975) The selective impairment of semantic memory. *Quarterly Journal of Experimental Psychology, 27*, 635–657.

Warrington, E. K. (1981a) Neuropsychological studies of verbal semantic systems. *Philosophical Transactions of the Royal Society of London, B295*, 411–423.

Warrington, E. K. (1981b) Concrete word dyslexia. *British Journal of Psychology, 72*, 175–196.

Warrington, E. K., & McCarthy, R. (1983) Category specific access dysphasia. *Brain, 106*, 859–878.

Warrington, E. K., & Shallice, T. (1979) Semantic access dyslexia. *Brain, 102*, 43–63.

Warrington, E. K., & Shallice, T. (1980) Word-form dyslexia. *Brain, 103*, 99–112.

Warrington, E. K., & Shallice, T. (1984) Category-specific semantic impairment. *Brain, 107*, 829–854.

Warrington, E. K., & Taylor, A. M. (1978) Two categorical stages of object recognition. *Perception, 7*, 695–705.

Weigl, E., & Bierwisch, M. (1970) Neuropsychology and linguistics: Topics of common research. *Foundations of Language, 6*, 1–18.

6 Contrasting Patterns of Sentence Comprehension Deficits in Aphasia

David Caplan
Montreal Neurological Institute, 3801 University Street, Montreal, Quebec, Canada

INTRODUCTION

In this paper I shall report on the ability of two aphasic patients to comprehend auditorily presented sentences. The data have been gathered as part of a project designed to investigate patients' abilities to use specific syntactic structures in the interpretation of sentences. Before presenting the data and analysing these performances, I shall briefly review pertinent aspects of the literature on this problem and present the rationale behind the choice of materials presented to these patients.

It has been known since Jackson (1974) that some aphasic patients have trouble comprehending and producing sentences in the absence of similar disturbances in the comprehension or production of words in isolation. The reasons behind this difficulty may lie in many spheres. Luria (1971, 1975) claimed that syntactic form was a factor influencing comprehensibility of sentences. Clear demonstration that some patients' failures were related to their ability to utilise syntactic structure to determine sentential aspects of meaning have been provided by Caramazza and Zurif (1976), Heilman and Scholes (1976), Schwartz, Saffran, and Marin (1980), Caramazza et al. (1981), and other investigators. These workers have shown that agrammatic Broca's aphasics and Conduction aphasics with short-term memory impairments have difficulty assigning thematic roles to noun phrases on the basis of the syntactic structure of sentences. The experiments show that, for a variety of sentence types, thematic roles are appropriately assigned when they are

129

uniquely determined by pragmatic constraints, but significantly misassigned when semantic constraints are absent and assignment must proceed entirely on the basis of syntactic structure.

One question which this research raises is whether disturbances of interpreting syntactic structures have an "all-or-none" character, and, if not, what patterns of misinterpretation are found in aphasic patients. Some authors have claimed that the parser fails as a whole in certain classes of patients, such as agrammatics (Berndt & Carmazza, 1980). However, the empirical basis for this claim is weak. For the most part, patients have been tested on complicated sentence types, such as subject-object relative clauses (Caramazza & Zurif, 1976); inner dative constructions (Heilman & Scholes, 1976); and complex sentences containing subordinate conjunctions (Saffran & Marin, 1975). Schwartz et al. (1980) did test five agrammatic patients on simple active transitive sentences and sentences with the copula verb and a locative preposition, as well as simple passive sentences, and claim that their cases could not interpret syntactic structures. Their analysis is questioned by Caplan (1983), and data from Ansell and Flowers (1982) contradict those of Schwartz et al. (1980), finding that Broca's aphasics interpret active transient sentences in a normal fashion but show increasing difficulty with passive and cleft object forms. Caplan, Matthew, and Gigley (1981) report that some Broca's aphasics comprehend gerunds correctly and others use a simple compensatory strategy to comprehend these forms. Overall, it appears that aphasic patients have trouble with more complex sentence forms, and adopt regular adaptive strategies to deal with forms they find difficult. The cases I shall present here also illustrate that the ability to interpret syntactic structures does not disintegrate in its entirety in at least some aphasic patients. The data also indicate that different patients show different disturbances with respect to their ability to interpret syntactic structure.

METHODS AND MATERIALS

The set of sentences that was presented to test syntactic comprehension is shown in Table 6.1. Sentences were chosen to test patients' abilities to appreciate a variety of features of syntactic structure.

Verb-argument structure is tested in the contrast between the two place verbs and three place verbs.

The ability to interpret *constituent order* is tested in three ways. The basic *canonical N-V-N structure* of English is tested in the active two-verb sentences. This basic order is also found in the active dative sentences, where a third noun appears in a prepositional phase in the verb phrase (VP) leading to an N-V-N-Prep-N sequence, and in the conjoined, subject-subject relatives and object-subject relatives, in which there is a second clause and where the

TABLE 6.1
Sentence Types Presented

One–verb sentences

  I. Two–place verbs
     Active: The frog hit the elephant
     Passive: The frog was hit by the elephant
     Cleft–object: It was the frog that the elephant hit
 II. Three–place verbs
     Active: The frog gave the elephant to the rabbit
     Passive: The frog was given to the elephant by the rabbit
     Cleft–object: It was the frog that the elephant gave to the rabbit

---

Two–verb sentences

Conjoined: The frog hit the elephant and kissed the rabbit
Subject–subject relatives: The frog that hit the elephant kissed the rabbit
Subject–object relatives: The frog that the elephant hit kissed the rabbit
Object–subject relatives: The frog hit the elephant that kissed the rabbit
Object–object relatives: The frog hit the elephant that the rabbit kissed

---

entire sentence has the form N-V-N-V-N. Second, passive sentences, both of two-place verbs and three-place verbs, also maintain the basic word order of English, but contain *special markers*—passive morphology in the form of the auxiliary and past participle, and the *by*-phrase—which indicate that the usual assignment of the pre-verbal subject noun as Agent or Instrument and the post-verbal object noun as Theme does not apply. Third, cleft-object sentences as well as subject-object and object-object relative clauses contain *sequences of the form N-N-V*, which violate the basic N-V-N order of English. The presence of these special markings (passive) and unusual word orders is known to lead to difficulty in sentence comprehension (Ansell & Flowers, 1981; Schwartz et al., 1980).

Subject-subject relatives and object-subject relatives contrast with the conjoined sentences insofar as they contain *embedded clauses*, while maintaining the same N-V-N-V-N sequence of lexical categories. The subject-subject relatives actually lead to the same assignment of thematic roles to each noun as the conjoined sentences. However, they contain a lexical sequence which could be a well-formed sentence but whose elements are not related thematically. This is illustrated in (1) where the sequence *the monkey bumped the bear* could be a well-formed sentence but where the structure of the sentence dictates that *the monkey* does not enter into thematic roles around the verb *bumped*.

  1. The frog that chased the monkey bumped the bear.

In the comparable conjoined sentence, (2), the thematic roles are the same as in (1) but there is no similar well-formed sequence. Thus, subject-subject relatives constitute a strong test of the ability of a patient to recognise embedded clauses. Object-subject relatives, such as (3), contrast with the conjoined and subject-subject sentences with respect to the assignment of thematic roles around the second verb, and their interpretation requires that a subject recognise that the second verb is embedded in a noun phrase whose head is the second noun.

2. *The frog chased the monkey and bumped the bear.*

3. *The frog chased the monkey that bumped the bear.*

Correct performance on all these sentence types would indicate that all these elements of syntactic structure are constructed and interpreted. Particular patterns of errors in assignment of thematic roles might be attributable to a failure to utilise one or another of these syntactic features for interpretive purposes. Linguistic analysis of patterns of error might reveal which syntactic elements are utilised in the construction of syntactic form, the nature of the syntactic structures constructed, the interpretive principles which apply to these structures, and the nature of the operations of a parser/interpreter.

The protocol utilised in the two cases to be presented consisted of six examples of each of the two-place verb and three-place verb sentences, and 10 examples of each of the two-verb sentences. In the case of S.P., several other sentence types were also tested. In the case of R.L., the sentences were presented in French, which is R.L.'s native tongue. The sentences were pseudo-randomised such that there were never more than two consecutive occurrences of a given sentence type on a list. The sentences were assigned to four test forms in the case of S.P., and three test forms in the case of R.L. S.P. was tested in two sessions, responding to two of the test forms in each session, and R.L. was tested in a single test session at his own request.

Testing consisted of reading each sentence aloud with a normal and neutral intonation, and requesting that the patient indicate thematic roles of each noun through the manipulation of toy animals. The animals required for each sentence were placed in random spatial order on a large working surface before the sentence was read. Sentences were not repeated. In the case of the patients reported here, responses were clear and immediate, and very few responses were changed by the patient. The results to be reported reflect the patients' preferred interpretation in cases where responses were changed.

The two patients represent two different aphasic syndromes. S.P. was a 41-year-old, right-handed female who had suffered a subarachnoid haemorrhage secondary to rupture of an anterior communicating artery aneurysm. As part of her treatment, the left internal carotid artery ligated. Six weeks after the ligation, she had a "predominantly expressive aphasia" and five months later, when she was tested on this protocol, her BDAE scores characterised her as an agrammatic Broca's aphasic. Melodic line was rated as 4, phase length as 5, articulatory ability as 5, and word finding at 5. Grammatical form was rated at 5, with the speech therapist's comments that agrammatic features were present in speech. She showed no phonemic paraphasias in speech. Auditory comprehension for words, body parts and commands, and single word reading comprehension were at ceiling, and she scored 7 on the "Complex Ideational Material" subtest of the BDAE. R.L., in contrast, was a 55-year-old, right-handed male who had a small temporal parietal stroke. Two months post-infarction, he showed fluent speech, with pauses before content words and numerous phonemic paraphasias. Single word, list, and sentence repetition was also marked by many phonemic paraphasias, as was oral reading. Confrontation naming showed phonemic paraphasias and occasional failures to name. Comprehension of single words presented auditorily and in printed form was at ceiling. Memory testing showed excellent recognition abilities, although free recall and repetition were impaired because of his output limitation (Caplan & Baker, 1983).

S.P.'s and R.L.'s performances in the object manipulation sentence comprehension test are shown in Tables 6.2 and 6.3.

Responses are scored according to the following notation. The nouns in each sentence are numbered sequentially, from left to right (that is, in their order of auditory occurrence). For each verb in a sentence, thematic roles are indicated in the order: Agent, Theme, Goal (where Goal is necessary). The noun used in each of these thematic roles is indicated by its number. Thus, in a sentence type such as an object-subject relative, illustrated in (4):

4. *The frog chased the monkey that bumped the bear.*

the correct response would be 1,2:2,3. This notation indicates that the first noun (the frog) is Agent of the first verb, and the second noun (the monkey) is its Theme, and that the second noun (the monkey) is Agent of the second verb and the third noun (the bear) is its Theme.

CASE S.P.

It is possible to analyse these patterns linguistically and in terms of a parser/interpreter. Turning first to the data of S.P., we begin by considering one-verb sentences. We note that the only sentences that S.P. consistently interprets correctly are the active forms of the two-place verb and three-place verb sentences. She interprets approximately half the passive and cleft-object forms correctly with both two-place verb and three-place verb sentences. These data suggest that S.P. is able to assign and interpret the basic N-V-N structure, including its extension to include a third noun in a prepositional phrase whose role is Goal. She interprets this structure by assigning Agent,

TABLE 6.2
Responses of Case 1 (S.P.)

One–verb sentences

	Two-place verbs			Three-place verbs		
Response type	*Active*	*Passive*	*Cleft–object*	*Active*	*Passive*	*Cleft–object*
1,2	*6/6	3/6	4/6			
2,1		*3/6	*2/6			
1,2,3				*6/6	4/6	3/6
1,3,2					1/6	
2,1,3						*3/6
3,1,2					*1/6	
3,2,1						

Two–verb sentences

Response type	*Conjoined*	*Subject–subject*	*Subject–object*	*Object–subject*	*Object–object*
1,2;1,3	*6/10	*5/10	2/10	5/11	1/9
1,2;2,3	4/10	5/10	5/10	*6/11	1/9
1,2;3,2					*7/9
1,3;3,2			1/10		
2,1;1,3			*2/10		
2,1;2,3					
1,2;1,2					
1,3;2,3					
2,3;1,3					

Note: For interpretation of notation, see text. Correct responses are indicated by *.

Theme, and Goal to N_1, N_2 and N_3 in sequences of the form N_1-V-N_2(-Prep-N_3). Moreover, she is sensitive to both passive markings and the N-N-V word order seen in cleft-object sentences. Both these sentence types are distinguished from the corresponding active and cleft-subject forms. However, S.P. does not interpret these sentences normally. She treats the passive and cleft-object two-place verbs and the cleft-object three place verbs as ambiguous between their normal meaning and the meaning these sentences would have if nouns were assigned their thematic roles in the linear fashion utilised in N-V-N (-Prep-N) structures.

TABLE 6.3
Responses of Case 2 (R.L.)

	One–verb sentences					
	Two-place verbs			Three-place verbs		
Response type	Active	Passive	Cleft–object	Active	Passive	Cleft–object
1,2	*6/6	2/6	2/6			
2,1		*4/6	*4/6			
1,2,3				*6/6	1/6	2/6
1,3,2					1/6	
2,1,3					1/6	*4/6
3,1,2					*3/6	
3,2,1						

	Two–verb sentences				
Response type	Conjoined	Subject–subject	Subject–object	Object–subject	Object–object
1,2;1,3	*8/10	*5/10	2/10	2/10	
1,2;2,3	2/10	2/10	2/10	*7/10	2/10
1,2;3,2					*8/10
1.3;3,2					
2,1;1,3		1/10	*2/10		
2,1;2,3			3/10		
1,2;1,2		1/10		1/10	
1,3;2,3		1/10			
2,3;1,3			1/10		

Note: For interpretation of notation, see text. Correct responses are indicated by *.

This pattern suggests that S.P. assigns N-V-N (-Prep-N) sequences and attempts to interpret them according to a principle which assigns the pre-verbal noun as Agent, the post-verbal noun as Theme and the post-prepositional noun as Goal. The presence of the passive morphology or the N-N-V sequence renders the syntactic structure ambiguous. There are two ways to account for this ambiguity. The first is to hypothesise that S.P. occasionally interprets passive morphology and the cleft-object configur-ration correctly, and that she fails to do so on other occasions. When she fails to interpret these features in a normal correct fashion, this account would postulate that she applies her linear interpretive strategy to the nouns of the sentence in the order she hears them, as a "compensatory" or "adaptive" mechanism. A second approach would be to account for her ambiguous interpretations by postulating that she constructs a syntactic representation which is itself ambiguous with respect to its semantic interpretation.

Grodzinsky (1984) has developed this second approach, suggesting that agrammatic patients assign traces (Chomsky, 1981) but cannot bind them.

5. [[The frog] was [[hit] NP*] [by[the elephant]]]
   S   NP   VP   V   PP NP

Consider (5), where NP* is the location of the trace which fails to be co-indexed. The resulting phrase marker for this passive sentence is ambiguous, since either the subject noun phrase or the NP in the by-phrase can be assigned as Agent, given that the subject NP does not receive its case through co-indexation with its trace, as usually occurs (Chomsky, 1981). This approach can also be extended to cleft-object forms, on the assumption that the failure to co-index the post-copula noun phrase with its trace results in its possible utilisation as an Agent, in the structure illustrated in (6).

6. It was [[the frog] [that [[the elephant] [[hit] NP*]]]]
       NP   NP S   S NP   VP   V

NP* is the location of the trace which fails to be co-indexed. At present, the data on the one-verb sentence types do not choose between these two analyses.

S.P.'s performance on these sentences containing a single verb suggests one feature of her parsing and interpretive processes. It appears that S.P. operates on longer sequences than N-V strings. If her parsing and interpretive processes consisted of assigning Agency to the immediately pre-verbal noun regardless of the overall configuration of the sentence, she would assign Agency consistently to the correct noun in cleft-object forms. This should lead to consistently correct interpretations in two-place verb cleft-object sentences, and to constant assignment of N_2 as Agent in three-place verb cleft-object sentences, neither of which is observed. If S.P. assigns the first noun she hears to the Agent role, she would consistently interpret all these sentences, and passives, incorrectly. It thus seems that the "window" over which the parser and interpreter operate in S.P. consists of more than just a verb with its immediately preceding noun. One possibility is that S.P. identifies the verb of each clause, and attempts to assign a syntactic structure and an interpretation to as many NP's as are required by the argument structure of the verb, thus operating on two or three nouns plus the verb, as the sentence and verb require.

Turning to S.P.'s performance on sentences with two verbs, we note that her interpretation of conjoined, subject-subject relative, and object-subject relative sentences is virtually identical. Each of these sentence types is for her ambiguous between an interpretation in which the first noun is Agent of both verbs and one in which the second noun is Agent of the second verb. As with the ambiguity of passive and cleft-object sentences, this pattern of interpretation might be due to an alternation between S.P.'s ability to assign a normal structure and her use of a compensatory strategy, or to her assignment of a structure which is inherently ambiguous. In the present case, there are several reasons to favour the second alternative.

First, if S.P. sometimes assigns a correct syntactic structure and interprets it normally, and sometimes resorts to compensatory strategies, it must be the case that she uses a variety of compensatory strategies. Thus, in conjoined sentences, this analysis would claim that S.P. assigns the correct 1,2;1,2 interpretation half the time (presumably after having constructed a normal phrase marker in which the VPs are conjoined) and, in the remaining cases, uses a 1,2;2,3 interpretive strategy, presumably as a natural extension of the N_1 is Agent, N_2 is Theme strategy found with N-V-N sequences. On the other hand, in the object-subject relatives, this analysis would have to claim that she assigns the 1,2;2,3 interpretation correctly in half the cases and resorts to a 1,2;1,3 compensatory interpretation in the other half of the sentences of this type. Though this is not impossible, it is somewhat counterintuitive.

Second, there is an analysis which can account for the observed alternation in responses and which is consistent with other aspects of S.P.'s performance. The three sentence types which show this systematic alternation between 1,2;1,3 and 1,2;2,3 interpretations—the conjoined, subject-subject, and object-subject relatives—all have the structural property of containing the sequence N-V-N-V-N. Suppose that S.P. represents the structure of these sentences as this linear string of lexical categories. Suppose also that S.P. interprets strings of this sort according to the interpretive principle suggested above, namely she assigns Agency and Theme to the pre- and post-verbal noun in a sequence of the form N-V-N. Suppose, further, that, having assigned a noun a thematic role in the argument structure of a verb, S.P. no longer considers that noun as a candidate for the assignment of a thematic role around a second. On these assumptions, S.P. would assign N_1 as agent of V_1, N_2 as Theme of V_1, and N_3 as Theme of V_2 in structures of the form N_1-V_1-N_2-V_2-N_3. She would be left with the problem of assigning the Agent of V_2. N_1 might be chosen for this function, either because of some special "saliency" attributable to sentence initial position (Goodglass, 1968) or through an application of a "parallel function" interpretative strategy (Volin, 1983). N_2 could be considered as Agent, in this "second-pass" portion of the interpretive process, because it is the immediately pre-verbal noun. S.P. chooses both nouns equally frequently.

If we assume that S.P. assigns the simplified syntactic structure just described, and uses the interpretive principles indicated above, we also can account for her performance on object-object and subject-object relatives. The former present no problem: the first clause would be interpreted normally, and N_3 would be assigned as Agent of the second verb, leaving N_2 as Theme of the second verb. This pattern is found in 7/9 sentences of this type. The remaining interpretations must be due to the application of the "linear order" and "parallel function" or "salient first noun" strategies. Subject-object relatives, however, should show considerable difficulty with respect to assignment of thematic roles around the first verb, where they resemble cleft-object forms, and with respect to assignment of the Agent of V_2 because of the presence of the sequence V-V-N. This is, in fact, observed.

Overall, the analysis two-verb sentences in S.P. suggests that this patient assigns linear strings of lexical categories and interprets these strings according to a simple interpretive strategy. There is no evidence that S.P. organises categories in hierarchies. The analysis is post-hoc, and could be confirmed by observation of S.P.'s performances on sentences such as (7):

7. *The lion that hit the tiger and the elephant pushed the monkey.*

where the prediction that N_3 will be regularly taken as Agent of V_2 is made by the analysis. Unfortunately, sentences of this type were not tested. Nonetheless, the analysis is empirically adequate for the data available.

The simplification of syntactic structure that I have suggested underlies S.P.'s interpretive strategies consists of the reduction of a phrase marker to a linear sequence of major lexical categories. This contrasts with Grodzinsky's (1984) analysis, according to which the abnormality in syntactic analysis found in S.P and other agrammatic patients consists of the failure to bind traces in a far more fully specified syntactic tree. Grodzinsky's analysis may account for S.P's performance in one-verb sentences, as noted above, and for her difficulty with subject-object relatives, but it cannot account for the consistency with which she assigns thematic roles around the second verb of object-object relative clauses.

If the present analysis is correct, it suggests that the portion of S.P.'s parser which is defective is quite specific: it would be restricted to operations which build phrasal and other non-lexical nodes. It is possible that this particular failure could be related to S.P.'s expressive agrammatism, since it could be the result of a failure to utilise function words and grammatical morphemes for structure building purposes. Whether the failure to construct phrasal nodes extends to sentences where such structures are not marked overtly by function words, such as (8), is not determined:

8. *The elephant saw the monkey hit the frog.*

On the present analysis, sentences such as (8) should show the same ambiguity as all other sentences of the form N-V-N-V-N, despite the fact that the embedding in (8) is signalled by the subcategorisation features of the main verb *saw*, rather than the relative pronoun *that*. This question remains unresolved at present.

CASE R.L.

Turning to the second case, we note the pattern shown in Table 6.3. R.L.'s performance on one-verb sentences is strikingly similar to that of S.P. However, he shows quite a different pattern in interpreting two-verb sentences.

R.L. interprets conjoined and object-subject relatives correctly in the majority of cases. Unlike S.P., he seems to appreciate the differences in structure indicated by the coordinate conjunction *and* and the relative pronoun *that*: he takes N_1 as Agent of V_2 in the former sentences and N_2 as Agent of V_2 in the latter. For R.L. these sentences do not have the ambiguity that they have for S.P. Subject-subject relatives are also interpreted differently by R.L. and S.P. These sentences are not ambiguous between *two* interpretations for R.L. Rather, R.L. interprets them correctly half the time, and the remaining responses show a wide scatter of interpretations. This suggests that he sometimes assigns a correct structure to subject-subject relatives and interprets that structure normally, and at other times fails to assign an interpretation to the sentence based on its syntactic structure and resorts to almost random assignment of thematic roles to noun phases. However, the single most common response for subject-subject relatives is correct, and it is a different response than the equally correct interpretation of object-subject relatives which R.L. produces on 7/10 presentations. Moreover, R.L. is far more accurate in conjoined sentences than subject-subject relatives. It thus appears that R.L. distinguishes these three sentence types, unlike S.P., and that he has particular trouble interpreting subject-subject relative clauses.

R.L. is quite accurate in the interpretation of object-object relatives. Subject-object relatives, however, produce almost random responses.

The fact that R.L. distinguishes conjoined sentences from object-subject relatives, and interprets both correctly in a majority of cases, indicates that he appreciates the difference in structure signalled by the coordinate conjunction and the relative pronoun. A similar conclusion can be reached on the basis of his superior performance with conjoined than subject-subject relatives. These differences would follow from R.L.'s appreciating the structural feature of embedding, signalled by the relative pronoun *that*. The suggestion is that R.L. constructs phrase markers such as those indicated in Fig. 6.1 in which sentences are embedded under noun-phases and can be conjoined. His grammar must therefore contain recursive rules elaborating phrase structures of the sort illustrated in 9, 10 and 11.

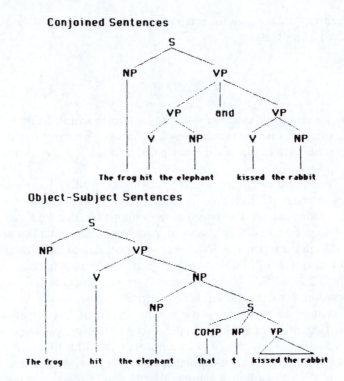

FIG. 6.1   Phrase markers constructed by R.L.

9.   S→NP+VP

10.   VP→VP+VP

11.   NP→NP+S

The principles whereby R.L. interprets structures such as those shown in Fig. 6.1 could well be the usual interpretive principles for these structures in English, including binding of traces and the assignment of thematic roles to NPs on the basis of the position of the traces with which they are co-indexed (Chomsky, 1981, 1982).

R.L.'s main difficulty lies with his ability to interpret relative clauses that occur on the subject NP of the sentence. As noted, he is virtually random in interpreting subject-object relatives and shows a wide scatter of errors in the subject-subject relatives, where he gets only 50% of the sentences correct. This difficulty cannot be accounted for in terms of the rules of R.L's grammar. There is no obvious way to restrict the generative capacity of rules such as those above to NPs in object position. If we accept these rules as a characterisation of R.L.'s knowledge of French, resulting in structures such as those shown in Fig. 6.1, we must attribute his difficulty with relative clauses in subject position to performance factors.

The most obvious factor is an increase in memory load which is due to the presence of a relative clause on the subject NP. This NP is required for later assignment to a thematic role around a second verb, and must be stored in memory until the second verb is identified and its morphology ascertained. If this is the reason for R.L.'s difficulty with these sentence types, it is interesting that he does not show a similar difficulty with the conjoined sentences, which also require the retention of the first NP in memory for assignment to a thematic role around the second verb. The difference between the conjoined sentences and sentences with relative clauses in subject position may be that relative clauses are marked by a relative pronoun, and thus signal the need for retention of the first NP in memory, while there is no such marking in the case of conjoined sentences. This sort of parsing operation is found in the HOLD operator of some ATNs (Wanner & Maratsos, 1978). The suggestion is, therefore, that R.L. has difficulty in the processing of thematic roles around the verb of a relative clause in a subject position because some portion of his parser/interpreter is devoted to the maintenance of the subject NP in memory, which diminishes his ability to process syntactic form and assign thematic roles within the relative clause.

If this analysis is correct, it suggests that R.L.'s parser/interpreter is easily over-burdened by sentences which impose certain types of memory loads. Given that R.L.'s recognition memory functions are excellent—R.L. has the "reproduction" type of conduction aphasia, not the "repetition" type (Shallice & Warrington, 1977)—it does not seem possible to attribute his difficulty to a failure of short-term memory functions *per se*. He thus contrasts with patient M.V., discussed in Chapter 4 by Bub, Black, Howell, and Kertesz. These authors argue that M.V. encountered difficulty in processing written sentences precisely because she could not store these in short-term memory (this being prevented by her severely impaired ability to rehearse). Furthermore, in addition to the highly particular memory disturbance which may underlie R.L.'s problems in comprehending subject relative clauses, R.L. also has some difficulty in processing the morphological markings of the passive and the non-canonical order of constituents in cleft-object sentences. There seems to be more than one problem underlying R.L.'s failure to utilise normal grammar as the determinant of sentence meaning.

CONCLUDING REMARKS

In summary, I have presented data regarding sentence comprehension in two aphasic patients. The sentences presented were all semantically reversible and required the assignment of syntactic structures for normal interpretation. Both patients show departures from normal comprehension. In neither case are the departures random, but rather occur in particular sentence types.

Post-hoc analyses of the syntactic structures that are constructed and interpreted are possible for both patients and, to a limited extent, different analyses can be formulated and compared on the basis of the data collected. Accepting one such analysis for each case, it is possible to suggest the nature of parsing and interpretation problems for each patient.

Many aspects of the disturbances in sentence comprehension in these patients, and in aphasics generally, require further investigation before answers to several fundamental questions can be provided. Whether the particular analyses suggested here are correct will require presenting patients materials specifically designed to test these hypotheses. I have suggested several specific tests of this sort above. Indeed, it would be important to *retest* patients on the same sentence types after a brief interval, to be sure that their patterns of responses remain stable. The relationship of the disturbances in sentence comprehension to other aphasic symptoms, notably expressive agrammatism and short-term memory limitations, requires data regarding patients' performances on specific sentence types designed to test utilisation of particular aspects of the function word vocabulary, the operations of memory in parsing and interpretation, and other abilities, as well as extensive testing of patients with other aphasic symptoms on the same material as controls. Research of this kind is reported by Berndt in Chapter 10.

Despite the preliminary nature of the data and analyses presented here, and the many questions which cannot be answered at present, these results do suggest several conclusions. First, the process of sentence interpretation does not seem to fail in all-or-none fashion. As far as can be told from the available data, different patients make use of different partial grammatical representations as the basis for sentence interpretation. Second, when the ability to assign and interpret syntactic structure breaks down, adaptive/compensatory strategies arise which, in many instances, can be seen as an attempt to apply quite elementary principles of structure building and interpretation to an input string that would ordinarily receive a more complex structural analysis. Third, the investigation of the syntactic structures that are assigned and interpreted requires an analysis of aphasics' errors in a variety of sentence types. Simply considering the number of sentences a patient interprets correctly as an index of his ability to understand a particular structure will often not reveal the details of the structures that he assigns and interprets. This error-analysis can lead to consideration of quite abstract linguistic structures and detailed parsing models as part of a patient's parsing and interpretive capacities. In turn, patterns of deficit seen in aphasics might provide evidence for or against particular grammatical analyses and parsing models. In sum, much remains to be learned through the detailed analysis of disturbances of syntactic comprehension in aphasic patients.

ACKNOWLEDGEMENTS

The research reported here was partially supported by the Medical Research Council of Canada (MRC-PG 28) and the Fonds de Recherche en Santé du Québec (Establishment Grant).

REFERENCES

Ansell, B., & Flowers, C. (1982) Aphasic adults use of heuristic and structural linguistic cues for sentence analysis. *Brain and Language, 16*, 61–72.

Berndt, R. S., & Caramazza, A. (1980) A re-definition of Broca's aphasia. *Journal of Applied Psycholinguistics, 1*, 225–278.

Caplan, D. (1983) A note on the "word order problem" in agrammatism. *Brain and Language, 10*, 155–165.

Caplan, D., Matthew, E., & Gigley, H. (1981) Comprehension of gerundive constructions by Broca's aphasics. *Brain and Language, 13*, 145–160.

Caplan, D., & Baker, C. (1983) Disturbances of sentence comprehension in absence of recognition memory deficit in a Conduction aphasic. Presented at Academy of Aphasia, Minneapolis.

Caramazza, A., & Zurif, E. B. (1976) Dissociation and algorithmic and heuristic processes in language comprehension: Evidence from aphasia. *Brain and Language, 3*, 572–582.

Caramazza, A., Basili, A., Koller, J., & Berndt, R. (1981) An investigation of repetition and language processing in a case of Conduction aphasia. *Brain and Language, 14*, 235–271.

Chomsky, N. (1981) *Lectures on government and binding.* Dordrecht: Foris.

Chomsky, N. (1982) *Concepts and consequences of the theory of government and binding.* Cambridge, Mass.: MIT Press.

Goodglass, H. (1968) Studies of the grammar of aphasics. In S. Rosenberg & J. H. Kopiin (Eds.), *Developments in applied psycholinguistic research.* N.Y.: Macmillan.

Grodzinsky, Y. (1984) Language deficits and the theory of syntax. Presented at BABBLE, Niagara Falls.

Heilman, K., & Scholes, R. A. (1976) The nature of comprehension errors in Broca's, Conduction, and Wernicke's aphasics. *Cortex, 12*, 258–265.

Jackson, J. K. (1874) On affection of speech from disease of the brain. Reprinted in *Brain, 38*, 1–190, 1915.

Luria, A. R. (1947) *Traumatic aphasia* (English Translation, 1971). The Hague: Mouton.

Luria, A. R. (1975) *The working brain.* New York: Basic Books.

Saffran, E., & Marin, O. (1975) STM deficit in a case of Conduction aphasia. *Brain and Language, 2*, 420–433.

Schwartz, M. F., Saffran, R. M., & Marin, O. (1980) The word-order problem in agrammatism I: Comprehension. *Brain and Language, 10*, 263–280.

Shallice, T. & Warrington, E. (1977) Auditory-verbal short-term memory impairment and Conduction aphasia. *Brain and Language, 4*, 479–491.

Volin, R. A. (1983) Agrammatics' perception of grammatical relations in relative clauses. Unpublished Ph.d. dissertation. Speech and Hearing Sciences, City University of New York.

Wanner, E., & Maratsos, M. (1978) An augmented transitional network model of relative clause comprehension. In J. Bresnan, M. Halle, & G. Miller (Eds.), *Psychological reality and generative grammar.* Cambridge, Mass.: MIT Press.

7 Spoken Language Comprehension in Aphasia: A Real-Time Processing Perspective

Lorraine K. Tyler
Max Planck Institute fur Psycholinguistik Nijmegen, The Netherlands;

and

MRC Applied Psychology Unit, Cambridge CB2 2EF, England

INTRODUCTION

In this chapter I will describe a particular approach to the study of language disorders. This approach has two major characteristics. First, it focusses on the real-time properties of language comprehension: by this I mean the set of mental processes which take place in the mind of the listener as he or she attempts to interpret a speech input. Second, the approach depends for its concepts and framework on a model of real-time language processing in normal listeners. I will begin by summarising the properties of this model.

The model (see, e.g., Marslen-Wilson & Tyler, 1981) starts from the assumption that the comprehension of a spoken utterance requires the listener to integrate several different types of knowledge about the properties of the utterance. These types of knowledge include the products of lexical, syntactic, semantic and pragmatic analyses. This analysis and integration is mediated by a set of mental processes which are automatic and obligatory, and which serve to transform the speech input into a meaningful representation. These "core" processes form the basis for the comprehension of speech by the normal listener, and are not open to conscious awareness or control. Once these automatic core processes have run through to completion, or have failed in some way, then the products of the processes become available for a variety of off-line analyses. These later analyses are not central to the normal processes of speech comprehension.

One important property of these core processes is that they are *optimally efficient*, in that they assign an analysis to the speech input at the theoretically earliest point at which the type of analysis in question can be assigned. Translated into the word recognition domain, this means that a spoken word is recognised at that point, starting from the beginning of the word, at which the word in question becomes uniquely distinguishable from all the other words in the language beginning with the same sound sequence. We have called this the "recognition point" (Marslen-Wilson & Tyler, 1980).

The core processes operate on the principle of *bottom-up priority*. This means that processes within any one knowledge source are initially determined by the bottom-up input to that source. In the case of auditory word recognition, the set of possible word-candidates is defined in the first instance by the sensory input to the auditory word recognition system. Top-down constraints do not restrict the set of possibilities in advance of the sensory input (Marslen-Wilson, 1984).

The third property of the core processes is that they are *obligatory*. Given that a knowledge source receives the input appropriate to it, it *must* run through its characteristic operations on this input. If a speaker utters a string of speech sounds that form a word in a language that the listener knows, then the listener must hear the input as constituting that word, and similarly for strings of words structured as grammatical and meaningful sentences.

These joint properties ensure that the speech input is rapidly projected onto higher levels of representation. After only about half a word has been heard (within an average of 250 msec from speech onset), the input has not only begun to be mapped onto the mental lexicon, but has also begun to be syntactically and semantically interpreted (Marslen-Wilson & Tyler, 1980). This means that words in context can be recognised before sufficient acoustic-phonetic input could have accumulated to uniquely specify what the word was solely on the basis of this input. Contextual information participates in the analysis process to provide the missing information. But for context to have an effect, the syntactic and semantic representations attached to each lexical entry must be activated in order for them to be assessed against contextual constraints. Without the activation of lexical representations, there would be no domain within which contextual evaluation could occur.

The system's efficient use of processing information as it becomes available in time, and the possibility of cooperative interactions between top-down and bottom-up sources of information, lead to a processing system in which the analysis of an utterance is always conducted with immediate reference to the discourse context in which it occurs. From the first word of an utterance, listeners construct an interpretative representation of the utterance. This representation is the outcome of an on-line integration of linguistic and non-linguistic analyses. Listeners integrate constraints derived from the specific discourse context, and constraints derived from their general knowledge of the world, with information derived from the linguistic properties of the utterance itself. As each word is heard and recognised, its semantic and syntactic properties become immediately available and are mapped onto this developing interpretative representation.

If we wish to use this model as a framework for studying disorders of spoken-language comprehension, we need to ask a number of basic questions. First, is the comprehension deficit due to a breakdown in the automatic processes underlying on-line language processing, or rather in the off-line processes which operate on the products of these core processes (as reflected in tasks such as question-answering and sentence-picture matching)? Second, is a patient's deficit due to a loss of stored information, or to difficulty with the processes that access this information? Shallice has discussed in Chapter Five some of the methods which may be used to distinguish between these two possibilities. If access is unimpaired, does the problem lie in the ability to use particular types of information to build a representation, or in the ability to integrate different types of analyses? Third, what specific aspect of the processing system is functioning abnormally? Fourth, if some aspect of the patient's processing system is selectively impaired, what implications does this have for the rest of the system? In normal language understanding, an incompletely specified input at one level of the system can be compensated for by constraints available at other levels (Tyler & Marslen-Wilson, 1982). Does the same kind of compensation— perhaps in a more extreme form—occur with language comprehension deficits?

To address these kinds of questions we have to use experimental tasks which tap the listener's representation of the input as it is being constructed on-line. The core processes operate upon a transient, continually-varying input—the speech signal—that is distributed over periods of time ranging from a few hundred milliseconds to several seconds. To determine what types of analysis the listener performs, and when he or she performs them, we have to use tasks which elicit fast timed responses which can be closely related in time to the speech input. We can then try to determine what kind of representation the listener has developed, given the input available at the point the response is made. In particular, we can determine whether, and to what extent, the internal representation can be accounted for strictly on the basis of the information carried by the available signal, and to what extent it is determined by internally generated knowledge. This kind of analysis crucially depends on the use of fast reaction-time tasks, because the closer in time the response is to the relevant stretches of the signal, the more closely we can specify the properties of the internal mapping processes involved.

My general strategy for studying real-time language processes in aphasic patients involves taking a mixed group and case-study approach and developing a "processing profile" for each patient. The profile attempts to cover the sequence of mental operations involved in on-line processing, and also includes performance in off-line tasks, in order to build up a picture of how a patient's language processing system functions. This approach enables us to study individual patients in depth. The important evidence is the pattern of results across a wide range of experiments, rather than data from a single study. Moreover, by developing tests designed to probe a range of processes involved in language comprehension, we can obtain sufficient information about a particular patient's language processing abilities to reduce the risk of drawing spurious inferences about the cause of a deficit.

Data from the individual experiments making up the processing profile will be combined for patients who cluster into the major syndrome categories. This allows us to evaluate the extent to which patients falling into one of the various syndrome groups show the same pattern of performance.

SELECTION OF PATIENTS

I decided to begin by examining in detail the performance of Broca and Wernicke patients, and then include patients whose deficits did not fall into one of the traditional categories. I took this approach because Broca's and Wernicke's aphasias have received more attention than any other type of aphasic disorder, and consequently there have been a number of theories attempting to account for these particular syndromes (e.g., Berndt & Caramazza, 1980; Blumstein, Milberg & Shrier, 1982; Bradley, Garrett, & Zurif, 1980; Kean, 1980; Schwartz, Chapter 8 in this volume; Zurif, 1982). I assumed that these theories would provide an initial framework for the interpretation of the on-line data, although as Berndt makes clear in Chapter 10, Broca's aphasia is not a single condition and cannot have a single explanation, since the set of symptoms traditionally characterising this syndrome dissociate in a variety of ways.

Patients were selected on the basis of the Boston Diagnostic Aphasia Exam. Only those patients who presented as relatively clear examples of either the Broca or Wernicke types were used as subjects. I selected subjects in this way because, at the same time as building up a picture of the real-time processing characteristics of an individual patient, I wanted to see whether the Boston diagnosis concurred with the description of the deficit based upon the on-line data. Also, I intended to compare those patients who, on the Boston, were classified as belonging to the same category of disorder, in order to evaluate the extent to which all members of a category behaved in the same way in the on-line tests.

One of the consequences of taking this approach is that patients who are being studied for their *comprehension* problems are selected as subjects primarily on the basis of their *production* deficits. This is particularly true for Broca's aphasics, whose diagnosis is based on the results of sub-tests which mainly focus on production skills. In the Boston exam, for example, only a small percentage of the tests are concerned with comprehension, and these only probe the most general distinctions between syntax and semantics. Moreover, subcategorising patients within one of the major categories—for example, determining whether or not a Broca patient is agrammatic—is done exclusively on the basis of an analysis of their spontaneous speech. But unless one wishes to test all patients who exhibit any kind of language disturbance (and I have already explained why I did not want to do this), it is not clear what the alternative selection criteria could be. Selecting patients exclusively on the basis of their performance on the comprehension sub-tests of the Boston or the Aachen exam, for example, would not solve the problem, since one would then be in danger of overlooking patients who, on more sensitive tests, *do* show evidence of subtle comprehension deficits.

In any case, selecting patients on the basis of their production deficits is not necessarily a drawback. It allows us to determine, first, whether a production deficit is always accompanied by a comprehension disorder and, second, the ways in which comprehension and production deficits are similar or different. This, in turn, means that we can evaluate those theories which make claims about relationships between production and comprehension disorders.

CURRENT RESEARCH

A number of Dutch and English patients have been tested on a variety of experiments probing various aspects of real-time language comprehension. I have examined the data both from an individual and group-study perspective. In general, the case-study data (which constitute individual processing profiles) has been the most informative in terms of answering specific questions and generating hypotheses. Therefore I will begin by describing in detail the initial processing profile of one patient and then briefly outline some of the group data.

Results of a Case-Study

The patient for whom I currently have the most on-line data is D.E. In 1970, when he was 16 years-old, D.E was involved in a motor-scooter accident. He suffered extensive, mostly anterior, left hemisphere damage, which was confirmed by CAT scan and behavioural examinations. When tested on the BDAE in 1975 and 1983, his profile was that of a "typical" agrammatic Broca patient. His repetition of single words is excellent, but of phrases and sentences is poor: he can only produce 3–4 words arranged in simple syntactic structures. His utterances contain few free grammatical and bound morphemes. According to the BDAE, his auditory comprehension is only slightly below normal, and in conversation his comprehension is very good. D.E.'s reading abilities have been extensively studied by Patterson (1978; 1979; 1981), and he shows the typical error pattern of a deep dyslexic.

The first question I asked of D.E. was a very general one: as he listens to an utterance, is he able to develop, on-line, normal syntactic and interpretative representations spanning the utterance? To answer this question I had D.E. monitor for target words occurring in three types of prose contexts— normal prose (where both syntactic and semantic structural information are available); semantically anomalous prose (which is syntactically correct but semantically anomalous); and scrambled strings (where there is neither syntactic nor semantic structural information). Examples of these three types of context, with target word underlined, are:

1. NORMAL PROSE: The church was broken into last night. Some thieves stole most of the *lead* off the roof.
2. SEMANTICALLY ANOMALOUS PROSE: The power was located in great water. No buns puzzle some in the *lead* off the roof.
3. SCRAMBLED STRINGS: In was power water the great located. Some the no puzzle buns in *lead* text the off.

I was able to track the availability of different sources of processing information across the input string by placing target words in different serial positions throughout each type of context. I used these particular contrasts because they have been shown to be sensitive to the global properties of on-line processing in normals (Marslen-Wilson & Tyler, 1975; 1980). When normal listeners were tested on these types of material, they produced faster monitoring RTs to target words heard in normal prose (275 msec) than in semantically anomalous prose (336 msec), and these in turn were faster than those in scrambled strings (360 msec). Also, RTs were faster to words occurring later in the sentence for both normal and semantically anomalous prose, but not for scrambled strings. We argued that this was because the interpretative and/or syntactic structure in normal and in semantically anomalous prose develops across the sentence and increasingly facilitates word recognition processes. In contrast, neither type of structure exists in scrambled strings and so there is no basis for facilitation to occur, even for targets occurring very late in the string.

These contrasts enable us to assess whether D.E. shows any abnormality in his on-line analysis of a spoken utterance, and, if so, whether his particular difficulty is in exploiting the syntactic or interpretative properties of utterances. Any deficit in the real-time processes involved should be reflected in his monitoring performance. If, for example, his main problem is in constructing a syntactic representation, as many people have argued is the underlying deficit in Broca's aphasia (e.g., Berndt & Caramazza, 1980), then his monitoring RTs should not become progressively faster across semantically anomalous prose utterance. If, on the other hand, Broca patients can perform syntactic analyses but cannot map these onto semantic roles (see, e.g., Linebarger, Schwartz, & Saffran,1983), then D.E.'s RTs in normal prose should not show the normal pattern.

D.E. performed very well on the monitoring task. He rarely missed a target, and his latencies were similar to those for normal young adults. His fast latencies for recognising target words showed that, like normal listeners, he was rapidly interpreting the speech input. Furthermore, he showed the normal pattern of faster responses (collapsing across word-positions) to targets in normal prose (258 msec) compared to the same targets in semantically anomalous prose (368 msec), with these in turn being faster than those in scrambled strings (409 msec).

Faster overall responses in normal prose compared to those in semantically anomalous prose suggests that D.E. is able to use semantic structural information in the on-line interpretation of an utterance. Moreover, this facilitation in normal prose is due to structural and not simply to lexical semantic information, since when the same words appear in a non-structured context (scrambled strings) latencies are slower. D.E can also use some kind of syntactic information, since his latencies in semantically anomalous prose are faster than those in scrambled strings. These overall latencies provide a general measure of his ability to use structural information. Latencies across word-positions tell us whether he is able to develop syntactic and interpretative representations across the course of an utterance.

D.E's data clearly deviate from normal in the effects of word-position in semantically anomalous prose. His latencies were the same whether the target occurred early, middle or late in an utterance; in contrast, normal listeners produce progressively faster latencies throughout a semantically anomalous prose sentence, closely paralleling their effects in normal prose. D.E's responses suggest that his use of syntactic information to construct a syntactic representation is deviant. But how is it deviant? Since D.E. does produce faster *overall* latencies to targets in semantically anomalous prose than to the same targets heard in a scrambled string, he must be able to use some aspects of syntactic information, but, presumably, not those which are necessary for the construction of a structural representation spanning an entire utterance.

In normal prose and scrambled strings, his latencies show the normal pattern. They decrease across word-positions in a normal prose sentence, but remain constant across a scrambled string. This contrast is important, because it is used to validate the claim that, for normal listeners, faster latencies across both normal and semantically anomalous prose utterances reflect the construction of structural representations rather than simply serial position effects. D.E.'s progressively faster responses across normal prose utterances must reflect his ability to develop an interpretative representation. From these data we cannot say whether, and how, this representation differs from normal. But given that D.E. cannot construct utterance-level syntactic representations, it is improbable that his interpretative representations are developed in the normal way. For this to be true, it would undermine the importance of syntactic structural information in the development of a meaningful interpretation of an utterance. It is plausible, then, that D.E.'s syntactic deficit means that he is unable to develop an interpretative representation in the same way as normal listeners. Perhaps he compensates for this by depending more heavily than normal upon pragmatic information. Since he does show a syntactic processing deficit, he presents a counter-example to the claim that agrammatism is characterised by a general inability to map correctly computed syntactic structures onto semantic roles (Linebarger et al., 1983).

To look more closely at D.E's ability to use specific types of syntactic and semantic information in the on-line processing of an utterance, I ran a second experiment. This study focussed on syntactic and semantic co-occurence relations between verbs and their arguments. Materials of the following type were constructed:

(a) The crowd was waiting eagerly. The young man grabbed the *guitar* and . . .
(b) The crowd was waiting eagerly. The young man buried the *guitar* and . . .
(c) The crowd was waiting eagerly. The young man drank the *guitar* and . . .
(d) The crowd was waiting eagerly. The young man slept the *guitar* and . . .

In each of these four examples, the first sentence provides a minimal context for the interpretation of each continuation sentence. The critical variable in the continuation sentence is the relationship between the verb and the following noun phrase. The relationship in (a) is perfectly normal, whereas in (b) it is pragmatically implausible, given the prior context. In (c) the object noun violates selection restrictions on the prior verb, ("drank the guitar") in that the argument slot for "drink" is restricted to a liquid substance. In (d) the noun also violates strict subcategorisation restrictions on the verb ("slept the guitar") because sleep is intransitive and cannot take a direct object. This means that the appropriate syntactic structure cannot be built, and also that there is no semantically interpretable relationship between noun and verb.

For normal listeners, all types of violation increase latencies to monitor for the target noun—"guitar" (Brown, Marslen-Wilson, & Tyler, in preparation). Latencies increase significantly to pragmatic violations, supporting earlier claims (e.g., Marslen-Wilson & Tyler, 1980; Tyler & Marslen-Wilson, 1982) that assessing the pragmatic plausibility of words with respect to the existing representation of the utterance in its discourse context is an essential part of normal language comprehension. They also show a substantial increase to both selection restriction and combined violations, with the largest effect for the combined anomaly. This suggests that when listeners encounter a verb, part of the lexical representation which they access includes the syntactic and semantic restrictions on the arguments which the verb can take. Constructing an on-line interpretation of the utterance is constrained by these lexical properties of the verb. The listener requires the object noun to fit both the syntactic and semantic constraints specified by the verb, so, when it does not, processing of the utterance is disrupted.

These various contrasts probe more specifically into D.E.'s comprehension deficit. The subcategorisation anomaly tests for his ability to use one type of syntactic structural information—combining verbs with their object nouns into syntactically permissible constituents. If D.E. is unable to use *any* type of syntactic information, he should be insensitive to the presence of subcategorisation anomalies. The two types of semantic anomaly test his ability to use both selection restriction and pragmatic information in the construction of a representation of an utterance. In general, to the extent that D.E. is sensitive to each type of constraint in his on-line interpretation of an utterance, monitoring latencies should increase when the constraints are violated.

D.E.'s monitoring latencies were again as fast and reliable as those of normal listeners of his age. Moreover, the pattern of his results was the same as for normals, except for one deviation. In normal listeners, pragmatic anomaly has the smallest disruptive effect, whereas for D.E. it has the largest (see Fig. 7.1). This suggests that he is more dependent than normal upon deriving a coherent pragmatic interpretation of an utterance, perhaps in compensation for his syntactic deficit.

This abnormally large disruptive effect of pragmatic anomaly in D.E.'s on-line processing contrasts with its effect (relative to the other conditions) when tested off-line. In the off-line test, D.E. merely had to say "good" or "bad" at the end of each sentence-pair, according to whether he thought there was anything wrong with the material. In this situation, D.E. correctly identified the three different types of violations with equal frequency. This contrast between the off- and on-line data raises an important point. To gain access to the range of processes involved in interpreting an utterance as it is being heard, one has to use tasks which more directly tap those processes. From D.E.'s off-line data alone—or merely by comparing his off-line data with that of normals—we could not have inferred that D.E. was abnormally dependent upon pragmatic information. To draw that conclusion we needed the on-line data.

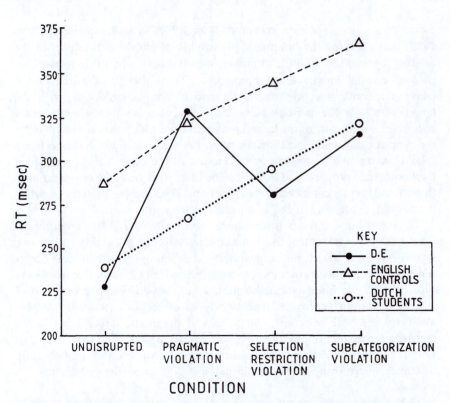

Fig. 7.1.   The mean latencies in each of the four experimental conditions for D.E., a group of English controls (mean age 53 years), and a group of Dutch students tested on the Dutch version of this experiment (mean age 23 years). Both control groups showed the same pattern of latencies although the groups vary in overall speed of response. D.E.'s pattern differs from both groups only in the pragmatic anomaly condition.

D.E.'s performance in these experiments suggests that he suffers from a disorder in syntactic processing. However, he clearly does not exhibit the complete breakdown in syntactic parsing routines which would have been expected on, for example, Berndt and Caramazza's (1980) account of agrammatism. Although unable to construct a normal syntactic representation of an utterance (no word position effect in semantically anomalous prose), he can use some kinds of syntactic information. He is faster to respond to targets in semantically anomalous prose than in scrambled strings, and he is sensitive to violations of subcategorisation restrictions between verbs and their arguments. This implies that he can construct at least some types of phrasal constituents which observe appropriate syntactic constraints.

Why does D.E. show no word-position effect in semantically anomalous prose? One possibility is that he is unable to construct a *global* syntactic representation spanning an entire clause or utterance, although he is still able to construct *local* syntactic phrases. This distinction between global and local can be thought of as the general distinction between syntactic representations in which phrases are related together into constituent hierarchies, and those which are confined to a small number of adjacent elements—such as prepositional phrases and noun phrases.

To test this hypothesis I carried out a third word monitoring study in which I manipulated the availability of local and global syntactic information. First, I constructed sentences which were semantically anomalous but grammatically well-formed (anomalous prose), in order to observe the effects of syntax without the additional effects of structural semantics. Within each sentence, words were grouped together into "phonological phrases" (cf. Gee & Grosjean, 1983).

Phonological phrases are groups of adjacent words which form syntactic and prosodic units. They are intermediate in size between the word and the syntactic phrase. There are two defining properties of phonological phrases. First, each one has a "head". The head is the main word around which the phrase is organised—for example, the head of a verb phrase is the main verb. All the other words in the phrase either modify, complement, or specify the head in some way. The second property of phonological phrases is that each has one major stress, and this stress is on the head. An example sentence, with phonological phrases marked off by slashed lines and target word in italics, follows:

(a) The book/ whose hair/ was heavy/ with bitter sunshine/ honestly protected/ a careful *ladder*/ who was waiting/ at an end/.

Using phonological phrases allowed me to examine two sorts of cue to local structural organisation—phonological and syntactic. The phonological cue is provided by the words within a phonological phrase being spoken as part of a rhythmical unit containing one major stress, and the syntactic cue is provided by the first word of the phonological phrase. In the example, the first word of the critical phonological phrase (containing the target) is the indefinite article, which cues listeners to the fact that they are hearing a noun phrase.

To determine whether D.E. was sensitive to these local structural cues, I introduced two other experimental conditions. In condition (b) I disrupted the syntactic organisation of the critical phonological phrase and removed the critical syntactic cue (the article). In the example, the phonological phrase was changed from "a careful ladder" to "careful quite ladder." In condition (c), phonological cues were disrupted by the simple method of splitting up the phonological phrase into two breath groups with the break occurring between the adjective ("careful") and the target noun ("ladder"). When normal listeners encounter these disruptions their latencies to monitor for the target increase. These increased RTs are assumed to reflect disrupted processing due to the lack of information which is normally used in on-line comprehension of an utterance. In this case, they indicate that listeners use both syntactic and phonological information in constructing local groupings. The question was whether D.E. would show a similar increase in latencies.

To test the other aspect of the hypothesis—namely, that D.E. cannot construct a global syntactic representation—I included condition (d). Here the critical phonological phrase occurred early in the sentence (as opposed to late in the sentence as in condition (a) above:

(d) A careful *ladder*/ whose hair/ was heavy with bitter sunshine/ honestly protected/ the book/ who was waiting/ at an end/.

If D.E. cannot construct a syntactic representation spanning an entire utterance, his latencies to early targets should be no different from those to late targets, thus replicating the lack of a word-position effect in anomalous prose in the first experiment. This is indeed what I found. D.E. showed no significant word-position effect—the difference in RTs to early (511 msec) and late (496 msec) targets was not significant. Normal listeners tested in this study (and in the prose experiment mentioned earlier) produce significantly faster latencies to late (377 msec) compared to early targets (437 msec).

Of the two types of local cue, only syntactic disruptions resulted in a significant increase in monitoring latencies. These increased latencies suggest that D.E. is able to group words together into local units on the basis of syntactic, but not phonological, cues. This syntactic grouping must be based on an interpretation of the structural implications of local syntactic cues (prepositions, determiners, etc.). This account conflicts with those theories of agrammatism which claim that the major source of the deficit is the ability to exploit the grammatical function (in either production or comprehension) of *all* function words (e.g., Bradley, Garrett, & Zurif, 1980), and is instead consistent with findings reported by Berndt in Chapter 10. She showed that some patients classified as Broca's aphasics have specific difficulties in processing preposition and determiners, but others do not. Analogous findings concerning other syntactic cues (function words and suffixes) are presented by Parisi in Chapter 9.

These on-line studies, then, suggest that D.E.'s syntactic processing deficit is primarily confined to an inability to construct a global syntactic representation of an utterance. His ability to use some other types of syntactic information is unimpaired. He is able to access the subcategorisation information attached to words and use it to constrain permissible verb-argument relations, and his knowledge of the local structural constraints marked by certain groups of function words remains intact. It is also clear that D.E. is able to construct a semantic representation of an utterance. In view of his syntactic deficit, this representation must be based on the joint products of various types of local syntactic information, the semantic properties of words, and his extensive use of pragmatic information. It remains to be seen whether the resulting representation is significantly different from normal.

Before leaving D.E. I should make one last point. The on-line data show that D.E. has a syntactic processing deficit in comprehension, and locates the deficit in his inability to construct global representations as opposed to local constituents. This is not something we would have known from the results of the Boston exam (on the basis of which he was diagnosed as having no significant comprehension deficit). This suggests that the Boston is not sufficiently sensitive to subtle disorders of auditory comprehension. The Boston contains few auditory comprehension sub-tests, which probe very general aspects of comprehension and are therefore only capable of diagnosing relatively severe and global comprehension deficits. Certainly, on the basis of the Boston alone, a patient cannot be safely diagnosed as having had essentially normal comprehension.

Results of Group Analyses

A number of Dutch and English patients have been tested on the first two experiments discussed earlier—the prose experiment and the verb-argument structure experiment. Although the data are preliminary, I will discuss them briefly because they illustrate the limitations of the major diagnostic exams.

Prose Experiment.   At present, only the English patient data are available for this study. The English patients were classified into aphasic sub-types on the basis of the Boston exam. Of special interest are the various types of Broca and Wernicke aphasics. First of all, I will discuss the Broca patients. These were judged on the basis of their spontaneous speech to be either agrammatic, non-agrammatic or as having a speech output restricted to 1–2 words. In terms of their overall latencies to monitor for target words in the three prose contexts (normal prose, semantically anomalous prose and scrambled strings), all three groups of patients behaved like normals. Their overall RTs in normal prose were faster than in semantically anomalous prose, which were faster again than RTs in scrambled strings. Where some patients differed from normal was with respect to their RTs across word positions. In particular, five out of the six agrammatic patients behaved like normals and differed from the other two groups of Brocas.[1] That is, while all

---

[1] The sixth patient was D.E., whose performance was described in detail earlier.

patients showed the normal pattern of word-position effects in normal prose and scrambled strings, only these five agrammatics showed the normal word-position facilitation in semantically anomalous prose. In contrast, the two non–agrammatics and the three patients who produced utterances restricted to 1–2 words showed no facilitation at all across word-positions in semantically anomalous prose—in spite of showing faster overall RTs in this material compared to scrambled strings.

These results suggest that these five agrammatics are able to construct a syntactic representation which spans an utterance. This global syntactic structure serves to facilitate responses to targets occurring later in a semantically anomalous prose sentence. In contrast, the non-agrammatic and 1–2 word utterance patients cannot take advantage of larger scale syntactic structure. However, they seem to be able to construct local syntactic groupings, as overall latencies in semantically anomalous prose are faster than those in scrambled strings.

These data suggest that a syntactic deficit in production is not necessarily accompanied by a syntactic deficit in comprehension; further evidence for this view is provided by Berndt in Chapter 10. Most of the Broca patients who were diagnosed as having agrammatic spontaneous speech showed no evidence of a syntactic comprehension deficit in the prose experiment. In contrast, patients who had a severely restricted, rather than syntactically deformed, speech output, could not correctly parse an utterance.

Unlike the Broca patients, the five Wernicke patients do not form a cohesive group, nor even a set of cohesive sub-groups, whether we examine their spontaneous speech or estimate the severity of their comprehension deficit on the basis of the Boston exam. The spontaneous speech of the five patients varies in fluency, presence of paraphasias or paragrammatism, severity of word-finding problems and frequency of circumlocutions.[2] Moreover, patients also vary in the severity of their comprehension deficit, as measured by the Boston.

Four of the Wernicke patients show the normal word-position effects in both normal and anomalous prose. The fifth (F.B.) does not. This patient produces fluent spontaneous speech which contains few paraphasias but shows some evidence of paragrammatism and word-finding problems. Unlike both normals and Brocas, he shows no significant word-position facilitation in either normal or anomalous prose. His data on scrambled strings are normal. If this pattern holds up in other experiments on this patient, then it suggests that he is unable to construct a normal interpretative representation of an utterance.

---

[2]Decisions about similarities and differences along these dimensions are problematical, as they have received scant attention. Consequently, they are difficult to define and quantify.

Anomalies Experiment.   A number of Dutch and English patients have been tested in the anomalies experiment. The Dutch patients were initially classified as either Broca or Wernicke on a diagnostic exam which is analogous to the Boston—the Aachen exam. Both the Dutch and English Brocas differed from normal in showing: (1) no added increase in RT for the combined violation over and above that for the selection restriction violation; (2) pragmatic anomalies had a large effect on increasing latencies; (3) both types of semantic anomaly—pragmatic and selection restrictions—had an equally disruptive effect.

This pattern suggests that the subcategorisation information attached to verbs does not function in the same way for these patients as for normal listeners. Either this particular type of lexical information is not accessed when a verb is recognised, or it is not used to constrain permissible verb-argument relations. These patients are also more dependent than normal upon pragmatic information. As was mentioned earlier, pragmatic anomalies only produce a small increase in RTs with normal listeners, but for Broca patients the increase was larger.

None of these patients produced exactly the same pattern of results as was shown by D.E.—the agrammatic patient whose data were described earlier. For D.E., pragmatic anomalies produced the largest increase in RTs, and I proposed that this might indicate that D.E. was more dependent than normal upon pragmatic information as compensation for his syntactic deficit. The fact that not all Brocas (even those who show no word-position effect in anomalous prose) were as disturbed by pragmatic anomalies as D.E., suggests that reliance upon pragmatic information might be an optional, rather than obligatory, response to a syntactic deficit.

The Dutch Wernicke results (no English Wernickes have yet been tested) mirror those of the Brocas with one exception. For the Wernickes, combined anomalies had a larger effect than did selection restriction violations, suggesting that like normal listeners, Wernicke patients do use subcategorisation information. The only way in which the Wernickes differed from normal is that selection restriction violations did not disrupt processing more than pragmatic violations—both types of semantic anomaly had equal effects on increasing latencies. This suggests that whatever semantic deficit these patients have, it is not a simple loss of the ability to use semantic or pragmatic information in immediate processing.

These data illustrate two difficulties. First, there is the problem of clustering patients into groups on the basis of the on-line data. Patients who perform similarly in one experiment, rarely cluster together in a second experiment. For example, the two groups of patients which emerged in the prose experiment (on the basis of the presence or absence of a word-position effect in anomalous prose), did not remain intact in the anomalies experiment. It was not possible to predict, on the basis of results in one study, which patients would cluster together in a second study. There may be two reasons for this. First, the two experiments might tap different aspects of syntactic analysis—lexical and structural. Second, each patient might not have one specific deficit. Rather, each patient may suffer from disruptions to a variety of processes. This is not implausible, given how rarely we find even two patients who perform similarly across a range of tests.

The second difficulty concerns the issue of grouping patients on the basis of a general diagnostic exam. The data collected so far indicate that there is a poor correspondence between the on-line data and the original classification of a patient as either a Broca or Wernicke. In the anomalies experiment, for example, the group data obscured individual differences. Not all patients showed the group pattern. One patient, for example, showed significantly increased latencies to combined violations over those to selection restriction violations alone. Another patient showed no significant effect of pragmatic anomalies. Such deviations from the group results cannot be dismissed on the grounds that they reflect normal individual variation. Presumably they show that these two patients are different from the other patients in the group. Since the groups were formed on the basis of the Boston exam, this suggests that the Boston is not sufficiently sensitive to comprehension disorders. Consequently, we should not expect patients falling within any one classificatory group to be homogeneous (cf. Caramazza, 1984). Nor should we expect the diagnostic exams to predict performance on anything other than the most general tests of language comprehension. That these points apply generally to research in cognitive neuropsychology, and not just specifically to the study of patterns of impaired comprehension of spoken language, is argued by Ellis in the final chapter of this book.

CONCLUSIONS

This work, although very preliminary, shows that on-line tasks, originally developed for use with normals, can be successfully adapted for use with patients. Whether one looks at individual patients or group data, probing the on-line processes involved in spoken language comprehension in aphasic patients is both feasible and informative. The majority of patients had no trouble in performing reliably on on-line tasks. Reaction times were usually within the normal range and reasonably stable. Moreover, since significant differences emerged between patients and normals, the experiments were successful in the ways in which they probed real-time language processes. The distinctions they contained tapped relevant aspects of the processing deficits in the various aphasic patients.

D.E.'s data from the three studies reported here indicate the advantages of developing a processing profile for each patient. Although the initial experiments were designed to probe general aspects of his real-time processing, on the basis of these data we were able to develop quite specific hypotheses about the type of syntactic deficit he might plausibly be suffering from, and to test these hypotheses in other on-line studies.

The group data, however, were less satisfactory. Although there were differences between groups, there were also differences within each group. In most group studies, such individual differences tend to be ignored. Reports of group data rarely include details of individual patients. Therefore, it is often not possible to assess the extent to which each member of the group follows the group pattern. While this approach might be justified in research on normals, it cannot be justified in patient research. It requires making assumptions about the effects of brain damage that we are not yet in a position to verify: for example, that differences within a group of patients reflect nothing more than statistical fluctuation; that the principles of statistical averaging are as applicable to brain damaged populations as they are to normal populations; that there is no meaningful individual variation in the response to the effects of brain damage.

Finally, we should consider how these data bear on models of normal language processing. Perhaps their most important contribution is that they offer a different way of validating distinctions between different knowledge types. From normal data we can only obtain quantitative evidence of such distinctions, whereas from patient data we can also obtain qualitative evidence. For example, the contrast between D.E.'s lack of a word-position effect in semantically anomalous prose, and its presence in normal listeners, is a qualitative difference which can be interpreted as evidence of a separate syntactic knowledge source[3] which, in D.E.'s case, has been selectively impaired. We can apply the same interpretation to the finding that some patients showed no effect of syntactic subcategorisation violations, although such anomalies significantly disrupt normal listeners. So, in this respect at least, patient data provides an invaluable source of data that helps to constrain the way in which we theorise about the organisation of knowledge types.

ACKNOWLEDGEMENTS

I wish to thank William Marslen-Wilson and Karalyn Patterson for helpful comments on the manuscript.

---

[3]One should keep in mind that evidence for the existence of distinct knowledge types is not necessarily evidence for distinct levels of processing analysis (Marslen-Wilson & Tyler, 1981; Tyler, 1982).

REFERENCES

Brown, C., Marslen-Wilson, W. D., & Tyler, L. K. (In preparation) *The role of lexical representations in spoken language comprehension.*

Berndt, R., & Caramazza, A. (1980) A redefinition of the syndrome of Broca's aphasia: Implications for a neuropsychological model of language. *Applied Psycholinguistics, 1*, 225–278.

Blumstein, S., Milberg, W., & Shrier, R. (1982) Semantic processing in aphasia: Evidence from an auditory lexical decision task. *Brain and Language, 17*, 301–315.

Bradley, D., Garrett, M., & Zurif, E. (1980) Syntactic deficits in Broca's aphasia. In D. Caplan (Ed.), *Biological studies of mental processes*. Cambridge, Mass.: MIT Press.

Caramazza, G. (1984) The logic of neuropsychological research and the problem of patient classification in aphasia. *Brain and Language, 21*, 9–20.

Gee, J., & Grosjean, F. (1983) Performance structures: A psycholinguistic and linguistic appraisal. *Cognitive Psychology, 15*, 411–459.

Kean, M-L. (1980) Grammatical representations and the description of language processing. In D. Caplan (Ed.), *Biological studies of mental processes*. Cambridge, Mass.: MIT Press.

Linebarger, M., Schwartz, M., & Saffran, E. (1983) Sensitivity to grammatical structure in so-called agrammatic aphasics. *Cognition, 13*, 361–392.

Marslen-Wilson, W. D. (1984) Function and process in spoken word-recognition. In H. Bouma & D. Bouwhuis (Eds.), *Attention and Performance X: Control of language processes*. Hillsdale, N. J.: Lawrence Erlbaum Associates.

Marslen-Wilson, W. D., & Tyler, L. K. (1975) Processing structure of sentence perception. *Nature, (London), 257*, 784–786.

Marslen-Wilson, W. D., & Tyler, L. K. (1980) The temporal structure of spoken language understanding. *Cognition, 8*, 1–71.

Marslen-Wilson, W. D., & Tyler, L. K. (1981) Central processes in speech understanding. *Philosophical Transactions of the Royal Society of London, B295*, 317–332.

Patterson, K. (1978) Phonemic dyslexia: Errors of meaning and the meaning of errors. *Quarterly Journal of Experimental Psychology, 30*, 587–607.

Patterson, K. (1979) What is right with "deep" dyslexic patients? *Brain and Language, 8*, 111–129.

Patterson, K. (1981) Neuropsychological approaches to the study of reading. *British Journal of Psychology, 72*, 151–174.

Tyler, L. K., & Marslen-Wilson, W. D. (1982) Processing utterances in discourse contexts. *Journal of Semantics, 1*, 297–314.

Zurif, E. (1982) The use of data from aphasia in constructing a performance model of language. In M. Arbib, D. Caplan, & J. Marshall (Eds.), *Neural models of language processes*. London: Academic Press.

8

Patterns of Speech Production Deficit Within and Across Aphasia Syndromes: Application of a Psycholinguistic Model

Myrna F. Schwartz
Moss Rehabilitation Hospital, 12th Street and Tabor Road, Philadelphia, Pennsylvania 19141, USA

INTRODUCTION

The goal of this chapter is to show how a particular psycholinguistic model of sentence planning, when applied to the phenomena of aphasic sentence production, brings coherence to a set of facts that went largely unexplained on the classical aphasia theory. The facts concern certain characteristics of aphasic speech: the varieties of error type; their distribution within the sentence, and their patterns of co-occurrence. The gain in coherence is reflected in our ability to explain these characteristics as non-arbitrary outcomes, given the stipulated functional architecture of the sentence production mechanism.

It is not at all my intention to argue for the correctness of this particular psycholinguistic model. In the first place, the model continues to undergo revision and elaboration in the hands of its creators and others, with the data from pathology serving as an increasingly rich source of input to its development. In the second place, there is as yet no consensus, even among like-minded aphasia researchers, on what are the essential facts to be explained by the model. Consider, for example, the pattern of co-occurring symptoms that has traditionally defined the syndrome of agrammatic Broca's aphasia, and that serves as the point of departure for this chapter. An accumulation of evidence from well-studied cases makes it clear that many, if not all, components of this syndrome are dissociable one from another (e.g. Miceli et al., 1983; Saffran, Schwartz, & Marin, 1980a; Tissot, Mounin, & Lhermitte, 1973; and in this volume, Chapter 9 by Parisi and Chapter 10 by

Berndt). This being the case, is the theorist under any obligation to account for the "prototypical" agrammatic pattern? (for a range of perspectives on this question, see Badecker & Caramazza, 1985; Caramazza, 1984; Good-glass & Menn, 1985; Schwartz, 1984).

It will be my contention in this chapter that a consideration of the phenomena that have traditionally characterised the syndrome of agrammatism, together with those that have characterised neologistic jargon in Wernicke's aphasia, yield important generalisations; that these generalisations eluded the classical aphasia theorists, whose model of the language system operated exclusively at the level of individual words and was grounded, by design, in neuroanatomical connectionist theory; and that these generalisations are naturally captured by a particular psycholinguistic model of sentence production by virtue of the assumptions it makes about the sequence of mental operations that underlie sentence planning, and the modular systems that effect these operations. It will be my further contention that such a model provides an invaluable tool for moving beyond the syndrome-based characterisation of aphasic disorders towards a psycho-linguistically oriented account phrased in the language of computational modules and their operation under states of normality and pathology.

To set the stage for the discussion of the model and its application, I will briefly characterise that general enterprise that goes under the heading of "the psycholinguistic approach to aphasic disorders" and contrast this approach with the classical neuroanatomical theory.

THE PSYCHOLINGUISTIC APPROACH TO APHASIA

In 1974, in their influential book, *The Psychology of Language*, Fodor, Bever, and Garrett posed the central question of psycholinguistic research: "How does the speaker-hearer employ the knowledge of his language represented by a grammar to effect the encoding and decoding of speech (p. 21)?" This formulation of the question entails two important theoretical commitments. First, language *knowledge* is to be characterised by the types of structural description that constitute the linguist's grammar. To know a language, on this view, is to know the rules that generate well-formed, meaningful sentences. The second commitment is to a characterisation of language use in terms of the ways in which this knowledge is brought to bear in the production and the interpretation of sentences.

The psycholinguistic approach to aphasia shares these theoretical commitments and makes an additional important assumption: that pathological language will best be explained with reference to these knowledge structures and the procedures that employ them (Caplan, 1981; Kean, 1980; LaPointe, 1983). It is this set of assumptions that differentiate the psycholinguistic approach to aphasia from the classical theory, which has dominated aphasiology for over 100 years, and which takes as its goal neuroanatomical explanation of the major aphasia syndromes.

THE CLASSICAL NEUROANATOMICAL THEORY OF THE APHASIAS

Developed in 1874 by the German neurologist Carl Wernicke (Wernicke, 1874), and elaborated and modified frequently thereafter (e.g., Geschwind, 1965; Lichtheim, 1885), the theory survives today because of its elegant

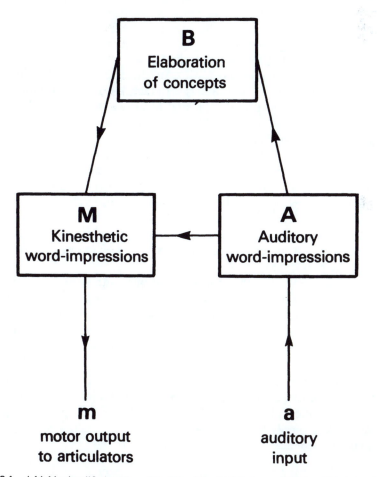

FIG. 8.1   A highly simplified outline of the Wernicke–Lichtheim model (after Lichtheim, 1885).

simplicity and its success in accomplishing its goals. This is a theory that attempts to explain the major symptom complexes in aphasia and their association with particular lesion sites.

The theory postulates one anatomically defined centre at **M**, supporting the motor memories corresponding to the word-as-spoken, and another centre at **A** for memory images representing the word-as-heard. An input channel, **a**, carries auditory impressions to **A**, and an output channel, **m**, conducts instructions to the muscles concerned with articulating speech. Auditory word impressions are given meaning through their association with **B**, the area or areas of the brain supporting the elaboration of object concepts. Thus, comprehension of spoken language is accomplished by means of the circuit **aAB**; volitional speech occurs over pathway **BMm**; repetition of heard speech over **aAMm**.

Broca's Aphasia

Let us now consider the theory's treatment of the so-called Broca's aphasia, named for the French physician who, in the late 1860s, described the syndrome and its neuroanatomical basis. In fact, Wernicke's account of this syndrome differed little from that offered by Broca himself: a lesion at **M** affects the memory for word articulations and hence any and all language functions requiring spoken output. Volitional speech is thus compromised, along with repetition and oral reading. Spared are those language functions that bypass **M**, most notably comprehension of spoken speech (**aAB**).

This characterisation captures well the non-fluency of the Broca's aphasic. Patients of this type speak little, and with great effort. The articulation of speech sounds undergoes distortion in the form of phonetic disintegration (Alajouanine, Ombredane, & Durand, 1939); and long interword pauses give the impression that speech prosody is absent (but see Cooper & Zurif, 1983; Danly & Shapiro, 1982).

What is not captured in this theoretical account is the striking breakdown in grammatical structure which so often accompanies the effortful speech of the Broca's aphasic. This breakdown, the so-called agrammatism of Broca's aphasia, has become the focus for contemporary linguistic and psycho-linguistic analyses (see Kean, 1985, and the contributions therein for an up-to-date perspective).

To illustrate the character of agrammatic speech, I have recorded the response of one of our patients, B.L., to the "cookie theft" picture of the Boston Diagnostic Aphasia Examination (Goodglass & Kaplan, 1972). The subject's task is simply to describe with complete sentences what he sees in the picture (reproduced in Fig. 8.2).

FIG. 8.2   The "cookie theft" picture from the Boston Diagnostic Aphasia Exam (Goodglass & Kaplan, 1972) (with permission from Lee & Febiger, Publishers).

B.L.:	Wife is dry dishes. Water down! Oh boy! O.K. Awright. O.K. . . . Cookie is down . . . fall, and girl, O.K., girl . . . boy . . . um . . .
Examiner:	What is the boy doing?
B.L.:	Cookie is . . . um . . . catch
Examiner:	Who is getting the cookies?
B.L.:	Girl, girl
Examiner:	Who is about to fall?
B.L.:	Boy . . . fall down!

The two characteristic attributes of agrammatic speech are evident in B.L.'s transcript:

1. The agrammatic's vocabulary is heavily weighted toward the major lexical items (nouns, verbs, adjectives), with a predominance of nouns that make concrete reference.

Notably absent are the "small words": the pronouns, prepositions, articles, auxiliary verbs, and conjunctions, which together bear so much of the burden of logical/syntactic communication. In addition, the nouns and verbs which do appear in speech are often stripped of their inflectional endings, or else inflected wrongly.

Note that it is not at all obvious, on the Wernicke theory, why these syntactic morphemes (i.e. free standing functors and bound inflections) should be particularly vulnerable to disruption by a lesion at **M**. Indeed, one might predict just the opposite: that since these constitute the most frequent forms in the lexical inventory, their motor representations should be particularly resistant to disruption. Attempts to explain this paradox generally invoke the "economy of effort" principle: syntactic morphemes are not selectively disrupted; rather, their omission reflects a strategy adopted by the patient, designed to maximise informativeness while minimising articulatory effort. Exploiting this strategy, the aphasic produces a sentence that is telegram-like in structure, in that it emphasises lexical content at the expense of (typically redundant) syntactic morphemes. A somewhat modified version of this thesis has recently been set forth by Kolk (1983; Kolk & Heeschen, 1985).

It should be apparent, from the excerpt given, that B.L.'s speech is not well captured by the telegram analogy. His restricted use of syntactic morphemes arises in a context of generally impoverished clause and phrase structures. To see this, consider that the left hand portion of the cookie theft picture could be described quite adequately by a telegram-like utterance of the sort, "girl want boy get cookies", in which the hierarchical structure of constituent phrases is given by lexical context and lexical order alone:

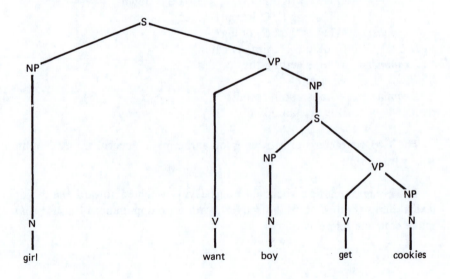

But "sentences" like these are never obtained from B.L. Like other agrammatics, B.L. rarely attempts multi-clause utterances. Typically, the construction of even simple sentences poses an insurmountable problem, and he is forced to rely on uncoordinated sentence fragments: NP–V; NP–NP; or V–NP combinations.

Thus we come to the second characteristic of agrammatic speech:

2. Agrammatic speech reflects a breakdown in the construction and coordination of constituent phrases.

Additional examples of this breakdown in phrase construction and coordination are given in Table 8.1, which records the attempts of ten agrammatic aphasics to describe a picture showing a girl handing a bouquet of flowers to her teacher.

Eight of these ten subjects fails in his or her attempts to construct a complete verb phrase (integrating verb, direct object, and indirect object), even though it is possible to do so by the serial ordering of major lexical elements alone: ". . . give teacher flowers". Subject #7 displays an additional problem, to do with the selection of the subject noun phrase, and it is possible to interpret the false start of subject #9, too, as showing a confusion over the ordering of noun phrases around the verb.

My colleagues and I have amassed additional evidence that agrammatic aphasics have difficulty exploiting word order to communicate thematic roles (that is, who or what is the agent of the action, the object of the action, and so forth). When we required them to describe a set of semantically reversible agent-action-object depictions (e.g., dog chasing cat) and a set depicting the locative relation of two inanimate objects (e.g., pencil in sink; shoe under

TABLE 8.1
Attempts at Picture Description by Ten Agrammatic Aphasics

Picture shows a young girl handing a bouquet of flowers to her teacher

---

(Pt. 1) "The young . . . the girl . . . the little girl is . . . the flower."

(Pt. 2) "The girl is flower the woman."

(Pt. 3) "Girl is . . . going to flowers."

(Pt. 4) "The girl is . . . is roses. The girl is rosing (/*rozin*/). The woman and the little girl was rosed."

(Pt. 5) "The girl is giving . . . giving the teacher . . . giving it teacher."

(Pt. 6) "The girl is flowering."

(Pt. 7) "The teacher is . . . the girl . . . giving the girl and the flowers."

(Pt. 8) "Girl is handing flowers to teacher."

(Pt. 9) "The flowers . . . the girl bringing the teacher."

(Pt. 10) "The girl is flowers . . . teachers."

table), eight agrammatic speakers reversed the order of subject and object nouns on approximately 40% of trials (Saffran, Schwartz, & Marin, 1980b).

The following summary description captures the speech of the "prototypical" agrammatic aphasic:

The agrammatic speaker experiences difficulty communicating those semantic distinctions that rest upon the proper configuration of grammatical morphemes and/or the linear order of constituent phrases.

The psycholinguistic approach to agrammatism starts with this characterisation and looks for explanations in terms of the knowledge structures and procedures assumed to underly the normal capacity to generate well-formed sentences.[1] I will elaborate on this endeavour further, but first it is necessary to return to the classical theory and to a consideration of its treatment of the second major aphasic syndrome.

Wernicke's Aphasia

It was Wernicke himself who first described the deficit in understanding speech that arises as a consequence of damage to the posterior temporal lobe of the left hemisphere, and this form of receptive aphasia has come to bear his name. The comprehension defect in Wernicke's aphasia is readily

---

[1] Throughout this chapter I will be concentrating on the production problem in agrammatic aphasics, but a comment is in order concerning the status of their receptive language. The reader will recall that the classical theory's treatment of Broca's aphasia was predicated on the notion that patients of this type did not experience difficulty in comprehending spoken language. And, indeed, a review of the exchange between B.L. and the examiner will confirm the standard clinical impression of preserved understanding in patients with non-fluent, agrammatic speech patterns. Over the past decade, however, substantial evidence has accumulated that shows that when patients of this type are tested formally, they frequently display problems in interpreting the information carried by the syntactic structure. This evidence for parallel difficulties in the expressive and receptive domain has given rise to a number of hypotheses affirming the existence of a "central" syntactic deficit playing a causal role in both the expressive and receptive manifestations of agrammatism (for a review of these hypotheses, see Schwartz, Linebarger, & Saffran, 1985). Of late, the enthusiasm for a central syntactic deficit account has diminished, largely as a result of evidence showing, first, that agrammatic speech is neither a necessary nor sufficient condition for agrammatic comprehension (e.g., Kolk, van Grunsven, & Keyser, 1985); and, second, that agrammatic comprehenders are for the most part sensitive to the well-formedness constraints of their language and to violations of those constraints in the sentences they hear (Crain, Shankweiler & Tuller, 1984; Linebarger, Schwartz, & Saffran, 1983; Lukatela, Crain, & Shankweiler, 1985). At this point in time, it is altogether unclear how to interpret the comprehension deficit that often, but not invariably, accompanies the agrammatic speech deficit. Additional discussion and evidence on the issue of the comprehension deficit in agrammatism is provided in this volume in the chapters by Caplan, Berndt, and Tyler.

captured by the theory; it is attributed to a breakdown at **A**, the auditory word centre, and to the resulting disruption of the **AB** associations.

More problematic for the theory is the explanation of the disturbances in speaking that reliably accompany the comprehension impairment.[2] Classical aphasiologists coined the term "paraphasic" to describe the resultant speech pattern, in which "wrong words are used, the words themselves are altered by the introduction of wrong syllables, occasionally to such an extent that language becomes wholly unintelligible (Lichtheim, 1885; p. 439)." In the modern literature, this pattern of minimally or wholly unintelligible speech in the Wernicke's aphasic is termed "jargon aphasia."

Why this impairment when the structural basis for volitional speech (**BMm**) remains intact? Wernicke's explanation invoked the notion that correct word choice and expression requires the arousal, during speech, of auditory memories stored at **A**. When this monitoring is disrupted by a lesion at **A**, speech output is distorted, though fluent.[3]

While certainly plausible and cogent, this account does not suffice to explain the form or the distribution of paraphasias in the speech of the Wernicke's aphasic. Consider the following sample of jargon aphasia elicited once again by the cookie theft picture (Fig. 8.2). This sample is excerpted from Buckingham, 1981, p. 54; the phonetic transcription of paraphasias recorded in the original text are transliterated here for the convenience of the reader.

C.B.:   (Looking at left side of picture) You mean like this boy? I mean *noy*, and this, uh, *meoy*. This is a *kay·nit, kah·ken*. I don't say it. I'm not getting anything from it. I'm getting. I'm *dime* from it, but I'm getting from it. There were *ek·spresh·ez, ah·grash·enz* and with the type of *mah·kan·ic* is standing like this ... and then the ,.. I don't know what she *go·in* other than [?] (*sic*) And this is *deh·lee*, this one is the one and this one and this one and ... I don't know.

---

[2] I do not mean to imply that the comprehension problem in Wernicke's aphasics is fully explained by this account. It is not. For example, Blumstein, Baker, and Goodglass (1977) failed to find the predicted association between patient's failures to discriminate and identify phonemes, on the one hand, and the severity of their comprehension problem, on the other. Lexical semantic deficits (e.g., Baker, Blumstein & Goodglass, 1981; Goodglass & Baker, 1976), and deficits and the level of phrasal and clausal analysis (Pate, 1985; Chapter 7 by Tyler) certainly contribute to the problem, in at least a subset of patients.

[3] Lichtheim (1885) modified this idea, suggesting that it was the entire **BMAB** circuit whose integrity guaranteed successful monitoring of speech output. On this view, a lesion anywhere along the circuit that did not entirely disrupt speech output would result in paraphasic speech. Lichtheim made this modification to account for the reliable occurrence of paraphasias in two other aphasic syndromes, conduction aphasia and transcortical sensory aphasia.

Examiner: (Indicating right side of the picture) Can you tell me what she's doing?

C.B.:   Anything [?] I mean, she is a beautiful girl. And this is the same with her. And now its coming there and [?] Now what about here or anything like that . . . what any.

Examiner: Anything else?

C.B.:   Nothing the *kee·ser·eez* the, these are *dav·ver·eez* and these and this one and these are living. This one's right in and these are . . . uh . . . and that's nothing, that's nothing . . . I can see things like this. You know, this type of thing. I can *dru·bit*, but so what.

Paraphasias in the speech of the Wernicke's aphasic take several forms. Most classifications distinguish:

1. *Unrelated verbal paraphasia*—the substitution of one word for another, where the substitute bears no relation in either form or meaning to the target. Examples from C.B.'s transcript are *dime* and *mah·kan·ic* (mechanic).

2. *Semantic paraphasia*—the substitution of one word for another where the substitute bears an obvious semantic relation to the target. In C.B.'s transcript, *go·in*, interpreted as *going*, might be considered a semantic paraphasia for *doing*. The range of documented semantic paraphasias is wide, as can be seen in Table 8.2.

3. *Phonemic paraphasia*—the occurrence of a word, or more commonly, a non-word, resulting from the obvious distortion of the segmental (i.e. phonemic) structure of the target word. These distortions can arise from the deletion, addition, substitution, or displacement of constituent phonemes (Lecours & Lhermitte, 1969). The occurence of *noy* in C.B.'s speech sample presumably reflects the substitution of *n* for *b* in the intended target, *boy*.

Occasionally, paraphasic distortions seem to suggest interactions among error types. Thus, on the assumption that C.B. was referring to the girl in the left-hand side of the picture when he said, "and this, uh, *meoy*" we might plausibly interpret his utterance as a complex phonemic paraphasia occurring on a semantic paraphasia: girl→boy→*meoy*.

4. *Neologisms*—literally, "new word"; the application of this term to the paraphasic speech of aphasic patients varies from researcher to researcher. Some (e.g. Butterworth, 1979; Ellis, Miller, & Sin, 1983; Lecours, 1980) admit into this category all word-like forms not found in the dictionary of the speaker's language. On this criterion, phonemic paraphasias like *noy* represent one subtype of neologism; items like *ek·spresh·ez* and *ah·grash·enz*, which contain recognisable pieces of words from the speaker's language (*expression, aggression*) represent a second subtype (labelled "monemic parapha-

TABLE 8.2
Semantic Paraphasias in Jargon Aphasia: Examples from the Literature

(from Buckingham, 1980):

south→north	sandwiches→crackers
ride→run	Easter→Christmas
green→red	sons→daughters
knuckles→finger	Florida→New York
cherries→apples	shoulder→mouth

(from Lecours & Rouillon, 1976; French)

le panier (basket)→le sac (bag); la bourse (purse)
Monsieur (Sir)→Mademoiselle (Miss)
Je suis tombé malade (I fell sick)→Je suis morte (I died)

(from Luria, 1976; Russian)

Kuvshin (jug)→mishka (basin); chashka (cup)
galka (crow)→belka (squirrel)
brosila (threw)→prinesla (brought)
bol'nitsa (hospital)→militsiya (police station)

sias" by Lecours & Rouillon, 1976; "morphemic deviations" by Lecours, 1980).

The third subtype of neologism, the so-called "abstruse" neologism, comprises that set of forms that has no recognisable source in the language of the speaker. Buckingham, in several published reports, limits his analysis of neologistic utterances to these alone, that is, to "phonological form(s) produced by the patient for which it is impossible to recover with any reasonable degree of certainty some single item or items in the vocabulary of the subject's language as it presumably existed prior to the onset of the disease" (Buckingham & Kertesz, 1976, p. 13). Examples of such abstruse neologisms in C.B.'s transcript include *kay·nit*, *kee·ser·eez*, and *dru·bit*.

Regardless of how broadly or narrowly one sets the definition, neologisms can be shown to display many interesting features. For example, although these utterances may look or sound quite bizarre on casual inspection, they turn out to be tightly rule-governed. Thus, the neologism of the paraphasic speaker of English will be constituted of English phonemes only, and these sequenced in such a way as to generally conform to the phonotactic constraints of English. For example, such a patient is unlikely to begin his neologistic utterance with *tl* or *zgr*, both of which are non-permissible consonant clusters in English.[4] Moreover, in the case of bi-syllabic neologisms, it tends to be the first syllable rather than the second that receives primary stress, consistent with the rules of noun stress assignment in English (Buckingham & Kertesz, 1976).

A second interesting feature of these neologisms is their distribution, which is to say, their overwhelming tendency to occur in sentence slots marked for major lexical items, and in particular, nouns.

It is not always possible to identify the grammatical category of neologisms. There are patients who produce extended strings of neologistic discourse which defy analysis of this kind (e.g., Perecman & Brown, 1981). However, not infrequently the Wernicke patient's neologistic paraphasias arise within phrasal contexts sufficiently well defined as to allow for grammatical tagging; and in these cases, the effect of grammatical category is striking. For example, Buckingham & Kertesz (1976) report of their patient B.F. that 182 of 209 neologisms could be identified as to grammatical category; and of those, 134 (73.6%) were nouns and 43 (23.6%) verbs. In Butterworth's (1979) analysis of patient, K.F., he reported that 61% of classifiable neologisms were nouns, 20% verbs, 14% adjectives. Further evidence for this powerful effect of grammatical category has been documented by Lecours (1980); that evidence is reproduced in Table 8.3. It appears, from all these studies, that major lexical content is particularly vulnerable to neologistic distortion, syntactic morphology much less so—just the converse of the pattern of vulnerabilities that characterise agrammatic aphasia.

This basic generalisation is clearly upheld in C.B.'s description of the cookie theft picture. In that speech sample paraphasic distortions, including

TABLE 8.3

Distribution by Grammatical Category of 447 Abstruse Neologisms Arising in the Speech of a Wernicke's Aphasic (after Lecours, 1980)

Category	No.	%	Category	No.	%
Nouns:	284	64	Articles:	0	0
Adjectives:	27	6	Pronouns:	0	0
Verbs:	74	17	Prepositions:	0	0
Names:	32	7	Conjunctions:	0	0
Lexical adverbs:	5	1	Relative pronouns:	0	0
Unclassifiable:	25	6			

---

[4]Fromkin (1971) points out that the explanation for the non-occurrence in the language of these sequences does not lie in their non-pronounceability, since both are uttered easily across word boundaries, e.g., girl's grades; at large.

abstruse neologisms, occur only in slots marked for nouns, adjectives, and verbs; or, to be more precise, the root morphemes of those categories. These root neologisms are inflected by bona fide affixes of the language (and see Buckingham & Kertesz, 1976; Butterworth, 1979; Caplan, Keller & Locke, 1972; Lecours & Rouillon, 1976); and while the particular inflection may not always be appropriate to the syntactic context, it is nevertheless the case that rule-governed constraints of their pronunciation do apply.

Thus, consider in C.B.'s transcript the neologisms *ek·spresh·ez* and *ah·grash·enz*. Judging from the prior context, "these were", these utterances represent iterated substitutions for an intended plural noun phrase, so that their underlying morphological structure can be construed to be of the form: *ek·spresh + pl.* and *ah·grash·en + pl.*[5] If this is so, it is of substantial interest that this plural affix is realised by different, and correct, pronunciations in the two cases, /əz/ in the first, /z/ in the second. It is the case in English that the pronunciation of the plural inflection is conditioned by preceding phonetic context, in accordance with a set of "morphophonemic" rules. These rules also determine the form of the indefinite article: /e/, /ʌ/, or /æn/, among other things. The fact that the lexically deformed speech of the Wernicke's aphasic tends to conform to these morphophonemic rules reinforces the general impression that the vocabulary of syntactic morphemes is somehow shielded from that mechanism or mechanisms that yields paraphasic distortion, just as it is selectively vulnerable to whatever process of deformation underlies agrammatism.

One further contrast between the agrammatic and paraphasic speaker concerns the status of syntactic structures. Earlier I indicated that one component of the agrammatic syndrome is a breakdown in the ability to construct noun and verb phrases and to coordinate these into well-formed clauses. In this context, it is noteworthy that whereas narratives produced by Wernicke patients generally reveal little in the way of syntactical complexity and diversity (Gleason et al, 1980), the occasional occurrence of well-formed constructions of considerable complexity attests to the integrity of the process by which constituent phrases are constructed and hierarchically integrated. Perhaps the most impressive demonstration comes from Buckingham & Kertesz's (1976) study of the spoken discourse of three jargon aphasics, which provided evidence that even where neologisms distort the target message beyond recognition, complex syntactic structures involving sentential coordination and subordination are still discernible. The following examples are taken from the Buckingham & Kertesz's monograph:

---

[5]There are other ways to interpret these neologisms. For example, *expreshez* might have arisen from a phonemic substitution on the target *expresses*, i.e., *express + 3rd person sing.* If so, however, it would violate the well supported generalisation that neologisms preserve the grammatical category of the target (see text).

1. It was quite a number of reeze down here and we flash done (p. 65).
2. I appreciate that farshethe, because they have protocertive (p. 66).
3. I have no one that's somebody that's no body that's doing, and I haven't anybody who die . . . (p. 68).
4. I would say that the mik daysis nosis or chpicters (p. 70).[6]

Summary

The phenomena of ´aphasic speech discussed so far clearly fall outside the scope of the classical neuroanatomical model. Because these phenomena tend to implicate linguistic phenomena at the level of phrase, clause and sentence, they require explanation within the context of a model of sentence production. Before turning to one such model, it is useful to review the facts to be accounted for.

There is, first of all, the distinction between two vocabulary types. One, the vocabulary of major lexical items (nouns, verbs, adjectives) communicates the major semantic and referential distinctions. The other, grammatical morphemes both free and bound, supports the syntactic organisation of the sentence. These two vocabularies behave differently from one another in agrammatism and again in Wernicke's aphasia.

Inability to access or articulate grammatical morphemes will necessarily impose a limit on sentence complexity and coherence; but many agrammatic aphasics seem to experience added difficulty in constructing phrases and clauses beyond that which can be attributed to the morphological impairment. For example, an ongoing cross-linguistic study of agrammatism reports that a particularly robust and ubiquitous characteristic of agrammatic narrative discourse is the absence of noun modifiers, including adjectives and other nouns (Obler, Menn, & Goodglass, 1983). My colleagues and I have confirmed this finding in a sentence repetition task: English speaking agrammatics made frequent errors repeating sentences with prenominal adjectives in subject or object noun phrases; their tendency was to omit these prenominal modifiers or transpose them into predicate-adjective forms (Ostrin, Schwartz, & Saffran, 1983).

Case study reports have shown that this sort of construction deficit can be doubly dissociated from the morphological simplification that is the hallmark of agrammatic aphasia (e.g., Miceli et al., 1963; Saffran et al., 1980a; Tissot et al., 1973). Nevertheless, there is a strong tendency for the two features to co-occur in the speech of patients classified as agrammatics, and

---

[6]This neologism, [tʃpɪktʏz], violates the generalisation, stated above, that non-permissible consonant clusters do not occur in neologistic jargon aphasia. The patient who uttered this sentence produced a total 37 neologisms beginning with consonant clusters; this was the only one that violated the sound-sequencing conventions of English.

for both features to be absent from the jargon-filled speech of the Wernicke aphasic.

The major lexical items undergo distortion in the speech of the jargon aphasic, but the nature of the distortion implicates several different aspects of lexical knowledge. Thus, the jargon aphasic tends to select words wrongly on the basis of their semantic descriptions and to distort the segmental phonemic structure of the targets he does retrieve; on the other hand, his speech does not violate those rules of the language that condition permissible segmental sequences by phonetic and syntactic context. In this respect, too, there is a marked contrast to be drawn with the agrammatic Broca's aphasic.

A PSYCHOLINGUISTIC MODEL OF SENTENCE PRODUCTION

With this summary in mind, we move on to consider an account of the process of sentence generation in normal speakers. This model owes its detailed articulation to psycholinguist Merrill Garrett, but the line of precursors is long (e.g., Fromkin, 1971; Goldman-Eisler, 1968; Lashley, 1951; Pick, 1931).

Garrett's characterisation of sentence production as a sequence of independent processing levels, each corresponding to one or more levels of linguistic representation (Fig. 8.3) falls well within the scope of a psycholinguistic theory, as defined in the introduction. It is not a complete theory, however, since Garrett has chosen to remain agnostic on the question of how these linguistic levels should be formally represented. The reason for this is not the unavailability of candidate formalisms, for candidates do exist. It is, rather, Garrett's firm commitment to build into the theory only as much detail as is warranted by the data base (Garrett, 1980, p. 215). I have allowed myself somewhat greater freedom in presenting Garrett's model here. Thus, in Figs. 8.4 and 8.5 and in the text below, assumptions are made about the form of the representations achieved at the various processing levels that go beyond Garrett's exposition. These notational details are added for clarity of explication. They are not strictly motivated by the data base.

What is the data base for a theory of production? How does an investigator gain insight into the sequence of mental operations that intervene between the thought and the articulation of a message? A surprisingly rich source of information has been slips-of-the-tongue, the speech errors that normal people occasionally make in otherwise fluent discourse. It has proven possible to classify these speech errors on the basis of their form, their distributional features, and the contexts in which they occur. From these facts about speech errors, inferences can be made about the underlying mental operations and the sequence in which they occur. Such is the

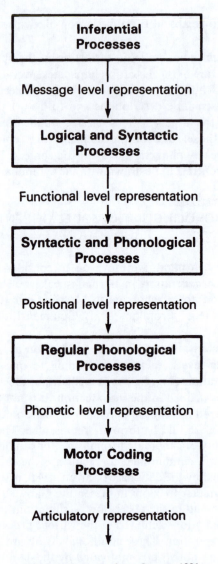

FIG. 8.3   Redrawn from Garrett, 1981.

endeavour that motivated the model of speech production presented in Figs. 8.3, 8.4, and 8.5.

Further discussion of these speech error facts would take us too far afield. The reader interested in more detailed exposition is referred to Garrett (1975; 1980). Additional discussion of the relation between speech errors and aphasic language is available in Buckingham (1980); Garrett (1981; 1982); Garnsey & Dell (1984). A general introduction to the subject of speech errors is available in Fromkin, 1973.

Let us consider now how this model would operate to generate the sentence "The girl gives flowers to the teacher" which, we saw earlier, posed so much difficulty for agrammatic aphasics (Table 8.1).

The process of sentence construction begins when the conceptual and inferential operations of the non-linguistic *message level* trigger a search through the mental lexicon. This lexical search, the first of two incorporated into the model, is responsive to the meaning of the lexical entries and to their grammatical category; it is not concerned with pronunciation. The outcome of this search is a set of abstract entities that correspond to the simple surface vocabulary of the language (Garrett, 1982) but are not yet specified for form. The entries so selected constitute the major lexical content of the sentence: the nouns, verbs, and adjectives that will carry the referential load of the utterance. In our example, this initial search through the lexicon will yield the verb *give*, and three nouns, *girl, flower, teacher*.

The selection of lexical content is one of three operations that characterise the *functional level* of representation. The second is the creation of a predicate/argument structure; the third, the assignment of lexical items to roles within that structure. Together, these operations yield a representation of the who-does-what-to-whom information to be communicated. In Fig. 8.4, what is specified is the action *giving* along with its three noun arguments: the agent of the action, *girl*, the object, *flowers*, and the beneficiary, *teacher*.

It is important to emphasise the abstractness of this functional level representation. The lexical content, to repeat, is not specified for pronunciation. And the argument structure is similarly indifferent to form, that is, to the serial order of the lexical items and to the details of the phrasal environments in which they will occur. The functional argument structure shown in Fig. 8.4 is compatible with a variety of surface manifestations: *the girl gives flowers to the teacher; flowers are given to the teacher by the girl; the girl gives the teacher flowers.*[7]

On the model, deciding how the argument structure will actually be expressed amounts to the selection of a particular *planning frame*. The presumption is that this selection is guided by various pragmatic and discourse considerations operating at the message level, as well as by

---

[7]Garrett does not commit himself to degree of correspondence between the functional structure and the surface manifestation. Indeed, he admits that certain considerations might lead one to argue for considerable similarity for the two, noting further that "There is little in the error process to deny such a move, one which "demotes" the functional level to a seemingly less abstract level (1980, p. 217)."

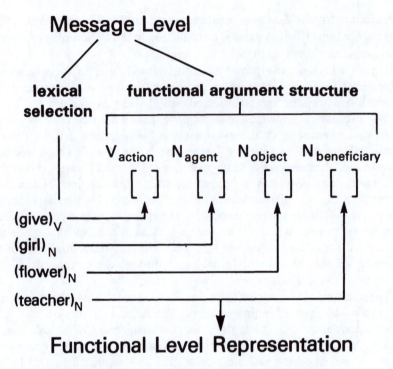

Message Level

lexical selection

functional argument structure

V_{action} N_{agent} N_{object} N_{beneficiary}

[ ]   [ ]   [ ]   [ ]

(give)_V

(girl)_N

(flower)_N

(teacher)_N

Functional Level Representation

FIG. 8.4   Redrawn, with modification, from Garrett, 1981.

functional level descriptions. Be that as it may, we have the characterisation of the planning frame as instantiating the specific phrasal geometry of the sentence through an ordered sequence of features and slots. The features of the frame are syntactic morphemes and markers of emphatic stress and sentence prosody. The slots designate points of insertion for the major lexical content. However, and this is a critical point, the entities targeted for slots are not those abstract formatives contacted on the first pass through the lexicon but rather phonemically interpreted versions of these. Thus, by this point in the construction of the sentence there has occurred a second pass through the mental lexicon, this time in search of the sound-based (segmental) forms corresponding to the abstract entities arrayed at the functional level. It is the output of this second search that gets inserted into the slots of the planning frame.

Shattuck-Hufnagel (1979; 1983) has used the evidence from speech errors to construct a "scan-copier" model of how these interpreted lexical items are inserted, phoneme by phoneme, into the planning frame. The evidence comes largely from the various sorts of errors that deform the phonemic structure of the target sentence, in particular, sound exchanges like "*putting and casting*" (for *cutting and pasting*). As noted by Garrett, these sound exchange errors display two important properties: they occur within phrases, and they tend to involve members of the open class vocabulary. These constraints on sound exchanges call for an account of lexical insertion that: (a) maintains the computational distinctiveness of the open and closed class vocabulary; and (b) recognises the phrase as the unit over which insertion takes place.

On Garrett's model, this act of inserting phonemically interpreted lexical items into a frame featuring syntactic morphemes amounts to one step in the creation of the *positional level*. As the lexical segments are copied into slots, the output is acted upon by lower level phonological processes that accomplish: (1) the phonetic encoding of the supporting syntactic elements; and (2) the detailed phonetic elaboration of the major lexical content. Why this sequence of events? The reasoning follows from our earlier discussion of the morphophonemic rules of English.

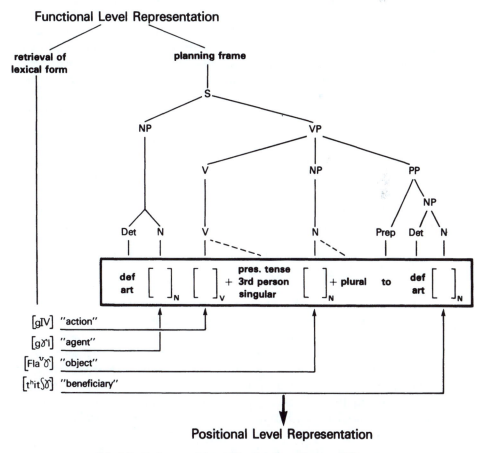

FIG. 8.5   Redrawn, with modification, from Garrett, 1981.

Consider the requirement for pluralisation marked in the planning frame of Fig. 8.5. How is that suffix to be phonetically realised? The answer will depend on what has been inserted into the preceding slot. If the slot has been filled by the lexical formative *flower* /flaʊɤ/, the final segment /ɤ/ will condition the voiced variant of the plural morpheme, i.e., /z/. Had the speaker instead selected the lexical formative *violet*, the final /t/ segment of that word would have conditioned instead the unvoiced variant of the plural, /s/.

In the slips-of-the-tongue that normal speakers make, it is quite clear that the phonetic specification of these syntactic elements arises late in the sentence planning process. Consider this speech error, discussed by Fromkin (1971):

> intended: *cow tracks*/træk + s/
> uttered: *track cows*/kaʊ + z/

This slip involves what Garrett calls a "stranding exchange": an exchange of two lexical formatives, presumably at the point of assignment to the planning frame (Garrett, 1980). The very fact that the exchange leaves behind, i.e., "strands" the plural inflection, supports the computational distinctiveness of lexical formatives and their bound affixes. The point at issue, however, is that the phonetic variant of the plural in the phrase uttered, /z/, is appropriate to the exchanged formative, *cow*, rather than the intended formative, *track*. This must mean that the relevant morphophonemic rules operated after the occurrence of the exchange, i.e., after /træk/ and /kaʊ/ had been assigned their erroneous positions within the positional representation.

This point can perhaps be made more clearly with the following slip, reported in Garrett (1975):

> intended: *an aunt's money*
> uttered: *a money's aunt*

Here again an exchange of lexical formatives has "stranded" an element of the planning frame, this time the possessive marker. The interesting point here, however, concerns the indefinite article. Had this element been spelled out prior to the occurrence of the exchange, the resulting utterance would have been of the form: *an money's aunt*. The fact that its morphophonemic form was instead conditioned by the post-exchange environment constitutes further evidence that the spelling out of these elements that define planning frames goes on *after* the creation of the positional level has begun.

These "accommodations" of syntactic morphology to the altered environments of slips-of-the-tongue are of course reminiscent of what we find in the neologistic jargon of the Wernicke's aphasic. There is a second parallel, too, having to do with the phonological well-formedness of speech errors; like neologisms, slips-of-the-tongue rarely violate the phonological conventions of the language spoken.

In his discussion of the speech error data, Garrett provides a single explanation for both the accommodations of syntactic morphology and the phonological well-formedness of slips. Both, he claims, result from the normal operation of "automatic rule-governed sequencing procedures" that apply to a positional representation underspecified for phonetic form. These sequencing procedures incorporate not only the morphophonemic rules that apply to syntactic elements, but also the phonological rules that determine the ultimate pronunciation of segments in combination. In both cases, that phonetic detail is supplied that is not tied to any particular lexical content, but is rather predictable from local phrasal and segmental environments (Garrett, 1980). It is uncertain whether these automatic sound-sequencing procedures operate in slips-of-the-tongue by rejecting error outputs that violate the morphological or phonological conventions of the language, or by converting those outputs into others that are well-formed. Either way, the conclusion is clear: these automatic sound-sequencing procedures can continue to operate unimpaired in jargon aphasia.

SENTENCE PRODUCTION IN WERNICKE'S APHASIA

In the preceding discussion I have focussed on what is right about sentence production in the jargon aphasic. The phonological well-formedness of the neologistic paraphasias and of the grammatical morphology uttered in the environment of neologisms both point to the preservation of the automatic, rule-governed sound sequencing operations that apply at the late stages of sentence planning in normal speakers. Where, then, does the planning process go awry for the Wernicke's aphasic? An obvious place to look is in the mechanisms of lexical retrieval.

Garrett's model incorporates a "dual retrieval" account of lexical selection, i.e., two passes through the mental lexicon. On the first pass, the match is made on the basis of meaning and category features, the output of the search assembled into the functional argument structure. The second pass through the lexicon involves a look-up for sound-based structures associated with the entries selected on the first pass. The outputs of that second search are assigned ordered positions via the planning frame.

The argument can be made that Wernicke's aphasics suffer a disruption of both stages of this dual retrieval process. When, on the first pass through the lexicon, the semantic and categorical specification fails to yield a correct match, the result is an unrelated verbal paraphasia (in those cases where selection has been totally unconstrained), or a semantic paraphasia (where selection has been imperfectly constrained). In contrast, paraphasias of the phonemic type arise later, at the second lexical pass, when selected lexical targets contact form-based representations that have been rendered unstable, or minimally degraded. Note that this dual model easily handles those cases in which a phonemic paraphasia occurs to a semantic substitution, as in the *girl→boy→meoy* case. Note, too, that a similar mechanism can be invoked to explain the origin of the so-called abstruse neologisms: if the output of the first lexical pass is an entity unrelated by meaning or perhaps even by category to the intended target, and if phonemic distortion of this entry occurs on the second retrieval phase, then the result will be likely to be unrecognisable to the listener. We need only postulate that the output of such a two-phase error will be subject to the rule-governed sound sequencing procedures that presumably block unlawful phonetic sequences, and we have a quite reasonable account of the form and variety of paraphasic utterances.

Even more impressive is the fact that the distribution of paraphasias in the speech of the jargon aphasic fall out as a necessary consequence of this account. Recall that the dual retrieval process applies only to major lexical items.[8] The syntactic morphemes are not targets of this search; presumably, the storage principles and access codes for these morphemes are of a very different sort.[9] Where one or both aspects of the dual retrieval process are compromised by brain damage, then, the consequences should be apparent in the deformation of the major lexical content but not those syntactic elements featured on planning frames.

---

[8]Complications arise when we consider the status of prepositions within this category of syntactic morphemes. While it is true that prepositions behave in many ways like other features of planning frames, it is also true that they engage in speech error "exchanges" otherwise restricted to nouns, verbs, and adjectives (Garrett, 1980). Moreover, there are good linguistic reasons for believing that prepositions are represented in deep (i.e., functional argument) structures, and stored lexically in much the same way as other major lexical formatives. These facts about prepositions may have important implications for the future elaboration of production models, and, ultimately, for a theory of agrammatism (Kean, 1979; 1980).

[9]These claims concerning the special status of grammatical morphemes in the mental lexicon are subjects of considerable dispute at the moment. For example, Bradley's 1978 dissertation work presented strong support in the form of evidence showing that (a) in a lexical decision task, reaction times for function words and content words showed different frequency sensitivity functions and (b) that the two vocabulary types behave differently with respect to the non-word interference effect. Both sets of findings have been challenged (Gordon & Caramazza, 1982; Kolk & Blomert, 1985; Segui et al., 1982). In particular, Gordon & Caramazza's evidence strongly suggests that Bradley's frequency finding is an artifact of the frequency ranges of the two vocabulary types, i.e., the over-representation of function words at the very high frequency end. This same fact has recently been appealed to by Ellis et al. (1983) as an alternative account for the non-participation of function words in the neologistic jargon of Wernicke's aphasics. Their evidence comes from one patient's performance on a single-word reading test, the findings being that for function words as well as concrete nouns, the likelihood of paraphasic distortion increased with decreasing word frequency. It is my view that single-word access tasks may have very little to tell us about the lexical search space and search operations employed in the process of sentence generation. For example, syntactic category information is not at issue in word recognition but it is the heart of the matter in sentence generation.

Let us return now to the consideration of where, in the sentence planning process, abstruse neologisms arise. In the two-stage account given above, abstruse neologisms are attributed to phonemic distortions of intended targets (e.g., Brown, 1977; Kertesz & Benson, 1970; Luria, 1970; Pick, 1931). But careful inspection of the neologistic utterances of jargon aphasics has demonstrated that this cannot be the complete account. One piece of evidence is that these entities often turn out to bear a sound-based relation not to any conceivable lexical target, but rather to *one another*. Thus, one hears from the Wernicke's aphasic stretches of neologistic jargon in which particular phonemic segments are repeated again and again, either in repetitive "chains", or in neologisms iterated across phrases or clauses (Buckingham & Kertesz, 1976; Buckingham, Whitaker, & Whitaker, 1978; Green, 1969). Indeed, Butterworth (1979) reports of a single jargon aphasic that phonologically related neologisms constituted the majority of all his neologisms uttered.

It is reasonable to suggest that neologisms of this sort arise under conditions in which the (second) dictionary look-up for lexical forms comes up empty, i.e., where no segmental information at all is available about a lexical target. How, on our model, could such lexical "gaps" arise? One possibility is that the failure occurs earlier, on the first lexical pass, such that there is no specification of the lexical targets available to the second pass operation (Buckingham, 1980; 1981). Alternatively, the lexical specification might be unimpaired, but the phonemic representation itself unavailable (Butterworth, Swallow, & Grimston, 1981; Ellis, Miller, & Sin, 1983).

The crucial point would seem to be that regardless of how they arise, such lexical gaps are filled, in jargon aphasia, by the output of some sort of neologism-producing "device" that selects units from the speaker's repertoire of phonemes (Butterworth, 1979) or syllables (Buckingham, 1981) and strings them together in accordance with the phonotactic constraints of the language.

A question of great importance is whether such a "device" can be accounted for in terms of the operation of those automatic sound-sequencing procedures described above. If not, we may be in the undesirable position of having to attribute to the jargon aphasic a unique language capacity which is not part of the normal sentence planning machinery, but which is rather created *de novo* as a consequence of the disease process. (For discussion of the status of these entities in neurolinguistic theory, see Caplan, 1981; and for arguments against their general applicability, Saffran, 1982).

The Uncoupling of Semantically- and Phonologically-Based Difficulties

We have seen that in order to account for the varieties of paraphasia in the speech of the Wernicke's aphasic it is necessary to postulate a breakdown in both phases of the dual retrieval system. The question arises whether this coupling is inevitable. If not, we should expect to see subgroups of patients showing one or another impairment; if so, we might want to question the model's assertion of strict independence between these retrieval operations.

In fact, Dell & Reich (1981) have challenged this aspect of Garrett's model on the basis of additional evidence from speech errors, natural and experimentally elicited. As an alternative to a lexicon structured into files with distinct access codes, these authors build into a Garrett-like model a lexicon organised in network fashion, with nodes representing linguistic units of all sorts: semantic features, words, morphemes, phonemes, phonemic features. Then:

> Retrieval processes in this lexical network occur by spreading activation with each activated node sending a proportion of its activation to all nodes connecting to it. Connections are assumed to reflect the composition of units, for example, semantic feature nodes connect to word nodes that define them, word nodes connect (*sic*) phoneme nodes that spell out the words, and phoneme nodes connect to their proper feature nodes (p. 627)

Descriptive constraints at the various levels of representation drive the retrieval process: message level descriptions drive the search for word units corresponding to particular semantic features; planning frames guide the search for words of particular grammatical class, and so on. However, at any level the targets that are available for selection will have been influenced by "irrelevant" factors as a result of spreading activation. Thus Dell & Reich give an example in which the activation of words targeted under a particular grammatical description results in the spread of activation to other words that do not necessarily share that grammatical description but that do have certain phoneme nodes in common. As an explanation for the observed phonological influences on errors presumed to arise at the functional level, they note that "a competing word will have more activation (and thus an increased chance of being mistakenly selected) if it is both semantically similar (sharing semantic nodes) and phonologically similar (sharing phonemic nodes) to the intended word (p. 628)".

At first blush such a model of lexical access would seem just the thing to handle the observed co-occurrence patterns in jargon aphasia. But let us take a closer look. Semantic paraphasias arise, on this model, when threshold activation is achieved by competing word units sharing semantic nodes with the target. This is most likely to happen when other, non-semantic, nodes are also shared. On the one hand, this provides a ready explanation for why semantic paraphasias respect grammatical role; on the other hand, it predicts a definite influence of phonological similarity on semantic paraphasias. Such an influence has yet to be demonstrated. Buckingham (1981, p. 202) presents the results of an analysis of 37 semantic paraphasias produced by a jargon speaker over four interview sessions. In only one case did the substituted word share the initial phoneme of the target; eight of the 37 substitutions also differed from the target in number of syllables. (These are the two most salient dimensions of phonological similarity reflected in normal speech error data.)

On this sort of spreading activation model of lexical access, it is natural to account for the prevalence of semantic paraphasias in jargon aphasia by postulating some problem with the activation process, perhaps some sort of imbalance between activating and inhibitory influences. There is no reason to suppose that such an imbalance would be selective for particular linguistic features and so the expectation is that retrieval processes responsive to phonological descriptions would be similarly compromised. Unfortunately, however, the types of phonological errors predicted do not correspond to what is actually observed.

On the analogy with semantic paraphasias, phonemic paraphasias should take the form of word substitutions, where the substituted word shares phonemic rather than semantic nodes. Buckingham (1981) reviewed the evidence for substitutions of this sort in jargon aphasia and finds remarkably few instances that merit classification as sound-based word substitutions. Diane Bloch, a graduate student at the University of Pennsylvania, has confirmed Buckingham's impression in her own analysis of the speech sample of two jargon aphasics. One type of analysis focussed on those instances in which a target word was replaced by another actual word of English. The first patient produced 38 such substitutions, of which nine were related by meaning and only one by form; the second made 58 substitutions, seven of them meaning related, one related by form (as well as meaning: "*next floor* (door) *we have.* . . .").

On the other hand, the sort of phonemic paraphasia that abounds in jargon aphasia, the sort that transforms the target word into a highly similar non-word, is not expected on the Dell & Reich model, which predicts strong lexical biases based on the notion that "spreading activation acts automatically as an editor and turns the pattern into a word (p. 628)".

Having seen, then, that the existing evidence offers little support to this alternative to the dual retrieval account of lexical access, we can turn attention to the possibility that semantic and phonological disturbances undergo dissociation in subsets of aphasic patients. In fact, Ellis et al. (1983) argue that such dissociations are observable even within the category of Wernicke's aphasia. It is their conclusion that a review of the literature reveals three "pure" varieties of Wernicke's aphasia, each characterised by one major symptom: conceptual disorder (manifested in well-formed but rambling, incoherent speech); verbal paraphasia (semantic and unrelated); and neologisms (including phonemic paraphasias). They offer their patient, R.D., as an example of this last, phonemically-based variety, and provide an account that corresponds quite closely to one proposed by Butterworth

(1979): these patients are capable of activating adequate semantic representations for target words but are often unable to fully activate the corresponding phonological form. In these instances where a partial phonological specification is achieved, and pronunciation nevertheless attempted, the result is a phonemic paraphasia ("target-related neologism", in their terminology). Where still less phonological detail is available, a neologism is "assembled."

It is my view that this variety of jargon aphasia can be "purified" still further, and this condition arises as part of an evolutionary process, when the jargon speaker begins to edit his or her output so as to censor blatant neologistic utterances. At that point, the lack of availability of full phonological specifications is more likely to result in fragmented pronunciations, in iterated approximations, or in attempts at pronunciation that may actually be quite far afield from the target. The characterisation I have in mind here is one that is frequently observed in the condition known as "conduction aphasia" (e.g., Goodglass & Kaplan, 1982; Kohn, 1984; Lecours, 1980).

Syntactic Processes in Jargonaphasia

Implicit in the discussion to this point is the claim that in Wernicke's aphasia the constructional aspects of sentence production are not compromised. Certainly, the complexity of phrase and clause structure in their language is compelling evidence, as is the preservation of syntactic morphology. It does not follow, however, that the sentences of these patients are, or should be on the model, syntactically well-formed. For example, the faulty selection of lexical items on the first lexical pass will result, in at least some cases, in the creation of anomalous functional argument structures in which selectional and subcategorisation constraints are violated. This may provide the explanation for the frequent violations of restrictions on permissible word sequences, e.g.,

Now, I've own the sun would quiet (Buckingham & Kertesz, 1976)

But errors like these constitute only a subset of the violations seen in jargon aphasia and grouped under the label "paragrammatism" (Goodglass, 1976). Other violations, especially those involving AUX-Verb morphology, are less obviously attributed to these "deeper" levels of sentence formation, e.g.,

Because ya know at one time I didn't have written (Caplan, Keller, & Locke, 1972)

It is the existence of errors like these that have led some to postulate syntactic processing deficits in jargon aphasia that are distinct from their problems in lexical selection and/or retrieval (e.g. Goodglass & Menn, 1985;

Menn at al., 1982; Parisi, Chapter 9). But this is a premature conclusion; until we can commit ourselves more definitively to the nature and form of information represented at the functional level; and until we can say just how it is that the programming of the planning frame is influenced by descriptive constraints represented at the functional level, it will not be possible to say with any assurance what are the necessary implications for syntactic well-formedness of an impairment arising at these "deeper" levels of sentence organisation (but see LaPointe, 1983 for some interesting suggestions). In the meantime it is crucial that we gather more data on the characteristics of paragrammatism occurring in patients with different degrees and different types of lexical access difficulties. For example, the move to relegate paragrammatism to a deficit in semantically-driven lexical access carries the prediction that lexical disorders of a strictly phonological type should not be associated with paragrammatism. It is my impression that is in fact true. There is particular need for longitudinal case studies charting the recovery process from jargon aphasia. The prediction from the present thesis is that recovery from paragrammatism will prove to be tightly coupled to the dropping out of verbal and semantic paraphasias, but not phonemic para-phasias.

Summary

It appears that the speech production problems in Wernicke's aphasia are readily explicated within this model of normal sentence production. The varieties of paraphasic distortions, and their distribution within the sentence, implicate the inventories that represent, on the one hand, the meanings and grammatical category of words, and on the other hand, their segmental form. The possibilities are that one or another (or both) of these knowledge stores contains impoverished information; or that the retrieval operations that draw upon this stored information are faulty. If history serves us right (see Coltheart's introduction), it will turn out to be necessary to invoke all possibilities in order to account for patterns of individual variation.

SENTENCE PRODUCTION DEFICITS IN AGRAMMATIC BROCA'S APHASICS

Perhaps the most striking characteristic of the production model under discussion is the sharp distinction it draws between the vocabulary of content words and the vocabulary of grammatical morphemes. These two vocabular-ies are computationally distinct; up through the creation of the phonological (i.e., positional) representation, they do not interact. Thus, grammatical morphemes are not retrieved from the mental dictionary along with the noun, verb, and adjective formatives. Instead, they are selected as part and parcel of that configuration that defines the phrasal geometry of the utterance (i.e., the planning frame). Furthermore, as discussed earlier, phonetic realisation of at least a subset of these grammatical morphemes occurs late in the course of sentence planning, via the application of the automatic sound-sequencing procedures that operate over positional representations. At the point at which such rules apply, the lexical formatives have been phonemically interpreted. The syntactic morphemes, on the other hand, are represented more abstractly. In Fig. 8.5 I have these specified at the positional level by definitional features, but this is another notional detail that is not strictly motivated by the data.

On this formulation, then, there are two distinct points in the sentence planning process at which a disruption, should it arise, would have the effect of selectively compromising the vocabulary of syntactic morphemes: the application of automatic sound-sequencing procedures, and the selection/ creation of planning frames.

In an earlier paper (Saffran et al., 1980a), my colleagues and I attributed the agrammatic's difficulty in realising syntactic morphemes to a breakdown at the level of the automatic sound-sequencing procedures. On this account, the morphemes are adequately specified at the positional level; however, they are not subject to translation into articulatory commands. A patient suffering from such an impairment would have in mind a model of the well-formed target, i.e., he would know what sort of inflection on the verb was appropriate to the intended message, even while leaving the verb uninflected. Thus the account readily captures the behaviour that many agrammatics display when speaking: the tendency to self-correct and to strive towards the well-formed target (Goodglass, Gleason, Bernholz, & Hyde, 1972). It is also consistent with the fact that the likelihood of omission of a syntactic morpheme is to a degree influenced by the phonological form of the morpheme (i.e., whether syllabic or non-syllabic) and by its relation to the stress contour of the sentence (Goodglass, 1968).

Another virtue of this account is the prediction it makes concerning the coupling of the morphological and phonetic deficits in agrammatism. Recall that in the earlier discussion of the automatic sound-sequencing procedures it was noted that these procedures not only spell out the phonetic variants of syntactic morphemes, they also specify the details of pronunciation for the major lexical formatives, for example, that the segment /p/ will be articulated with aspiration when it occurs in word- or syllable-initial position but without aspiration when it occurs within a syllable. As shown in Fig. 8.3, the output of these sound-sequencing procedures (the phonetic level representation), is acted upon by motor-coding processes to accomplish the sequence of articulatory gestures. It follows, then, that a deficit that compromises these sound-sequencing operations will necessarily result in impaired articulation.

If the account just given succeeds in explaining why it is that the tendency to omit grammatical morphemes arises so often in conjunction with the articulation problem that defines Broca's aphasia, it fares less well in explaining why it is that these two features of agrammatism so often co-occur with a third: the difficulty in phrasal construction. In Saffran et al., 1980a we suggested that the morphological and constructional aspects implicate different levels of the speech production system. In attempting to characterise the latter, we relied heavily on a patient who appeared to show agrammatic-like constructional difficulties in the absence of morphological simplification or phonetic disintegration. The patient in question had difficulty generating complete phrases, in particular verb phrases, and even more difficulty coordinating these phrases at the level of the clause. His problems frequently involved the failure to access verbs and locative prepositions. Here, for example, is his attempt to describe a picture showing a cat peeping out from behind an armchair:

> *"The sofa . . . the . . . cat leans the . . . the cat leans the sofa up . . . the cat and the sofa and the sofa . . . the cat un-under the sofa." (p. 235)*

In Saffran et al. (1980a), we went on to pinpoint a locus for this constructional deficit in the creation of functional argument structures: "In general, it can be said that the (agrammatic) patients have difficulty producing linguistic structures that encode relations, whether these structures are morphemes—verbs or prepositions—or sentences. Thus they are unable to 'propositionise', to use Jackson's (1878) early characterisation of the deficit (p. 239)."

I would like to offer now an alternative conception of the constructional deficit in agrammatism, whereby it comes about as a necessary accompaniment to a morphological impairment operating at the level of planning frames. In setting forth this account, I will be relying on the theoretical work of Steven LaPointe, although my account diverges from his at several points, as will be clear below.

LaPointe (1983), in an attempt to formalise the morphological properties of items inserted into syntactic frames, has provided some very interesting suggestions about how a deficit in creating planning frames might arise, and what its consequences would be. On his account, the processes that construct positional representations have access to a store of "prepackaged fragments of morphosyntactic structures, with the fragments consisting of minimal lexically-headed phrases (NP, VP, etc.) containing a lexical head stem, various grammatical markers, and positions indicating where other fragments are to be attached (p. 31)." "Lexical head stems" are the entities stored in the mental lexicon. They are the entities to which productive affixation applies; that is to say, they are the stems to which inflectional and derivational affixes will attach.

Here are two of LaPointe's examples of prepackaged VP fragments, illustrating different degrees of morphosyntactic complexity:

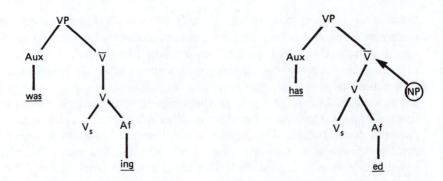

Fragments like these are retrieved and integrated on the basis of the semantic information provided at the functional level. Lexical stem nodes (e.g. V_s) mark the insertion points for phonemically interpreted lexical formatives made available by the second search through the lexicon. The circled NP in the right-hand fragment indicates that an NP fragment is to be attached at this point.

To account for the agrammatic's tendency to omit syntactic morphemes, LaPointe postulates "disruption in the ability to output these fragments from the fragment store, such that the more complex the fragment in terms of more fully elaborated morphosyntactic structure, the more difficult it is to output, although the information from the Functional Level about *which* fragments are to be selected is not itself impaired (p. 33)." As a consequence of this disruption, "whatever fragments are produced will be simplified both in terms of the relative absence of grammatical markers and in terms of the markers indicating where complement and modifier phrases are supposed to be attached (p. 33)."

This account succeeds in capturing several aspects of the agrammatic's morphological deficit, e.g., the preference for simple over complex auxiliaries; the tendency to substitute singular for plural nouns; the omission of determiners. Other aspects are more problematic. In B.L.'s utterance "Wife is dry dishes" we have an example of the omission of a verb inflection that is obligatory given the presence of the aux. Here, the presumption would have to be that the structure retrieved for output is of the form:

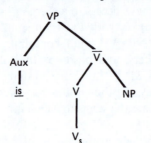

but there is no independent reason for including this structure in the inventory of English VPs. Thus, if LaPointe's account is to accommodate phenomena like these (which are extremely common in agrammatism) it is necessary to postulate not only that the inventory of available morphosyntactic fragments is restricted to the less complex forms, but, in addition, those forms that do remain available are pathologically degraded or simplified still further.

Be that as it may, the account also seems to have important implications for various aspects of phrasal construction and coordination. (These implications are not recognised by LaPointe.) As I interpret it, the proposed restriction in the fragment inventory to morphosyntactically simpler forms implies a bias in the direction of unexpanded phrases. For example, since NP fragments that contain adjective phrase nodes are more complex than those that do not (other things being equal), it should be the case that the latter will sometimes be retrieved for output even where the functional level description calls for the noun to be modified. This would account for the underuse of prenominal modifiers by agrammatic speakers noted earlier. Similarly, since intransitive verb fragments are simpler *ceterus parabus* than transitive fragments, the search for the latter will not infrequently turn up the former. Consider such a situation arising where the target utterance is "The boy is kissing the girl." I presume that under the guidance of the functional level description, and operating within the constraint of a limited fragment inventory, three morphosyntactic fragments are selected, and filled, as follows:

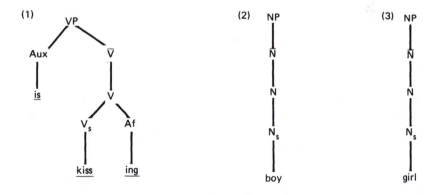

The problem comes at the point of assembling these fragments at the positional level. The direct object has not been integrated into the verb phrase (which does not contain a NP node) and hence there are two NPs available for selection as grammatical subject. Conceivably, this is the locus of the word order problem discussed earlier. Let us see how this might work.

At the functional level *boy* is labelled as the agent of the kissing action; but this information does not by itself constrain the choice of the grammatical subject. The choice is governed in addition by the type of VP fragment (i.e., passive VP fragment calls for the assignment of patient to subject position). Now, it would seem that the VP fragment shown above, were it to be selected, should suffice to mark the active voice form of the verb, and hence the selection of *boy* as subject. If so, there should be no word order problem here, although there might well be in those cases where the VP fragment retrieved for output is underspecified for aux or for inflectional affix, or where it is inappropriate to the intended message. On the other hand, it is possible that some additional set of markers on the VP fragment is necessary to guarantee smooth mapping from argument positions to grammatical roles, and that the agrammatic fragments, which I suggested above are occasionally missing nodes and branches, may be similarly underspecified for these.

If this is the locus of the agrammatic word order problem, we must go on to ask why it is that the semantic character of the agent and object, specifically whether they are of like or contrasting animacy, has a determining influence (Saffran et al., 1980b). An important consideration is that word order errors to semantically irreversible sentences in which only the agent is animate result in sentences that are semantically implausible:

> e.g. The boy is eating the apple → *The apple is eating the boy*
> The wagon is pulled by the boy → *The boy is pulled by the*
> *wagon*

It has been suggested by Garnsey & Dell, 1984 that the normal speech production mechanism incorporates a prearticulatory editor that operates to screen out or censor anomalous messages like these, and that such an editing device might well operate in agrammatic sentence production as well. This is consistent with the recent findings of Ostrin & Schwartz (1986) showing that such a plausibility bias influences the sentence repetition performance of agrammatic speakers. Thus we might speculate that word order errors *are* generated to semantically non-reversible messages, at the point where morphosyntactic fragments are retrieved for output and integrated into a positional representation, but that these are suppressed or edited by means of a device sensitive to the semantic well-formedness of the utterance.

This marks the end of the discussion of the origin of the morphological deficit in agrammatism. Two possibilities have been suggested, both of which carry predictions for co-occurrence with other symptoms. The first account locates the deficit at the level of automatic sound-sequencing procedures. Such a deficit would prevent the phonetic realisation of at least those syntactic morphemes whose phonemic form is conditioned by prior context;

it also prevents the adequate phonetic realisation of other words; and conceivably the assignment of those prosodic features that are arrived at by algorithm from the characteristics of the planning frame. All of these phenomena show "accommodation" to speech errors (Garrett, 1980). On the other hand, a deficit at this level carries no negative implications for the earlier stages of sentence planning and, in particular, the construction of planning frames.

The second account of the morphological deficit in agrammatism locates the problem in the prepackaged morphosyntactic fragments that constitute the building blocks of planning frames. The idea here (after LaPointe), is that agrammatic patients have difficulty retrieving for output the more complex of these fragments, and they tend to substitute structures that are morphosyntactically simpler. As I interpret this proposal, the implication is that the fragments selected for output by agrammatic speakers will also contain few branching nodes and few sites of attachments for other fragments; hence their sentences will be markedly simplified in terms of phrase and clause structure.

Thus, this second account predicts a necessary co-occurrence of the morphological and constructional aspects of agrammatism. Agrammatics who produce morphologically simplified utterances should also have difficulty incorporating into their speech prenominal modifiers, S and NP complements, and so on. Furthermore, following the exposition above, their output should, under some conditions, be subject to error in the assignment of arguments to surface grammatical roles.

This is not the time to debate which of these is the better explanation. In view of the diversity that is increasingly being revealed in case study reports, it is most unlikely that one explanation will suffice. Indeed, there is reason to believe that even the two accounts presented here will not together account for the full range of intra-syndrome variability: consider Case 2 of Miceli et al. (1983) in which there occurred substantial omission of grammatical morphemes, free and bound, without concomitant articulatory impairment (ruling out an explanation in terms of automatic sound sequencing procedures) and without obvious difficulties in phrasal construction (hence, no problem retrieving complex morphosyntactic fragments). The fact that this was a highly unusual case, a transient aphasic in whom recovery was complete within a month's time, does not mitigate the impact of the observation: circumscribed morphological omissions can arise under some conditions and it is not apparent how this is to be handled on the model (but for suggestions from outside the model, see Caramazza & Berndt, 1985; Kolk et al., 1985).

If it is true, and I believe it is, that the tendency to omit syntactic morphemes (and other major symptoms of agrammatism) can arise under a variety of circumstances, following disruption to the production system at one of a number of different points, it is crucial that criteria be established for fixing the locus of the deficit. Such an enterprise will have to be guided by a model of the production system more detailed than what I've offered here; one that specifies more precisely the form and content of the information available at each level of the planning process, and the nature of the processes that map from one level to another. I am impressed by the elaborations of the Garrett model that have already appeared (e.g. Dell & Reich, 1981; Shattuck-Hufnagel, 1983) and by the appearance of alternative candidates that incorporate many features of that model (e.g., Parisi, Chapter 9). It is certain that the immediate future will witness the application of these detailed models to analytic studies of impaired speech in individual cases. I would hope that these studies would also incorporate a longitudinal perspective, which has proved invaluable in other areas of cognitive neuropsychology, and a much-needed input from efforts at remediation (cf., Byng, 1985). It will be these studies that propel us beyond the syndrome characterisation in the direction of a psycholinguistic theory of speech production deficits.

ACKNOWLEDGEMENTS

This is an updated and revised version of an unpublished manuscript written in 1982 and circulated under the title, "Classification of language disorders from a psycholinguistic viewpoint." Several readers made helpful comments on that manuscript, and I wish to thank in particular Eleanor Saffran, Hugh Buckingham, and Merrill Garrett. Preparation of this chapter was supported by NIH research grants AG02231 and NS18429.

REFERENCES

Alajouanine, T., Ombredane, A., & Durand, M. (1939) *Le syndrome de desintegration phonétique dans l'aphasia.* Paris: Masson.

Badecker, W., & Caramazza, A. (1985) On considerations of method and theory governing the use of clinical categories in neurolinguistics and cognitive neuropsychology: The case against agrammatism. *Cognition, 20,* 97–126.

Baker, E., Blumstein, S. E., & Goodglass, H. (1981) Interaction between phonological and semantic factors in auditory comprehension. *Neuropsychologia, 19,* 1–15.

Blumstein, S. E., Baker, E., & Goodglass, H. (1977) Phonological factors in auditory comprehension in aphasia. *Neuropsychologia, 15,* 19–30.

Bradley, D. B. (1978) *Computational distinctions of vocabulary type.* Ph.D. Dissertation, M.I.T., Cambridge, MA.

Brown, J. W. (1977) *Mind, brain and consciousness: The neuropsychology of cognition.* New York: Academic Press.

Buckingham, H. W. (1980) On correlating aphasic errors with slips-of-the-tongue. *Applied Psycholinguistics, 1,* 199–220.

Buckingham, H. W. (1981) Where do neologisms come from? In J. W. Brown (Ed.), *Jargon-aphasia*. New York: Academic Press.

Buckingham, H. W., & Kertesz, A. (1976) *Neologistic jargon aphasia*. Amsterdam: Swets & Zeitlinger.

Buckingham, H. W., Whitaker, H., & Whitaker, H. A. (1978) Alliteration and assonance in neologistic aphasia. *Cortex, 14*, 365–380.

Butterworth, B. (1979) Hesitation and the production of verbal paraphasias and neologisms in jargon aphasia. *Brain and Language, 8*, 133–161.

Butterworth, B., Swallow, J., & Grimston, M. (1981) Gestures and lexical processes in jargonaphasia. In J. W. Brown (Ed.), *Jargonaphasia*. New York: Academic Press.

Byng, S. (1985) *Sentence comprehension deficit: Theoretical analysis and remediation*. Paper presented at the 2nd Venice Conference on Cognitive Neuropsychology, March, 1985.

Caplan, D. (1981) On the cerebral localisation of linguistic functions: Logical and empirical causes surrounding deficit analyses and functional localisation. *Brain and Language, 14*, 120–137.

Caplan, D., Kellar, L., & Locke, S. (1972) Inflection of neologisms in aphasia. *Brain, 95*, 169–172.

Caramazza, A. (1984) The logic of neuropsychological research and the problem of patient classification in aphasia. *Brain and Language, 21*, 9–20.

Caramazza, A., & Berndt, R. S. (1985) A multi-component deficit view of agrammatic Broca's aphasia. In M. L. Kean (Ed.), *Agrammatism*. New York: Academic Press.

Cooper, W. E., & Zurif, E. B. (1983) Aphasia: Information processing in language production and reception. In B. Butterworth (Ed.), *Language Production II*. London: Academic Press.

Crain, S., Shankweiler, D., & Tuller, B. (1984) *Preservation of sensitivity to closed-class items in agrammatism*. Presented at a meeting of the Academy of Aphasia, Los Angeles, October 1984.

Danly, M., & Shapiro, B. (1982) Speech prosody in Broca's aphasia. *Brain and Language, 16*, 171–190.

Dell, G. S., & Reich, P. A. (1981) Stages in sentence production: An analysis of speech error data. *Journal of Verbal Learning and Verbal Behaviour, 20*, 611–629.

Ellis, A. W., Miller, D., & Sin, G. (1983) Wernicke's aphasia and normal language processing: A case study in cognitive neuropsychology. *Cognition, 15*, 111–144.

Fodor, J., Bever, T., & Garrett, M. (1974) *The psychology of language: An introduction to psycholinguistics and generative grammar*. New York: McGraw-Hill.

Fromkin, V. A. (1971) The non-anomalous nature of anomalous utterances. *Language, 47*, 27–52.

Fromkin, V. A. (1973) *Speech errors as linguistic evidence*. The Hague: Mouton.

Garnsey, S. M. & Dell, G. S. (1984) Some neurolinguistic implications of prearticulatory editing in production. *Brain and Language, 23*, 64–73.

Garrett, M. F. (1975) The analysis of sentence production. In G. Bower (Ed.), *Psychology of learning and motivation, vol. 9*. New York: Academic Press.

Garrett, M. F. (1980) Levels of processing in sentence production. In B. Butterworth (Ed.), *Language Production I*. New York: Academic Press.

Garrett, M. F. (1981) *The organisation of processing structure for language production: Applications to aphasic speech*. Conference on Biological Perspectives on Language. Montreal, May 17–20, 1981.

Garrett, M. F. (1982) Production of speech: Observations from normal and pathological language use. In A. Ellis (Ed.), *Normality and pathology in cognitive functions*. London: Academic Press.

Geschwind, N. (1965) Disconnexion syndromes in animals and man. *Brain, 88*, 237–294; 585–644.

Gleason, J., Goodglass, H., Obler, L., Green, E., Ackerman, N., Hyde, M. R., & Weintraub,

S. (1980) Narrative strategies of aphasic and normal-speaking adults. *Journal of Speech and Hearing Research, 23,* 370–382.

Goldman-Eisler, F. (1968) *Psycholinguistics.* London: Academic Press.

Goodglass, H. (1968) Studies on the grammar of aphasics. In S. Rosenberg & J. Koplin (Eds.), *Developments in applied psycholinguistic research.* New York: Macmillan.

Goodglass, H. (1976) Agrammatism. In H. Whitaker & H. A. Whitaker (Eds.), *Studies in neurolinguistics, vol. 1.* New York: Academic Press.

Goodglass, H. & Baker, E. (1976) Semantic field, auditory comprehension and naming in aphasia. *Brain and Language, 3,* 359–374.

Goodglass, H., Gleason, J. B., Bernholtz, N. A., & Hyde, M. R. (1972) Some linguistic structures in the speech of a Broca's aphasic. *Cortex, 8,* 191–211.

Goodglass, H., & Kaplan, E. (1972) *The assessment of aphasia and related disorders.* Philadelphia: Lea & Fiebiger.

Goodglass, H., & Menn, L. (1985) Is agrammatism a unitary phenomenon? In M. L. Kean (Ed.), *Agrammatism.* New York: Academic Press.

Gordon, B., & Caramazza, A. (1982) Lexical decision for open- and closed-class items: Failure to replicate differential sensitivity. *Brain and Language, 15,* 146–160.

Green, E. (1969) Phonological and grammatical aspects of jargon in an aphasic patient: A case study. *Language and Speech, 12,* 103–118.

Jackson, J. H. (1878) On affections of speech from disease of the brain. *Brain, 1,* 304–330.

Kean, M. L. (1979) Agrammatism: A phonological deficit? *Cognition, 7,* 69–84.

Kean, M. L. (1980) Grammatical representations and the description of language processes. In D. Caplan (Ed.), *Biological studies of mental processes.* Cambridge, MA: MIT Press.

Kean, M. L. (1985) *Agrammatism.* New York: Academic Press.

Kertesz, A., & Benson, D. F. (1970) Neologistic jargon: A clinicopathological study. *Cortex, 6,* 362–386.

Kohn, S. E. (1984) The nature of the phonological disorder in conduction aphasia. *Brain and Language, 23,* 97–115.

Kolk, H. H. J. (1983) *Agrammatic processing of word order.* Paper presented at a meeting of the Academy of Aphasia, October 1983, Los Angeles, California.

Kolk, H. H. J., & Blomert, L. (1985) On the Bradley hypothesis concerning agrammatism: The non-word interference effect. *Brain and Language, 26,* 94–105.

Kolk, H. H. J., & Heeschen, C. (1985) *Agrammatism versus paragrammatism: a shift of behavioral control.* Presented at a meeting of the Academy of Aphasia, October 1985, Pittsburgh, Pa.

Kolk, H. H. J., van Grunsven, M. F., & Keyser, A. (1985) On parallelism between production and comprehension in agrammatism. In M. L. Kean (Ed.), *Agrammatism.* New York: Academic Press.

LaPointe, S. (1983) Some issues in the linguistic description of agrammatism. *Cognition, 14,* 1–40.

Lashley, K. S. (1951) The problem of serial order in behavior. In L. A. Jeffress (Ed.), *Cerebral mechanisms in behavior.* New York: Wiley.

Lecours, A. R. (1980) *On neologisms.* Paper presented to the Conference of the CNRS. Abbé Royamount, June 1980.

Lecours, A. R. & Lhermitte, F. (1969) Phonemic paraphasias: Linguistic structures and tentative hypotheses. *Cortex, 5,* 193–228.

Lecours, A. R. & Rouillon, F. (1976) Neurolinguistic analysis of jargonaphasia and jargonagraphia. In H. Whitaker & H. A. Whitaker (Eds.), *Studies in neurolinguistics, vol. 2.* New York: Academic Press.

Lichtheim, L. (1885) On aphasia. *Brain, 2,* 433–484.

Linebarger, M., Schwartz, M. F., & Saffran, E. M. (1983) Sensitivity to grammatical structure in so-called agrammatic aphasics. *Cognition, 13,* 361–392.

Lukatela, K., Crain, S., & Shankweiler, D. (1985) *Sensitivity to closed-class items in Serbo-Croat agrammatics*. Presented at a meeting of the Academy of Aphasia, October 1985, Pittsburgh, Pa.

Luria, A. R. (1970) *Traumatic aphasia*. The Hague: Mouton.

Luria, A. R. (1976) *Basic problems of neurolinguistics*. The Hague: Mouton.

Menn, L., Powelson, J., Miceli, G., Williams, E. & Zurif, E. B. (1982) *A psycholinguistic model for paragrammatic speech*. Paper presented at the B.A.B.B.L.E. meeting, March 1982, Niagara Falls, Ontario.

Miceli, G., Mazzucci, A., Menn, L., & Goodglass, H. (1983) Contrasting cases of Italian agrammatic aphasia without comprehension disorder. *Brain and Language, 19*, 65–97.

Obler, L. K., Menn, L., & Goodglass, H. (1983) *Agrammatism: Why cross-language approaches*. Paper presented at a meeting of the Academy of Aphasia, October 1983, Los Angeles, California.

Ostrin, R. K., & Schwartz, M. F. (1986) Reconstructing from a degraded trace: A study of sentence repetition in agrammatism. *Brain and Language, 28*, 328–345.

Ostrin, R. K., Schwartz, M. F., & Saffran, E. M. (1983) *The influence of syntactic complexity in the elicited production of agrammatic aphasics*. Paper presented at a meeting of the Academy of Aphasia, October 1983, Loss Angeles, California.

Pate, D. S. (1985) *The syntactic sensitivity of a Wernicke's aphasic: A case report*. Presented at a meeting of the Academy of Aphasia, October 1985, Pittsburgh, Pa.

Perecman, E., & Brown, J. W. (1981) Phonemic jargon: A case report. In J. W. Brown (Ed.), *Jargonaphasia*. New York, Academic Press.

Pick, A. (1931) *Aphasia*. Translated by J. W. Brown. Springfield: Thomas.

Saffran, E. M. (1982) Neuropsychological approaches to the study of language. *British Journal of Psychology, 73*, 317–337.

Saffran, E. M., Schwartz, M. F., & Marin, O. S. M. (1980a) Evidence from aphasia: Isolating the components of a production model. In B. Butterworth (Ed.), *Language production*. London: Academic Press.

Saffran, E. M., Schwartz, M. F., & Marin, O. S. M. (1980b) The word order problem in agrammatism: Production. *Brain and Language, 10*, 249–262.

Schwartz, M. F. (1984) What the classical aphasia categories can't do for us, and why. *Brain and Language, 21*, 3–8.

Schwartz, M. F., Linebarger, M. C., & Saffran, E. M. (1985) The status of the syntactic deficit theory of agrammatism. In M. L. Kean (Ed.), *Agrammatism*. New York: Academic Press.

Segui, J., Mehler, J., Frauenfelder, U., & Morton, J. (1982) The word frequency effect and lexical access. *Neuropsychologia, 20*, 615–627.

Shattuck-Hufnagel, S. (1979) Speech errors as evidence for a serial-ordering mechanism in sentence production. In W. E. Cooper & E. C. T. Walker (Eds.), *Sentence processing: Psycholinguistic studies presented to Merrill Garrett*. Hillside, N.J.: Erlbaum.

Shattuck-Hufnagel, S. (1983) Sublexical units and suprasegmental structure in speech production planning. In P. F. MacNeilage (Ed.), *The production of speech*. New York: Springer-Verlag.

Tissot, R. J., Mounin, G., & Lhermitte, F. (1973) *L'Agrammatisme*. Brussels: Dessart.

Wernicke, C. (1874) The aphasia symptom complex: A psychological study on an anatomical basis. Reprinted in G. H. Eggert (Ed. and Trans.), *Wernicke's works on aphasia*. The Hague: Mouton, 1977.

9 Grammatical Disturbances of Speech Production

Domenico Parisi
*Istituto di Psicologia, C.N.R., Reparto Processi Cognitivi e
Intelligenza Artificiale, Via dei Monti Tiburtini, 509, 00157–Roma,
Italy*

INTRODUCTION

The purpose of this paper is to examine a number of theoretical and methodological issues related to grammatical disturbances of spontaneous speech and to propose an interpretation of some of these disturbances. The issues are traditionally discussed under the labels of agrammatism and sometimes paragrammatism. We think we should avoid using these categories since they are not very well-defined and concentrate on identifying theoretically justified dimensions of grammatical impairment. More specifically, we intend: (1) to show that a disturbance of syntactic constructional ability is a basic dimension of some forms of aphasia, quite apart from problems with so-called function or closed class words; (2) to give a definition of a function word within a procedural model of sentence production, in contrast to purely linguistic definitions as proposed by Kean and others.

THE CONSTRUCTION OF A SENTENCE'S MEANING

A basic aspect of the language production capacity is the ability to produce not isolated words but syntactic constructions, i.e. sequences of words which are part of syntactic structures. Traditionally recognised syntactic structures are phrases, clauses, and sentences. These structures are organised hierarchically: words occur in phrases, phrases in clauses, clauses in sentences. In

201

actual speech all types of structures may sometimes occur in isolation, even single words (e.g. in replies to questions). However, if a normal speaker produces anything which is not a complete sentence, this usually happens with the speaker being able to control the context so that the hearer can recover complete "thoughts" using the syntactic fragments and the context.

The ability to produce sentences—and sometimes smaller constructions that are, however, part of sentences for both the speaker and the hearer—can be described as the possession of a "sentence production procedure" (plus of course the ability of actually executing the procedure). The minimal requirements for such a procedure are: (1) that it must be able to extract from the speaker's store of knowledge about the world the appropriate content to be expressed in a sentence; and (2) that it must be able to select the words and their sequential ordering which constitute an appropriate sentence for that content.

Consider the first task or sub-procedure. This is the task of extracting the appropriate knowledge items from the knowledge store of the speaker so that a well-formed sentence will result. This may be referred to as the construction of the sentence's meaning. From the point of view of the speaker syntax is first of all a procedure (i.e. a set of sequential constraints) for selecting the next knowledge item, given the items already selected. The speaker "knows" that a first requirement is that the sentence must contain a "verbal complex", i.e. a word or set of words expressing: (1) a temporal event; (2) the time in which the event takes place. Instances of "verbal complexes" are: "is sleeping," "ate," "was on," "is nice." A second requirement is that, assuming that all words express predicate-argument structures, no argument that is marked as obligatorily fillable in the lexicon can remain unfilled. For instance, if I have decided to express a piece of knowledge with the word "explain," I am obliged to select and express two more knowledge items describing who explains and what is explained. If I have decided to say that something was done "in order to" something else, I must specify what this something else is.

Furthermore, syntax prescribes what sort of lexical material must be selected to fill up arguments, i.e. either nouns or clauses as a function of the particular lexical entry expressing the predicate.

Not all decision points in the sentence construction procedure are under the control of syntax. Syntax specifies how to say something, not what to say. At a higher level the sentence production process is under the control of a goal-pursuing mechanism which specifies what a speaker is interested in saying at any particular time as a function of the speaker's goals and knowledge. Syntax may dictate that a noun must be selected at a certain point, but not which specific noun. Some additions to the sentence meaning are syntactically optional, as is typically the case for noun modifiers and for adverbials. However, once the decision to add more information to a head noun or to a verbal complex has been adopted—on syntactically independent

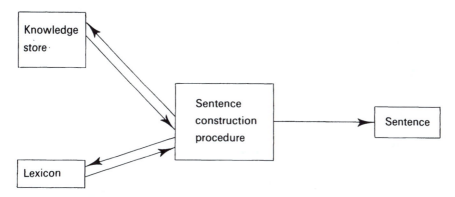

FIG. 9.1   Overall schema of the sentence construction procedure.

grounds—syntax dictates the "form" of these additions. A verbal complex can be further qualified only by selecting a particular class of lexical entries, i.e. adverbs, adverbial prepositions, or subordinating conjunctions. A head noun can only be modified by relative clauses and related constructions.

These contraints on the sentence construction process can be precisely described by designing a computational procedure which takes a knowledge store and a lexicon as input and gives sententially expressible meanings as output. One such procedure has been presented in Parisi and Giorgi (1985). We will give a much simplified version of that procedure here.

The overall design of the sentence construction procedure is schematised in Fig. 9.1. Let us examine the content of the various boxes more closely.

The Knowledge Store is a more or less permanent memory of what the speaker knows about the world (and what can be generated from it through inference). Knowledge in the store can be more permanent—as the knowledge that Paris is in France, or that dogs generally chase cats and not vice versa—or brief, temporary knowledge—as the knowledge that a car is coming or that a particular dog is chasing a particular cat at this very moment. Formally, all knowledge is represented as a set of propositional units forming a network because of the units' shared arguments. A propositional unit is made up of: (1) a predicate; (2) one or more arguments (X or C) as required by the predicate; (3) the unit's identifying label (C). Arguments and labels have code numbers to specify whether they refer to the same entity (same code) or to different entities (different codes). A unit's label may recur as an argument of another unit—this being the basis for producing adverbials and subordinate clauses.

A miniature knowledge store is represented on the left of Fig. 9.2. The speaker knows that there is an entity X1 that is a dog, and that chases another entity X2, that is a cat. The chasing takes place in a third entity X3

Lexicon

Knowledge store		Meaning			Signal
		Content units	Control units	Assembly instructions	
C1: X1 CHASE X2 C2: X1 DOG C3: X2 CAT	1	CA: XA CHASE XB	CB: CA TEMP	SATARG(XA) SATARG(XB)	chases
	2	CA: XA DOG	CB: XA HEAD		dog
	3	CA: XA CAT	CB: XA HEAD		cat
C4: C1 IN X3 C5: X3 STREET	4	CA: CB IN XA		SATARG(XA)	in
	5	CA: XA STREET	CB: XA HEAD		street
	6	CA: XA SAY CB	CB: CA TEMP	SATARG(XA) SATCARG(CB)	says
C6: X4 MARY C7: X4 SAY C8 C8: X5 SLEEP C9: X5 CHILD	7	CA: XA SLEEP	CB: CA TEMP	SATARG(XA)	sleeps
	8	CA: XA MARY	CB: XA HEAD		Mary
	9	CA: XA CHILD	CB: XA HEAD		child

FIG. 9.2   A miniature knowledge store and lexicon.

that is a street. Moreover the speaker knows that there is a fourth entity X4 that is called Mary, and that says that a fifth entity X5 sleeps, and this fifth entity is a child.

On the basis of this knowledge a number of sentences can be produced, e.g., "The dog chases the cat;" "The cat is chased by the dog in the street;" "The chasing of the cat by the dog takes place in the street;" "Mary says that the child sleeps;" "As Mary says the child sleeps;" etc. (Notice that the units stating the time in which events take place are omitted in the knowledge store of Fig. 9.2.)

The lexicon that is necessary to produce some of the above sentences is represented on the right of Fig. 9.2. The lexicon is a set of lexical entries. Each lexical entry is made up of a meaning and a signal. The signal is a small procedure for producing the appropriate sounds. The meaning of a lexical entry has three components, with some lexical entries lacking one or another of these components: (1) one or more content units; (2) one or more control units; (3) one or more assembly instructions. The content and control units are propositional units. The only difference with respect to the propositional units in the knowledge store is that arguments and labels have literal codes and not number codes. (Number codes are valid throughout the knowledge store. Literal codes are only valid within each separate lexical entry.)

The difference between content and control units is that content units correspond to units in the knowledge store (they have the same predicates, e.g., "chase," "street," "say") while control units are found only in the lexicon (e.g., "temp," "head"). The role of the control units will become clear in a moment.

We don't need to say in detail what assembly instructions actually are. (This can only be explained with reference to language comprehension, not language production.) Suffice it to say that their role in sentence production is to identify "unsaturated" arguments. An assembly instruction is "on" a specific argument. For example, "satarg" (XA) is "on" argument XA. If an argument in a lexical entry has an assembly instruction on it, the argument is said to be unsaturated. This means that the argument must be "saturated" by selecting another lexical entry on the same argument. For example, the entry "chases" has two unsaturated arguments which are saturated in the sentence "The dog chases the cat." We will discuss the role of unsaturated arguments below.

Now that we have described in sufficient detail the contents of the two boxes "Knowledge Store" and "Lexicon", we can go on to examining the sentence construction procedure which uses the knowledge store and the lexicon to construct a sentence's meaning. The procedure is schematised in Fig. 9.3.

Let us assume that as a starting point the system is given a specific argument to say something about. The first step of the procedure is to select in the knowledge store a propositional unit with two constraints: (1) the proposition must mention the argument; (2) the lexicon must contain a lexical entry with a corresponding content unit and with the proposition's label marked with the control predicate "temp." (The predicate "temp" is found with verbs, adjectives, and prepositions, at least in some uses of prepositions.)

If we assume that in a specific instance of producing a sentence the starting argument is X1 (the dog), this first step of the procedure concludes with the selection of proposition C1 in the knowledge store, and of lexical entry 1 in the lexicon. In this way the system progressively constructs the sentence's meaning and simultaneously lexicalises the constructed meaning with the appropriate lexical entries.

The next step is a question: Are there unsaturated arguments in the just-selected lexical entry? As we already know, an unsaturated argument is an argument on which there is an assembly instruction. In our case there are two such arguments, XA and XB. The system chooses one of the two and proceeds to the third step: to select in the knowledge store a proposition which mentions the argument and which can be expressed by a lexical entry marking the argument with the control predicate "head."

This is repeated twice (one for XA and one for XB), and it leads to the selection of propositions C2 and C3 and of lexical entries 2 and 3.

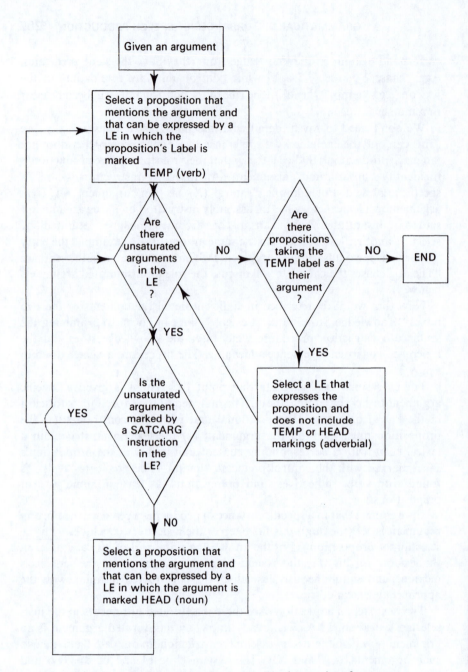

FIG. 9.3 A partial procedure for constructing the meaning of a sentence.

At this point the meaning of the sentence "The dog chases the cat" has been constructed, i.e. extracted from the knowledge store. By continuing with the application of the procedures the adverbial "in the street" might be added to this meaning. (The "temp" label is the label marked with the predicate "temp." In our case the "temp" label is C1.)

If we should start with another argument, say X4 (Mary), the procedure will construct the meaning of the complex sentence "Mary says that the child sleeps." Notice the role of the assembly instruction "satcarg" carried by the second argument (CB) of "says," which triggers the re-application of the whole procedure (see Fig. 9.3) and hence the construction of the subordinate clause "that the child sleeps."

As mentioned, the procedure described is a simplified version of an actual procedure for the various sentence types of English. For example, sentences containing relative clauses or pronouns have not been considered. However, we believe that what has been said is sufficient to show that some such procedure must be available to a speaker in order to extract syntactically well-formed meanings from the knowledge store and to express them in appropriate syntactic constructions.

If a sentence construction procedure like the one we have outlined above is an important part of the capacity of producing speech, disruption of the procedure (or of the ability to execute it) will result in speech which is different from normal speech in its syntactic constructions. We may assume that a complete unavailability of the procedure would make speech a sequence of isolated words. Content would still be somehow communicated but with no syntactic constructions. The language production ability in such cases would be reduced to extracting a piece of knowledge—say, one proposition—that the speaker wants to communicate and finding a word that can communicate it in the lexicon, repeating the operation a number of times. However, there would be no overarching procedure guiding the selection of content and its expression in syntactic constructions.

This is an extreme case. What is more likely to occur is that the sentence construction procedure (or the ability to carry it out) will be only partially disrupted. This may mean a number of different things: some specific operations prescribed by the procedure are not executed, or the path through the procedure is interrupted, or the procedure is entered at inappropriate points. In all such cases the speech that is produced would contain syntactic fragments and restricted constructions. More specifically, we would find: (1) sub-sentential constructions (clauses, phrases, or even isolated words); (2) incomplete constructions (constructions lacking obligatory elements); (3) basic constructions (constructions with no optional elements).

It has already been observed that constructions other than complete sentences may also occur in normal speech. However, the incidence of such non-sentence constructions should be higher in pathological than in normal speech. Moreover, pathological speech should be less comprehensible than normal speech because the patient is not using the normal strategy of non-sentential speech plus control of the context.

If we want to examine the syntactic constructions produced by an aphasic patient as a clue to the impairment or lack of impairment of his sentence construction procedure, we must first solve a number of methodological problems: which type of speech to examine; how to identify syntactic constructions; how to "measure" these constructions.

The procedural model that we have outlined is only appropriate for a specific "task," that of producing sentences based on the speaker's past experience. What is critical in this task is that the speaker has no external help in constructing and lexicalising the meaning of the sentences he produces. The type of speech to which the model should be applied is therefore spontaneous speech, such as describing daily activities, telling the story of illness, etc. Ruled out are not only, obviously, sentence repetition and sentence anagram tasks, but also picture description tasks. In picture description the perceptual and linguistic abilities of the patient must interact and the visual input to the patient may help or perhaps interfere with his sentence construction behaviour. Therefore, to study picture description we need a procedural model of picture description.

A second problem is how to identify syntactic constructions. We believe that we should identify them in aphasic speech as much as possible in the same way as we identify them in normal speech: by using the syntactic and semantic cues that are actually present in the speech. More objective criteria like pause length are: (1) arbitrary (which pause length should we use in separating two constructions?); (2) not necessarily valid (two words may be in construction—in the sense of being produced by a continuing application of the sentence construction procedure—and still be separated by a supra-threshold pause); (3) difficult to adhere to consistently (e.g. Goodglass, Quadfasel, & Timberlake, 1964, use both pause length and beginning of a new sentence as separation points).

Another approach is to accept a structural notion of a syntactic construction but to take into account only a subset of the constructions that are found in a text. A typical choice is to consider only the constructions which contain a verb. If no clear explanation is given for such a choice, this solution is arbitrary and should be discarded. Two patients may behave similarly with regard to verb-containing constructions—i.e., their verb-containing constructions are of the same average length—but differently with regard to constructions that do not contain a verb, e.g. noun phrases or prepositional phrases. Therefore, measuring their ability in the former case is not measuring their overall syntactic constructional ability.

A third problem is how to measure the syntactic constructions in a sample of speech once they have been identified. One solution is to take the proportion of words in a text that belong to constructions out of the total number of words. It is not clear why this solution should be proposed. In any case, it has nothing to recommend itself. Consider the hypothetical case of two patients who produce the same total number of words, say 10. One patient has two constructions in his text, each of five words. The other patient has five constructions, each of two words. The proportion of words-in-context would be one in both cases (10/10). However, we certainly would want to say that the first patient has a better constructional ability than the second one.

A better and more natural approach to measuring constructions in a text is to take the average length of these constructions in some kind of units. All constructions that result from a disrupted sentence construction procedure are reduced constructions, i.e. constructions which are on the average shorter than constructions found in normal speech. Constructions below the sentence level tend to be shorter than sentences; incomplete and basic constructions are by definition shorter than complete constructions and constructions with optional elements, respectively. Hence, while more sophisticated measures could be devised (for example, by separating the three cases of sub-sentential, incomplete, and basic constructions), a fundamental and theoretically important dimension of aphasic speech should be the average length of the syntactic constructions which are produced.

But if we want to measure the length of constructions in a text we need to know which units to count. Three alternatives are open: words, morphemes (both free and bound), content words. We are going to argue that if we are interested in measuring the length of constructions as a clue to the degree of disruption of the sentence construction procedure, the third alternative—content words—is the correct one. However, in order to define the notion of a content word—and the complementary notion of a function word—within our procedural model of sentence production we need to say something more about the model.

THE PRODUCTION OF CONTENT AND FUNCTION WORDS

The sentence construction procedure outlined in Fig. 9.3 only prescribes what can be said next given what has already been said. However, producing an actual sentence also involves the selection of the words making up the sentence and their correct sequential ordering. We won't say anything in the present paper on the sequential ordering of words and its possible disturbances. With regard to the selection of lexical entries we have already seen that constructing the meaning of a sentence necessarily implies the lexicalisation of the meaning progressively extracted from the knowledge store, i.e., the selection of the lexical entries that express the various parts of the constructed meaning. However, not all the lexical entries making up the final sentence are lexicalisations of the meaning extracted from the knowledge store. Some of these lexical entries lexicalise not content units (i.e., units corresponding to units in the knowledge store) but other types of unit—control units or, as we will see, discourse units. The lexical entries which lexicalise content units are roughly equivalent to the so-called content words, the lexical entries which lexicalise control or discourse units to the so-called function words.

Why should a sentence bother to include function words in addition to content words, as after all the final purpose of communicating with a sentence is to transfer knowledge from the speaker's knowledge store to the hearer's knowledge store? The answer can only be found within a procedural model of sentence comprehension. Briefly stated, content words communicate to the hearer the separate pieces of meaning of the sentence. However, to understand the sentence the hearer must assemble these various pieces together, and furthermore he must assemble the knowledge items expressed by the sentence with the knowledge already contained in his knowledge store. Function words play a role—but by all means not an exclusive one—in allowing the hearer to execute these assembling operations. Function words which lexicalise control units play a role in assembling together the separate meanings of the sentence's content words (e.g., "agreement" suffixes or argument-marking by grammatical cases or prepositions). Function words which lexicalise discourse units help in assembling the sentence's meaning with the hearer's previous knowledge (e.g. articles and perhaps pronouns).

Content and function words, therefore, are lexicalised through different mechanisms. Content words are lexicalised as part of the sentence construction process. They lexicalise information residing in the speaker's knowledge store. Disruption of the sentence construction procedure may interfere with the production of content words as part of syntactic constructions, but not with the production of content words as such.

Function words, on the other hand, are not lexicalised as an automatic consequence of the sentence construction process. They must be lexicalised by additional operations not described in the procedure of Fig. 9.3. The lexicon used by that procedure was a word lexicon (see Fig. 9.2). The actual lexicon for a language like English or Italian is a morphological lexicon, i.e., a lexicon with lexical entries corresponding to morphemes (e.g., root and affixes). The content "words" lexicalised as part of the sentence construction process are often simple roots to which suffixes must be added. Both free and bound function "words" lexicalise information (the control and discourse units) that is not found in the speaker's knowledge store, but must be generated within the sentence construction process.

We won't be more specific here on the procedure for lexicalising function words. This procedure is described in Parisi and Giorgi (1981) and some consequences of its disruption in aphasic speech are discussed in Parisi (1983). What has already been said seems to be sufficient to conclude that only content words should be counted in measuring the length of constructions, as only content words are lexicalised as an integral part of the sentence construction process.

However, the preceding discussion has also shown that the lexicalisation of function words is another fundamental component of the sentence production process—conceptually distinct from, even if perhaps not structurally or empirically independent of, the sentence construction component. This function word component can be disrupted and its disruption may result in disturbances in the production of function words. If the information which is lexicalised by function words (the control and discourse units) is not appropriately generated during the sentence production process, two types of disturbances in the production of function words can be predicted: they may not be produced at all (omissions) or the correct function word may be replaced by an incorrect one (errors).

We have presented a procedural model of the production of sentences. This model has (at least) two components: a component which extracts from a knowledge store and lexicalises the meaning of a sentence (content words); and a component which generates the information to be lexicalised by the sentence's function words. We believe that the model may have some usefulness in interpreting grammatical disturbances in aphasic speech. In the following section we will present some data based on transcriptions of aphasic speech to show how the model makes contact with such data.

SOME DATA ON GRAMMATICALLY DISTURBED SPONTANEOUS SPEECH

The data have been obtained from 10 Italian aphasics, eight of whom are clinically classified as "agrammatic", and two as "paragrammatic" (F.S. and F.D.). For five patients the data from two different time intervals post-onset were available (mostly, around three months and one year and three months). Because in all five cases clear improvements in spontaneous speech were observable from one session to the other one year later, each of these patients has been considered as two separate "data points" (e.g., C.D.A.1 and C.D.A.2).

The tapes of seven of these patients were kindly supplied by Gabriele Miceli, Neuropsychology Section, Catholic University of Rome. Patients G.G. and G.F. have already been described and analysed in Miceli, Mazzucchi, Menn and Goodglass (1983). The remaining three patients (G.J., B.W., and A.S.) are from the Neuropsychology Section, University of Milan, and

TABLE 9.1

Spontaneous Speech Data From Ten (Five Tested Twice) Italian Aphasics

Patient	Total words	No. of constructions	Average length (CW)	Proportion embedded clauses	CW/FW ratio	Proportion omissions FW	Proportion suffix errors V	Proportion suffix errors N	Proportion N	Proportion V
C.D.A.1	236	189	1.11	0.00	42.00	0.94	0.00	0.00	0.64	0.04
G.J.1	49	30	1.37	0.00	5.86	0.50	0.00	0.00	0.47	0.24
B.W.1	95	59	1.49	0.00	12.57	0.53	0.89	0.02	0.58	0.25
F.G.1	133	62	1.61	0.04	3.85	0.49	0.41	0.07	0.32	0.20
C.D.A.2	318	117	1.76	0.03	2.54	0.29	0.00	0.01	0.27	0.19
G.G.1	196	73	2.21	0.12	5.37	0.73	0.51	0.00	0.39	0.25
G.G.2	213	61	2.44	0.16	2.76	0.31	0.22	0.00	0.21	0.17
F.G.2	245	63	2.49	0.03	2.09	0.07	0.16	0.02	0.22	0.16
A.S.	55	13	2.62	0.23	1.89	0.00	0.23	0.00	0.22	0.31
G.J.2	40	10	2.70	0.40	2.45	0.00	0.00	0.00	0.27	0.32
B.W.2	114	21	3.38	0.33	1.77	0.05	0.00	0.00	0.27	0.22
C.D.	457	86	3.45	0.17	2.15	0.07	0.14	0.02	0.30	0.27
F.S.	184	34	3.62	0.29	2.20	0.24	0.44	0.17	0.32	0.16
F.S.	745	133	3.86	0.39	2.66	0.27	0.05	0.07	0.18	0.21
G.F.	491	91	4.07	0.22	4.20	0.51	0.71	0.00	0.22	0.18
Controls	1,016	92	6.50	0.59	2.01				0.20	0.16

their transcriptions have been made available through courtesy of Anna Basso.

Only spontaneous speech data were used in the analyses. For the Rome aphasics three types of spontaneous speech were available: daily activities, history of illness, description of a typical activity (shaving for men, cooking *pasta* for women). For the Milan patients only descriptions of typical activities were available.

The same types of spontaneous speech data were obtained from four non-neurological control patients matched for age and education. The data were collected with the help of Gabriele Miceli and are included in Table 9.1 collectively as controls.

The spontaneous speech of the Rome patients has been transcribed and analysed by Gabriele Miceli and Rosaria Cafiero. The speech of the Milan patients has been transcribed by Marcella Laiacana and analysed by her and Rosaria Cafiero.

For each patient the following data are listed in Table 9.1:

1. Total number of words.
2. Total number of syntactic constructions. (As already noted, two adjacent words are considered "in construction" if there are syntactic and semantic reasons for doing so. Two words are not considered in construction if this would require supplying a content word supposedly missing from the text. E.g. two adjacent nouns are not considered a single construction with a missing verb.)
3. Average length of construction in content words (CW).
4. Proportion of constructions with an embedded clause.
5. Content/function word ratio (CW/FW).
6. Proportion of omitted free function words in obligatory contexts. (Free function words include articles, grammatical prepositions, copula, and auxiliary verbs. Grammatical prepositions are those prepositions which are required as markings on a verb's or noun's argument, e.g., "to dream of;" "Mary's love for music." Pronouns were not included among either content or function words because: (1) they make comparison between Italian and English difficult in that they are often optional in Italian and obligatory in English; and (2) it is not clear whether they should be classified as content or function words for the present purposes.)
7. Proportion of incorrect verb suffixes. In Italian verb suffixes are obligatory.
8. Proportion of incorrect nominal suffixes. (Nominal suffixes are suffixes of nouns, articles, and attributive adjectives. In Italian articles and adjectives "agree" with the noun.)
9. Proportion of nouns out of total words.
10. Proportion of verbs out of total words.

The average length of syntactic constructions in content words (CW) is considered here as a measure of disruption of the sentence construction procedure. The patients place themselves on a continuum on this dimension, from a minimum of 1.11 content words per construction to 4.07 content words, compared with a measure of 6.50 for non-aphasic controls. The data show no discontinuity in the average construction length, thus offering no basis for a distinction between agrammatism and paragrammatism. Notice that the patient with the longest average length (G.F.) is one of those having the most severe problems with function words (CW/FW = 4.20; proportion of omissions = .51; proportion errors in verb suffixes = .71).

Another measure that may reflect the degree of disruption of the sentence construction procedure is the proportion of constructions with embedded clauses. In fact this measure shows a rank correlation of .84 (p < .01) with the average length of constructions.

Turning now to measures that are intended to tap the patients' problems with function words, we observe that on all four measures, except perhaps errors on nominal suffixes, this group of aphasics shows an impaired performance with respect to controls.

Problems with function words can manifest themselves as omissions or as errors. Omissions are captured by two measures: the ratio content/function words and the proportion of omissions in obligatory contexts. (The correlation between these two measures is .93, p < .01). In both cases the correlation with construction length is only moderate. The rank correlation between CW and CW/FW is .58 (p < .05) and between CW and proportion of omissions is .53 (p < .05). This seems to indicate that the two measures refer to distinct aspects of the capacity of producing sentences.

Errors on bound morphemes are captured by proportion of errors on verb suffixes and on nominal suffixes. The performance of these aphasics appears much more impaired on the first measure than on the second. The mean proportion of errors on verb suffixes for the whole groups is .25, while the mean proportion of errors for nominal suffixes is only .02. An attempt at explaining this marked difference in error rate for verbal vs. nominal suffixes has been made in Parisi (1983), based on the differential complexity of the operations required for lexicalising verbal and nominal suffixes as described by the function word lexicalisation procedure (see the Discussion section).

Limiting our attention to the more substantive measure of errors on verb suffixes, it turns out that this measure is not correlated with either length of syntactic constructions (.18) or to omission of function words (− .29).

Finally, the proportion of nouns and proportion of verbs out of total words were computed for each patient's speech sample. The correlation of this measure with construction length is .45 for nouns (just barely significant) and .15 for verbs (not significant).

DISCUSSION OF THE DATA

As already noted, disruption of the sentence construction procedure should result in constructions which are on the average shorter than normal constructions. If a patient's language production behaviour is only partially guided by the sequential constraints that make up the procedure, he will produce a more or less large number of incomplete, basic, and sub-sentential constructions. As a consequence, his average construction length will be reduced. This reduced construction length should be observable even when measured in content words, i.e. leaving function words out and therefore quite apart from any consideration of problems that the patient may have with function words.

The data indicate that a group of 15 aphasic patients (more exactly, 10 patients tested once plus retest of 5 of them) place themselves quite nicely on a dimension of construction length measured in content words, from a patient with construction length close to 1 (almost all constructions are isolated words) to patients with a substantial construction length even if still reduced with respect to controls. The data give no indication of a bi-modal distribution on which to base a possible distinction between "agrammatic" and "paragrammatic" patients. All that can be said, it appears, is that the sentence construction procedure may be more or less disrupted—and that patients can recover from a more radical disruption to a less severe one (see the patients with two "data points").

A disrupted sentence construction procedure should have special difficulties in generating meanings of subordinate clauses that imply especially long sequential constraints. In fact, the constructions of the most severely impaired patients show no traces of embedded clauses. More generally, the proportion of constructions with embedded clauses increases with average construction length. This does not seem to be entirely due to the fact that a construction containing an embedded clause tends to be longer than a construction without embedded clauses.

Our patients show quite clearly another aspect of impaired performance: they have problems in producing function words. This is indicated by the ratio content/function words, which tends to be higher than in controls, and by the omission of function words in contexts that obligatorily require them. According to our model, this implies that another component of the overall procedure for producing sentences is more or less disrupted in these patients, i.e., the component that generates the control and discourse units and lexicalises these units with the appropriate lexical forms.

The rank orderings of the patients on the construction length dimension, on the one hand, and on these two measures of function word behaviour, on the other, show a correlation which is statistically significant but not more than just moderate. This seems to indicate two things. To be able to produce function words is not the same thing as to be able to put content words in syntactic constructions. These seem to be two distinct components of the sentence production capacity. On the other hand, they are not two procedurally, completely independent components. Disruption of one component tends to be accompanied by the disruption of the other, at least within limits.

The conclusion of a distinction and partial independence of the two components is supported by an analysis of single patients. We have already mentioned patient G.F., who has the longest average construction length but omits more function words than most other patients. Another interesting case is patient G.G.1, who shows a very high proportion of function-word omissions but has not an especially short construction length. These two patients are those analysed by Miceli et al. (1983). It is interesting that in the Miceli et al. paper G.F. is contrasted with G.G. as being a "morphological" patient (long construction length and problems with function words), while G.G. is seen as a "syntactic" patient (short construction length and less problems with function words). However, this difference of classification notwithstanding, probably due to the larger sample of patients examined here, the distinction made in the present paper between two components of the language production capacity goes in the same direction as the distinction between "morphological" and "syntactic" aphasics used in the Miceli et al. paper and in other work cited there.

An American aphasic patient, obviously not included in our sample but analysed in the same way as our patients, shows an opposite pattern with respect to G.F. and G.G.1. This patient, M.F., and five other American patients to be mentioned later, have been observed by Eleanor Saffran and Myrna Schwartz and the transcriptions of their speech have been provided to the author through their courtesy. M.F. has an average construction length of 1.73 content words and a ratio content/function words of 1.79. He seems, therefore, to be comparatively less impaired in his function word behaviour than in his constructional ability.

Even if conceptually, and in part even empirically, distinct, the two components of the language production capacity show a significant correlation in our data. Furthermore, it seems to be general experience that reduced construction length in spontaneous speech tends to be accompanied by problems with function words. Our procedural model suggests two ways—not necessarily mutually exclusive—of explaining this relationship.

As will be recalled, the correct functioning of the sentence construction procedure critically depends on the availability and use of control unit information as carried by such predicates as "temp" and "head" and by information carried by assembly instructions in the lexical entries. Thus, one interpretation of the disruption of this procedure is that this non-content information is not available to the system, either because it is degenerated in the lexicon or because, while not degenerated, for some reason the system is not able to process it. The only information which is available to and processable by the system is content information, i.e. information in its store of knowledge about the world.

If we turn to function words, we may also recall that their correct production depends on non-content information, i.e., control and discourse unit information. If we assume that non-content information is partially unavailable or difficult to process for the system, we may see here a possible explanation for the observed relationship between reduced construction length and problems with function words.

In the above interpretation reduced construction length and problems with function words go together, not because one causes the other, but because both are at least partially caused by the unavailability of non-content information. Another line of reasoning suggests that problems with function words may be caused by a disrupted construction procedure. In fact some control unit information which is needed for the appropriate selection of function words is only generated if content words are produced as part of syntactic constructions. Consider prepositions that mark arguments, so-called grammatical prepositions. In order for a noun to be preceded by the correct grammatical preposition, the noun must be produced as part of a syntactic construction with its governing verb or noun (e.g., "Bill thinks of Mary;" "the director of the company"). Only if this is the case will the lexicalisation of the verb ("think") or noun ("director") generate the control unit information that the argument-filling noun ("Mary" or "the company") must be preceded by a specific preposition ("of").

Or consider verb suffixes. Their correct selection often, at least in Italian, depends on control unit information generated with lexicalisation of the subject of the verb. For example, taking an English example, the suffix "-s" of "chases" can only be selected if the system knows that the subject of the verb is "third person" and is "singular" (two control units). But if the verb is not produced in construction with the subject noun, this transfer of information from the noun to the verb cannot occur. On the other hand, selection of noun suffixes does not depend on control unit information generated with the lexicalisation of other words, at least in Italian, and this may explain why errors in noun suffixes are rare as compared with errors in verb suffixes. In German, where noun suffixes depend on control unit (grammatical case) information generated with the lexicalisation of verbs and other content words, errors in noun suffixes appear to be more frequent.

Problems with function "words" express themselves in omissions of free forms and in errors of bound forms. (In Italian a bound form cannot be omitted. Even in English it might be that a bound form is never omitted but only replaced by an incorrect zero form.) The results concerning errors in verb suffixes (errors in nominal suffixes are very infrequent and are not considered here) give us two sorts of indications. One is that there is no increase of these errors with increased construction length. This subtracts another ground for making a distinction between "agrammatism" and "paragrammatism", in that it goes against the traditional idea that errors in function words are typical of patients with longer construction length.

The second indication is that the proportion of errors in verb suffixes is a measure not correlated with omission of function words. The only (negative) conclusion that we are prepared to draw from this empirical observation is that whatever the disrupted mechanism responsible for omission of free function words and for its moderate correlation with construction length, it cannot be identical to the disruption underlying errors in verb suffixes. Further evidence for this conclusion is provided by Berndt in Chapter 10: her patient F.M. omitted determiners very frequently but there were no instances of verb suffix omissions in her spoken productions.

We now turn to the last result that we want to discuss: the proportion of nouns and verbs in our patients' speech.

With respect to nouns, the results seem to indicate that their proportion is abnormally higher than in controls only in the patients with very short construction length. This is confirmed by two additional American patients, E.G. and J.E., (data provided by Eleanor Saffran and Myrna Schwartz, as already mentioned) with an average construction length of 1.12 and 1.55 and a proportion of nouns of .50 and .42, respectively. As soon as a construction length of 1.61 is reached (patient F.G.1), the proportion of nouns is not very different than that of controls and it does not seem to be affected by further increases in construction length.

A similar picture emerges for verbs. Only the patient with the shortest construction length (C.D.A.1) has a reduced proportion of verbs with respect to controls. The same is true for the "worst" American patient, E.G.—one out of six—with a proportion of verbs of .13. All the other patients use verbs more or less in the same proportion as controls do.

Patients like the ones whose spontaneous speech is being analysed in the present paper are said sometimes to have special problems with verbs (see, e.g., Saffran, Schwartz, & Marin, 1980). If this is taken to mean that they have difficulties in producing verbs, our results appear to contradict this assumption. All our patients except one produce an equal or larger proportion of verbs out of total words as the controls' proportion (.16). However, it is interesting that for the patient with the most severe impairment in construction ability (and the same appears to be true for the American patient E.G.), the proportion of verbs is less than in controls. In other words, when the average construction length approximates 1 (isolated words), verbs tend to disappear and most produced words are nouns.

It is possible that these changes in the proportion of nouns and verbs in the patients with the very shortest construction length can be explained as consequences of the same impairment that produces a reduced construction length: an impairment of the sentence construction procedure. As it will be recalled, the first step of this procedure is the extraction and lexicalisation of the meaning of the verb of the future clause or sentence. A moderate impairment of the procedure creates problems in the further construction of the meaning of the sentence but leaves this first step undisturbed. However, when the impairment is very severe, it reaches back to the very first step of the procedure and sentences are not even started off with verbs.

Finally, the data presented in Table 9.1 make it abundantly clear that within a group of patients all classified as agrammatic there are substantial differences from patient to patient in the severity—or even the presence—of the symptoms traditionally taken to characterise agrammatism; symptoms such as function-word omission, verb suffix omission and syntactic simplification. The next chapter demonstrates this point equally clearly.

REFERENCES

Goodglass, H., Quadfasel, F. A., & Timberlake, W. H. (1964) Phrase length and the type and severity of aphasia. *Cortex, 1*, 133–153.

Miceli, G., Mazzucchi, A., Menn, L., & Goodglass, H. (1983) Contrasting cases of Italian agrammatic aphasia without comprehension disorders. *Brain and Language, 19*, 65–97.

Parisi, D. (1983) A procedural approach to the study of aphasia. Submitted to *Brain and Language*.

Parisi, D., & Giorgi, A. (1981) *A procedure for the production of sentences*. Technical Report PCIA/1. Istituto di Psicologia, C.N.R.

Parisi, D., & Giorgi, A. (1985) GEMS: A model of sentence production. *Proceedings of the Second Conference of the European Chapter Association for Confutational Linguistics.* Geneva.

Saffran, E. M., Schwartz, M. F., & Marin, O. S. M. (1980) Evidence from aphasia: Isolating the components of a production model. In B. Butterworth (Ed.), *Language production, vol. 1: Speech and talk*. London: Academic Press.

10 Symptom Co-Occurrence and Dissociation in the Interpretation of Agrammatism

Rita Sloan Berndt
*Department of Neurology, University of Maryland School of
Medicine, 22 S. Greene Street, Baltimore, Maryland 21201, USA*

INTRODUCTION

Much of the aphasia research that has been carried out from the perspective of cognitive neuropsychology has been focussed on the syndrome of agrammatic Broca's aphasia. Interest in patients exhibiting agrammatic sentence production has been generated by an apparent relationship between the primary agrammatic deficit—systematic omission of the grammatical morphemes of sentences—and a theoretically-defined processing mechanism that interprets and assigns sentence structures on the basis of these grammatical elements.

Although the omission of grammatical morphemes has been taken to be the cardinal feature of agrammatism, there are other deficits of sentence production that have been viewed as part of the general clinical picture of agrammatism (Goodglass, 1968). As a rule, patients who are called agrammatic produce grossly simplified sentence structure and rarely produce even minimally complex sentences. The grammatical marker omissions and structural simplification of agrammatism occur within a context of effortful, dysprosodic, misarticulated speech and short utterance length. Together with a clinical description of relatively preserved auditory comprehension, these productive symptoms constitute the classical syndrome of Broca's aphasia (Goodglass & Kaplan, 1972; see also Schwartz, Chapter 8 of this volume).

All of the various hypotheses that have been offered to account for the aphasic symptom of grammatical marker omission in speech have rested upon a strong assumption that various of these symptoms *must* co-occur. For example, one widely-accepted view held that grammatical markers were dropped to accommodate the increased effort accompanying the co-occur-

221

ring articulation disorder (Lennenberg, 1973). Thus, grammatical marker omission should not be found in patients without effortful, poorly-articulated speech.

More recent interpretations of agrammatism have similarly rested on a strong interpretation of the necessity of symptom co-occurrences, including a recently-described deficit of auditory comprehension for sentences. Several studies reported in recent years have shown that agrammatic patients fail to understand sentences that require analysis of sentence structure in addition to interpretation of lexical meaning. For example, semantically reversible sentences such as "The lion is chased by the tiger" can be understood only if the syntactic elements, i.e., the grammatical morphemes and the order of noun phrases (NPs), are correctly interpreted as assigning agent status to the second NP. In contrast, semantically non-reversible sentences such as "The letter is mailed by the man" can be readily understood without interpretation of structural markers simply by understanding the relationships that are *possible* among the major lexical items. In a variety of picture pointing tasks manipulating this factor of semantic reversibility, agrammatic patients have been shown to perform poorly when comprehension requires interpretation of structural cues (see Berndt & Caramazza, 1980, for review).

In the last several years, hypotheses have been offered to account for agrammatism as resulting from a deficit to a single processing mechanism (Berndt & Caramazza, 1980; Kean, 1978; Schwartz, Saffran & Marin, 1980; Zurif, 1980). With the exception of Kean's proposal, all of these hypotheses rest upon a strong interpretation of the co-occurrence of productive and receptive symptoms in agrammatism. That is, the omission of grammatical morphemes in *production* has been linked strongly in these theories to a failure to appreciate syntactic markers in *comprehension*, and both symptoms have been attributed to the same underlying deficit.

More detailed studies of individual cases, however, have revealed that the productive and receptive symptoms of agrammatism can be dissociated. Kolk, Van Grunsven, and Keyser (1985) and Miceli, Mazzucchi, Menn, and Goodglass (1983) have reported detailed investigations of Dutch-speaking and Italian-speaking patients who frequently omit grammatical morphemes in sentence production, but who show no difficulty understanding sentences that require syntactic analysis. In both case reports, sentence comprehension was assessed with a variety of tasks employing syntactically reversible sentences, and the patients performed very well. These studies, along with several other recent developments, have forced a reconsideration of the unitary nature of agrammatism (Caramazza & Berndt, 1985; Schwartz, Linebarger, & Saffran, 1985). If the symptoms can dissociate, they must arise from deficits to processing mechanisms that can be separately disrupted.

Since these co-occurrences and dissociations are so important in the formulation of an explanation for agrammatism, it is necessary to develop a method for characterising more clearly the deficits believed to co-occur with and to dissociate from one another. This paper is part of an effort to develop such a method through a detailed study of the sentence production of patients classified as Broca's aphasics. The goal is to describe objectively the production characteristics that have been taken to be symptomatic of agrammatism: fluency, phrase length, structural complexity, and the presence/absence of grammatical markers in expected contexts. If these production characteristics can be shown to dissociate, it will be necessary to re-examine existing accounts of agrammatism that are based on strong assumptions of symptom co-occurrences.

METHODS

Subjects

Data are presented from two normal control subjects and six patients classified as Broca's aphasics on the Boston Diagnostic Aphasia Examination (Goodglass & Kaplan, 1972). As suggested by that classification, all of the aphasic patients produce non-fluent, effortful speech with short, pause-defined phrases and relatively intact comprehension. All patients are right-handed, chronic aphasics with left hemisphere damage and without history of psychopathology, drug abuse or alcoholism. Additional information about these subjects is available in Table 10.1.

TABLE 10.1
Description of Patients and Control Subjects

Patient	Sex	Age	Time post–onset	Education	Occupation	Etiology
V.S.	F	61	12 years	12 years	Legal secretary	LCVA
F.M.	M	39	18 months	12 years	Truck driver	LCVA
J.R.	M	30	7 years	13 years	Florist assistant	(Closed) Head trauma; LCVA
P.D.	F	30	2 years	14 years	Bookkeeper	LCVA
C.G.	M	53	3 years	10 years +GED	Machine operator	LCVA
J.D.	M	38	4 years	14 years	Communications technician	LCVA
M.C.	F	60	control	13 years	Secretary	—
E.F.	F	32	control	18 years	Psychologist	—

Sentence Production

Procedure.   Speech samples were obtained using a story-telling procedure. After some preliminary discussion to refresh their memories, patients were asked to tell a classic, popular fairy tale. This procedure was chosen to provide a relatively constrained speech sample (for which intended targets would be more or less known), without using picture description, which often seems to elicit serial naming. Minimum target sample was five minutes, but this goal was not reached in all cases (e.g., V.S., J.R.).

Tape-recordings of the samples were transcribed verbatim, and all pauses longer than two seconds were timed. Interpretable articulatory distortions and phonemic paraphasias were transcribed as their intended target, and neologisms were noted in the transcripts as such. A second transcription was subsequently made containing only the core of the patient's narrative, excluding perseverations, fillers, comments on the procedures, answers to direct questions, etc.

Several analyses were performed on this core of "narrative" words. Form class counts were made of nouns, verbs, pronouns, other closed class and other open class words. Examination of the corpus for obligatory contexts for determiners, prepositions, and the possessive morpheme was carried out, and omission rates were obtained for those contexts. In addition, utterances were isolated and determined to be minimal "sentences" if they comprised one of the following:

> noun + main verb
> noun + copula + adjective
> noun + copula + prepositional phrase

or

> main verb + noun

Several additional analyses were performed on these "sentence" segments, including determination of mean number of words in sentences, number of clauses, number of NP nodes, and intactness of verb morphology. "Well-formed" sentences were determined to be those with no structural error or omission.

Results.   The six patients have been grouped into three pairs on the basis of some shared characteristics of their sentence production. Table 10.2 lists some of the parameters that might be used as indices of agrammatism, and it is clear that not all of these Broca's aphasics display all of the markers of agrammatism.

TABLE 10.2
Summary of "Agrammatism" Indices

	Rate of speech words/min	'Closed class' words/total	Proportion of nouns/pronouns	Number of determiner omissions/ obligatory contexts	Number of preposition omissions/ obligatory contexts	Verb morphology omission (or error) or auxiliary omission/ total no. sentences
V.S.	16.2	.24	(7/0)	6/7	0/0	4/4
F.M.	23.4	.36	12.7	17/26	0/0	0/7
J.R.	40.8	.43	3.3	1/13	0/3	2/6
P.D.	66.6	.57	.81	0/11	0/0	1/11
C.G.	13.8	.61	1.7	0/19	1/14	2/15
J.D.	38.0	.50	1.3	4/41	2/18	4/39
M.C.	108.0	.57	2.4	0/48	0/25	0/19
E.F.[a]	—	.57	1.5	0/67	0/35	1/43
(controls)						

[a] Control E.F. was tested by the Temple/Penn group, who generously made her data available. All other calculations were done according to the procedures here, but rate of speech was not calculated.

225

TABLE 10.3
Summary of Structural Indices

	Proportion of words in "sentences"	Proportion of "sentences" well-formed	Mean length of sentences	Mean clauses/ sentence	Mean no. noun phrases/clause
V.S.	.57	.00	3.0	1.0	1.0
F.M.	.21	.86	3.1	1.1	.75
J.R.	.38	.50	3.1	1.0	1.7
P.D.	.53	.55	4.0	1.0	1.6
C.G.	.86	.75	7.5	1.2	2.0
J.D.	.80	.72	6.0	1.2	2.0
M.C.	.99	.99	17.0	2.8	1.8
E.F.	1.00	.98	12.2	2.0	2.0

V.S. and F.M. can be viewed as prototypical (severe) agrammatics with a small proportion of closed class words, the production of many more nouns than pronouns, a substantial number of determiner omissions and a failure to produce any prepositions. In addition, all four of V.S.'s "sentences" showed an auxiliary omission. The fact that F.M.'s "sentences" appear to contain well-formed verbs is somewhat misleading: most of his sentences were imperatives (e.g., "wait"; "try it on") that are correct in their uninflected form with no auxiliary. He produced no verb inflections and no auxiliary verb in his seven "sentences," but neither did he produce contexts that required them.

The remaining four patients show a scattering of omissions, but also produce many of the elements that should be omitted in agrammatism (e.g. determiners). P.D., for example, produces many pronouns and auxiliaries. C.G. and J.D. produce many pronouns, determiners, prepositions, and auxiliary verbs. Both of these patients omitted several bound morphemes from verbs (e.g., "he dance with her"), but the omission of these minimal elements is difficult to interpret in patients with articulation disorder. It must be emphasised when reviewing these data that C.G., especially, is extremely non-fluent, with effortful, dysprosodic speech and many distortions. Yet he produces a relatively full complement of grammatical elements in his sentences.

Table 10.3 summarises the structural complexity indices and further clarifies the basis for the subgrouping of patients. V.S. and F.M. (the prototypical agrammatics) show the sparse syntax that has been taken to be one of the defining symptoms of agrammatism—short, single-clause sentences, typically ill-formed, with a single noun phrase. J.R. and P.D., who do not tend to omit grammatical morphemes, show a very similar structural pattern. Despite their fairly frequent correct production of a variety of grammatical markers (Table 10.2), these patients are not able to produce sentences of more than minimal complexity. C.G. and J.D., despite their non-fluency, do a considerably better job producing well-formed sentences of some length. A sample of the narrative produced by G.C., which has been edited to exclude distortions, perseverations and false starts, is reproduced in Table 10.4. C.G. and J.D. do not produce sentences that are as long and complex as those produced by the control subjects, but in light of their marked articulation deficits, what they do produce is remarkably complex and well-formed. For example, C.G.'s sentences produced in Table 10.4 took over one minute and unmeasurable effort for him to produce.

The data from these six aphasic patients, when compared with data obtained from the patients of Miceli et al. and of Kolk et al., reveal several possible ways for dysfluency, agrammatism and structural simplification of

TABLE 10.4
Transcription of Portion of Speech Sample—C.G.

the man (3 sec.) was trying the
slipper (7 sec.) on the girls (9 sec.)
then he (5 sec.) saw (3 sec.)
Cinderella (5 sec.) by herself

Total time: 63 seconds

sentences to co-occur.[1] The prototypical case is for all three to occur together
(V.S. and F.M.), but it appears that even severe dysfluency need not be
accompanied either by agrammatism or by gross structural simplification
(C.G. and J.D.). The most interesting cases involve dissociation between
grammatical marker omission and the production of simplified structures,
and it appears that a double dissociation is possible. J.R. and P.D. show
structural simplification but do not grossly omit grammatical markers; the
Italian and Dutch cases omit grammatical markers but produce relatively
normal structures.

These findings present very serious obstacles to accounts of agrammatism
that would attribute both of the productive symptoms to an impairment of
the same processing mechanism. Instead, they suggest that the syntactic
process underlying the creation of sentence structure in language production
is independent of the mechanism that assigns (or realises) the grammatical
morphemes.

The two productive symptoms of grammatical marker omission and
structural simplification, because they were believed to be necessarily linked,
have been tied as a unit to the frequently co-occurring symptom of
"asyntactic" comprehension. Since the productive symptoms dissociate from
one another, it is possible that the disorder of comprehension can be shown
to remain strongly tied to one of the productive symptoms but not to the
other. This possibility was addressed for the patients included in this study.

Auditory Comprehension of Sentences

Procedure.   The comprehension impairment that has been described
among agrammatic aphasics is operationally defined as a relative failure to
interpret semantically reversible sentences with transitive verbs in a sentence-
picture matching task, co-occurring with good comprehension of semantically non-reversible sentences. As part of a larger study of syntactic process-

---

[1] The fact that the patients of Miceli et al. and Kolk et al. are not speakers of English undermines
my own interpretation of their sentence production. The characterisations offered here are made
by the authors of the case reports, or are inferred from the authors' interpretations.

ing in aphasia, the patients reported here were presented with a variety of such sentences, interspersed randomly with many other types of constructions that were of interest, over a period of several months of testing. In all cases, patients were presented with two pictures—the correct choice and a single distractor. In the semantically reversible cases, the distractor pictured a reversal of subject and object roles; in the non-reversible cases a reasonable lexical substitution of one of the elements (noun or verb) was pictured. One set of 32 active-voice reversible sentences was included that probed all possible combinations of animate and inanimate subject and object nouns (e.g., "the girl hits the rock"; "the rock hits the girl"; "the rock hits the car"; "the girl hits the boy"). This manipulation of the animacy of subjects and objects was employed because a previous study had demonstrated that animacy is often a factor in agrammatic patients' assignment of sentence subject in comprehension (Schwartz, Saffran & Marin, 1980). Eight additional active and eight passive reversible sentences, matched to 12 active and 12 passive non-reversible sentences, were included as well.

Results.   Data are presented in Table 10.5, collapsed over all sentences within the categories of reversible and non-reversible items. These results, showing all patients performing better than chance, must be interpreted in light of patients' response biases and strategies. These factors, which differ from patient to patient, somewhat distort the picture when data are collapsed. For example, if a patient has a strategy of choosing animate nouns as agents (cf. Schwartz, Saffran & Marin, 1980) or of choosing the first noun heard as agent (patients' own reports), performance will be very good on some sentences and at chance on others. Actually, the pattern of comprehension failure for these patients is almost as complicated as the pattern of their

TABLE 10.5
Proportion Correct, Sentence–Picture Matching,
Active and Passive Sentences

	Sentence type	
	Reversible (N = 48)	Non–reversible (N = 24)
V.S.	.73	.96
F.M.	.60	.92
J.R.	.78	1.00
P.D.	.75	1.00
C.G.	1.00	1.00
J.D.	1.00	1.00

production deficit, but for purposes of this discussion it is enough to distinguish patients who have some trouble with the reversible sentences from those who appear to have *no* comprehension impairment. It must be emphasised that *all* patients were judged to have good comprehension on clinical testing, but nonetheless demonstrated considerable difficulty interpreting these simple sentences.

If we assume that the Italian and Dutch cases (whose comprehension was rigorously tested) would have performed perfectly on our tests, then it is possible to argue for a new pattern of co-occurrence between comprehension and production deficits. As shown in Table 10.6, difficulty with syntactic comprehension co-occurs with marked structural simplification of sentences, neither of which necessarily co-occurs with dysfluency or with tendency to omit the grammatical morphemes.

DISCUSSION

These results, though clearly preliminary, raise some interesting points to be considered in the formulation of explanations for the variety of deficits that are apparent here. The pattern of symptom dissociations allows the exclusion of several classes of hypotheses about the nature of these sentence processing deficits.

First, the dissociation of *dysfluency from omission of grammatical markers and from gross structural simplification* indicates that the latter two symptoms are not the result of patients' efforts to compensate for their difficulty in speaking. C.G. and J.D., who speak with great effort, produce relatively normal sentence structures and a full complement of grammatical markers.

TABLE 10.6
Summary of Co–Occurrence/Dissociations of Dysfluency, Agrammatism, Structural Simplicity and Syntactic Comprehension Disorder

	Dysfluency	*Agrammatism*	*Structural simplicity*	*"Asyntactic" comprehension*
V.S.	+	+	+	+
F.M.	+	+	+	+
J.R.	+	−	+	+
P.D.	+	−	+	+
C.G.	+	−	−	−
J.D.	+	−	−	−
Miceli's case	−	+	−	−
Kolk's case	−	+	−	−

Although the complexity and length of utterances of these patients are not perfectly normal (as compared to the two control subjects tested here), a transcript of their narrative appears to be quite unremarkable once it has been edited of distortions and abnormal pauses. It may be that severe fluency disorder has a negative impact on length and complexity in the upper limits of the normal production range. Nonetheless, the quality of the sentences produced by these two patients is much more like normal than like "agrammatic" speech.

Second, the dissociation of *structural abnormalities from omission of grammatical markers* undermines hypotheses that have sought to explain both symptoms as manifestations of a central syntactic deficit (e.g., Berndt & Caramazza, 1980; Saffran, Schwartz & Marin, 1980). In addition, since the data presented here support a double dissociation of these symptoms, it is not possible to support this hypothesis with an argument based on level of severity. That is, the syntactic deficit hypothesis could have been maintained if only one of the patterns of dissociation had been found. For example, patients like J.R. and P.D. might be viewed as less severely impaired counterparts of V.S. and F.M. The Italian and Dutch cases might also be viewed as "mild" cases of agrammatism. This account does not work when both pairs of patients are viewed together. Instead, separable processing mechanisms appear necessarily to be involved. The results of Parisi, described in Chapter 9, also lead to this conclusion.

Third, dissociation of *omission of grammatical markers from "asyntactic" comprehension* weighs against arguments that the comprehension disorder can be causally linked to the omission of grammatical markers in production (Kean, 1978). Again, a double dissociation has been demonstrated. Patients who omit grammatical markers do not necessarily have difficulty with structural cues in comprehension (Italian and Dutch cases); patients with comprehension disorder do not necessarily omit grammatical markers in sentence production (J.R. and P.D.). Thus, the two deficits must arise from impairments to different processing mechanisms.

Aside from these negative implications, these results leave us with one interesting co-occurrence of symptoms and several unanswered questions. The interesting co-occurence is that of structural simplification in production with difficulty interpreting structural cues in comprehension. If this co-occurrence can be upheld by further testing (that is, if no instances of dissociation of these symptoms are reported), then the possibility must be entertained that both symptoms arise from the same underlying deficit. In that case, it will not be unreasonable to revive aspects of previous explanations that viewed the productive and receptive aspects of agrammatism as stemming from a central disruption of the mechanisms responsible for assigning and interpreting syntactic structures.

Clearly, such arguments would have to be modified to deal with the fact that the grammatical marker system need not be affected. At the present time, there is no model of sentence processing available that would provide a reasonable basis for such an account. That is, the assignment of sentence structure (in comprehension and in production) has been viewed as importantly involving access to and production of the grammatical morphemes. If the grammatical marker system is intact, it is unclear what mechanism could be offered to account for major structural problems in comprehension and production. By the same token, disruption of the grammatical marker system (as shown in the Dutch and Italian cases) would be predicted by existing models to have a negative impact on other aspects of sentence processing. These predictions were apparently not upheld in the investigation of these two cases.

Finally, it is important not to lose sight of the fact that we are still unable to account for the original phenomenon that sparked interest in agrammatism: the relative omission of grammatical morphemes in sentence production. It is helpful that we are accumulating information about what other problems can be expected to go along with this deficit. Nonetheless, the question of why the grammatical morphemes are particularly vulnerable in some syndromes probably cannot be answered by research with agrammatic patients alone. Instead, we will need to consider data gathered in research on sentence processing with normal subjects, studies of form class and inflectional disturbances in acquired dyslexia, and research on lexical processing in normal and in brain-damaged subjects. Information seems to be converging on the view that the grammatical morphemes are a special class of lexical items in some important sense and are selectively subject to disruption in a variety of ways.

ACKNOWLEDGEMENTS

The research reported here was supported by NINCDS Grant No. NS-21054 to The University of Maryland School of Medicine. The scoring procedure discussed here was developed collaboratively with Eleanor Saffran and Alfonso Caramazza. Domenico Parisi and Christina Burani also contributed helpful comments to its development. Transcription of tapes, timing of utterances, and initial analyses were done by Celia Basich, whose contribution is gratefully acknowledged.

REFERENCES

Berndt, R. S., & Caramazza, A. (1980) A redefinition of the syndrome of Broca's aphasia: Implications for a neuropsychological model of language. *Applied Psycholinguistics, 1*, 225–278.

Caramazza, A., & Berndt, R. S. (1985) A multi-component view of agrammatic Broca's aphasia. In M. L. Kean (Ed.), *Agrammatism*. New York: Academic Press.

Goodglass, H. (1968) Studies on the grammar of aphasics. In S. Rosenberg & K. Joplin (Eds.), *Developments in applied psycholinguistics research*. New York: Macmillan.

Goodglass, H., & Kaplan, E. (1972) *The assessment of aphasia and related disorders*. Philadelphia: Lea & Febiger.

Kean, M. L. (1978) The linguistic interpretation of aphasic syndrome. In E. Walker (Ed.), *Explorations in the biology of language*. Montgomery, Vt.: Bradford Books.

Kolk, H. H. J., Van Grunsven, M. J. F., & Keyser, A. (1985) On parallelism between production and comprehension in agrammatism. In M. L. Kean (Ed.), *Agrammatism*. London: Academic Press.

Lennenberg, E. H. (1983) The neurology of language. *Daedulus, 102*, 115–133.

Miceli, G., Mazzucchi, A., Menn, L., & Goodglass, H. (1983) Contrasting cases of Italian agrammatic aphasia without comprehension disorder. *Brain and Language, 19*, 65–97.

Saffran, E. M., Schwartz, M. F., & Marin, O. S. M. (1980) Evidence from aphasia: Isolating the components of a production model. In B. Butterworth (Eds.), *Language production vol. 1*. London: Academic Press.

Schwartz, M. F., Linebarger, M., & Saffran, E. (in press) The status of the syntactic theory of agrammatism. In M. L. Kean (Ed.), *Agrammatism*. London: Academic Press.

Schwartz, M. F., Saffran, E. M., & Marin, O. S. M. (1980) The word order problem in agrammatism: 1. comprehension. *Brain and Language, 10*, 249–262.

Zurif, E. B. (1980) Language mechanisms: A neuropsychological perspective. *American Scientist, 68*, 305–311.

11 The Role of the Phoneme–to–Grapheme Conversion System and of the Graphemic Output Buffer in Writing

Gabriele Miceli
Servizio di Neuropsicologia, Università Cattolica, Roma, Italia;
Istituto di Psicologia, C.N.R., Roma, Italia

Maria Caterina Silveri
Servizio di Neuropsicologia, Università Cattolica, Roma, Italia

Alfonso Caramazza
The Johns Hopkins University, Baltimore, Maryland, USA.

INTRODUCTION

The typology of acquired dysgraphias has been enriched greatly by the careful description of the writing impairment in selected brain-damaged patients. Patients with phonological (P.R.—Shallice, 1981), surface (R.G.— Beauvois & Derouesné, 1981; T.P—Hatfield & Patterson, 1983) and deep dysgraphia (J.C.—Bub & Kertesz, 1982b; V.S.—Nolan & Caramazza, 1983) have been reported.

The pattern of errors described in phonological agraphia demonstrates that non-word writing can be virtually abolished in the presence of an almost normal ability to write words. Conversely, the type of writing impairment shown in surface dysgraphia shows that the ability to write words requiring the application of exceptional (or multiple) phoneme-to-grapheme conversion rules can be severely impaired, while stimuli (both words and non-words) that can be written by the application of unambiguous phoneme-to-grapheme mappings are produced quite accurately.

235

The existence of these two forms of dysgraphia has been taken as support for dual-route models of writing (Bub & Kertesz, 1982; Ellis, 1982; Morton, 1980; Shallice, 1981). In these models, the writing of words takes place via a direct (lexical) route, by activation of an abstract, orthographic entry in a Graphemic Output Lexicon (GOL). The activated graphemic representation is placed in a Graphemic Output Buffer (GOB) where it is held for subsequent allographic and motoric stages of processing (Ellis, 1982). Writing non-words involves a nonlexical route in which a Phoneme-to-Grapheme Conversion system (PGC) parses the input phonological string and maps the phonological segments onto corresponding abstract graphemic forms that are then processed further in a manner similar to words.

Dual-route models of writing satisfactorily account for the major patterns of dysgraphia. Thus, for example, the selective inability to write non-words in the phonological agraphic patient P.R. (Shallice, 1981), can be explained by assuming a selective impairment of the PGC, with preservation of the "direct" (lexical) route. In contrast, damage to both the PGC system and to the lexical route (the lexicon) must be assumed to explain the "deep dysgraphic" pattern found in J.C. (Bub & Kertesz, 1982). This patient was unable to write non-words, made semantic errors (e.g., chair→"table") and functor substitutions (e.g., our→"my") in writing words to dictation; and wrote concrete words better than abstract words.

Another error pattern consistent with a dual-route model is that shown by patients with surface dysgraphia (R.G.—Beauvois & Derouesné, 1979; T.P.—Hatfield & Patterson, 1983). These patients produced phonological spelling errors (e.g., "suttle" or "suttel" for *subtle*) when writing irregular words or words involving ambiguous phoneme-to-grapheme mappings. The loss or the unavailability of lexical orthographic information, coupled with a normal ability to write using the indirect (phonological) route can account for the error pattern found in surface dysgraphia.

Much less clear is the status of other error types, such as the visually-related, non-phonological spelling errors (e.g. "elpanch" for *elephant*), frequently found in the written production of aphasic patients (e.g., A.F.—Hier & Mohr, 1977; J.S.—Caramazza, Berndt, & Basili, 1983; R.D.—Ellis, Miller, & Sin, 1983 and Miller & Ellis, this volume). Accurate study of this type of error has been made difficult by the co-occurrence of other error types in most dysgraphic patients, making it impossible to unambiguously attribute visual spelling errors to the disruption of a specific mechanism. The case of pure dysgraphia reported here (also described in Miceli, Silveri, & Caramazza, 1985) produced only visual spelling errors, thus offering an excellent opportunity to explore the mechanism(s) responsible for visual, non-phonological spelling errors. We will discuss here three possibilities: damage to the Graphemic Output Lexicon (GOL); to the Phoneme-to-Grapheme Conversion system (PGC); and to the Grapheme Output Buffer (GOB).

1. Damage to the Graphemic Output Lexicon (GOL)

The possibility that damage to the GOL determines spelling errors of the visual (non-phonological) type has been entertained by Ellis (1982).

Different predictions can be made concerning the consequences of a selective impairment to the GOL in languages with "opaque" vs. "transparent" phoneme-to-grapheme conversion rules. Conversion rules in "opaque" languages such as English or French are characterised by the fact that the same phoneme maps into more than one grapheme (or graphemic sequence)—consider for example the orthographic equivalents of the phoneme /i/ in words like *beef*, *dean*, *scene*, *chief*, etc. In an opaque language, if lexical-orthographic information is disrupted or inaccessible, but the Phonological Output Lexicon and the PGC system are intact, a surface dysgraphic pattern with spelling errors of the phonological type is expected. In the absence of orthographic information, stimuli are written via the PGC system, and errors of the type subtle→suttel should be produced. If damage to orthographic representations is only partial and letter order information is retained, the "orthographic gaps" in the representation may still be filled by the PGC system but, again, phonological spelling errors should result. By contrast, damage to the GOL will go unnoticed in languages with "transparent" conversion rules (like Italian or Serbo-Croatian), where phoneme-to-grapheme mapping is unambiguous. Thus, provided that phonological word representations are intact and accessible, the intact PGC system will always supply the appropriate graphemes, even in the absence of word-specific orthographic information.

If damage or inaccessibility of lexical orthographic representations is coupled with impairment of the PGC system, writing errors of the non-phonological type are expected in all types of languages, independent of the complexity of conversion rules. When this combination of impairments is considered to be responsible for non-phonological spelling errors, a consistent pattern of errors is expected. Upon repeated presentation of the same word list, the patient should demonstrate a significant tendency to make errors on the same "affected" items, and to produce correct responses to the same "unaffected" words. The implications of such consistency effects are considered further by Shallice in Chapter Five.

2. Damage to the Phoneme-to-Grapheme Conversion system (PGC)

A second possible source of spelling errors is a disruption of the Phoneme-to-Grapheme Conversion system (PGC). In most dual-route models (Bub & Kertesz, 1982; Ellis, 1982; Morton, 1980; Shallice, 1981) the "phonological" route is entirely independent of the "lexical" route, its only function being to allow writing of non-words. According to these models, then, impairment of the PGC system should cause spelling errors of the visual type, but only on non-words.

Recently, a dual-route model of writing that postulates a different relationship between the "lexical" and the "phonological" route has been proposed (Nolan & Caramazza, 1983). The model is based on the assumption that graphemic information in the Graphemic Output Buffer (GOB) decays very rapidly and has to be "refreshed" for normal writing. According to Nolan and Caramazza, dictation of a word activates concurrently an orthographic entry in the GOL and a phonological entry in the Phonological Output Lexicon (POL). The phonological and the orthographic representations are then placed in the Phonological Output Buffer (POB) and in the GOB, respectively. Information in the GOB decays very rapidly, but the phonological entry can be rehearsed in the POB, converted into graphemic information by the PGC system, and can "refresh" the decaying information stored in the GOB. According to this model, then, the two routes are not independent, at least in the sense that in order to write words both the "direct" route (through which lexical entries are placed in the GOB) and the "indirect" route (through which the same entries are refreshed) are needed.

This model predicts that a patient with a selective impairment in the PGC will make errors on both words and non-words in writing to dictation. Patients of this type should not present with "lexical" effects (e.g., effects of frequency, abstractness vs. concreteness, or word class) in writing words. Furthermore, since damage to the same mechanism is responsible for the inability to write both words and non-words, errors should be qualitatively similar in these two types of stimuli. As to the type of errors, they should be mostly of the visual type: they originate from the faulty application of phoneme-to-grapheme conversions.

As originally formulated, this model cannot account for cases like P.R. (Shallice, 1981), who are very poor at writing non-words, but nonetheless write words with a negligible number of spelling errors. Miceli, Silveri, & Caramazza (1985) proposed that cases like P.R. can be accommodated in the Nolan and Caramazza model by assuming that other refreshing mechanisms, in addition to that via the POB, are available and may be spared in patient P.R. At least two possibilities may be entertained: (1) an orthographic-lexical refreshing mechanism: the entry stored in the Grapheme Output Buffer (GOB) is refreshed directly from the Graphemic Output Lexicon (GOL), perhaps by repeatedly reactivating the lexical entry that can be placed in the GOB; (2) a phonological-lexical refreshing mechanism: the phonological entry in the POB, subvocally rehearsed, is used to reactivate the lexical entry corresponding to the dictated word. The reactivation keeps the entry in the GOL and the corresponding entry in the POL activated, thus refreshing the GOB and POB, respectively.

3. Damage to the Grapheme Output Buffer (GOB)

Impairment of the Grapheme Output Buffer (GOB) is another potential source of non-phonological misspellings. The GOB is a stage of processing common to both words and non-words; hence, damage to the GOB must affect the writing of words and non-words similarly. Total absence of lexical effects is predicted in the case of a selective impairment to the GOB, but a length effect must be present. Furthermore, since the graphemic information in the GOB is addressed serially and from "left to right" (Ellis, 1982), an error position effect should be observed: errors should occur least often in the initial, more often in the middle, and most often in the final positions of the stimulus. In addition, an equal number of errors should be found in words and non-words. Finally, in terms of the qualitative features of the performance of a patient with a selective deficit in the GOB, the expectation is that errors should be of the visual, non-phonological type, as in the case of damage to the PGC system.

In this paper we analyse the basis for the visual errors in writing in an Italian dysgraphic patient. We attempt to identify the locus of deficit to the writing system in terms of a disruption to one of the three processing components discussed; that is, in terms of a deficit to the GOL, the PGC, or the GOB.

A particularly interesting feature of this report is the fact that, unlike other cases of dysgraphia in the literature, who were speakers and writers of languages with "opaque" phoneme-to-grapheme correspondences, like English and French, our patient's mother tongue was Italian, that is, language with "transparent" phoneme-to-grapheme mappings.

In "opaque" languages, with a large number of irregular words and complex conversion rules, only a processing unit with access to orthographic information about lexical items can ensure normal word writing. The need for two separate routes is much less clear in "transparent" languages where all words can be written normally by the correct application of conversion rules. The study of an Italian dysgraphic patient will give us the opportunity to consider whether in phonologically "transparent" languages a lexical route must be postulated in addition to a phonological route.

CASE REPORT

F.V. is a right-handed lawyer in his early sixties, a native of Rome who had a stroke in November, 1982. He was fully right-handed and an excellent speller prior to his accident.

In the acute stage he was found to be affected by a very mild conduction aphasia, from which he recovered promptly.

The patient was studied within approximately a two-month period, starting at 45 days post-onset. His condition remained stable throughout the period of the study.

The neurological exam was unremarkable, except for F.V.'s complaint of pareasthesias in the right hand, and the finding of a very mild disorder of two-point discrimination in the same hand. The patient could discriminate two points at 2mm distance in his left hand, but at 4mm distance in his right hand.

A CT scan showed a very small, hypodense area involving the superior parietal lobule and perhaps the superior portion of the angular gyrus.

Neuropsychological and Language Exam

paraesthesias in the right hand, and the finding of a very mild disorder of two-elsewhere (Miceli, Silveri, & Caramazza, 1985). Memory, praxis and "general intellectual abilities" were entirely preserved. The following scores were obtained on the WAIS: total IQ:119; verbal IQ:119; performance IQ:117. He scored 132 on the Wechsler Memory Scale. The only abnormality discovered after thorough testing was a very mild tactile agnosia in the right hand: F.V. recognised 12/12 objects placed in his left hand, but only 10/12 objects placed in the right hand. The patient's performance of language tasks was, except for writing, well within normal limits. Of particular relevance, reading was intact for connected text and for isolated words and non-words.

From the start it was evident that only writing posed severe difficulties to F.V. A careful exploration of his spelling abilities was thus started.

EXPERIMENTAL STUDY

1. Oral Spelling

Given the "transparency" of conversion rules in Italian, oral spelling is virtually non-existent: it is not taught in school and is not used in adult life. Tests of oral spelling sound awkward to Italian speakers, and F.V. refused to perform these tasks. We did manage to get him to spell 15 words and 5 non-words presented auditorily. He spelled correctly 13 words and 4 non-words.

2. Written Spelling

A summary of the results obtained by F.V. in various writing tasks is presented in Table 11.1. A complete list of writing errors made by the patient is reported in Miceli, Silveri, & Caramazza (1985).

In various types of tests requiring the production of words (writing sentences to dictation, written naming, written narrative) F.V. made errors on approximately 30% of the items in each test. To appreciate the purity of the dysgraphic disorder consider the results obtained by F.V. on the Boston Naming Test (Goodglass & Kaplan, 1978). When the test was administered for oral naming, the patient made no errors; however, when it was given as a test of written naming, 26/85 stimuli were produced incorrectly (30.6%). Our patient thus provides an extreme contrast with the patient described by Kremin in Chapter 14, whose written naming was vastly superior to his oral naming.

In a test of writing words and non-words to dictation, F.V. wrote incorrectly 63/283 words (22.3%) and 41/133 non-words (30.8%). There was no effect of frequency, concreteness/abstractness, or of part-of-speech in his writing performance. Errors consistently occurred on longer words both in the dictation and written naming task. In the written naming task the mean length of stimuli written correctly was 7.2 letters and that of stimuli written incorrectly was 9.2 letters ($t = 3.519$; $p < .001$); in the writing-to-dictation task the mean length of words written correctly and incorrectly was 5.8 and 6.3 letters, respectively ($t = 2.479$; $p < .02$) and the mean length of non-words written correctly and incorrectly was 5.8 and 6.6 letters, respectively ($t = 3.687$; $p < .001$).

F.V. wrote fluently and appeared to be aware of most of his errors. Letters were well-formed and his handwriting after the CVA was indistinguishable from his handwriting premorbidly.

F.V. produced only visual spelling errors of the non-phonological type. The vast majority of errors on both words and non-words were non-words. For the most part they involved substitutions (finestra [window]→"firestra"; faspedio→"faspenio"); insertions (piede [foot]→"piedre"; turmilo→"sturm-ilo"); or deletions (dieta [diet]→"deta"; delba→"deba") of a single letter of the stimulus. The remaining errors were transpositions of two letters (fanale [streetlamp]→"falane"; no such errors were found on non-words) or

TABLE 11.1
Tests Exploring F.V.'s Writing Abilities: Error Rates Obtained on the Various Tests

	Words		*Non-words*	
Spontaneous written narrative	32/121	(26.4%)		
Written naming	26/85	(30.6%)		
Writing to dictation				
(b) sentences	32/160	(20%)		
(b) individual stimuli	63/283	(22.3%)	41/133	(30.8%)
Copy				
(a) immediate	0/24		0/24	
(b) delayed (3 secs)	1/94	(0.9%)	0/53	
(c) delayed (10 secs)	1/24	(4%)	1/24	(4%)

combinations of two "simple" errors (pudore [modesty]→ "purdode"; beritto → "pertitto"). An isolated "gap" error was noted (invano [in vain]→ "inva o"). Interestingly enough, the distribution of error types was remarkably similar in words and non-words.

The results obtained in this first group of tests, together with the data of the language exam, clearly demonstrate a pure dysgraphia of moderate severity.

The Relationship Between Agraphia and Disorders of Visually-Guided Behaviour.   In at least one published case (Auerbach & Alexander, 1981) a reasonably pure dysgraphia was associated with disorders of visually-guided behaviour. This patient produced spelling errors, like F.V., but his handwriting was very ill-informed and tests of copying figures were executed sloppily. Visually-guided hand movements—especially with the right hand in the right hemifield—were severely impaired, apparently in the absence of disorders of limb praxis. The authors conclude that in their case "pour agraphia . . . may be partly produced by a general difficulty in visually-guided hand movements."

F.V. was submitted to tests of reaching under visual guidance with either hand in either hemifield, in the horizontal and in the vertical plane, similar to those described by Levine, Kaufman, and Mohr (1978). No difference between hands, hemifields or planes was found, and the patient's performance did not differ from normal controls. This result rules out the interpretation that the dysgraphic disorder in our patient was in any way influenced by deficits of visually-guided hand movements. The interpretation of Auerbach and Alexander's data we favour is that in their patient the disorder of reaching was responsible only for the poor execution of figure copying and for the ill-formedness of his handwriting, but not for the spelling errors. The two cases together seem to indicate that visually-guided hand movements and some aspects of writing abilities are anatomically contiguous but psychologically independent functions.

The Relationship Between Agraphia and Disorders of Sensation.   A major complaint of our patient was the presence of paresthesias in the right hand; the only neurological abnormality was a mild disturbance of two-point discrimination in the right hand; the only neuropsychological abnormality besides agraphia was a mild tactual agnosia for objects placed in the right hand. Thus, even if the possibility was very weak, it could not be ruled out without further testing that the sensory defect in the right hand influenced in some way the writing performance—for example, by inducing the patient to inadvertently produce hand gestures that, although belonging to the group of motor patterns necessary for the production of letters, did not correspond to the appropriate letter.

To exclude this possibility, we exploited the fact that prior to his accident F.V. was able to type and asked him to type words and non-words to dictation. It was reasoned that if a sensory defect was the cause of spelling errors in handwriting, F.V. should not make errors when typing (remember that visually-guided hand movements were normal). On this test, F.V. made errors on 21/72 words (29%) and on 19/42 non-words (45%). Not only was his performance on typing similar to that obtained in writing to dictation (actually, it was slightly worse), but the distribution of error types in the two tests was identical, with "simple" errors comprising the majority of misspellings. This result rules out the right-hand sensory deficit as the cause of spelling errors in F.V.

Since spelling errors could not be attributed to disorders of sensation, limb praxis or visually-guided hand movements, the rest of the study focussed on the assessment of various hypotheses that located F.V.'s disorder at different stages of processing within the writing system proper.

The consistent absence of word class, abstractness/concreteness and frequency effects is straightforward evidence against the hypothesis that damage to the lexicon is responsible for F.V.'s dysgraphia. Thus, other possible sources of spelling errors will now be considered.

We will focus on the lexical route (partial damage to the Graphemic Output Lexicon [GOL]), the phonological route (damage to the Phoneme-to-Grapheme Conversion system [PGC]) and the graphemic working memory (damage to the Graphemic Output Buffer [GOB]).

The Graphemic Output Lexicon (GOL) Deficit Hypothesis.   It has been argued by Ellis (1982) that partial loss of word-specific (lexical) orthographic information can be responsible for visual spelling errors of the non-phonological type. To explore this possibility, F.V. was submitted to several tests aimed at ascertaining the status of the orthographic representation of the stimuli he had been unable to write to dictation. A summary of the patient's performance on these tests is shown in Table 11.2.

A visual lexical decision test was prepared, with four sets of stimuli. The first set consisted of 63 words that F.V. had written incorrectly (e.g., palazzo (building)), and the second of the 63 non-words he had produced as incorrect responses (e.g., palozzo). The third set consisted of 63 words that F.V. had written correctly (e.g., ragazzo (boy)); and the fourth of 63 non-words created by the examiner to match F.V.'s non-word errors to the words included in the first set (e.g., ragozzo). The items in the four sets were matched for length and were administered in random order. F.V. performed very well on this task, making only two errors out of 252 stimuli (he failed to recognise one of the words from the first set, and failed to reject one of the non-words from the second set).

To explore more directly F.V.'s knowledge of orthographic information

TABLE 11.2

Tests Aimed at Exploring the Status of the Internal Representations of Words That F.V. Had Been Unable to Write

Errors on visual lexical decision	Words: 1/126; Non-words: 1/126

Ability to correct on sight non-word errors (N = 75) produced as responses to dictated words

(a)	F.V. produced the correct word	47/75	63%
(b)	F.V. produced another word (equally or more similar to the non-word error than the target)	14/75	19%
(c)	F.V. produced another non-word	5/75	7%
(d)	F.V. could not guess at a reasonable target	6/75	8%

Ability to correct upon auditory presentation non-word errors produced as responses to dictated words (N = 28) and non-words (N = 56)

		Words		Non-words	
(a)	F.V. produced the correct target	24/28	(86%)	47/56	(84%)
(b)	F.V. produced another non-word error	3/28	(10.7%)	9/56	(16%)
(c)	F.V. failed to correct the error	1/28	(3.3%)		

on the words he had written incorrectly, his ability to correct on sight errors made in writing to dictation was explored. Seventy-five non-word errors produced as responses to words in writing to dictation were typed and presented to the patient, who was invited to guess at the original stimulus and to write it correctly. The patient produced the correct response to 47 stimuli (62.7%). On 14 occasions (18.7%) he made an incorrect guess, but the guessed word was closer to the presented non-word than the non-word was to the original stimulus (for example, fontana [fountain] was written as "fortona", and corrected as "fortuna" [fortune]). Eight attempts at correction (10.7%) gave rise to other spelling errors (three of which were identical to those F.V. had produced originally). F.V. was unable to think of a word for 6 stimuli (8%).

In a later test session F.V. was asked to correct upon auditory presentation of the target response the 28 errors he had been unable to correct on sight. The examiner pronounced the target response while F.V. looked at a card on which the incorrectly spelled word had been typed. He corrected 24/28 errors (86%). This procedure was also used with errors (56) F.V. had produced as responses to non-words. He achieved a success rate similar to words—47 corrections: 84%.

The second test administered to obtain information on the status of orthographic lexical representation consisted of asking F.V. to write to dictation words (N = 36) and non-words (N = 21) he had written incorrectly on a previous occasion, and the same number of words and non-words, matched for length, to which he had previously responded correctly. Of the stimuli previously written correctly, four words and eight non-words were written incorrectly. Of the stimuli previously written incorrectly, eight words and 11 non-words were written incorrectly—approximately equal level of performance.

The hypothesis that spelling errors derive from partial disruption of orthographic representations predicts regularities of error patterns. Upon repeated presentation of the same word list, the patient should consistently deal easily with items whose orthographic representation is intact, and consistently encounter difficulties with words whose orthographic representations are impaired.

None of the results we reported support this interpretation, as F.V.: (1) easily distinguishes his own errors from correct stimuli on a lexical decision test; (2) is able to correct a substantial proportion of incorrect responses; and (3) has an inconsistent error pattern on tests where rewriting of previously presented items is required.

Further disconfirmation of the hypothesis that spelling errors in our case originate from partial damage to orthographic representations lies in the observation that the error pattern on words and non-words is the same (see also the next section). If the hypothesis were to be correct, differences in the incidence of various error types on words and non-words should have been found. None were.

Having excluded damage to the GOL as an explanation for F.V.'s pattern of errors, we can turn to the analysis of two other mechanisms that, if damaged, could be responsible for the error pattern found in our patient: the Phoneme-to-Grapheme Conversion system (PGC) and the Graphemic Output Buffer (GOB).

The Phoneme-to-Grapheme Conversion System (PGC) Deficit and the Grapheme Output Buffer (GOB) Deficit Hypotheses. Further testing was conducted and more detailed analyses of F.V.'s errors were made in order to investigate the possibility of a deficit either to the Phoneme-to-Grapheme Conversion system (PGC) or the Grapheme Output Buffer (GOB).

The first set of tests explored F.V.'s ability to copy words and non-words under three separate conditions.

In the first test, words (N = 24) and non-words (N = 24) typed in upper case were presented and F.V. was asked to copy the stimuli left in view. His performance on this test was flawless.

In the second test, words (N = 94) and non-words (N = 53) typed in upper case were presented. F.V. was asked to inspect the stimulus and to remove it when he felt confident that he could copy it. The patient was allowed to start to copy three seconds after the stimulus had been removed. Ninety-three words (99.1%) and all non-words were copied correctly.

Finally, words (N = 24) and non-words (N = 24) typed in upper case were presented with a procedure identical to that used in the previous test. Ten seconds after the stimulus had been removed, F.V. was allowed to copy the stimulus that had been presented. Twenty-three words and 23 non-words (96%) were copied correctly.

Two tasks that required writing words and non-words during concurrent articulation were also administered.

In the first test, words (N = 36) and non-words (N = 36) were dictated. Half of the words were of high (> 100/million), half were of low frequency (> 5/million). Within each frequency range, six stimuli were four or five; six stimuli were six or seven; six were eight or nine letters long. Non-words were constructed by substituting one or two letters in the word stimuli, and were matched with words in length. Stimuli were presented in random order. After each stimulus had been dictated, F.V. was instructed to articulate a meaning-less CVCV sequence, and to begin writing after initiating concurrent articulation.

The results are shown in Table 11.3. F.V. made 10/36 errors on words (27.8%)—a performance comparable to that obtained in writing to dictation. F.V. made errors on 3/18 high-frequency words (16.7%), and on 7/18 low-frequency stimuli (38.9%). On low-frequency items, a moderate effect of length was found. By contrast, performance on non-words was very poor: 27/36 items were written incorrectly (75%). A length effect was also noticed as none of the 8–9 letter long non-words were written correctly.

In the second test, the stimuli to be written during concurrent articulation were presented visually. The same number of stimuli as in the previous test was administered, and the same variables were controlled for. This time, the stimuli presented to the patient were typed individually in upper case on a card. F.V. was instructed to inspect each stimulus until he felt ready to

TABLE 11.3
Writing under Concurrent Articulation

		Errors		
		Words		Non-words
	Stimulus length	H.F.	L.F.	
(a) Auditory presentation	4–5	1/6	1/6	7/12
	6–7	1/6	2/6	8/12
	8–9	1/6	4/6	12/12
(b) Visual presentation	4–5	0/6	0/6	2/12
	6–7	0/6	0/6	3/12
	8–9	1/6	0/6	6/12

reproduce it. The patient himself removed the stimulus, started to articulate a meaningless CVCV sequence and subsequently began to write.

The results obtained by F.V. on this test are also shown in Table 11.3. F.V. wrote words very well (one error out of 36 items: 2.8%). Performance on non-words was markedly poorer (10 errors: 27.8%). A clear length effect was present, as the patient made errors on two of the shortest and six of the longest items.

Finally, in order to obtain more information on other aspects of F.V.'s dysgraphia, a qualitative analysis of errors was carried out.

F.V. made the same type of errors in all the tests that were administered, independent of whether he was required to produce words or non-words and, within words, of the lexical features of the stimulus. All the errors, with the exception of a neologism produced in the spontaneous narrative, were close approximations to the target, all of them being classifiable as substitutions, insertions, deletions or transpositions of letters, or as combinations of two of the above varieties. The distribution of errors on words and non-words is shown in Table 11.4. The similarity of error type distribution on words and non-words is striking.

In all tests, the incidence of writing errors was mildly but consistently higher on non-words than on words.

Most of the errors made by F.V. were non-words (115/129 in the corpus reported in Miceli, Silveri, & Caramazza, 1985—89%). All errors were obviously of the visual, non-phonological type—phonological misspellings are impossible in languages with "transparent" conversion rules. Most errors preserved the orthographic structure of the stimulus (i.e., vowels substituted for vowels, consonants substituted for consonants) as approximately half of them were substitutions of single letters. Substitutions involved consonants more often than vowels (70 and 15, respectively), and in 97% of the instances vowels substituted vowels and consonants substituted consonants. Only

TABLE 11.4
Incidence of the Various Error Types in Writing to Dictation
(From Miceli, Silveri, & Caramazza, 1985)

	Stimulus			
	Words		Non-words	
Substitutions	63	(46%)	19	(46%)
Insertions	22	(16%)	4	(10%)
Deletions	10	(7%)	4	(10%)
Transpositions	4	(3%)	—	
Gap	2	(1%)	—	
Mixed	37	(27%)	14	(34%)

8/129 errors in the published corpus contained illegal graphemic sequences (6.2%)—that is, resulted in illegal letter strings (e.g., discorso [discourse] →"dirscorso"; ambulmo→"amnulmo"). These orthographically illegal responses occurred equally often with words and non-words.

An analysis of the position of errors in F.V.'s responses was carried out, and the results are shown in Table 11.5. It is evident that errors occurred equally often in all positions within the stimulus, be it a word or a non-word.

F.V.'s performance on the tests reported in this section can be summarised briefly as follows: (1) immediate and delayed copying are executed flawlessly; (2) concurrent articulation while writing to dictation results in more misspellings on non-words than on words. Within words, a mild frequency effect and a clearer length effect were found; (3) concurrent articulation with delayed copying of visually presented stimuli affects only non-word writing. A qualitative error analysis shows that the patient produces misspellings of the same type in all tests, on both words and non-words—slightly but consistently more on the latter. The only lexical variable that influences writing is stimulus length. All the errors are very near misses and occur in all positions of the response.

TABLE 11.5
Error Position Effect: Position of the First Error in Word and Non-Word Stimuli

Stimulus length	Error position									
	1	2	3	4	5	6	7	8	9	10
Words										
4	1	2	4	1						
5	9	4	4	4	1					
6	7	2	12	1	2	1				
7	2	4	5	2	2	1	1			
8	1	4	4	5		2	1	1		
9		1	3		1	1	2	1		
10	1	1	1	1		1				
11				2	1			1	1	
12				1					1	
13			1							

Stimulus length	1	2	3	4	5	6	7	8
Non-words								
4		1	1					
5	2	1	2	2				
6	2	2			1			
7	2	5	2	2	3	2		
8	2	2	1	2	1	1		
9	1							

F.V.'s performance, while easy to summarise, is difficult to interpret within the framework of currently available models of writing. Specifically, it is difficult to ascribe the demonstrated error pattern to the impairment of either the Phoneme-to-Grapheme Conversion system (PGC) or the Grapheme Output Buffer (GOB). Our results do not allow clearcut conclusions with respect to these two alternatives.

The GOB deficit hypothesis predicts that errors: (1) should be of the visual, non-phonological type; (2) should occur with longer stimuli; (3) should be equally frequent on words and non-words; (4) should occur more frequently in middle and final than in initial letter positions. It also predicts that: (5) direct copying should be intact, while delayed copying should be as poor as writing to dictation.

Our results meet predictions (1) and (2), but are at variance with predictions (3), (4) and (5).

The mild advantage of word over non-word writing might be ascribed to the presence of unusual, although permissible, letter sequences in our non-word lists. This explanation is not entirely tenable since, even though letter transition probabilities in non-words were not calculated, all items were constructed by changing only one or two letters in real words and unusual sequences were avoided.

The lack of an error position effect is also hard to explain, unless one admits that damage to the GOB resulted both in a reduced graphemic working memory and in the loss of the "directional polarisation" (Seymour & Porpodas, 1980) or the "directional scanning" (Ellis, 1982) of the graphemic information.

The good performance on delayed copying is even harder to reconcile with the GOB deficit hypothesis. It might be argued that visual presentation allows to bypass the GOB by activating a non-linguistic, visual memory system that treats the stimulus as a graphic (as opposed to graphemic) pattern. However, the stimuli to be copied were typed in upper case and the patient copied them in script—which means that F.V. treated the presented stimulus as a graphemic (and not graphic) pattern.

Thus, even if it is not possible to reject the GOB deficit hypothesis altogether, too many *ad hoc* adjustments would have to be made to render it a satisfactory explanation of the pure dysgraphia found in our patient.

Let us consider now whether the Phoneme-to-Grapheme Conversion system (PGC) deficit hypothesis constitutes a better explanation of the disorder shown by our patient.

As noted in the Introduction, most dual-route models (e.g., Bub & Kertesz, 1982; Ellis, 1982; Morton, 1980; Shallice, 1981) postulate that the lexical and phonological routes are totally independent. Evidence in favour of these models comes from phonological agraphic patient P.R. (Shallice, 1981), who wrote correctly most words, with a negligible percentage of spelling errors, and yet managed to write only 18% of the (very easy) non-words that were dictated to him. In the case of an isolated PGC impairment, this model predicts that: (1) word writing should be normal; (2) non-word writing should be poor, with spelling errors—if PGC damage is not too severe; (3) under concurrent articulation, word writing should be unaffected while non-word writing should be severely disrupted.

The model of writing proposed by Nolan & Caramazza (1983), on the other hand, postulates that the direct and the indirect route are not independent, since word writing requires refreshing of the rapidly-decaying graphemic information stored in the GOB, through the Phonological Output Buffer. Within this model, since writing of both words and non-words requires the PGC system, selective damage to the PGC predicts that: (1) spelling errors should occur with both words and non-words; (2) should be of the same type; (3) a length effect should be demonstrated; (4) concurrent articulation should affect the writing of both words and non-words.

Neither model offers a satisfactory account of F.V.'s pattern of errors as a consequence of PGC impairments: dual-route models of the first type cannot explain misspelling on words; the second model cannot explain the mild but consistent advantage of word over non-word writing and the outcome of tests of writing during concurrent articulation, where non-word writing was disproportionately affected with respect to words. Furthermore, the latter model in its original formulation also encounter difficulties with case P.R., who does not show the predicted errors on words.

The inability of the Nolan & Caramazza model to explain F.V.'s behaviour can be remedied by making two not unreasonable assumptions. The first is that for word writing, refreshing of information in the GOB can be accomplished by the POB, but also directly from the Graphemic Output Lexicon (GOL). This kind of buffer refreshing from lexical output systems is also proposed by Bub, Black, Howell, and Kertesz (see Chapter 4) and Miller and Ellis (Chapter 12). Still another refreshing mechanism could involve the Phonological Output Lexicon (POL) that through subvocally rehearsed information in the POB, can be used to "re-enter" the lexicon. The second assumption is that subjects differ with respect to the extent to which they rely on the direct vs. the indirect route. With these assumptions it is possible to explain both the word advantage and the pattern of errors produced in writing during concurrent articulation. The discrepancies between case P.R. (Shallice, 1981) and our patient F.V. can be resolved: P.R. relied heavily on the direct route, while F.V. relied heavily on the indirect route. Consequently, it could be argued that damage to the PGC caused a selective impairment of word writing in P.R., and of both word and non-word writing in F.V.

It is appropriate, at this point, to ask whether the fact that our patient is a speaker of Italian might not have contributed significantly in determining the particular pattern of his writing deficit; that is, whether the fact that Italian is characterised by a "transparent" orthography might not be a critical factor in determining the extent of reliance in the PGC system in writing.

The need for postulating extensive reliance on the lexical route in order to write words correctly in "opaque" languages seems self-evident: the PGC system alone would never be able to map /jɔt/ onto "yacht," nor would it be able, given /sɛnt/ to choose the correct alternative among "sent," "cent," and "scent." In "transparent" languages, by contrast, exclusive reliance on phonological information (i.e., on a single-route process) would ensure normal writing of all stimuli. In other words, the issue here is whether the existence of two routes in the writing system is language-independent (i.e., cognitively necessary) or language-specific (i.e., induced by features peculiar to each language). Considerable cross-language research on the forms of dysgraphia in different languages needs to be undertaken to resolve this issue.

ACKNOWLEDGEMENTS

The work reported here was supported in part by NIH grant number NS 14099 to The Johns Hopkins University and a grant from the CNR (Italy).

REFERENCES

Auerbach, S. H., & Alexander, M. P. (1981) Pure agraphia and unilateral optic ataxia associated with a left superior parietal lobule lesion. *Journal of Neurology, Neurosurgery, and Psychiatry, 44*, 430–432.

Beauvois, M. F., & Derouesné, J. (1981) Lexical or orthographic agraphia. *Brain, 104*, 21–49.

Bub, D., & Kertesz, A. (1982) Deep agraphia. *Brain and Language, 17*, 147–166.

Caramazza, A., Berndt, R. S., & Basili, A. (1983) The selective impairment of phonological processing: A case study. *Brain and Language, 18*, 128–174.

Ellis, A. W. (1982) Spelling and writing (and reading and speaking). In A. W. Ellis (Ed.), *Normality and pathology in cognitive functions*. London: Academic Press.

Ellis, A. W., Miller, D., & Sin, G. (1983) Wernicke's aphasia and normal language processing: A case study in cognitive neuropsychology. *Cognition, 15*, 111–144.

Hatfield, M., & Patterson, K. E. (1983) Phonological spelling. *Quarterly Journal of Experimental Psychology, 35*, 451–468.

Hier, D. B., & Mohr, J. P. (1977) Incongruous oral and written naming: Evidence for a subdivision of the syndrome of Wernicke's aphasia. *Brain and Language, 4*, 115–126.

Levine, D., Kaufman, K. J., & Mohr, J. P. (1978) Inaccurate reaching associated with a superior parietal lobule tumor. *Neurology, 23*, 556–561.

Miceli, G., Silveri, M. C., & Caramazza, A. (1985) Cognitive analysis of a case of pure agraphia. *Brain and Language, 25*, 187–212.

Morton, J. (1980) The logogen model and orthographic structure. In U. Frith (Ed.), *Cognitive processes in spelling*. London: Academic Press.

Nolan, K. A., & Caramazza, A. (1983) An analysis of writing in a case of deep dyslexia. *Brain and Language, 20*, 305–328.

CNL–I*

Seymour, P. H. K., & Porpodas, C. D. (1980) Lexical and non-lexical processing of spelling in dyslexia. In U. Frith (Ed.), *Cognitive processes in spelling*. London: Academic Press.

Shallice, T. (1981) Phonological agraphia and the lexical route in writing. *Brain, 104*, 413–429.

12

Speech and Writing Errors in "Neologistic Jargonaphasia": A Lexical Activation Hypothesis

Diane Miller
Andrew W. Ellis
Department of Psychology, University of Lancaster, Lancaster, LA1 4YF, England

INTRODUCTION

Neologisms, or literal paraphasias, occur commonly in the speech of many patients with Wernicke's (alias "receptive," "fluent" or "sensory") aphasia. Very often these neologisms are reasonably close approximations to some identifiable target word, for example, "skut" (/skʌt/) for the target *scout*, or "stringt" (/strɪŋt/) for the target word *stream*. The term *neologistic jargonaphasia* has been applied to patients in whom the neologism is the predominant error form (see Buckingham & Kertesz, 1976; Butterworth, 1979; Caramazza, Berndt, & Basili, 1983; Ellis, Miller, & Sin, 1983; Miller, 1983).

Patient J.S. reported by Caramazza et al. (1983) and patient R.D. of Miller (1983) and Ellis, Miller, and Sin (1983) are remarkably alike in several respects, despite the fact that Caramazza et al. label J.S. as a case of "pure word deafness" because of their focus on his speech perception difficulties rather than language production problems. The similarities include:

1. The speech of both patients was replete with neologisms, most of which occupied content-word "slots." However J.S.'s speech, unlike R.D.'s, was also syntactically disordered and made hesitant by prolonged anomic pauses.

2. The neologisms of both patients were mostly still identifiable as distortions of target words: thus they usually contained the correct number of syllables and some correct phonemes (discussed later). The neologisms rarely resulted in sequences of phonemes that are illegal in English.

3. Both patients made more errors to low than high frequency target words. J.S. read 13/23 high-frequency, concrete nouns correctly vs. 5/23 low-frequency nouns; while R.D. named correctly 33/46 pictures with high-frequency names vs. 11/46 pictures with low-frequency names. (In both cases the comprehension of pictures and single written words was intact.)

4. Both patients made spelling errors which, like the neologisms in speech, bore a recognisable resemblance to the target word. In the case of the spelling errors, however, the resemblance was orthographic rather than phonological: the attempts shared letters in common with targets, including elements of a word's spelling that are not predictable from its pronunciation. The errors did not sound like the target word and were not transcriptions of the patient's attempt to say the word. R.D.'s spelling errors included "thunb" for *thumb*, "sicesse" for *scissors*, "leopald" for *leopard*, "forg" for *frog*, and "zebare" for *zebra*; while J.S. produced "pyminia" for *pyramid*, "escallion" for *escalator*, and "opuspus" for *octopus*.

5. Despite their errors in writing, both patients showed better written than spoken naming (both would spontaneously write down words they could not produce in ordinary conversation). In one task R.D. named and wrote correctly only 5/30 picture names, but managed to write a further 12 names he could not say correctly. J.S. showed a trend in the same direction (spoken naming of pictures 11/35, written naming 6/35), and his spelling errors give the impression of being closer approximations to their targets than do his spoken neologisms.

6. Both patients had a severe auditory comprehension deficit. J.S.'s hearing was within normal limits on audiological testing and he could identify evironmental sounds well, but he was found to have a severe deficit at the linguistic-phonetic level. R.D.'s auditory impairment almost entirely prevented him from repeating words or phrases, matching words heard to pictures, or answering simple Yes/No questions. Unfortunately, more systematic investigations were not carried out with R.D., and the locus of his speech comprehension deficit remained uncertain.

7. In contrast to their poor to non-existent speech comprehension, both J.S. and R.D. had good reading comprehension. They scored highly on matching written words to pictures, synonym matching, semantic categorisation, and comprehension of simple sentences (though J.S. was shown to have some syntactic problems).

8. Despite their intact comprehension of single written words, both patients made neologisms when attempting to read aloud. The neologisms to written word targets were closely similar to neologisms in picture-naming (Miller, 1983).

In this paper we shall present additional data on R.D.'s speech and writing errors. We shall further discuss how the pattern of symptoms shown by R.D. and J.S. can be assimilated to, and perhaps illuminate, models of normal language processing. In particular we shall emphasise the compatibility of their symptoms with activation models of language production such as the one put forward by Stemberger (1982; 1984; 1985).

R.D.'s ERRORS IN SPEECH AND WRITING

1. Serial Position Effects in R.D's Neologisms and the (Non)viability of a Phonological Decay Explanation

If the phonological forms of words are subject to decay before articulation, with perhaps an accelerated decay rate in neologistic jargonaphasics, then neologisms could reflect the patient's attempt to construct a pronunciation on the basis of a rapidly vanishing phonological trace. There is independent motivation from studies of speech errors and verbal short-term memory for a pre-articulatory phonological storage capacity which might be subject to decay in normals (Ellis, 1979; 1980; Morton, 1970). The less time an item spends in storage the more likely it will be to be outputted correctly. In general, early phonemes in words will be less prone to decay than later ones, so should be more accurately reproduced.

This prediction was tested on R.D.'s neologisms using a method devised by Wing and Baddeley (1980). The method assigns items in strings of any length to one of five serial positions according to the procedure shown in Table 12.1. Sixty of R.D.'s spoken neologisms were randomly selected from

TABLE 12.1
Method of Assigning n Elements to Five Serial Positions (from Wing & Baddeley, 1980)

Total no. of elements in string	Serial position in string				
	1	*2*	*3*	*4*	*5*
1	—	—	1	—	—
2	1	—	—	—	2
3	1	—	2	—	3
4	1	2	—	3	4
5	1	2	3	4	5
6	1	2	3,4	5	6
7	1,2	3	4	5	6,7
8	1,2	3	4,5	6	7,8
9	1,2	3,4	5	6,7	8,9
10	1,2	3,4	5,6	7,8	9,10
11	1,2	3,4	5,6,7	8,9	10,11
etc.					

picture-naming responses. The correct versions of the 60 target words contained 292 phonemes whose distribution across the five serial positions is shown in line A of Table 12.2.

Each target-neologism pair was inspected to see which of the target phonemes occurred in the neologism. For those that did occur a mark was given to one of the five positions according to the location of the correctly reproduced phonemes in the target word. So, if we consider the target-neologism pair

Target: /pensɪl/ (pencil)
Neologism: /pezʌl/

we see that the phonemes /p/, /e/ and /l/ from the target also occurred in the neologism. Their positions in the target are 1, 2 and 5 respectively, so those positions received one credit each. In the pair bishop—/gɪmɪst/ only position 2 gains a credit. One hundred and eighty-two phonemes from target words also occurred in the neologisms, and their distribution across serial positions is shown in line B of Table 12.2. From line A we can compute the distribution of correct phonemes that would be expected by chance if serial position played no part in determining whether a phoneme is accurately reproduced or not. That chance distribution is shown in line C of Table 12.2. Although there is a tendency for position 1 accuracy to be higher than expected, the observed and chance distributions do not differ significantly (chi-square = 3.30, df = 4), and the decline from positions 2 to 5 that one would predict on the decay hypothesis is certainly not present.

TABLE 12.2

Distribution of Phonemes Across Five Serial Regions in 60 Target Words and Neologisms
(Patient R.D.)

		Position					
		1	2	3	4	5	Total
A.	Target phonemes	73	30	86	30	73	292
B.	Phonemes correctly reproduced in neologisms	56	18	50	17	41	182
C.	Expected-by-chance distribution of 182 phonemes from neologisms	45	19	54	19	45	182

2. Serial Position and Decay Explanations of R.D's Spelling Errors

An explanation of the characteristic spelling errors of J.S. and R.D. in terms of decay might propose that the decay occurs at a graphemic level where words are represented as letter strings, possibly in the graphemic buffer posited by Morton (1980) and Ellis (1982). To be viable such a theory must also explain why the patients cannot overcome decay by simply reactivating the appropriate lexical entry, thereby refreshing the contents of the buffer. Caramazza et al. (1983) and Nolan and Caramazza (1982) suggest that refreshment may normally come to the graphemic buffer from rehearsal at the phonemic level, via nonlexical phoneme-grapheme conversion. Their proposal, as we understand it, is that in normal spelling only those parts of a longer word's spelling that are not predictable with certainty by phoneme-grapheme conversion procedures are retrieved from a lexical store; the remaining parts being supplied (and refreshed) by phoneme-grapheme conversion (cf. similar proposals by Dodd, 1980; Frith, 1980; Weigl, 1975). If a patient is no longer able to rehearse items in the phonemic buffer, and is therefore unable to refresh the contents of the graphemic buffer via pho-neme-grapheme conversion, then Caramazza et al. argue that errors like those of J.S. and R.D. might arise. We can see two problems for this particular theory. First, patients have been reported who can still spell well despite having no demonstrable access to the phonological forms of the words they could spell (Bub & Kertesz, 1982; Levine, Calvanio, & Popovics, 1982). Second, Shallice's (1981) case of "phonological dysgraphia" could still spell the majority of words with which he was familiar before his stroke, but had an impairment of phoneme-grapheme conversion which meant that he could no longer assemble plausible spellings for new or non-words he could nevertheless repeat aloud (and could therefore both hear and say). Despite this impairment to phoneme-grapheme conversion, which should according to Caramazza et al.'s theory have prevented the refreshment of the graphe-mic buffer, Shallice's patient did not make spelling errors of the sort made by J.S. and R.D.

A decay theory of J.S.'s and R.D.'s spelling errors should also predict a serial position effect (possibly an exaggerated one given the slower produc-tion of writing than speech), with early letters being more accurately reproduced than later ones. An analysis similar to that done earlier on R.S.'s neologisms was carried out on 36 of his spelling errors (from Ellis et al., 1983, Table 9). There were 186 target letters in the 36 words, and their distribution across serial positions is shown in line A of Table 12.3. One hundred and thirty-one of those letters were correctly reproduced in the errors, and line B of Table 12.3 shows their distribution across serial positions. The distribu-tion that would be expected by chance if position played no part in

TABLE 12.3

Distribution of Letters Across Five Serial Regions in 36 Spelling Errors (Patient R.D., from Ellis, Miller, & Sin, 1983, Table 9)

		Position				
		1	*2*	*3*	*4*	*5*	*Total*
A.	Target letters	42	24	54	24	42	186
B.	Letters correctly reproduced in errors	32	20	38	15	26	131
C.	Expected-by-chance distribution of 131 correct letters in errors	29.5	17	38	17	29.5	131

determining whether or not a letter is correctly reproduced is given in line C of Table 12.3. Once again there was no significant difference between observed and expected distributions (chi-square $= 1.4$, df $= 4$). Thus we could find no empirical support for a decay explanation of R.D.'s spelling errors.

3. Real and Random Transpositions and Substitutions in Neologisms

The 60 picture-naming errors made by R.D. that were earlier analysed for serial position effects contained 121 incorrect phonemes. Of these, 22 (18%) could be classified as transpositions (i.e., movement of a phoneme from one position in the target word to another in the neologism), while the remaining 99 (82%) were substitutions by phonemes not found anywhere in the target word. Though it is common practice to analyse incorrect phonemes into transpositions and substitutions it is clear that if substitution is the *only* process going on, then a proportion of those substitutions will result in apparent transpositions because the error phoneme will, by chance, be a phoneme which occurs elsewhere in the target word. To test whether this hypothesis could account for the 18% of apparent transpositions in R.D.'s 60 picture-naming neologisms all the error phonemes were extracted then randomly reassigned back to the vacant slots in the neologisms. The number of pseudo-substitutions and pseudo-transpositions were then counted. This reassignment was performed three times with the result that the mean number of pseudo-transpositions in the false corpus was found to be exactly the same as the number of apparent "transpositions" in the genuine corpus, 22 in both cases. We conclude from this that substitutions are the *only* type of error needing to be explained in R.D.'s neologisms, and that if a patient makes both apparent substitution and transposition errors then the proportion of transpositions must be substantially over 20% before one can conclude with confidence that genuine phoneme movements are occurring.

4. Phonetic Similarity and Phoneme Substitutions

R.D. made 71 errors to consonant targets in the 60 picture-naming neologisms. Casual inspection suggested that in a high proportion of cases the correct phoneme and the substituted phoneme were phonetically similar, differing on only one or two distinctive features. At the same time it was not clear to us what proportion of errors one would expect to be so close to their targets if phonetic similarity played no part whatsoever in determining which consonants substitute for which others.

The phonetic similarity of the target and error phonemes was compared by means of a four-feature system of "place," "manner," "voicing," and "oral/nasal" (from Trost & Canter, 1974). The three random phoneme redistributions as in the previous section provided a corpus of 194 pseudo-errors that preserved any general biases R.D. may have had towards the production of some phonemes rather than others in his neologisms. Table 12.4 shows the number of genuine consonant substitutions and the mean number of pseudo-substitutions that differed from their targets by 1, 2, 3 or 4 distinctive features.

We note that other investigators have claimed in the past that phonemes substituted in aphasic paraphasias tend to differ from the correct targets by only one or two distinctive features (e.g., Green, 1969; Martin & Rigrodsky, 1974; Trost & Canter, 1974), but we also note that such studies have typically not generated a corpus of pseudo-errors to obtain chance estimates against which to compare the apparent influence of phonetic similarity. It is clear from Table 12.4 that for R.D. both genuine *and* pseudo-errors tended to differ from their targets by only one or two distinctive features, and the

TABLE 12.4

Number of Distinctive Feature Differences Between Target and Error Phonemes in 71 Genuine Substitutions by R.D. and 194 Pseudo-Substitutions (See Text for Details)

		Number of distinctive features different between target and error				
		1	*2*	*3*	*4*	*Total*
Genuine consonant substitutions	No.	23	34	14	0	71
	Prop.	.32	.48	.20	0	
Pseudo-substitutions	No.	55	86	47	6	194
	Prop.	.28	.44	.24	.03	

observed distribution of the genuine errors did not in fact differ significantly from the distribution one would predict by chance on the basis of the pseudo-errors (chi-square = 3.38, df = 3). We conclude, therefore, that the case for a phonetic similarity effect in aphasic phoneme substitution remains, at present, not proven, though we are willing to believe that genuine effects may exist, particularly for Broca's aphasics, where phonetic problems are often compounded with phonemic ones.

5. Successive Approximations to Target Words

Aphasic patients often make more than one attempt at a target word. Joanette, Keller, and Lecours (1980) found that aphasics with relatively intact speech comprehension tended to move closer toward the target in a series of approximations while Wernicke's aphasics with comprehension deficits did not show this consistent progression. From the various picture-naming tasks carried out on R.D. we had 43 sequences that consisted of more than one attempt at the target. The first and the final attempts were compared for their proximity to the target in terms of number of syllables, consonant-vowel structure, and number of phonemes correct. On each measure two points were distributed between the two attempts, with both receiving one point if they were both equally close approximations to the target, and one attempt receiving two points and the other none if one was a closer approximation than the other. On number of syllables, if one attempt contained the correct number and the other an incorrect number, then the former gained two points and the latter none; otherwise both gained one point each. On consonant-vowel structure, if only one attempt had the same structure as the target word it gained both points; otherwise both attempts gained one point each. The number of target phonemes correctly reproduced in each attempt were also counted. If one attempt had more correct phonemes than the other it gained two points and the other none; otherwise both gained one point. Finally, the points gained by each attempt were summed to yield a total approximation score for each initial and final neologism.

Three of R.D.'s 43 sequences (7%) ended with the target being correctly spoken. Nine other sequences (21%) moved towards the target, ending with a neologism which was a closer approximation to the target than was the first attempt. Nine sequences (a further 21%) had initial and final attempts which were equally good (or bad) approximations, while in the remaining 22 sequences (51%) the final attempt was a *worse* approximation to the target than was the initial attempt. Overall, 12 "corrections" moved closer to the target and 22 moved further away. On a binomial test this represents a significant bias towards doing *worse* (p = .032), which is what one would predict if the major determinant of a "correction" is, in fact, random.

6. Target Relatedness in R.D.'s Neologisms

We have just demonstrated that when R.D. substituted one phoneme for another there was no tendency for the substituted and substituting phonemes to be phonetically similar. We have also shown that there was no tendency for multiple attempts to move any closer towards the target. At this point the reader may be querying the status of the second of our original list of claims about R.D., namely that his neologisms were usually fairly close approximations to identifiable targets. Table 1 of Ellis, Miller, and Sin (1983) provides a transcript of R.D.'s attempt to describe a picture depicting the goings-on around a scout camp. R.D.'s three attempts at *scout* were /skɜt/, /skʌt/, and /skrʌt/, all recognisable approximations. Other close approximations included /bʌn/ and /bʌk/ for *bull*, /strɪŋt/ for *stream*, /trəʊlvɒt/ for *trivet*, and /pləʊɪŋ/ for *blowing*.

In Study 6 reported by Ellis et al. (1983) R.D. was asked to name 10 pictures with one-syllable names, 10 with two-syllable names, and 10 with three-syllable names. He named five correctly. Of the 25 neologistic errors, 20 (80%) contained the correct number of syllables and none was more than one syllable different from the target (see Ellis et al., Table 8).

To confirm the claim of target relatedness we took the 60 target-neologism pairs used in the earlier analyses, separated the neologisms from their original targets, shuffled them, and randomly reassigned them back to the targets as "pseudo-errors."[1] We then counted, irrespective of positions, the number of phonemes shared in common by genuine and pseudo- target-error pairs. For 51 of the targets (85%) the real error shared more phonemes in common with the target than did the pseudo-error: there were 7 ties (12%) and only 2 cases (3%) in which the pseudo-error turned out to be a closer "approximation" to the target than had been the real neologism R.D. gave as an attempt at it. This greater phonemic relatedness of real neologisms than pseudo-errors is highly significant (p < .0001 by sign test).

We also looked at the extent to which real and pseudo-errors tended to have the same number of syllables as their targets. Tables 12.5a and 12.5b show the results of these two analyses. For the genuine target-error pairs the tendency for the two to share the same number of syllables was once again significant (chi-square = 103, df = 4,p < .001) thereby replicating on a fresh sample of errors the result reported by Ellis et al. (1983). For the pseudo-errors there was no such tendency (chi-square = 7.51, df = 4).

Thus, despite the lack of evidence for a phonetic similarity effect in R.D.'s phoneme substitutions, or any tendency for second and third attempts at a target to be closer than the first, there can be no disputing the claim that the great majority of R.D.'s neologisms *were* target-related. We shall now turn to

---

[1] This analysis was suggested by Max Coltheart.

TABLE 12.5A
Number of Syllables in Target Words and 60 (Genuine)
Neologisms Made by Patient R.D.

		Number of syllables in target		
		1	2	3
Number of	1	27	0	0
syllables in	2	1	19	1
error	3	0	1	11

TABLE 12.5B
Number of Syllables in Target Words and 60 "Pseudo-
Errors" Derived by Randomly Reassigning R.D.'s Original
Neologisms Back to the Targets

		Number of syllables in target		
		1	2	3
Number of	1	10	9	7
syllables in	2	11	8	3
pseudo-error	3	7	3	2

considering how this symptom-pattern might best be explained, and what implications it might have for theories of normal language processing.

INTERPRETATION AND IMPLICATIONS

Neologistic Jargonaphasia as a Selective Impairment of a "Phonological Component"

Caramazza, Berndt, and Basili (1983) proposed that their patient J.S. suffers from "a severe impairment of the phonological processing system." While we have nothing but admiration for the quality of the analysis in that paper, we should like to take brief issue with Caramazza et al.'s concluding diagnosis as applied to J.S. and R.D. First, in the sort of information-processing models we find congenial (e.g., Ellis, 1984; Morton & Patterson, 1980; Newcombe & Marshall, 1980) it is not at all clear what one would point to and say "that is *the* phonological processing system." Instead of being one phonological processing system, there are many processing components whose operations involve representations that linguists would call phonological. In the logogen model (Morton, 1980; Morton & Patterson, 1980) these include the speech output logogen system, the response buffer, grapheme-phoneme conversion, phoneme-grapheme conversion, auditory analysis, the auditory input logogen system, and auditory-phonological conversion (at least). We are loath, without very compelling evidence, to combine these various components into a phonological super-module and claim that that component is impaired in J.S. and R.D. Our reluctance is reinforced by our second objection, which is to note the number of language disorders already known to us in which some of these components are impaired but not others. Grapheme-phoneme conversion may be uniquely impaired in phonological dysgraphia (Shallice, 1981); phoneme-grapheme conversion uniquely disturbed in phonological dyslexia (Beauvois & Derouesné, 1979; Funnell, 1983; Patterson, 1982); and auditory-phonological conversion uniquely disturbed in auditory phonological agnosia (Beauvois, Derouesné, & Bastard, 1980). Most importantly, patients with *very* pure word deafness may have problems with auditory analysis alone and show none of the neologisms which so disrupted the speech of J.S. and R.D. (e.g., Hemphill & Stengel, 1940; Klein & Harper, 1956; Saffran, Marin, & Yeni-Komshian, 1976). That is, we already have sufficient evidence to fractionate the phonological component, so we would suggest that it is perhaps unwise, even as an opening gambit, to explain an observed pattern of performance in terms of impairment to such a component.

Our third and fourth objections can be stated together. The third is that there is at least one component impaired in J.S. and R.D. that we do not consider to be phonological; and the fourth is that there are processes *intact* in patients like J.S. and R.D. that we consider to be indisputably phonological. The impaired non-phonological process in question is the activation or retrieval of the graphemic forms of words for writing. We stated earlier our objections to interpreting R.D.'s and J.S.'s spelling errors in terms of a failure of phonologically-mediated refreshment. Our preferred interpretation given in Ellis et al. (1983) and elaborated upon further in this paper is in terms of a problem in activating lexical entries within an orthographic lexicon akin to Morton's (1980) graphemic output logogen system. We see no reason for including that orthographic component within a larger "phonological processing system."

The phonological component thought to be *intact* in neologistic jargonaphasics like R.D. and J.S. is the inflectional system. When an inflected word is distorted in a neologism the inflection itself is claimed to be: (1) preserved; and (2) accommodated to the neologised form of the root (Buckingham & Kertesz, 1976; Butterworth, 1979; Caplan, Kellar, & Locke, 1972; Garrett, 1982). Thus, if the neologised word is a plural, then the form the plural inflection takes (/s/, /z/, or /ɪz/) will depend not on the correct version of the root but on its neologised form. This implies that the inflectional processes which may be impaired in some "agrammatic" patients (see Berndt, this volume) are spared in neologistic jargonaphasia (though admittedly neither Caramazza et al. nor Ellis et al. tested this directly on their patients).

There seems to us to be no viable alternative to analysing the impairments shown by J.S. and R.D. in terms of damage to several (at least three) different processing systems. Those whose impairment results in the loss of speech comprehension and the neologisms in speech can reasonably be called phonological, but other phonological components may be intact, and at least one non-phonological component (the orthographic output lexicon) is impaired.

Neologisms and Lexical Activation in Speech Production

Neologisms require explanation in terms of a cognitive theory of normal speech production. They are clearly not caused by a semantic deficit, because both J.S. and R.D. could successfully carry out a variety of semantic tasks where written words and/or pictures were used as stimuli. We would also argue that neologisms are not due to a selective impairment in the use of content (alias open-class or major words).

Although R.D.'s reading comprehension was good, he produced neologisms when trying to read words aloud. These neologisms were virtually indistinguishable from those made in spontaneous speech or object naming (Miller, 1983). It was possible, therefore, to use reading aloud to assess the relevance of the content/function word distinction in this type of aphasia. Once content and function words were matched on frequency of usage, R.D. was no more successful at reading aloud function words than content words, and made neologistic errors to both (Ellis, Miller, & Sin, 1983, Studies 9 and 10). The content-function word distinction might be relevant to the description and explanation of some aphasic patterns, but we would argue that neologistic jargonaphasia is not one of them, and that previous claims to that effect have arisen artefactually because neologisms tend to occur on less frequently used words, and content words tend to be less common in usage than function words. The lack of a serial position effect in R.D.'s neologisms argues against an explanation in terms of decay at a pre-articulatory phonemic stage. The absence of genuine phoneme transpositions and the apparent lack of an effect of distinctive feature similarity on phoneme errors also argues against localising the deficit at the same phonological level held responsible for phonemic slips of the tongue where both transpositions and phonetic similarity effects are clearly present (Ellis, 1979; 1980).

Ellis, Miller, and Sin (1983) followed Buckingham (1979) and Butterworth (1979) in interpreting neologisms as due to a problem with activating entries in a speech lexicon. The lexicon in question contains one entry (or "node") for each word in a speaker's vocabulary. The entry for a particular word is activated in speaking by the prior activation of the semantic representation of the word's meaning. On being activated, the lexical entry releases or activates the spoken form of the word as a sequence of phonemes that can then be articulated. Thus if you wish to talk about a large, humped desert animal, the semantic representation of that concept will activate the appropriate node in the speech output lexicon that will, in turn, release or activate the phoneme sequence which can then be articulated ("camel").

The speech output lexicon obviously corresponds in many respects to the speech output logogen system in the post-1979 version of Morton's logogen model (Morton, 1979; Morton & Patterson, 1980), but we believe that the existence of neologisms necessitates certain revisions to that model. Logogens are word production (or recognition) units which are activated by their various inputs (in speech production the activation to the speech output logogens comes from the semantic system). Each logogen has a threshold. It accumulates activation until that threshold is exceeded, whereupon the logogen releases its output code (a phonemic code in the present instance). The threshold assumption makes logogens all-or-nothing units: a logogen's activation is either less than threshold, in which case none of its content is released, or it is more than threshold, in which case all of its content is released. In logogen theory, there should be no such state as one in which part, but not all, of the information encoded in a logogen is available to a speaker, yet that is precisely what appears to happen to J.S. and R.D. The neologisms of those two patients are predominantly "target-related" in Butterworth's (1979) terms; that is, they typically have the same number of syllables as the target word and share a substantial proportion of phonemes in common with it. If our interpretation of such neologisms as indicators of an impairment of the speech output logogen system is correct, then the errors imply that a logogen may on occasion release some but not all of its contents in violation of the all-or-nothing principle. Normal speakers may experience the same state when groping for a little used word that is caught on the "tip of the tongue" (see Ellis et al., 1983, pp. 140–141).

Though we have no quarrel with the overall functional architecture of the logogen model, we would suggest that logogens should take on some of the attributes of word-level nodes in interactive activation models of language processing (e.g., McClelland & Rumelhart, 1981; Stemberger, 1982; 1984; 1985). Stemberger's attempt to apply activation concepts to modelling speech production is particularly relevant. In Stemberger's model lexical units are activated from above by inputs from syntax and semantics, and they in turn feed activation down to the phoneme level. Thus the conceptual or semantic entry *two-humped desert dweller* will strongly activate the lexical unit for *camel*, and weakly activate the entries for conceptually related words like *oasis*, *dune* or *nomad*. In addition to being activated from above, lexical units inhibit one another until one of them—hopefully the right one—emerges maximally active from the fluctuating background noise. Units also differ in their quiescent resting levels of activation. Whereas in Morton's logogen model each firing of a logogen lowers its threshold, in activation models the frequency of usage of a lexical unit affects its resting level of activation. Words a speaker uses often have higher resting levels of activation and so require less input from above to become maximally active (they are also more efficient inhibitors of other units).

As the activation level in a lexical unit rises it begins to activate the appropriate phoneme-level units. Activation also flows back up from the phoneme level to the lexical level, providing a form of positive feedback (N.B. in this sort of model *codes* do not pass between components, only activation and inhibition). Phoneme units also inhibit one another until—again hopefully—the correct set of phonemes is activated. Activation can then flow down to lower processing levels, resulting ultimately in the word being articulated.

How might neologisms of the sort made by R.D. and J.S. arise within such a model? Recall that Ellis et al. (1983) found high frequency words that R.D. had used many, many times in his life were likely to be correctly spoken and that neologisms tended to afflict words he would have used less often. In terms of Stemberger's model this pattern seems most readily interpretable as a *difficulty in activating lexical units in the speech output lexicon*. Where activation should be cascading down from the semantic level to the lexical level (McClelland, 1979), in neologistic jargonaphasics that flow is reduced to a trickle. The trickle is sufficient to activate lexical units whose resting level of activation is already high (common words, including most of the function words), but lexical units for less common words never achieve maximal activation.

Weak lexical activation will mean weakened activation at all subsequent levels. Phoneme-level units for lower frequency words will consequently be only weakly activated (and inappropriate ones only weakly inhibited). The patient will thus be obliged to produce attempts in which some of the phonemes will be correct (because they managed to be sufficiently activated to be discriminable against the background noise level), but other slots will be filled by inappropriate phonemes. The analyses presented earlier suggest that for R.D. initial and final phonemes have no special status; they are not activated any more strongly than medial ones. The lack of an apparent phonetic similarity effect suggests that substitutions are more or less random (though consonant or vowel status tended to be preserved), and the fact that "transpositions" occurred only at chance level suggests that activation problems are a *sufficient* explanation: we do not need to postulate any additional serial ordering deficit.

Each attempt at a word will be a fresh attempt to activate lexical and phonemic units. The element of randomness explains why a word may be correctly articulated on one occasion but not on another. Presumably as a consequence of his severe speech perception deficit R.D. did not appear to know when he had correctly spoken a word, and he would sometimes produce the correct version flanked on either side by neologistic approximations. As we have seen, his successive attempts at words did not tend to result in closer approximations. In contrast, patient I.S. discussed by Miller (1983) showed reasonable comprehension of single spoken words, and her successive attempts *did* tend to get closer to the target, often culminating in the correct pronunciation.

Some patients who produce large numbers of neologisms tend to perseverate phonemes between one neologism and the next (e.g., Buckingham, Whitaker, & Whitaker, 1979). Though not a salient feature of R.D.'s speech, this tendency may be explicable within our interpretation of Stemberger's model. If activation of the phoneme level by the lexical level is weak, then inhibition between phonemes will be weak too. A phoneme unit which has chanced to dominate over its neighbours and become highly activated will not be inhibited as it should be by later words. Thus when the patient is having difficulty activating the phoneme units for a particular word, the phoneme units from previous neologisms may still have fairly high activation levels and so be erroneously incorporated in the present attempt, resulting in a tendency to between-word (or between-neologism) perseverations.

Errors of Partial Lexical Knowledge in Spelling and Normal Lexical Activation in Writing

Our current best guess, then, is that neologisms reflect problems in lexical activation. A similar explanation may be possible for the spelling errors of R.D. and J.S. (e.g., "castin" for *cactus*, "harf" for *harp*, "escatlon" for *escalator*, "sigil" for *squirrel*, and "bashel" for *basket*). Ellis (1982) argued that such errors reflect "partial lexical knowledge": the patient has access to *some* spelling information specific to the word being presented, but not enough to permit the word to be spelled correctly.

The source of that word-specific spelling knowledge (at least for spellers of English) is an orthographic output lexicon, similar in function to the speech output lexicon but a distinct and separate cognitive component. Recent neuropsychological analyses of spelling point firmly towards the conclusion that writers of English must retrieve (or activate) the spellings of familiar words from a lexical store (e.g., Bub & Kertesz, 1982; Ellis, 1982, 1984; Hatfield & Patterson, 1983; Shallice, 1981). The spelling lexicon may be the same lexicon as that used in reading (Allport & Funnell, 1981), or may be specific to orthographic *output* (Morton, 1980). Either way, we would propose that it operates on activation principles. In writing, lexical units of the orthographic lexicon are activated by inputs from the semantic system, and also possibly by inputs from the corresponding units of the speech lexicon (Ellis, 1982; 1984; Morton, 1980). As a lexical unit is activated, it in turn activates the appropriate letter-level units (graphemes), and inhibits unwanted letters. If all goes well, the correct set of graphemes—and *only* the correct set of graphemes—is activated, and the word should be written correctly.

All does not go well, however, when patients like R.D. and J.S. produce their spelling errors. If in normals some activation for the orthographic output lexicon comes from the speech output lexicon, that activation will be attenuated (at least for many words) because of the problems discussed earlier. However, it seems likely that input from semantics can be enough to permit correct spelling. Patient M.H. of Bub and Kertesz (1982) was anomic in speech, yet could write correctly many words of whose pronunciations she seemed to have no knowledge (see also patient E.B. of Levine, Calvanio, & Popovics, 1982). Thus we seem to be obliged to argue that in R.D. and J.S. there is also an attentuation of the activation coming to the orthographic lexicon from the semantic system. As a consequence of the weak activation of orthographic lexical units, grapheme units are only weakly activated, making it hard for the patient to discern which are the correct graphemes against the background of noise. The resultant spelling errors therefore contain a mixture of correct letters and incorrectly selected ones. Again, initial and final positions do not seem to be privileged in any way.

Errors of partial lexical knowledge, due, we believe, to weak activation of units in the graphemic output lexicon, are not specific to jargonaphasics. They have been reported in a variety of patients with a variety of other speech and writing symptoms (e.g., Bub & Kertesz, 1982; Clark & Grossfeld, 1983; Hatfield & Patterson, 1983; Hier & Mohr, 1977; Morton, 1980). So while a problem in activating units in the orthographic output lexicon may be characteristic of neologistic jargonaphasia, that problem is not unique to that type of patient.

In conclusion, we believe that the neologism and spelling errors of patients like R.D. and J.S. are readily explicable in terms of activation models like that of Stemberger (1982; 1984; 1985), and that such errors create difficulties for threshold based models such as Morton's logogen model. At present, our best explanation of R.D. and J.S. postulates similar deficits afflicting two distinct output lexicons. Spelling errors showing partial lexical knowledge can occur without neologisms, but the reverse dissociation (which we would predict) has not, as far as we are aware, yet been reported.

ACKNOWLEDGEMENTS

We would like to thank Max Coltheart and Joe Stemberger for comments on an earlier draft of this chapter. We are very grateful to the speech therapists of the Lancaster Moor Hospital, Maureen Millar, Shân Hallam and Garry Withnell, for their permission to test R.D., and for many helpful comments and suggestions. We should also like to thank the consultants and the District Administration Team for their consent and support. The data were collected while the first author was a postgraduate student funded by the Social Science Research Council, and the preparation of this paper was assisted by grant number G8305511N from the Medical Research Council and a grant from the University of Lancaster Research Fund. Finally, we owe a debt of gratitude to R.D. and his wife for their cheerful cooperation throughout.

REFERENCES

Allport, D. A., & Funnell, E. (1981) Components of the mental lexicon. *Philosophical Transactions of the Royal Society of London, B295*, 317–410.

Beauvois, M. F., & Derouesné, J. (1979) Phonological alexia: Three dissociations. *Journal of Neurology, Neurosurgery and Psychiatry, 42*, 1115–1124.

Beauvois, M. F., Derouesné, J., & Bastard, V. (1980) *Auditory parallel to phonological alexia.* Paper presented at the Third European Conference of the International Neuropsychological Society, Chianciano, Italy, June, 1980.

Bub, D., & Kertesz, A. (1982) Evidence for lexicographic processing in a patient with preserved written over oral single word naming. *Brain, 105*, 697–717.

Buckingham, H. W. (1979) Linguistic aspects of lexical retrieval disturbances in the posterior fluent aphasias. In H. Whitaker & H. A. Whitaker (Eds.), *Studies in neurolinguistics, vol 4.* New York: Academic Press.

Buckingham, H. W., & Kertesz, A. (1976) *Neologistic jargon aphasia.* Amsterdam: Swets and Zeitlinger.

Buckingham, H. W., Whitaker, H., & Whitaker, H. A. (1979) On linguistic perseveration. In H. Whitaker & H. A. Whitaker (Eds.), *Studies in neurolinguistics, vol 4.* New York: Academic Press.

Butterworth, B. (1979) Hesitation and the production of verbal paraphasias and neologisms in jargon aphasia. *Brain and Language, 8*, 133–161.

Caplan, D., Kellar, L., & Locke, S. (1972) Inflection of neologisms in aphasia. *Brain, 95*, 169–172.

Caramazza, A. Berndt, R. S., & Basili, A. G. (1983) The selective impairment of phonological processing: A case study. *Brain and Language*, 18, 128–174.

Clark, L. W., & Grossfeld, M. L. (1983) Nature of spelling errors in transcortical sensory aphasia: A case study. *Brain and Language, 18*, 47–56.

Dodd, B. (1980) The spelling abilities of profoundly pre-lingually deaf children. In U. Frith (Ed.), *Cognitive process in spelling.* London: Academic Press.

Ellis, A. W. (1979) Speech production and short-term memory. In J. Morton & J. C. Marshall (Eds.), *Psycholinguistics series vol 2: structures and processes.* London: Elek Science; and Cambridge, Mass.: MIT Press.

Ellis, A. W. (1980) Errors in speech and short-term memory: The effects of phonemic similarity and syllable position. *Journal of Verbal Learning and Verbal Behaviour, 19*, 624–634.

Ellis, A. W. (1982) Spelling and writing (and reading and speaking). In A. W. Ellis (Ed.), *Normality and pathology in cognitive functions.* London: Academic Press.

Ellis, A. W. (1984) *Reading, writing and dyslexia: a cognitive analysis.* London: Lawrence Erlbaum Associates.

Ellis, A. W., Miller, D. & Sin, G. (1983) Wernicke's aphasia and normal language processing: A case study in cognitive neuropsychology. *Cognition, 15,* 111–114.

Frith, U. (1980) Unexpected spelling problems. In U. Frith (Ed.), *Cognitive processes in spelling.* London: Academic Press.

Funnell, E. (1983) Phonological processes in reading: New evidence from acquired dyslexia. *British Journal of Psychology, 74,* 159–180.

Garrett, M. F. (1982) Production of speech: Observations from normal and pathological language use. In A. W. Ellis (Ed.), *Normality and pathology in cognitive functions.* London: Academic Press.

Green, E. (1969) Phonological and grammatical aspects of jargon in an aphasic patient: A case study. *Language and Speech, 12,* 103–118.

Hatfield, F. M., & Patterson, K. E. (1983) Phonological spelling. *Quarterly Journal of Experimental Psychology, 35A,* 451–468.

Hemphill, R. E., & Stengel, E. (1940) A study of pure word-deafness. *Journal of Neurology, Neurosurgery and Psychiatry, 3,* 251–262.

Hier, D. B., & Mohr, J. P. (1977) Incongruous oral and written naming: Evidence for a subdivision of the syndrome of Wernicke's aphasia. *Brain and Language, 4,* 115–126.

Joanette, Y., Keller, E., & Lecours, A. R. (1980) Sequences of phonemic approximation in aphasia. *Brain and Language, 11,* 30–44.

Klein, R., & Harper, J. (1956) The problem of agnosia in the light of a case of pure word deafness. *Journal of Mental Science, 102,* 112–20.

Levine, D. N., Calvanio, R., & Popovics, A. (1982) Language in the absence of inner speech. *Neuropsychologia, 20,* 391–409.

Martin, A. D., & Rigrodsky, S. (1974) An investigation of phonological impairment in aphasia, part 2: Distinctive feature analysis of phonemic commutation errors in aphasia. *Cortex, 10,* 329–346.

McClelland, J. L. (1979) On the time relations of mental processes: An examination of systems of processes in cascade. *Psychological Review, 86,* 287–330.

McClelland, J. L., & Rumelhart, D. E. (1981) An interactive activation model of context effects in letter perception: Part 1. An account of basic findings. *Psychological Review, 88,* 375–407.

Miller, D. (1983) *Word finding difficulties in aphasia.* Unpublished Ph.D. thesis, University of Lancaster, England.

Morton, J. (1970) A functional model for memory. In D. A. Norman (Ed.), *Models of human memory.* New York: Academic Press.

Morton, J. (1979) Facilitation in word recognition: Experiments causing change in the logogen model. In P. A. Kolers, M. Wrolstad, & H. Bouma (Eds.), *Processing of visible language, vol 1.* New York: Plenum.

Morton, J. (1980) The logogen model and orthographic structure. In U. Frith (Ed.), *Cognitive processes in spelling.* London: Academic Press.

Morton, J., & Patterson, K. E. (1980) A new attempt at an interpretation, or, an attempt at a new interpretation. In M. Coltheart, K. E. Patterson, & J. C. Marshall (Eds.), *Deep dyslexia.* London: Routledge & Kegan Paul.

Newcombe, F., & Marshall, J. C. (1980) Transcoding and lexical stabilisation in deep dyslexia. In M. Coltheart, K. E. Patterson, & J. C. Marshall (Eds.), *Deep dyslexia.* London: Routledge & Kegan Paul.

Nolan, K. A., & Caramazza, A. (1982) Modality-independent impairments in word processing in a deep dyslexic patient. *Brain and Language, 16,* 237–264.

Patterson, K. E. (1982) The relation between reading and phonological coding. In A. W. Ellis (Ed.), *Normality and pathology in cognitive functions.* London: Academic Press.

Saffran, E. M., Marin, O. S. M., & Yeni-Komshian, G. (1976) An analysis of speech perception in word deafness. *Brain and Language, 3*, 209–228.

Shallice, T. (1981) Phonological agraphia and the lexical route in writing. *Brain, 104*, 413–429.

Stemberger, J. P. (1982) *The lexicon in a model of language production.* Unpublished doctoral dissertation, University of California at San Diego, USA.

Stemberger, J. P. (1984) Structural errors in normal and and agrammatic speech. *Cognitive Neuropsychology, 1*, 281–313.

Stemberger, J. P. (1985) An interactive activation model of language production. In A. W. Ellis (Ed.), *Progress in the psychology of language, vol 1.* London: Lawrence Erlbaum Associates.

Trost, J. E., & Canter, G. J. (1974) Apraxia of speech in patients with Broca's aphasia: A study of phoneme production accuracy and error patterns. *Brain and Language, 1*, 63–79.

Weigl, E. (1975) On written language: Its acquisition and its alexic-agraphic disturbance. In E. Lenneberg & E. H. Lenneberg (Eds.), *Foundations of language development: A multi-disciplinary approach, vol 2.* New York: Academic Press.

Wing, A. M., & Baddeley, A. D. (1980) Spelling errors in handwriting: A corpus and a distributional analysis. In U. Frith (Ed.), *Cognitive processes in spelling.* London: Academic Press.

13 Speak and Spell: Dissociations and Word-Class Effects

Karalyn Patterson
MRC Applied Psychology Unit, Cambridge CB2 2EF, England.

Christina Shewell
Addenbrooke's Hospital, Cambridge CB2 2QQ, England.

INTRODUCTION

In the 1970s, neuropsychologists were busy discovering, or at least demonstrating, that it is possible to read without phonology, in two senses. Firstly, in order to read a whole familiar word aloud, it is not necessary to be able to assign phonology to individual graphemes; thus a patient who, given the printed word *try*, cannot respond with /tə, rə, ai/ may easily be able to produce "try" (see, for example, Beauvois & Derouesné, 1979). Secondly, in order to comprehend a written word, it is not necessary to know anything about its corresponding phonology; thus a patient who, given *try*, cannot respond /tə, rə, ai/ or respond "try", or judge that it rhymes with *high*, may still know what *try* means (see, for example, Saffran & Marin, 1977).

In the first few years of the 1980s, neuropsychologists have been busy discovering that it is possible to spell without phonology. In a way, this demonstration may surprise more than its reading counterpart, possibly because whilst one rarely observes direct influences of phonology in everyday fluent reading, there is evidence to suggest a continually active role for phonology in spelling: phonological spelling errors are a commonplace occurrence for many normal adult spellers. Of course, the neuropsychological observation that a skill (such as reading or spelling) may operate without the functional intactness of a particular routine (such as a phonological

273

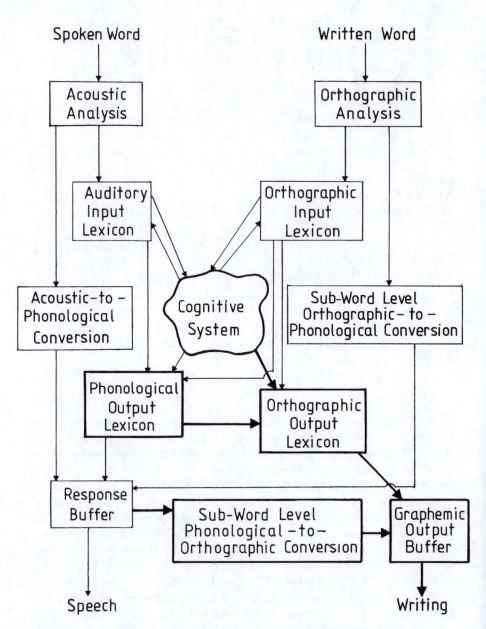

FIG. 13.1 A simple process model for the recognition, comprehension and production of spoken and written words and non-words.

process) does not conflict with the view that the skill *normally* involves this process.

As with reading (though perhaps also with some significant variations attributable to the differing natures and purposes of reading and spelling), spelling without phonology may take several different forms. Considering for the moment only spelling to dictation, this task requires on the model in Fig. 13.1 that the subject proceed from the process represented in the upper left-hand corner, acoustic analysis of the spoken word, to the process represented in the lower right-hand corner, output from the grapheme buffer. If a patient cannot use sub-word conversion from phonology to orthography to enter the graphemic output buffer, yet can spell to dictation, this is one form of spelling without phonology. Shallice (1981) described such a patient, P.R., who could spell real words with considerable success (though with a little sensitivity to frequency, concreteness and/or word class) but failed almost entirely to spell simple non-words (which he could repeat correctly). Bub and Kertesz (1982) also presented a patient, M.H., characterised by this basic pattern of phonological dysgraphia though with some differences from P.R. (particularly concerning the influence of stimulus dimensions on spelling and also with a different pattern of reading performance). In these phonological dysgraphic patients, spelling appears to be accomplished with a more-or-less intact orthographic output lexicon accessed by the cognitive system and/or possibly by representations in the phonological output lexicon.

In addition to a deficit compromising sub-word level phonological-to-orthographic conversion, a patient may also have such an impaired phonological output lexicon that a representation in the orthographic output lexicon *could not* be accessed by its corresponding entry in the phonological output lexicon. If the patient is still able to achieve some success in spelling, this is another form of spelling without phonology. Patients with this general pattern have been described by Hier and Mohr (1977, patient A.F.); Assal, Buttet and Jolivet (1981, J.F.M.); Ellis, Miller, and Sin (1983, R.D.: see also Miller and Ellis, this volume). Evidence of the patients' sub-word translation deficit typically derives from complete failure to write non-words to dictation (as in phonological dysgraphia, above) whilst their lexical phonological impairment is signalled by poor or abolished oral naming of pictures (though the pictures are comprehended). In these cases, spelling appears to be accomplished solely by access from representations in the cognitive system to entries in the orthographic output lexicon. Some, though not all, of this latter group produce semantic paragraphic errors in spelling, and are accordingly labelled deep dysgraphic patients.

The patient to be described here, G.A., is a patient whose spelling ability is severely impaired yet sufficient to provoke an inquiry as to how it is accomplished. It is clear that phonology, either at a whole-word or a sub-word level, makes no contribution to G.A.'s spelling. One of the features of her performance supporting this claim is the fact that, as implied by the title of the chapter, G.A.'s speech and spelling present entirely different patterns.

CASE REPORT

G.A. is a 76 year-old right-handed woman who worked prior to retirement in the medical records department of a large hospital. She had a history of known hypertension, with a minor transient cerebral ischaemic episode in 1974, and in May 1981 suffered a major CVA. Although unconfirmed by CT scan or other definitive neurological assessment, the damage was undoubtedly in the region of the mid-posterior left cerebral hemisphere. This left her with a minor right-hand weakness and a major dysphasia.

Initially her fluent speech contained many neologisms; her sentences were long and syntactically complex but were, and remain, classically empty of content words, although replete with pronouns, general nouns ("something," "thing"), general verbs ("have," "go," "was") and grammatical function words. An alternative but equally accurate description recommended by Ellis et al. (1983) is that G.A.'s speech is restricted to approximately the first 200 words in the Kucera and Francis (1967) frequency list.

G.A. had twice weekly speech therapy for the first eighteen months after her CVA. For most of that time, she was unable to repeat any words or speech sounds other than a simple vowel (e.g., "aah," "ooh"), and therefore work concentrated on written language with the aim of enabling her to write single key content words to convey basic information. She was well-motivated to achieve this and worked with great energy and concentration, both in the clinic and at home with a speech-therapy volunteer. Repetition of any words other than those of a simple phonological structure remains grossly impaired.

G.A. can now usually convey her intended meaning by writing a key word (often misspelt but recognisable) and accompanies this by a flow of speech with a range of facial expression, intonation and gesture to help illustrate her meaning. However, the following transcription of her description of a picture sequence illustrating the fable of "The Hare and the Tortoise" will demonstrate how "empty" her spoken language remains:

Two things today, the gon man and a little tiny soo. He said I will go, and the man said, I will. Today the big one is going ever so much, but the little tiny sooin, he couldn't do at all. So the old man said I'm arafe from him so I will have, I will something to eat co he would be here for a long while. But the little man, he said I will go. He got right out and was there waiting for the ban.

BACKGROUND TESTS

Oral Output

1. Repetition.   As indicated in the case report, G.A.'s ability to repeat at the single word level is severely impaired. With high-frequency single-syllable words, she correctly reproduced 13/60 = .22; with single-syllable nonsense words, her performance dropped to 2/30 = .07. In word repetition, errors were paraphasias and jargon (no omissions) and were also very perservera-tive. Her response to the word "why" was /nais/; her response to "them" was /nais/; in fact 10/60 repetition responses were /nais/ (though "nice" was not a stimulus word).

2. Naming.   G.A. fails almost completely to name objects or pictures: 3/50 = .06 correct on pictures of common objects. Her performance in various tests involving pictures (discussed later) demonstrates that the naming deficit is not attributable to difficulty in picture recognition. Her errors in naming, unlike those in word repetition, contain only a few literal paraphasias and instances of jargon; the majority are omissions (either a shrug-and-a-smile, or, for example, for a picture of a mop: "I don't know what they call those things . . . I don't much like 'em!").

3. Oral reading.   Very little work was done on this task since G.A. was extremely poor at oral reading. Given single words, most of her reading responses were jargon (e.g., *walk*→/ʌfnən/) though some were paraphasias (e.g., *garden*→"garben," *coming*→"humming"). A small amount of data from oral reading of short sentences will be presented later in connection with G.A.'s word class effects.

Short-Term Memory

Not surprisingly, given the single-word repetition impairment described above, G.A.'s immediate auditory-verbal memory span (digits) is less than 1.

She does, however, apart from this output limitation, have a genuine and severe deficit in immediate auditory memory: her pointing span is 1.5 digits. Her visual span has not been properly tested, but she can reliably reproduce (in writing) a 4-digit number after it has been shown to her for 1–2 seconds.

It should be emphasised that G.A.'s failure to repeat words and digits genuinely reflects problems with auditory memory and phonological output rather than any major deficit in processing of the spoken input. While not brilliant, her performance on tests involving acoustic analysis of verbal input was fair. For example, she was asked to judge whether spoken pairs of non-words (rather than words, to prevent decisions based on lexical or semantic information) were the same (e.g., /keid, keid/) or different (e.g., /keid, kaid/). She had a bias for responding "yes," missing only one matching pair (hit rate = .98) and accepting a lot of mismatches (false positive rate = .49), but her resulting discrimination between same and different pairs (d' = 2.08) was considerably better than chance. She was also asked to judge whether spoken pairs of words rhymed. Her judgements were correct on 50/60 pairs; this is 83% correct or, in terms of discrimination between rhyming and non-rhyming pairs, d' = 2.40. However, when the rhyme task was repeated several weeks later with the introduction of a memory component (a 3-sec pause between presentation of the two words to be judged for rhyme), G.A's performance dropped sharply: 68% correct, d' = 1.20.

Calculations

No experimental study was made of this skill but, in the light of G.A.'s severe deficits in both phonology and short-term memory, it may be of interest to note that she was generally accurate in simple written calculations. She could do both addition and subtraction of double-digit numbers requiring a "carry" and could add up columns of four single digit numbers. It is a common subjective experience that such calculations involve, indeed depend upon, the ability to keep track of one's progress with "inner speech." Like the patient studied by Levine, Calvanio and Popovics (1982), it seems clear that G.A. had no such inner speech to rely upon. Though her calculation ability was probably not at its pre-morbid level of skill (since, though *generally* accurate, she made some errors and performed rather slowly), it may be surprising that she could do it at all.

Lexical Decision

In lexical decision, G.A. showed major effects of both familiarity and imageability. Her results (measured by d') on a test designed by Rickard (personal communication) to evaluate these two dimensions are shown in Table 13.1. This test has been given only with visual presentation. More lexical decision data in both modalities will be offered later.

Comprehension

Table 13.2 displays results from six comprehension tests, several performed with both auditory and visual presentation.

1. The Bishop word-picture matching test (Bishop & Byng, 1984) involves selection of one of either four or eight pictures to match a single word. (The value given for chance performance is an average between 1/4 and 1/8.) The

TABLE 13.1
G.A.'s Visual Lexical Decision Performance (d') on Rickard's
Test (S. Rickard, Birkbeck College, London). The Number of
Items Per Cell Varies Between 30 and 50 (Half Words, Half Non-
Words). The Total Test Has 240 Words and 240 Non-Words

	Familiarity		
	Low	Medium	High
Imageability			
Very low	0.36	1.68	2.48
Low	1.30	1.96	2.60
Medium	1.57	2.12	3.60
High	2.56	3.96	3.36

test includes trials with a distractor item which is (a) visually similar to the
target, or (b) semantically related to the target or (c) visually *and* semantically
similar to the target. In both modalities, G.A. performed well but made a few
errors, almost all of which were choices of a distractor of type (b) or (c).

2. The Shallice-McGill test (Shallice, personal communication) requires
selection of one of four pictures to match a concrete word (e.g., *parachute*),
an abstract word (e.g., *disparity*: the correct picture shows two gloves of
different sizes), or an emotional word (e.g., *hostility*: two people in an angry
argument). G.A. showed fairly good success with the concrete words, almost
complete failure on the abstract words and (as in the preceding test) no
modality effect.

TABLE 13.2
G.A.'s Performance on Various Tests of Comprehension

Test	(N)	(Chance)	Auditory	Visual
1. Bishop word–picture matching	(80)	(.19)	.90	.93
2. Shallice–McGill word–picture				
Concrete	(30)	(.25)	.90	.83
Abstract	(30)	(.25)	.30	.37
Emotional	(15)	(.25)	.67	.47
3. Howard & Orchard–Lisle				
Picture–Picture	(60)	(.50)	—	.90
Word–Word	(60)	(.50)	—	.95
4. Coltheart synonym judgement				
Imageable	(36)	(.50)	—	.89
Abstract	(36)	(.50)	—	.58
5. Morton–Patterson spatial				
prepositions	(14)	(.50)	.57	.93
6. Bishop sentence–picture	(40)	(.25)	.68	.58

3. The Howard and Orchard-Lisle (1984) test assesses somewhat more sophisticated knowledge about concrete words or objects than the simple referential information required by word-picture matching. The test material can be pictures or words (performance for each is shown in Table 13.2) or indeed a mixture of the two. Each trial requires choice of one of two pictures (or printed words) to go with a third. For example, either *palm tree* or *pine tree* must be selected to go with *pyramids*; either *dragonfly* or *butterfly* must be selected to go with *caterpillar*. G.A. succeeded reasonably well on this test, whether operating with pictures or (several weeks later) words.

4. Coltheart's synonym judgement test (Coltheart, personal communication) requires a person to judge whether two printed words have approximately the same meaning. G.A.'s performance here confirms the message from the Shallice-McGill test results: considerable (though not perfect) success with imageable or concrete words but scarcely better than chance on abstract words.

5. The Morton-Patterson (1980a) test assesses ability to match a spatial preposition to one element of a picture. For example, a picture of two cars (one following the other) is presented with the word *behind* (spoken or written); a picture of two aeroplanes (one above the other) is presented with the word *over*. There is not enough data here to support any firm conclusion, but the indication is that G.A. understands written but not spoken spatial prepositions.

6. Finally, G.A.'s ability to match spoken or written sentences to pictures (Bishop, 1982: Test for Reception of Grammar) is clearly impaired.

Rhyme Judgements.   A 60-pair rhyme test was constructed as follows: 10 rhyming orthographically similar pairs (e.g., *pipe—ripe*); 10 non-rhyming orthographically dissimilar pairs (*tile—heel*); 20 rhyming orthographically dissimilar pairs (*blown—cone*) and 20 non-rhyming orthographically similar pairs (*pint—lint*). This test was used for both auditory and visual rhyme judgements and, as already mentioned, with auditory presentation, G.A.'s performance was 50/60 correct = .83. She rejected one spoken rhyming pair ("burn—learn") and incorrectly accepted nine non-rhymes, eight of which were orthographically similar (e.g. "could—mould"). This may suggest that her *auditory* rhyme judgements are influenced by the target words' orthography (as demonstrated for normals by Seidenberg & Tanenhaus, 1979), though it should be noted (a) that G.A. would not be able to produce correct spellings of many of these words and (b) that of the non-rhyme pairs in this list, twice as many *are* orthographically similar as dissimilar. With visual presentation, G.A.'s performance was 26/60 = .33 correct. This reflects almost total reliance on orthographic similarity: her probabilities of responding "yes" to a visually similar pair and "no" to a visually dissimilar pair (independent of actual rhyme status) were both .90.

Auditory-Visual Matching.   On two separate occasions, 200 printed noun pairs (taken from ratings of synonymity by Wilding & Mohindra, 1981) were presented to G.A., each pair on an index card. One of the two words was spoken aloud and she was to point to the matching printed word. In one session, the pairs were synonyms (e.g., *sweat—perspiration*; *pal—chum*; *error—mistake*); in the other session, the 400 words were reassembled into non-synonym pairs (e.g., *sweat—error*; *chum—jail*, etc.). G.A.'s proportion of correct auditory-visual matches was .98 for the non-synonyms and .66 for the synonyms; the latter is significantly better than chance (.5) but obviously represents abysmal performance. On the assumption that the synonym pairs cannot have been any more orthographically/phonologically confusable than the non-synonym pairs, the contrast between her performance on the two versions of the test suggests that she has essentially no reliable ability or strategy for converting between orthographic and phonological codes and that her auditory-visual word matching relies primarily on cognitive (semantic) codes. G.A. is not the first patient for whom this effect has been demonstrated. Allport and Funnell's (1981) patient A.L. was perfect (16/16) at auditory-visual matching even if the two printed words (one of which matched the spoken word) came from the same object category (e.g., *sock* and *glove*). If the written words were synonyms, however, (e.g., *dress* and *frock*), A.L.'s auditory-visual matching was at chance (9/16).

The next section will focus on G.A.'s spelling ability, but a tentative summary of her pattern of retained and lost sub-skills, as suggested by the background tests, can now be offered with reference to Fig. 13.1. To begin with, it should be emphasised that G.A.'s impairments are very severe indeed, and one could not claim normal functioning for *any* sub-component represented in Fig. 13.1. In other words, for G.A. even more than most neurological cases, "retained" has a very relative status. With this caveat in mind, we suggest that she has no major deficit in acoustic analysis or the auditory input lexicon (since her auditory rhyme judgements and auditory word-picture matching were fair) nor any major deficit in the corresponding analysis and lexicon for written words (given her performance in visual word-picture matching, the word-word version of Howard & Orchard-Lisle's test and visually presented lexical decision). It is undeniable that her d' for some of the cells in Table 13.1 (lexical decision) is very low and, depending on one's view of the basis for lexical decisions, this might cast doubt on the relative intactness of the input lexicon(s). However, her probability of a correct positive lexical decision was a function of the word's imageability (as well as its familiarity). In a model like Fig. 13.1, which is clearly a logogen model (Morton, 1969, 1979), it is assumed that semantic distinctions amongst words such as their imageability value are to be found *subsequent* to the input lexicon. Since G.A.'s imageability effect in lexical decision was most pronounced for relatively unfamiliar words, and since normal subjects show at least a significant if small latency disadvantage for abstract words of low frequency (James, 1975), both of these effects may signal consultation of the cognitive system in lexical decisions for less common words. An alternative view championed by Sartori, Masterson and Job in Chapter Three is that semantic distinctions amongst words, such as their imageability value, *are* represented at the input-lexicon level.

Although there may be no glaring deficits for G.A. in processing up to the point of the input lexicon in either modality, every subsequent sub-component in Fig. 13.1 is disturbed for her. One finds a large advantage for concrete over abstract words in G.A.'s performance of any task which taps word comprehension, whether with auditory or visual input. As in the models proposed by Warrington (1975), Morton & Patterson (1980b) and others, this suggests a separability between concrete and abstract semantics in the cognitive system. Whilst G.A.'s semantic representations for concrete words are competent (though not perfect: note her occasional semantic errors in word-picture matching), those for abstract words, at least at the level required for the "comments" about meaning involved in synonym judgements and word-picture matching, seem to be altogether abolished. The only evidence to suggest a glimmer of comprehension for some abstract words comes, via a complicated argument, from G.A.'s performance in auditory-visual word matching. Since she was little better than chance when the word pairs were synonyms but virtually perfect when they were unrelated, we argued that G.A. has none of the various options (whole-word or segmental) available to a normal reader/speller for converting between phonological and orthographic codes and relies instead on comparing the cognitive/semantic codes for the spoken and written words. When the two printed words were synonyms (e.g., *riches* and *wealth*), therefore, she could not reliably determine which of them corresponds to the spoken word ("riches"). This interpretation does, however, predict that, if G.A. has no semantic representations for abstract words, then she should fail in auditory-visual matching with pairs of abstract words even if these are *not* synonym pairs.[1] No prospective test of this prediction has been done; a post-hoc analysis of the non-synonym pairs reveals about 22/200 items in which (by our own subjective assessment) both members of the pair were abstract (e.g., *agreement/chance*; *confusion/regulation*; *wit/cost*, etc.). G.A.'s choice was correct on 21/22 of these.[2] This does not constitute a large enough sample to support

---

[1] We are grateful to the editors of the book for drawing our attention to this point.

[2] Her four errors (out of 200) in auditory-visual matching of non-synonym pairs occurred on the following items, of which we consider the first pair to consist of both abstract words:

fame—satisfaction   mass—dampness
cart—stove   beginning—revolt

In these examples we have placed first the printed word which was also the spoken word, though of course in the actual test the spoken word corresponded to the first printed word for exactly one-half of the pairs.

any theorising; but it may suggest that vestiges of meaning for abstract words, insufficient to support a reflective judgement *about* meaning (as in synonym *judgements*) can assist G.A.'s auditory-visual matching.

G.A.'s abysmal performance in single-word repetition (which cannot be attributed to articulatory problems: her articulation in spontaneous speech is clear and effortless) suggests severe impairment of both, or indeed all three, of the routines assumed to permit repetition. That is (1) having analysed a word or word-like sound acoustically, she cannot manage acoustic-to-phonological conversion. Having accessed the appropriate element for a spoken word in the auditory input lexicon, she cannot then address its corresponding unit in the phonological output lexicon either (2) directly or (3) via the cognitive system. Since word repetition, though very poor indeed ($\approx.22$), was more successful than non-word repetition ($\approx.07$), G.A's attempts at word repetition probably reflect limited use of routine (2) or (3) rather than (1).

Analysis of G.A.'s spontaneous speech may suggest that only words which are extremely high frequency (and possibly short as well) remain in her phonological output lexicon. Furthermore, while the majority of G.A.'s pre-morbid vocabulary appears to be permanently lost from her output lexicon (because it cannot be elicited at any time or in any task—spontaneous speech, oral reading, oral naming or repetition), those few high frequency elements which remain are themselves only unreliably accessible. Words which she manages to repeat on one occasion may be failed on another. More strikingly, the "cognitive support" (semantic, syntactic, prosodic, etc.) involved in spontaneous speech enables G.A. to use words when speaking which she fails to repeat in the more artificial task of single-word repetition. This phenomenon, though little understood or discussed (but see Lesser, 1978, pp. 65–69) is surely characteristic of many aphasic patients.

SPELLING

As mentioned in the case report, given G.A.'s very limited success in any task requiring phonological output, both therapy and research with her concentrated on writing. She writes with her right (dominant) hand and always prints in upper-case letters. All evidence suggests that G.A.'s limited writing ability reflects use of a single routine: from semantic representations in the cognitive system to the orthographic output lexicon. At the letter level, G.A. correctly wrote 15/26 single letters to dictation of their names and 11/18 single letters to dictation of their sounds. The partial phonological success indicated by writing letters to sounds ($/f\vartheta/\rightarrow F$) may be based on lexical knowledge: that is, she may be able to think of a word which begins with that sound and write its first letter. Whatever its basis, this ability does not extend to larger units: G.A. wrote 0/20 single-syllable non-words to dictation, and while a few of her responses bore some resemblance to the stimulus (e.g., /beim/→*babe*; /riːt/→*creep*), the majority did not (e.g., /trid/→*laugh*; /neis/ →*yeser*; plus a number of omissions).

What about G.A.'s word writing? Over a number of sessions, she has twice been asked to write the names of a set of 85 objects; on one occasion, the name of the object was dictated to her; on the other, a picture of the object was shown to her for written naming. Table 13.3 presents a profile of her spelling performance from these sessions.

Considering only exactly correct responses, her spelling is scarcely brilliant; on the other hand, three categories of error response (namely, partial lexical knowledge [Ellis' term, 1982], semantic paragraphias and inflectional/ derivational paragraphias) seem to reflect *partially* preserved spelling ability. If these three categories are added to correct responses, then the proportion of occasions on which she can produce something more-or-less meaningful in spelling is .72 for written naming and .71 for spelling to dictation.

To ascertain whether her pattern of spelling performance differs in the two conditions (dictation and picture naming), two analyses were performed. Firstly, the simple proportions in the various response categories (Table 13.3) for the two conditions were compared and revealed no statistically significant difference, X^2 (5df) = 7.5, p > .1. Secondly, since the words for the two conditions were identical, an analysis for matched pairs (using X^2 as an

TABLE 13.3

G.A.'s Written Spelling of 85 Words in Picture-Naming and to Dictation: Numbers and Proportions of Various Response Types, and Examples of Errors. In the Examples, a Stimulus Word With Quotation Marks Denotes Dictation, While One Without Denotes Naming

	Naming		Dictation	
	Number	*Proportion*	*Number*	*Proportion*
Correct spelling	30	.35	27	.32
Partial lexical knowledge	18	.21	25	.29
e.g., balloon→*ballon*				
"tortoise"→*torter*				
Semantic paragraphia	10	.12	4	.05
e.g., hose→*water*				
"torch"→*lighting*				
Inflectional/derivational	3	.04	4	.05
e.g., knitting→*knitter*				
"eyes"→*eye*				
Single letter or ?	11	.13	18	.21
e.g., car→*front*				
"anchor"→*Y*				
Omission	13	.15	7	.08

extended McNemar statistic)[3] confirmed that there was no significant difference in pattern of performance for the two conditions, X^2 (13df) = 17.3, p > .1.

The stimulus input for the two conditions (written naming and writing to dictation) is, of course, very different. G.A. cannot provide the phonological name of an object for herself; if she were able, in spelling, to make any use of the phonological information provided by dictation of the word, then these two stimulus conditions should produce different patterns of performance. The absence of this difference is one line of evidence that G.A. is spelling without phonology.

WORD-CLASS EFFECTS

A second line of evidence for G.A.'s spelling without phonology is to be found in a contrast between her success in speaking and in spelling as a function of word class. This contrast is apparent in tests both of single words and of short sentences. The former used a list of 120 words (from Patterson, 1982), 3–6 letters in length, consisting of 60 content words and 60 function words. Items from the two word classes were balanced for length (number of letters) and, while not exactly balanced for frequency, they were all exceedingly high in frequency (> 350 per million in the Kucera and Francis list). In an initial test, 60 three-and-four letter words (half content, half function) were randomised and dictated to G.A. on two different occasions, once for oral repetition and once for written spelling. A subsequent test used the same procedure but with all 120 items. The results are shown in Table 13.4, which also presents the data from a less controlled test involving a set of 35 short sentences (like "Come into the garden," "He travelled from London," "She combed her hair," etc.). These sentences, which contained a total of 63 content words and 73 function words (balanced for neither length nor frequency), were presented to G.A. on three occasions: once spoken for her to repeat, once spoken for her to write to dictation, and once written for her to read aloud.

Table 13.4 shows that whenever G.A.'s output was in speech (whether repetition or oral reading, whether individual words or short sentences), she fared rather better on the function than the content words. When her output

---

[3]This analysis (see Bishop, Fienberg, & Holland, 1975) takes the 6 × 6 matrix of possible outcomes (correct responses plus five error types) for each word in the two conditions. Ignoring the diagonal (that is, where both tasks produced the same outcome), the analysis looks at matched pairs on the two tasks (e.g., outcome A in naming, outcome B in writing to dictation matched with outcome B in naming, A in dictation) and asks whether the tasks yielded significantly different patterns. The degrees of freedom, which should be 15 ([36–6]/2), are reduced to 13 because of empty cells in the data matrix for two matched pairs.

TABLE 13.4
A Contrast Between G.A.'s Speaking and Spelling as a Function of Word
Class

Proportion correct on words dictated in isolation for repetition or writing

	Content	Function
3–4 letter words	(N = 30)	(N = 30)
Repetition	.13	.30
Writing	.27	.03
3–6 letter words	(N = 60)	(N = 60)
Repetition	.28	.38
Writing	.17	.07

*Proportion correct on words in 35 short sentences presented for repetition,
oral reading or writing*

	Content	Function
	(N = 63)	(N = 73)
Repetition	.17	.60
Oral reading	.08	.70
Writing	.38	.11
Example: *"Come into the garden"*		
Repetition: "Come into the /roudən/"		
Reading: "Some into the /slʌmben/"		
Writing: *"I was up garden"*		

was in writing (again, individual words or sentences), the advantage was reversed. Of the seven specific word-class contrasts in Table 13.4, four are statistically reliable by X^2 tests: repetition of sentences ($X^2 = 25.73$, $p < .001$), oral reading of sentences ($X^2 = 53.54$, $p < .001$), writing of sentences ($X^2 = 13.84$, $p < .001$) and writing of 3–4 letter content and function words ($N = 30$ each) ($X^2 = 6.41$, $p < .01$). The remaining three comparisons failed to reach significance: repetition of 3–4 letter words ($N = 30$ each) ($X^2 = 2.47$, $p = .117$), writing of the full set of individual words ($N = 60$ each) ($X^2 = 2.91$, $p = .08$), and repetition of the full set of individual words ($X^2 = 1.35$, $p = .245$). A slightly more sensitive statistical analysis takes the 95% confidence intervals for the difference between word classes compared across modality of output. Of the four contrasts possible here (repetition vs writing of sentences; oral reading vs writing of sentences; repetition vs writing of individual words ($N = 30$ each); and repetition vs writing of words ($N = 60$ each), the first three of these show completely non-overlapping confidence intervals whilst the last again fails to reveal a significant difference.

It is essential to acknowledge that G.A.'s apparent function word advantage in oral output may not be a genuine word-class effect. Ellis, Miller &

Sin's (1983) conclusion with respect to their patient R.D. applies equally to G.A.'s performance here. Function words as a class are higher in frequency and shorter in length than content words, and short, frequent words are more likely to be spared in the severely compromised phonological output lexicon characteristic of fluent, anomic posterior aphasics like G.A. This valid alternative explanation of the effect for speech does not, we believe, alter the point that we wish to make about the implications of the double dissociation[4] for an interpretation of G.A.'s spelling. If the words that she can speak and those that she can spell are different sub-sets of words (whether on the basis of grammatical class or frequency or whatever), it is unlikely that her spelling of a word makes any use of its phonology.

Whilst not especially germane to the main message of the data in Table 13.4, it is of interest to note G.A.'s substantially augmented success in oral output of function words when she was producing sentences rather than single words. This presumably reflects either the higher predictability of these words in context, or the greater similarity of sentence repetition/oral reading to spontaneous speech (with its aforementioned "cognitive support") or both.

The set of 35 sentences was presented to G.A. on yet one further occasion for delayed copying. Each sentence, written on a card, was shown to her for several seconds, then removed, and she was asked to write what she had seen. If her success on this task is analysed once again for a word class effect, it appears at first glance that there was none: over the sentences as a whole, G.A.'s "memory" writing correctly produced .59 of the 63 content words and .52 of the 73 function words. Her performance showed a strong primacy effect, however, benefitting the first word of each sentence whatever it happened to be—and in 28 of the 35 sentences, the first word was a function word. If sentence-initial words are dropped from the analysis, the expected word class effect re-emerges: for content words (now N = 56), .55 correct; for function words (now N = 45), .29 correct. This effect is similar to that demonstrated by Caramazza, Berndt and Basili (1983) for their patient J.S.: his short-term written free recall for three-word sequences of either content or function words showed a significant advantage for the former. The interpretation given by Caramazza et al. to this phenomenon is that a phonological representation of a word string, which is an efficient code for remembering the string until it can be produced, is especially helpful or necessary in the case of words without a good solid semantic representation. Since neither J.S. nor G.A. can reliably generate phonological represen-

---

[4]It may not be altogether appropriate to call this pattern a double dissociation since, in both instances, performance in the relatively "preserved" task was in fact very severely deficient (Shallice, 1985).

tations of written words, their short-term memory for these will be biased in favour of content words and against function words.

The data just presented concern word-class effects in G.A.'s output. There is also some indication of a word-class effect in a task relating more to input, namely lexical decision. A lexical decision test was constructed consisting of 76 single-syllable, 3–5 letter words, plus 76 non-words, each differing by just a single letter from one of the stimulus words. Of the words, half were content and half were function words; as in the lists used for repetition and writing to dictation, words in the two classes were balanced exactly for length and approximately for frequency (in fact, the 38 words of each class for lexical decision were a sub-set of the 60 words in each class from the preceding tests). A randomised order of all 152 words and non-words was presented for lexical decision on two different occasions, once with spoken input and once with the items printed individually on cards. G.A.'s performance on these tests appears in Table 13.5, which also repeats (for comparison purposes) her scores on the first test from Table 13.4. Although in phonological output (repetition) G.A. had an advantage on function words > content words, in auditory lexical decision her advantage is the other way round, content words > function words. Her hit rates (auditory) for the two word classes differ significantly, X^2 (ldf) = 6.13, p = .01. The comparison for orthography is less interesting because, while it also reveals a slight crossover (in the opposite direction), there was no significant word class effect for visual lexical decision. The difference between word classes in auditory lexical decision is not interpretable in terms of a frequency effect (as the previous result for output tasks may have been) since here it is the content—i.e., somewhat *lower* frequency—words which fared better.

TABLE 13.5

G.A.'s Performance on Content and Function Words in Tasks Relating to Phonological Input/Output and Orthographic Input/Output

	Content	Function
Phonology		
Output: single word repetition	.13	.30
Input: auditory lexical decision		
hit rate	.89	.66
FP rate	.37	.34
d′	1.56	0.82
Orthography		
Output: writing to dictation	.27	.03
Input: visual lexical decision		
hit rate	.84	.87
FP rate	.11	.08
d′	2.22	2.53

The feature of this word-class effect which merits comment is a confirmation and extension of the conclusion drawn by Allport and Funnell (1981): word-class effects can be a function of task and modality. The fact that some patients show consistent effects across task and modality (e.g., B.L., studied by Nolan & Caramazza, 1982, displayed a content > function word advantage in spontaneous speech, repetition, oral reading, writing, comprehension, indeed everything except lexical decision) does not constitute evidence for a single, central locus in our models where such effects arise. The patient studied by Allport and Funnell who provoked them to emphasise this point showed one pattern of task-specific effects. A.L.'s fluent, anomic spontaneous speech was composed almost exclusively of function words plus a few general content words ("thing" and "stuff," "make" and "do," etc.). His oral reading, on the other hand, was agrammatic rather than anomic: he failed to read function words but achieved a medium degree of success in reading the sort of concrete object names which were entirely lacking in his spontaneous speech. G.A. showed a somewhat different pattern. Her speech was like A.L.'s except that specific content words were sometimes replaced with jargon rather than nonspecific "thing" words. The preponderance of function > content words was, however, consistently characteristic of her performance so long as the task involved spoken output. Thus for G.A. word-class effects in spontaneous speech and oral reading were associated, while for A.L. these dissociated. The reversal in pattern of word-class advantage for G.A is to be found instead when one contrasts either *output modalities* (oral vs written) or *input and output tasks* (auditory lexical decision vs phonological output).

What appears to be a major difference between the patterns shown by these two patients may be explicable in terms of a single component in the model in Fig. 13.1: the phonological output lexicon. We have already suggested that for G.A., the primary deficit here is to be characterised not as a problem of access or retrieval but a genuine loss of representations. Thus, apart from a few hundred of the most frequent words in the language, G.A.'s speech output lexicon has been abolished: no task or condition can alter this. For A.L., on the other hand, the primary deficit here must be one of access.[5] His relative success in oral reading of content words (object names) demonstrates that these representations have not been abolished from his phonological output lexicon. They were apparently not accessible solely on the basis of cognitive codes: hence his severe anomia in spontaneous speech and his almost total failure in object naming. A printed word, however, could

---

[5]We do not intend this claim to apply to A.L.'s entire pre-morbid speech lexicon. It may be that some or many words were, for him as for G.A., unavailable rather than just inaccessible. The contrast between the patients should perhaps be taken as applying to some middle frequency range of words in which, for example, the names of many common objects are found.

apparently address its available but relatively inaccessible counterpart in the phonological output lexicon. A.L.'s oral reading, which could not have involved sub-word level conversion of orthography to phonology (e.g., he scored 0% in non-word reading), presumably reflects use of one of the two routines linking the orthographic input lexicon with the phonological output lexicon. If this were the "direct" (non-semantic) routine, one would require an account of A.L.'s failure to read function words aloud. If, as seems much more likely, A.L.'s oral reading relied on the routine involving the cognitive system,[6] then his word-class effect in reading is unproblematical, indeed predictable. This solution does, however, require an account of why printed words (names) can be so much better than their corresponding pictures at arousing cognitive codes sufficiently specific to address the appropriate output phonology. Howard (1985) discusses this issue with reference to a number of deep dyslexic patients who are significantly more successful in reading written object names than in naming the corresponding pictures.

The suggestion, then, is that G.A. and A.L. show very similar patterns of deficit up to the point (in Fig. 13.1) of the phonological output lexicon. Neither patient retains any ability to translate an input string (*acoustic or orthographic*) to an output code (phonological or orthographic) except with reference to the cognitive system. Due either to deficits in the cognitive system, or possibly to the nature of routines through the cognitive system when intact but unconfirmed by the other "supporting" routines (an unresolved issue: see Morton & Patterson, 1980b, and Newcombe & Marshall, 1980 for some dicusssion), both of these patients show advantages for content > function words and/or concrete > abstract words in any task which relies on mapping from input lexicon to cognitive system (e.g., auditory-visual matching, lexical decision, word-picture matching, etc.). For A.L. this same advantage is still manifest at output, provided that the task begins with this mapping from the input lexicon (i.e., oral reading as opposed to spontaneous speech). For G.A., the content > function advantage is still present for output in *writing*; for a task involving *speech output*, however, even if it begins with the same input mapping characterised by content-word superiority, the advantage reverses. We have suggested that this can be explained in terms of a severe depletion of G.A.'s speech output lexicon leaving virtually only function words. But will this account actually predict the reversal? The following piece of arithmetic suggests that it will.[7]

If essentially all tasks for G.A. are routed through the cognitive system, then her hit rate in auditory lexical decision might be taken as a rough

---

[6] Reading via semantics was our interpretation of A.L. based on the limited data presented for him by Allport & Funnell (1981); more significantly, it was also Funnell's interpretation of A.L. based upon an extensive case study (Funnell, 1983).

[7] We are grateful to Max Coltheart for devising this analysis.

measure of the success of mapping from auditory input lexicon to cognitive system.[8] In auditory lexical decision, the hit rates = .89 for content words and .66 for function words. For repetition to be successful, however, the appropriate routine must include not only the input lexicon and the cognitive system but also the output lexicon. Let x be the probability that a content word still exists in the output lexicon, and y be the probability that a function word still exists in the output lexicon. For content words, then, the probability of successful repetition = (.89) × (x) and for function words = (.66) × (y). Since our estimate of the probability of correctly repeating a content word = .13, we have .89 x = .13, i.e., x = .15. The probability of correctly repeating a function word = .30; if .66 y = .30, then y = .45. This suggests that G.A.'s phonological output lexicon represents 45% of the original function words in her pre-morbid speech, but only 15% of the original content words. The actual numbers are, of course, somewhat arbitrary; but the principle of the analysis reconciles an advantage for content > function words in an input task with an advantage for function- > content words (in the *same* modality of input) in an output task.

CONCLUDING COMMENTS

The conclusions to be drawn from this study of a severely aphasic patient are rather modest. This is because the intriguing features of her case are either effects of considerable magnitude that are not novel or novel effects that are not of striking magnitude. The case does, nonetheless, have several characteristics germane to issues of current theoretical interest.

Firstly, although G.A.'s ability to communicate was severely impaired in all respects, she managed to use writing rather effectively, either on its own or as a complement to her impoverished speech and her non-verbal expression. Writing is often considered the verbal skill most vulnerable to aphasic impairment and, whilst G.A. is certainly not the first patient known to succeed in writing on occasions when she fails to communicate in any other way (see, for example, Ellis, Miller, & Sin, 1983; Michel, 1979), this contrast is still sufficiently rare to allow interest in some further case studies.

Secondly, G.A.'s admittedly limited writing skill constitutes an unequivocal demonstration of spelling without any assistance from or involvement of phonology. (See Patterson, in preparation, for some further discussion of

---

[8] These hit rates might instead be interpreted as reflecting the relative depletion, at the input lexicon level, of content (or concrete) words versus function (or abstract) words, if one took the position adopted by Sartori, Masterson, and Job in Chapter 3 that distinctions such as concrete/ abstract or content/function word are permissible at this level. Whichever view is adopted, the arithmetical analysis carried out here is appropriate.

various patterns of impaired spelling which do or do not rely on one or more varieties of phonological processing.) Again, spelling without phonology has not been discovered with G.A. Various forms of evidence for this phenomenon are already available, including a dissociation between spelling words and non-words (Bub & Kertesz, 1982; Shallice, 1981) or between written and oral naming (Ellis et al., 1983; Hier & Mohr, 1977). The result of particular note in G.A.'s case (which may have been present but not analysed in previous studies) is the almost complete lack of overlap between the words which she was able to speak and those which she could spell.

Thirdly, G.A. provides another pattern of word-class effects to reinforce and extend the conclusions of Allport and Funnell (1981) with regard to such effects. These conclusions were: (a) that the specificity rather than independence of word-class effects with respect to task and modality in some patients prevents any kind of global characterisation of the patients as anomic or agrammatic: the same patient can be anomic in one task and agrammatic in another; (b) that one must query the assumption that word-class effects, even carefully specified ones, reflect syntactic distinctions amongst words. The advantage for content > function words shown by A.L. (Allport & Funnell, 1981) and G.A. in "input" tasks like lexical decision or auditory-visual matching may reflect the way in which these word groups, differing in imageability/concreteness, map onto cognitive, semantic codes. The advantage for function > content words shown by G.A. in an output task like repetition may reflect the bias in her output lexicon for short, high frequency words (this point is also emphasised by Ellis et al., 1983). Neither of these effects would concern what one normally thinks of as the essential linguistic difference between content and function words.

Finally, considerable space has been devoted to a comparison of two patients, A.L. and G.A. If required to justify this attention, we would do so with the claim that the similarities and differences between these two patients are only interpretable when one relates each patient's entire pattern of performance to a single well-specified process model.

REFERENCES

Allport, D. A., & Funnell, E. (1981) Components of the mental lexicon. In H. C. Longuet-Higgins, J. Lyons, & D. E. Broadbent, (Eds.), *The psychological mechanisms of language.* London: The Royal Society.

Assal, G., Buttet, J., & Jolivet, R. (1981) Dissociations in aphasia: A case report. *Brain and Language, 13,* 223–240.

Beauvois, M. F., & Derouesné, J. (1979) Phonological alexia: Three dissociations. *Journal of Neurology, Neurosurgery and Psychiatry, 42,* 1115–1124.

Bishop, D. (1982) *TROG: Test for reception of grammar.* Abingdon, Oxon: Thomas Leach (for the Medical Research Council).

Bishop, D., & Byng, S. (1984) Assessing semantic comprehension: Methodological considerations, and a new clinical test. *Cognitive Neuropsychology, 1*, 233–244.

Bishop, Y. M. M., Fienberg, S. E., & Holland, P. W. (1975) *Discrete multivariate analysis.* Cambridge, Mass: MIT Press.

Bub, D., & Kertesz, A. (1982) Evidence for lexicographic processing in a patient with preserved written over oral single word naming. *Brain, 105*, 697–717.

Caramazza, A., Berndt, R. S., & Basili, A. G. (1983) The selective impairment of phonological processing: A case study. *Brain and Language, 18*, 128–174.

Ellis, A. W. (1982) Spelling and writing (and reading and speaking). In A. W. Ellis (Ed.), *Normality and pathology in cognitive functions.* London: Academic Press.

Ellis, A. W., Miller, D., & Sin, G. (1983) Wernicke's aphasia and normal language processing: A case study in cognitive neuropsychology. *Cognition, 15*, 111–144.

Funnell, E. (1983) *Ideographic communication and word-class effects in aphasia.* Unpublished Ph.D. thesis, University of Reading, England.

Hier, D. B., & Mohr, J. P. (1977) Incongruous oral and written naming: Evidence for a subdivision of the syndrome of Wernicke's aphasia. *Brain and Language, 4*, 115–126.

Howard, D. (1985) *The semantic organisation of the lexicon: Evidence from aphasia.* Unpublished PhD dissertation, University College, London.

Howard, D., & Orchard-Lisle, V. (1984) On the origin of semantic errors in naming: Evidence from the case of a global aphasic. *Cognitive Neuropsychology, 1*, 163–190.

James, C. T. (1975) The role of semantic information in lexical decisions. *Journal of Experimental Psychology: Human Perception and Performance, 104*, 130–136.

Kucera, H., & Francis, W. N. (1967) *Computational analysis of present-day American English.* Providence, Rhode Island: Brown University Press.

Lesser, R. (1978) *Linguistic investigations of aphasia.* London: Edward Arnold.

Levine, D. N., Calvanio, R., & Popovics, A. (1982) Language in the absence of inner speech. *Neuropsychologia, 20*, 391–409.

Michel, F. (1979) Preservation du langage écrit malgré un deficit majeur du langage oral. *Lyon Medical, 241*, 141–149.

Morton, J. (1969) The interaction of information in word recognition. *Psychological Review, 76*, 165–178.

Morton, J. (1979) Facilitation in word recognition: Experiments causing change in the logogen model. In P. A. Kolers, M. E. Wrolstad, & H. Bouma (Eds.), *Processing of visible language, vol 1.* New York: Plenum.

Morton, J., & Patterson, K. (1980a) 'Little words—No!'. In M. Coltheart, K. Patterson, & J. C. Marshall (Eds.), *Deep dyslexia.* London: Routledge & Kegan Paul.

Morton, J., & Patterson, K. (1980b) A new attempt at an interpretation, or, an attempt at a new interpretation. In M. Coltheart, K. Patterson, & J. C. Marshall (Eds.), *Deep dyslexia.* London: Routledge & Kegan Paul.

Newcombe, F., & Marshall, J. C. (1980) Transcoding and lexical stabilisation in deep dyslexia. In M. Coltheart, K. Patterson, & J. C. Marshall (Eds.), *Deep dyslexia.* London: Routledge & Kegan Paul.

Nolan, K. A., & Caramazza, A. (1982) Modality-independent impairments in word processing in a deep dyslexic patient. *Brain and Language, 16*, 237–264.

Patterson, K. E. (1982) The relation between reading and phonological coding: Further neuropsychological observations. In A. W. Ellis (Ed.), *Normality and pathology in cognitive functions.* London: Academic Press.

Patterson, K. E. (in preparation) Acquired disorders of spelling. In G. Denes, C. Semenza, P. Bisiacchi, & E. Andreewsky, (Eds.), *Perspectives in cognitive neuropsychology.* London: Lawrence Erlbaum Associates.

Saffran, E. M., & Marin, O. S. M. (1977) Reading without phonology: Evidence from aphasia. *Quarterly Journal of Experimental Psychology, 29*, 515–525.

Seidenberg, M. S., & Tanenhaus, M. K. (1979) Orthographic effects on rhyme monitoring. *Journal of Experimental Psychology: Human Learning and Memory, 5*, 546–554.

Shallice, T. (1981) Phonological agraphia and the lexical route in writing. *Brain, 104*, 413–429.

Shallice, T. (1985) *Single cases and/or group studies.* Paper presented to the Third European Workshop on Cognitive Neuropsychology, Bressanone, January 1985.

Warrington, E. K. (1975) The selective impairment of semantic memory. *Quarterly Journal of Experimental Psychology, 27*, 635–657.

Wilding, J., & Mohindra, N. (1981) Ratings of the degree of synonymity of 279 noun pairs. *British Journal of Psychology, 72*, 231–240.

14

Is There More Than Ah-oh-oh? Alternative Strategies for Writing and Repeating Lexically

Helgard Kremin
Chargée de Recherche au C.N.R.S., Unité 111 de l'I.N.S.E.R.M., E.R.A. 274 du C.N.R.S., 2ᵗᵉʳ rue d'Alésia, 75014 Paris (France)

This paper will concern the neurolinguistic status of a patient whose spontaneous output is limited to "ah-oh-oh." Although "ah-oh-oh" is Michel's permanent verbal stereotypy, this meaningless sequence carries many different expressive values, such as question, astonishment, sadness, etc. Communication with the very motivated patient is relatively easy, since Michel responds (adequately) with "yes" and "no" to questions. Moreover, Michel has a highly-developed way of expressing himself by gesture.

The first observation of a similar patient was given by Broca (1861), describing his patient Leborgne, who retained only the stereotyped expression "tan-tan." Broca termed this total loss of output of speech *aphemia*, to distinguish it from other types of aphasic disorder. This variety of stereotypical language production—later called "recurrent utterances" by Jackson (1879–1880)—seems to be relatively rare. Poeck, De Bleser, and Keyserlinck (1984) point out that patients with recurrent utterances constitute about 1% of their aphasic population.

According to Broca, true aphemia does not mean loss of language but, rather, loss of speech (due to damage to the third convolution of the frontal lobe) without paralysis of the organs of articulation, and without destruction of intelligence. Broca explicitly states:

La faculté du langage persiste évidemment toute entière, puisque les malades comprennent parfaitement le langage articulé et le langage écrit; puisque ceux qui ne savent pas ou ne peuvent pas écrire ont assez d'intelligence (et il en faut en pareil cas) pour trouver le moyen de communiquer leur pensée, et puisque enfin ceux qui sont lettrés, et qui ont le libre usage de leurs mains, mettent nettement leurs idées sur le papier. Ils connaissent donc le sens et la valeur des mots, sous la forme auditive comme sous la forme graphique. (Broca, 1865, cité d'après Hécaen & Dubois, 1969, p. 64).

The obvious interpretation of such verbal behaviour is that patients suffering from aphemia have access to concepts, given visual and/or auditory input, but cannot attain phonological codes directly from conceptual ones, for oral output. Broca's early comments, furthermore, entail the possibility of total independence of oral and written production. Such a state of affairs is currently accounted for by separate logogen systems for speech output and for graphemic output (Ellis, 1982; Morton, 1980a).

Although some general observations are available on the basis of group studies of patients with recurrent utterances (Alajouanine, 1956; Poeck et al., 1984), no detailed neurolinguistic case study of such a patient exists in the literature. The purpose of this paper is thus twofold: on the one hand, it furnishes experimental data on one of these rare patients whose spontaneous output is limited to a recurrent utterance; on the other hand, the disorder will be analysed from an information processing framework. Special attention will be given to the mechanisms underlying writing.

CASE DESCRIPTION OF A PATIENT WITH RECURRENT UTTERANCE

Michel, 34 years old, right-handed, has a degree in history and was teaching till his cerebral accident in 1980. A standard neuropsychological examination (see Boller & Hécaen, 1979) conducted in September 1982 showed that the patient was well oriented in time and space. There were no signs of apraxia or agnosia, and no visual field defect, but the patient was hemiplegic. The standard examination further revealed that Michel had no acalculia (except for difficulty with division), and that his verbal comprehension in terms of execution of commands was impaired, but was somewhat better for visual (76% correct including self-correction) than for auditory presentation (52% correct). The patient's spontaneous language was limited to the verbal stereotypy "ah-oh-oh," and oral naming was severely impaired. Repetition and reading aloud were impossible. The patient could write his address, correctly copy text, and write a short sentence from dictation (with his left hand). Oral spelling even of three letter words was impossible both ways (R.U.E. → rue; rue → R.U.E.).

Auditory memory span was also impaired. The patient could correctly repeat digits only when they were presented in isolation; he was, however, capable of repeating up to two words (of a series of two or more). Given the patient's general problems with oral output, memory span was also assessed independently of oral production: when a series of spoken words had to be matched by pointing to the corresponding written words, the patient correctly identified 93% of the items in series of three words (14/15).

The CT scan showed a (superficial) engagement of the left Sylvian territory, extending from the temporo-parietal region to the frontal lobe.

More formal assessment of language function was carried out in December 1982 and in March and October 1983 and will be described in more detail.

A. Study of Oral Output

1. Spontaneous Language and Oral Naming. For more than three years now, Michel's spontaneous oral output has been limited to the stereotypy "ah-oh-oh," which shows up at every attempt to speak. In fact during the many hours I spent with him the patient uttered a few isolated words spontaneously: *"mer"* (sea) (the patient lives close to the ocean); *"maman"* (mummy); *"pisser"* (to piss); the name of the city where he lives; and the first name of his therapist. Although these isolated words were uttered in a syllabic manner and on rare occasions only (and somewhat to the patient's own surprise) I think, however, that these words were being used as propositions. The same is true for the utterances "yes" and "no," which were used with full and definite propositional intent. The adequate use of these particles is indeed considered to be the simplest and most definite example of the evolution of a stereotypy (see Jackson, 1879–1880).

Oral naming was severely impaired in all modalities (vision, sound, and touch) ranging from 0–25% correct for the different tasks and sessions. There was no improvement over the testing period. It should be stressed, however, that oral naming hardly ever resulted in omissions (only 5% of total trials). Rather, the patient was desperately trying out different soundforms that had more or less resemblance with the target word, e.g.:

> *pyramide* (pyramid) → "spi-ra-ble pi-ra-ble pi-ra-le non!
>   pri ... pi-ra-le pi-rab-la non!"
> *harpe* (harp) → "ar ... *harpe* ... har-ple ... har-ble"
> *joug* (yoke) " ... chau ... chou .. non! .... sou .. chou ..
>   jou .. zou non!"

The phonetic production appeared normal; oral production was, however, effortful and took place in a syllabic manner.

2. Reading and Repetition.   When given the Standard Reading Test (see Hécaen & Kremin, 1976) the patient appeared to be incapable of reading aloud. He correctly reproduced only 10% of the isolated words, 10% of the nonsense syllables, and no sentence at all. His oral reading of isolated letters was 45% correct. Pointing (upon oral request) to letters (n = 20) and to content words (n = 20) was executed without error even on initial testing in December 1982; pointing to function words (n = 20) was correct taking into account spontaneous self-correction; pointing to nonsense syllables (n = 10), however, yielded 30% errors.

Broca (1865) observed that one of his patients with aphemia was well capable of reproducing stimuli when these were limited to one syllable, but never succeeded in combining sequences into longer words. We thus hypothesised that—for whatever reason—output in oral production tasks such as reading and repetition may be affected by the length of the stimuli. This phenomenon, although often stated with language disturbances of the conduction type—where the same pattern of difficulty, due to increase of the number of syllables of the target words, may be observed in oral repetition as well as in naming (see Yamadori & Ikumura, 1975)—is not generally considered for studies of aphasic performances. The length of the stimuli (as well as their syllabic composition) may, however, be crucial in order to distinguish among different factors possibly underlying severely impaired oral output (see Derouesné, Beauvois, & Ranty, 1977).

For the following testing sessions we therefore constructed lists to control for the problems of oral output. The patient's oral reading performances stayed unchanged from March to October 1983.

The most complete and strictly controlled data from October 1983 are represented in Table 14.1. (Only monosyllabic items controlled for frequency were administered: the length of the stimuli ranged from a minimum of two to a maximum of six letters.) It can be seen from Table 14.1 that Michel was indeed able to produce oral output for reading. In fact, he read (short) content and function words of same (high) frequency equally well (Standard

TABLE 14.1
Oral Reading and Repetition of Monosyllabic Items (% correct)

	Reading	Repetition
High frequency content words (n = 60)	72 / 78[a]	72 / 83[a]
High frequency function words (n = 30)	50 / 80	70 / 87
Low frequency content words (n = 40)	35 / 50	33 / 48
Nonsense syllables (n = 15)	27 / 40	73 / 93

[a] First percentage refers to first response correct; second percentage refers to total correct including spontaneous selfcorrections.

Bayesian Inference on the difference of two proportions was not significant with p = .435). The frequency of the presented written words nevertheless did play an important role (test of difference between proportions of high vs low frequency content words yielded a significant difference with p = .002).

Although no imageability ratings of the target words were available, it can nevertheless be inferred that imageability did not influence Michel's oral reading performance: function words which are generally of low imageability were as well read as content words of same frequency and even better than low frequency content words. On the other hand, function words were, however, significantly better read than nonsense syllables (p = .004). With regard to oral reading, it should be emphasised that the patient never (that is, from December 1982 to October 1983) produced a semantic paralexia. Frank omissions hardly ever occurred; instead the patient struggled for the adequate soundform of the target words, e.g.:

feuille (leaf) → ".. foi foi ... non ... veuille veuille non"
plus (plus) → "pli plu blu ... *plus.*"

These "attempts after soundform" eventually resulted in other existing words (for the cited examples: "foi," "veuille," "pli," "plu") which were, however, rejected or successfully self-corrected. Similar attempts after the correct soundform occasionally also yielded the production of a real word while reading nonsense syllables. On the mentioned list (October 1983) there were two such errors, e.g., *quain*→/kə/ /kəl/* ... *quain* (*could be "quel").

The patient's oral repetition performance on the same items (in October 1983) is also represented in Table 14.1. Again, there is no significant difference in performance with regard to grammatical class (test of difference between proportions of content vs function words of high frequency yielded p = .349). However, as for oral reading, word frequency constitutes a crucial variable. (The difference between repetition performance of high vs low frequency content words is highly significant with p = .001). In contrast to reading, however, the meaningfulness of the presented stimuli had no influence on oral repetition: nonsense syllables were as well reproduced as words of high frequency (both content and function words). In fact, nonwords were even more successfully reproduced than real words with low frequency of occurrence (p = .001).

It should also be pointed out that the patient *never* produced any semantic error while repeating content words, nor did he ever produce substitution errors while repeating function words. On rare occasions the repetition of nonsense syllables resulted—I think by chance—in real word responses. On the mentioned list (October 1983) there were two errors of this sort, e.g.:

gu→glu* *gu* ku* glu* (*could be "glue" and "cul").

Throughout the testing period the patient remained incapable of repeating and of reading aloud even short sentences.

B. Word Recognition and Comprehension

In this section we will describe the patient's capacities to access information at the level of isolated words.

1. Lexical Decisions.   Visual lexical decision performance was good (90% correct) for both content and function words of high frequency in March 1983 (80 items had to be judged). Because of the patient's problems in writing from dictation (discussed later), more data concerning both visual and auditory input modality were collected in October 1983. A lexical decision test was constructed consisting of 40 nonsense syllables and 30 concrete and 30 abstract words (of various but balanced frequencies). To control for the possible influence of stimulus length, half of the items in each category were monosyllabic, the other half consisting of items with more than one syllable. It can be seen from Table 14.2 that neither the length nor the concrete/abstract dimension of the stimuli had an influence on the patient's performance in lexical decisions: with visual presentation Michel scored 92% correct and with auditory presentation 80%. This difference is statistically significant (p = .011; Standard Bayesian Inference on the difference of two proportions).

2. Word Comprehension.   The patient's comprehension of nouns was checked by various matching tasks:

1. Matching of a spoken word with the corresponding picture was performed flawlessly. (The patient had to match a spoken word (n = 20) with the corresponding picture in a multiple choice of four pictures all of which had names similar in sound.)

TABLE 14.2
Visual and Auditory Lexical Decisions (Score Correct)

	Concrete words		Abstract words		Nonsense syllables	
	Visual	Auditory	Visual	Auditory	Visual	Auditory
Monosyllabic items	13/15	11/15	13/15	12/15	18/20	16/20
Multisyllabic items	15/15	13/15	13/15	11/15	20/20	17/20
Total	28/30	24/30	26/30	24/30	38/40	33/40

2. The patient also performed flawlessly in matching a given object (n = 20) with its corresponding written name in a multiple choice of four words (target, semantic distractor, phonological distractor, word without any relationship).

3. A semantic categorisation task was administered in March 1983: the patient had to match a given written word with the only semantically-related candidate among a multiple choice of five written words. The patient's performance was flawless on the 25 concrete word pairs (e.g., fork—knife) and also correct on the 25 abstract words pairs (e.g., punishment—justice) allowing two self-corrections. (Note that this test of word association does not require detailed specific knowledge of each referent. However, it should also be noted that Michel's performance is far better than the average performance of aphasic subjects (n = 19) who correctly classified only 82% of the concrete words and 69% of the abstract words).

4. In October 1983 the patient was also administered a French version of one of the synonym comprehension tests used by Allport and Funnell (1981) and by Funnell (1983): the "two word—word matching test" with related pairs, e.g., *soulier* (shoe): *chaussure* (shoe)—*bas* (stocking). The patient scored 13/15 (86.6%) correct with visual presentation and 9/15 (60%) correct with auditory input.

The patient's comprehension of function words was also studied. We asked the patient to execute five semi-complex commands, all of which contained two content words and one preposition, e.g., "put the key into the ashtray." (Two out of five objects lying in front of the patient had to be manipulated with respect to the correct sequence of objects and to one of five prepositions: on, under, into, in front of, beside). All sentences were presented in both spoken and in written form. The patient's execution (March 1983) of both versions was deficient with regard to his understanding of the function words. He succeeded indeed with all objects/content words for the written material and with 8/10 object names on oral request. However, he "executed" none of the functors in the written version (three omissions, two errors) and only 1/5 in the auditory version (two omissions, two errors).

3. Simultaneous Comprehension of the Presented Stimuli. Because of the patient's limited verbal output, we could not check for word comprehension by asking him to give definitions. Because of the breakdown in the patient's verbal comprehension at the level of sentences, it was also impossible to test comprehension of words vs definitions by a forced choice paradigm. We therefore decided to look at the patient's own judgements of his comprehension (YES/NO decision) while reading and while repeating isolated words. Although this way of testing may seem to be rather subjective, at least the

NO-responses can be trusted: it is difficult to imagine that a patient would pretend not to understand a given word although he actually fully grasps its meaning. We thus checked the patient's *simultaneous* comprehension of the presented stimuli.

(a) *While reading aloud*: Immediately after the patient had read aloud a presented stimulus word (concrete and abstract), we asked the patient whether he understood the word he had just read. Twenty-six words were checked in this way for simultaneous reading comprehension, but of the 12 correctly-read words the patient judged himself to correctly understand 11. Out of 14 words that he did not read successfully, the patient judged that he nevertheless understood 12 words. In other words: except for three items (out of 26) the patient's written comprehension of isolated words seemed to be preserved. Reading comprehension while reading aloud appeared to be independent of success and/or failure in oral reading. There was only one (abstract) word which the patient claimed not to understand even though he read it correctly.

(b) *While repeating isolated words*: Immediately after repetition of a target word (concrete and abstract) we asked the patient for his auditory comprehension. Thirty-eight items were checked in this way for simultaneous understanding during repetion. Out of 24 correctly repeated words the patient claimed to understand only 15; that is, he said he did not understand 9/24 words in spite of repeating them perfectly. Out of 14 words that were not correctly repeated he still understood four (as compared with 10 that he did not understand). Presented with another list of words, the patient claimed to have no auditory comprehension for 14 out of 36 items. Interestingly enough, 13/14 were not understood in spite of correct oral repetition.

4. Orthographic Knowledge. We already mentioned that Michel was unable to orally spell even three-letter words: he could neither name the word corresponding to the sequence of letter names spoken by the experimentor, nor could he spell out the component letters of auditory presented words. It is possible, however, that performance in oral spelling is interfered with by poor memory span and/or by the patient's ability to correctly "name" letters (from the "inner screen" of an internal visual representation). We therefore asked Michel to make lexical decisions on the orthography of words. Ninety items had to be judged: words (*stylo, étain*, etc.); pseudo-homophones of words (*stilault, ethin*); and legal nonsense syllables (*stilotte, ethine*). The patient made only 8.9% errors (two omissions on words; three false recognitions of pseudo-homophones; and three accepted nonsense syllables).

5. Phonological Knowledge. Michel's performance in oral reading, although astonishing in the light of the absence of any spontaneous language, was, nonetheless, far from perfect for both words and nonsense syllables. To assess the patient's phonological knowledge we administered a homophone recognition test (forced choice condition) for (a) real words; (b) nonsense syllables; (c) words paired with nonsense syllables. (Chance level for all three conditions is 10.)

In judging homophones of real words (e.g., *porc = port*; *port ≠ porte*) Michel made three errors on 20 trials. (All errors were omissions.) His recognition of homophonic nonsense syllables (e.g. *trin = traint*; *trein ≠ treinte*) was more impaired: he committed five errors (two omissions; three false alarms).

Michel thus shows a far better performance on homophone recognition than do deep dyslexic patients. In fact, he even preserves some knowledge of the soundform of meaningless letter strings. Judging homophony between real words and pseudowords (e.g., *repos = repau*; *bas ≠ bau*) however was very deficient: his performance was at chance level (11 errors on 20 trials). At the moment I cannot conceive of an explanation of this performance pattern, although it does not seem to be idiosyncratic as similar results have been obtained with another patient who has a difficulty similar to Michel's. One possibility that could be tentatively advanced is that the phonological codes for a word and for a nonsense syllable are not judged at the same level of comparison within the language system: worse performance would thus be due to "noise" resulting from switching from one code (output logogen?) to another (response buffer or later for nonsense syllables?).

C. Study of Written Output

1. Spontaneous Writing and Written Naming. We have already mentioned that the patient could write his address and copy text correctly. Spontaneous writing, however, was very poor and stayed telegraphic. Once he described, for example, the night he spent before (watching a TV programme on channel 1) in the following way: Mozart
TF1
20 h.

In contrast with oral naming, the patient's written naming of the same objects turned out to be fairly well preserved. The patient's naming performance stayed stable during testing periods: he thus named only 2/20 objects orally but 18/20 by writing in December 1982 and 3/20 orally but 17/20 by writing in October 1983. In contrast the patient described by Miceli, Silveri, and Caramazza in Chapter 11 made no errors in oral naming but 30% errors in written naming. Error analysis of written naming reveals one semantic error (or visual misperception?): *vis* (screw)→*clou* (nail); two of the remaining errors were frank omissions—*trépied* (tripod) and *éponge* (sponge); the other two pictures were approximated by listing words "in the sphere" (e.g., *palette→dessin peinture* (drawing painting), but the patient *knew* that these words were not adequate. It is noteworthy that the patient did not produce any gap errors and that the rare mispellings were mostly corrected (e.g., *prise→*"pise *prise*"; *pyramide→*"pyrm pyra pymide *pyramide*").

The dissociation of (impaired) oral naming and (preserved) written naming demonstrates again the relative independence of both functions which has previously been described in some case studies (see Bub & Kertesz, 1982b; Ellis, Miller, & Sin, 1983; Hier & Mohr, 1977; L'Hermitte & Derouesné, 1974; Michel, 1979). These data from pathology are thus in accordance with the theoretical notion of a separate graphemic output logogen system that contains the orthographic codes of words and that can be accessed directly from representation in the cognitive system (see Ellis, 1982; Miller & Ellis, this volume; Morton, 1980a; Patterson & Shewell, this volume).

2. Writing to Dictation.   From the onset of testing the patient was able to write isolated letters from dictation, averaging 80% correct across different sessions. However, he never succeeded in reproducing even short nonsense syllables. Writing words from dictation was always possible but prone to error. For illustration and comparison the patient's performance in writing to dictation the same items (monosyllabic words and non-words) given for oral reading and repetition (see Table 14.1) at the same time of testing (October 1983) are represented in Table 14.3.

Comparison of the patient's performances in writing from dictation with his oral production (see Table 14.1) shows a clear dissociation: although Michel could repeat 93% of the presented monosyllabic non-words, he could not write any to dictation. The patient was also unable to write many of the

TABLE 14.3
Writing from Dictation of Monosyllabic and Multisyllabic Items

	% Correct			
	Monosyllabic		*Multisyllabic*	
High frequency content words	70%	(42/60)	50%	(20/40)
High frequency function words	27%	(8/30)	20%	(6/30)
Low frequency content words	47%	(19/40)	40%	(16/40)
Nonsense syllables	0%	(0/10)	0%	(0/10)

function words that he successfully repeated and/or read. However, mono-syllabic function words were more successfully written to dictation than nonsense syllables (p = .012). The part of speech effect was highly significant for writing from dictation (test for difference between proportions of monosyllabic function vs content words of same frequency yielded p < .001), and the frequency of the dictated words also played a significant role (monosyllabic high vs low frequency content words yielded p = .012). A very similar pattern is shown in writing to dictation by patient G.A., described by Patterson and Shewell in Chapter 13.

Since the patient's performance in written naming did not seem to depend on the length of the stimuli, words with more than one syllable were also administered for writing from dictation. The scores of correct writings of long words are also represented in Table 14.3. It is evident from Table 14.3 that the length of the stimuli plays only a minor role for writing from dictation: indeed, only the writing of high frequency content words is affected by length (p = .022). Writing of multisyllabic words shows again the influence of grammatical class on writing from dictation (p = .005), and again multisyllabic function words are better written than nonsense syllables of comparable length (p = .046). Frequency of occurrence, however, does not affect the writing of long content words (p = .185)—(although it did for the writing of short content words).

The patient's performance pattern suggests indeed that the writing disturbance does not so much originate from problems at the level of the grapheme buffer—although there is a certain "weakness" as shown by better writing of short (as compared to long) high frequency content words—but, rather, from a central disturbance as shown by the influence of lexical variables such as the part-of-speech dimension. In fact, not only were function words constantly written with less success than content words, but abstract words were also more error prone than concrete ones. Both deficits stayed unchanged over the different testing periods. *In spite of quantitatively stable performances there seemed to be a change* in the patient's writing from dictation *with regard to the error pattern* on content words. The production of semantic paragraphias, which was rather pronounced in the initial stage, seemed to become less frequent and/or "shift" to errors which were both semantically and structurally related to the stimulus. For illustration some examples of both types of errors:

semantic errors:	*mixed errors* (semantically and structurally related to the stimulus):
"fatigue"→*dormir* (sleep)	"porte" (door)→*porche* (porch)
"aiguille" (needle)→*fil* (thread)	"feuille" (leaf)→*fleur* (flower)

"corbeau" (crow)→*hibou* (owl)

"cordon" (twist of rope)→*corde* (rope)

"bonnet" (cap)→*gantelet* (gauntlet)

"peloton" (ball, clew)→*pelote* (ball, clew)

"bâton" (stick)→*canne* (walking stick)

"coup" (stroke)→*couteau* (knife)

"coussin" (cushion)→*soie* (silk)

"mois" (month)→*mai* (May) etc.

Unfortunately we did not present the same lists for writing from dictation in March and in October. Two of the presented lists included, however, concrete and abstract words (predominantly multisyllabic) which are closely balanced for length in terms of number of constituent letters. The lists differ with regard to their frequency: list I (March 1983) contained concrete and abstract words of various frequencies, but individually matched concrete/abstract pairs; list II (October 1983) also comprises an equal number of concrete and abstract words, half of which were of high frequency (taken from the first 500 words of Juilland, Brodin, & Davidivitch, 1970) and half of which of lower frequency (taken from the tenth 500 words). The error analysis of the patient's writing from dictation in March and in October 1983 is given in Table 14.4.[1] Inspection of Table 14.4 seems to confirm our

---

[1]The term "gap error" is taken from Nolan and Caramazza's (1983) description of a case with deep dysgraphia. We use it to describe incomplete productions which indicate, however, that the patient has some partial knowledge about the stimulus, e.g., (essaim)→... sai; (corps)→o r; (problème)→pro b leme; (élément)→e lé me.

Note that such "gap writing" resulted on only two occasions in correct responses, e.g., (dame→d a m e ; (porc)→p o r c. Such "pictorial" writing that does not respect the conventional left-to-right order has been reported for another patient with deep dysgraphia (see Hatfield, 1982b). Nolan and Caramazza (1983) consider gap errors to result from a breakdown that occurs fairly late in the writing process, at the level of the grapheme buffer. Ellis (1982) also considers gap errors to result from a post-lexical disturbance. Nolan and Caramazza as well as Ellis think that "gaps" need to be filled in by use of the non-lexical route for writing.

Under "miscellaneous", we grouped all errors which could not be classified in the considered error types. Thus this group of miscellaneous errors is not necessarily homogeneous. It comprises however mainly two error types:

1. "Gap" errors that are close to omissions in that the response reproduces only one (or two) letter(s) of the target word, e.g., (travers)→.. v; (caractère)→a .. ; (fin)→f .. ; (force)→F | V | ?

2. "Deviant productions" such as, e.g., (brosse)→p ei s ; (bâton)→pad ; (idylle)→ilvi ; (synthèse)→sem ; (raison)→rasu.

I think indeed that the majority (if not all) errors classified under miscellaneous reflect the patient's unsuccessful attempts to write by phoneme-grapheme conversion. Some of the patient's writing errors may even be taken to suggest that the borderline between "gap" errors and "miscellaneous", that is, between writing with (partial) lexical knowledge and non-lexical

subjective impression with regard to the production of semantic errors during the course of illness. A high proportion of the errors on concrete words (6/9) consisted of semantic errors in the initial testing period. However, when Michel was seen again seven months later, in October 1983, semantic paragraphias constituted only 11% of total errors. Even considering the total amount of semantically related errors (semantic, derivational, and mixed), the diminution is still considerable: only 27% in October as compared to 66% in March. (That the diminution of semantic errors was real, and is not due to an artifact of list comparison, can be inferred from comparison of the two subsets of list II: high frequency concrete words yielded two semantically related errors, and concrete words of lower frequency yielded three semantically related errors). The patient's tendency to produce fewer semantically related errors becomes also apparent—although less pronounced—when considering the reproduction of abstract words in March vs October 1983.

Another prominent feature of the diachronic error pattern is the virtual absence of gap errors and of errors termed miscellaneous in the initial stage. These types of errors constitute, however, approximately half of all writing errors in the later stages of the illness. In contrast, semantically unrelated whole word errors seem to become less frequent with time (as do semantic whole word errors). The percentage of omissions (which mainly occurred with abstract words) hardly varied with time. This analysis of the patient's writing performances is summarised in Table 14.5, which clearly shows that

---

writing, is rather unclear. The patient wrote, for example: (question)→(cesu) e ⸬ ion ; (confins)→ c $\begin{vmatrix} g \end{vmatrix}_2$ on f $\begin{vmatrix} v \end{vmatrix}_3$.

Semantically unrelated whole word substitutions are a well defined category of errors, e.g., (milieu)→mieux ; (aube)→robe ; (contrôle)→rôle .

Note a certain structural similarity between erroneous response and target word. Such structural, non-semantic relation may well be taken to reflect the patient's specific problems of accessing information given auditory input. (This point will be discussed later in more detail.) Note, however, that the relation between purely structural and true semantic components of the word to be written to dictation may be more complex than usually thought of for the interpretation of the deep dysgraphic syndrome. On one occasion the patient wrote indeed: "sandale" (sandal)→*salade chaussure (salad shoe)*.

If deep dysgraphic patients solely rely on "writing through semantics" it is not easy to conceive of an explanation how Michel reproduced "sandal," which was dictated only once, as "salad" and then as "shoe," knowing, moreover, that the first realisation was wrong. In this case it will be argued that the first realisation of *sandal* as *salad* is due to lexical nonsemantic writing; but it was rejected as the information forthcoming from semantics was something like "you wear it on your foot." Consequently Michel wrote "shoe," which is both more frequent and its superordinate.

CNL-K

TABLE 14.4

Analysis of Writing Errors (Dictation) Produced in March 1983 and in October 1983

	Concrete words		Abstract words	
Period	March 1983	October 1983	March 1983	October 1983
Number of items	list I: n = 20	list II: n = 40	list I: n = 20	list II: n = 40
Correct responses	75%	60%	30%	28.5%
Total errors[a]	9	18	14	31
Error analysis:				
1. Omissions	0%	11.1%	57.1%	41.9%
2. Semantically related errors				
(a) semantic	66.6%	11.1%	0%	3.2%[b]
(b) derivational	0%	5.5%	0%	3.2%[b]
(c) mixed (semantically and structurally related)	0%	11.1%	7.1%	0%
3. Other word	22.9%	5.5%	14.2%	9.6%
4. Gap errors	0%	27.7%	7.1%	22.5%
5. Miscellaneous	11.1%	27.7%	0%	19.3%

[a]Total of errors refers to *all* errors produced, thus including multiple responses that are produced on rare occasions, e.g., "sandale" → *salade chaussure*; the response *salade* being classified as "other word" and the response *chaussure* being classified as "semantic error."
[b]The patient rejected these semantic errors as wrong productions.

there is a significant change over time in the patient's writing from dictation: whole word substitutions (with and without semantic relation to the stimulus) diminish, whereas gap errors and miscellaneous productions become more frequent. (Note that this *qualitative* change in the error pattern did not affect the patient's quantitative writing performance which stayed stable across different testing periods.)

D. Summary and Discussion

Michel is a patient without any spontaneous output other than "ah-oh-oh." Oral naming is also close to zero. It should be emphasised, however, that oral naming is not characterised by omissions as in the cases of Hier and Mohr (1977) and of Bub and Kertesz (1982b). Michel is, instead, desperately trying out different soundforms which more or less resemble the target word.

Although these "attempts after soundform" contrast with his almost

TABLE 14.5
Relative Distribution of Different Types of Writing Errors (Dictation) in
March 1983 and October 1983

	March 1983 List I (n=40)		October 1983 List II (n=80)	
Total of errors	23		49	
Omissions	(8/23)	34.78%	(15/49)	30.61%
		ns (p= .359)		
Whole word substitutions (with and without semantic relation to the stimulus)	(13/23)	56.52%	(11/49)	22.45%
		sig. (p= .013)		
Partial writings (gap errors and miscellaneous)	(2/23)	8.70%	(23/49)	46.94%
		sig. (p= .001)		

entire absence of spontaneous speech, I will, for the purpose of this paper[2] accept Warren and Morton's (1982) assumption that there is no direct connection between the picture recognition system and the phonological output lexicon. This would mean that patients like Michel have a problem getting from the cognitive system to the phonological output logogen system. This statement, then, should also hold for both oral reading and repetition by means of semantics. Michel does, however, read and repeat isolated words (whereas he is indeed totally incapable of orally reproducing sentences). There are two other methods by which a patient can attempt the reading and repetition of isolated words according to the current version of the logogen model (Morton & Patterson, 1980): by direct input/output logogen connections and/or by peripheral strategies. Since Michel had (for reasons I am ignoring for the present) a dramatic damage to the process of articulation (with regard to the *length* of the stimuli), the main concern of testing was to investigate the patient's spared reproduction capacities on short stimuli. For this reason the question of "which strategy was used for oral reading" cannot

---

[2]The discrepancy between total lack of output for spontaneous language and frequent (but unsuccessful) attempts of sounding out the target word for oral naming may indeed be taken to constitute another argument for my assumption (based on experimental data, see Kremin, 1984) that direct input/output connections (which bypass semantics) exist for oral naming also. A resolution of this question, however, is not required by the proposed interpretation that the patient cannot derive phonology solely from *semantics*.

be answered from the patient's performance on regular vs irregular words; not enough short words were found to test this dimension. Looking more closely at the obtained reading data should nonetheless permit a conclusive comment.

On the one hand, although Michel is capable of doing some grapheme-to-phoneme conversion (since he reads some nonsense syllables), he reads short lexical items more successfully than short nonsense syllables. This means that he is using at least in part a lexical route for reading. On the other hand, the part-of-speech dimension—which is so crucial for the oral reading perfor-mance of patients who obtain lexical phonology through semantics (see Coltheart, Patterson, & Marshall, 1980)—does not play a role for Michel's oral production of visually presented words. This pattern of performance is compatible with the use of the direct lexical (non-semantic) pathway for oral reading (from visual input logogens to phonological output logogens). That the visual input logogens are accessed is also evident from the patient's good performance on visual lexical decisions for all types of words (concrete and abstract content words as well as function words). Lisa, the patient described by Sartori, Masterson, and Job in Chapter Three, also relied on the direct lexical non-semantic pathway for reading aloud, but for a different reason. The semantic pathway was unavailable for Michel because the semantic system could not access output phonology, whereas it was unavailable for Lisa because the semantic system itself was severely damaged.

In any case, in the light of the initial assumption with regard to oral naming and spontaneous oral output (i.e., supposed disruption between cognitive system and phonological output logogens) use of the direct pathway constitutes the only possibility which is left to gain access of phonological output logogens. Michel's good recognition of visually pre-sented homophones seems to be another argument against the use of the semantic pathway (which should result in the same [bad] performances for oral reading as for oral naming and spontaneous speech). The semantic pathway is furthermore supposed by some, e.g., Newcombe and Marshall (1980), to have the characteristic of provoking substitution and/or semantic errors, and these *never* occurred in Michel's oral reading. To conclude: it seems plausible that Michel uses the direct pathway for the oral reading of all kinds of real words. Written words also gain access to the cognitive system. However, only content words are relatively well understood, whereas the understanding of function words is severely impaired (although function words are read well aloud and well recognised as words).

A similar, although more complex, interpretation fits Michel's spared ability to repeat short items. Again, there is no influence of the part-of-speech dimension. In contrast to oral reading, however, nonsense syllables are as easily reproduced as are lexical items of high frequency. However, from the experimental data it is nevertheless clear that the repetition of words cannot solely (or not at all!) rely on acoustic-to-phoneme conversion since words of low frequency are *significantly less well* repeated than meaningless stimuli of comparable length. This pattern of performance clearly demonstrates that words (at least when they are of *low* frequency) are treated differently from nonsense syllables. Indeed, Michel does not seem to make use of the (in his case) more "successful" strategy of acoustic-to-phoneme conversion; he, rather, uses the more "adequate" strategy for the repetition of real words, that is: direct input/output connections. Note also that—as in reading aloud—the patient *never* produced any semantic error. Finally, there was simultaneous understanding of many (but not all!) words while repeating them.

Michel's good (although not perfect) auditory lexical decisions constitute another argument in favour of the phonological input logogen system being intact. The patient's access to semantics seems, however, to be less efficient given auditory compared to visual input. And yet, as with visual input, the understanding of functors is severely impaired. But in contrast to reading the patient also seems to have problems of auditorily accessing the meaning of content words.

The patient's writing to dictation of isolated words is—especially in the initial stage—characterised by a specific error pattern which is usually termed "deep dysgraphia." Like deep dyslexic reading (see Coltheart, Patterson, & Marshall, 1980), deep dysgraphic writing is mainly characterised by a nonlexical phonological impairment (unavailability of phoneme-grapheme conversion for writing nonsense syllables from dictation); the presence of semantic errors (which, as for reading, constitute the crucial variable for defining the syndrome), better performance on concrete than abstract words, and poor transcription of function words as compared to content words (Bub & Kertesz, 1982a; Hatfield, 1982a; Nolan & Caramazza, 1983). This specific pattern of writing is taken to reflect the patient's reliance on the pathway through semantics. Other forms of non-lexical phonological writing impairment have been described as "phonological agraphia" (Bub & Kertesz, 1982a; Roeltgen, Sevush, & Heilman, 1983; Shallice, 1981). It should be emphasised, though, that the published cases of phonological agraphia, which are usually characterised by the absence of semantic paragraphias, vary with regard to the patient's performances in writing grammatical particles from dictation: P.R. (Shallice, 1981) did have a deficit in writing function words whereas M.H. (Bub & Kertesz, 1982b) wrote them with high accuracy.

All published observations on non-lexical phonological writing impairments are compatible with writing solely by the semantic route. They are indeed interpreted in this frame of reference by the authors.

Recent research on *reading* disorders, however, has experimentally established that there is another method of word production: the non-semantic but lexical pathway for reading aloud (Funnell, 1983; Schwartz, Saffran, & Marin, 1980). According to Morton's logogen model, such a lexical but non-semantic pathway should exit not only for reading aloud but also for repetition and for writing words to dictation. Morton (1980a) has indeed theoretically argued that the graphemic output logogens (that is, the ortho-graphic codes for words) can be accessed by two different modes: directly from the cognitive system *or* via the output logogen system and then to the graphemic output logogen system. Since on the logogen model information can flow *directly* (that is without semantic access) from the phonological input logogens to the phonological output logogens, and then to the graphemic output logogens, there should be patients who are able to write words from dictation they do not understand. Such patients should thus rely on a purely lexical strategy for written production (that is, without semantic access and without any use of peripheral writing by phoneme-grapheme conversion).

The relative contribution of these two ways of accessing information in the graphemic output logogen has been considered by Shallice (1981), who concluded re his patient P.R.: "In his case ... his ability to write a word seemed to depend heavily on his ability to understand it (p. 425)." It is noteworthy, however, that P.R. correctly wrote almost half (6/14) of those abstract words whose meaning was "not grasped at all." P.R. also correctly wrote from dictation 14 function words he did not understand (as shown by inappropriate or no use of the same words in a sentence production task), as compared to 13 function words that he failed to write (and to understand). Although the occurrence of correct writing of words that were not under-stood was relatively uncommon in P.R.'s case, I would like to stress the theoretical importance of such writing behaviour: it lends, indeed, some experimental support to the notion of a lexical but non-semantic pathway for writing words from dictation. Lexical but non-semantic writing would be achieved by connections from the auditory input logogens via the phonologi-cal output logogens to the orthographic code (graphemic output logogen). We mentioned before that our patient was often able to repeat words he claimed not to understand. On five occasions Michel *thereafter wrote down the target word*, and tried to indicate that, when he *sees* the *written form* understanding becomes possible.

Since the patient himself indicated that his comprehension of words was better with visual than with auditory presentation, it seemed necessary to try to elucidate the relations between repetition, comprehension, and writing from dictation more precisely. We tried to assess the possible relations and interdependences among these functions in the following test periods (end of October 1983 and March 1984).

FURTHER INVESTIGATION OF WRITING WITHOUT
PHONEME-GRAPHEME CONVERSION

Auditory Lexical Access: "Wordness" Versus Semantic Comprehension

Word recognition is not an all-or-none process, but involves various subprocesses: tapped by various tasks such as lexical decision, category verification, etc. (see Balota & Chumbley, 1984). These different stages of information processing may be selectively disturbed by pathology. For example, Sartori, Masterson, and Job (this volume) describe a patient with good performance on visual lexical decision tests in spite of very impaired comprehension of written words. Such dissolution would reflect that the visual input logogen system is functioning (in spite of impaired semantics, or impaired access to semantics from the visual input logogens). According to the logogen model, the same dissociation is theoretically possible given auditory input. Because of our patient's complaint that he often did not correctly "hear" (by pointing to his head rather than to his ears) we compared his performances on lexical decisions and the understanding of the same words presented auditorily.

A list consisting of 120 items: 40 multisyllabic content words of low frequency (20 concrete and 20 abstract nouns), 20 high frequency function words, and 60 nonsense syllables was presented in two different conditions:

A. The patient had to make lexical decisions by YES/NO responses (October 1983).

B. The patient had to indicate his "degree of comprehension" of the same items by pointing to one of the cards lying in front of him (March 1984):

(1) + + + je comprends parfaitement (I understand perfectly);
(2)   + je comprends un peu mais pas vraiment (I understand a bit but not quite);
(3)   − je ne comprends pas du tout (I do not understand at all).

The comparison of the patient's performances on both tasks (condition A and B) with regard to judgements on "wordness" is represented in Table 14.6 (Judgements in condition B referring to wordness only constitute the sum of (1) I perfectly understand and (2) I understand a bit but not quite.) Table 14.6 shows that there is a great consistency in auditory lexical decisions with regard to the recognition of "wordness": 14 errors in condition A and 16 errors in condition B, false recognitions being the main source of errors. However, when considering the "degree of comprehension" of the 58/60 recognised words in condition B it turns out that: the patient fully under-

TABLE 14.6
Auditory "Lexical Decisions" on Low Frequency Multisyllabic Words

(Score correct)	Condition A (October 83) Lexical decisions	Condition B (March 84) Judgements from understanding
Words	58/60	58/60
Non-words	48/60	46/60

stood only 41.3% of the recognised words (24/58). These were 19/20 concrete words, 3/20 abstract words and 2/20 function words; the patient understood "a bit but not quite" 58.7% of the recognised words (34/58). These were 1/20 concrete words, 17/20 abstract words and 16/20 function words. (Two [function] words were "not understood at all").

To resume: the patient recognised fairly well and with a high degree of consistency the "wordness" of auditorily presented stimuli. However, for more than half of the items that were well recognised as words he admitted to have no precise and full semantic understanding. (Note also that the patient judged himself to understand concrete words much better than abstract and/ or function words.)

Comprehension of Concrete and Abstract Nouns and of Function Words

We decided to assess the patient's comprehension of words more formally with regard to the possible influence of linguistic variables. To test for the influence of the concrete/abstract dimension of words the "two word—word matching" test with related pairs (see Funnell, 1983) was extended to include abstract nouns also. On each trial, the patient was given a target word, e.g., *entrave* (hindrance) and then a pair of words, one synonymous with the target, e.g., *obstacle* (obstacle) and the other closely related but not synonymous, e.g., *difficulté* (difficulty). The task was to indicate which member of the pair was closest in meaning to the target word. Since the patient seemed to have more difficulties in accessing the meaning of words when they were given auditorily, our presentation of the word triads was, in contrast to Funnell's (1983) cross-modal presentation, purely visual (three written words) or purely auditory (three spoken words).

Thus 15 triads of concrete words (which had been administered before) and 15 triads of abstract words had to be judged. All triads were presented three times on different sessions. The patient's performance on this synonym comprehension task is shown in Table 14.7. It is clear from Table 14.7 that the patient performs significantly better with visual than with auditory input (p = .001). Note that the patient's difficulty on the auditory version of this synonym comprehension test should not be due to problems with the sensory

TABLE 14.7
Synonym Comprehension (Two Word/Word Matching Task)

(% correct)	Presentation			
	Visual		Auditory	
Concrete words (45 trials)	88.8%	(40/45)	62.2%	(28/45)
Abstract words (45 trials)	80.0%	(36/45)	77.7%	(35/45)
Total	84.4%	(76/90)	70.0%	(63/90)

attributes of the input since, as we mentioned above, auditory lexical decisions were well executed even with *low* frequency multisyllabic words, both abstract and concrete.

It may seem surprising that the patient seemed to understand abstract words better than concrete ones given auditory input. An item analysis suggests, however, that Michel's performance was somewhat inconsistent from trial to trial. Indeed, the response consistency for the average synonym pairs (in terms of target pair correct on all three trials) is 20/30 correct with visual and 14/30 correct with auditory presentation. (This difference falls short of significance with $p = .06$).

To resume: the patient exhibits comprehension deficits in both modalities. Problems of semantic access are, however, more severe given auditory input. Analysis of the patient's response consistency (along with other results mentioned before) may be taken to indicate that the comprehension deficit for nouns when writing from dictation is only partly a consequence of *general* degradation of the verbal semantic system. The patient suffers as well from a *specific* inability to access stored information efficiently given auditory (as compared to visual) input. In the framework of the "semantic attainment theory", Shallice and Coughlan (1980) argued for the possibility of modality specific comprehension deficits. Their patient showed, however, the reverse of the pattern observed with Michel, performing significantly better on several word comprehension tasks given auditory as compared to visual input.

The comprehension of function words was also more formally tested in October 1983, that is independently of any executive commands. The patient had to decide whether a sentence correctly described a picture with the following sentences:

* les pommes sont du panier
* les pommes sont auprès du panier
  les pommes sont dans le panier (correct sentence)
* les pommes sont au panier.

CNL-K*

Twenty-five pictures had thus to be judged upon in both written and auditory presentation. Michel recognised only 8/25 adequate prepositions on the auditory version and 11/25 adequate function words with visual presentation. Since the patient moreover *often* accepted ungrammatical sentences, we conclude that his comprehension of the semantico-syntactical value of prepositions was disturbed with both visual and auditory input.

Writing to Dictation and Comprehension

On another session the patient was to write from dictation the same 120 items that had been presented for lexical decisions and judgements of comprehension. Comparison of auditory comprehension and writing from dictation of the same words (but on different occasions) reveals that:

1. 83.3% of the "perfectly understood" words were correctly written from dictation (20/24). Two of the remaining four words were semantic/visual word errors (*bracelet→bague; fillette→fille*); the other two words were tried out without any success.

2. 35.3% of the words which were "understood a bit not quite" were correctly written from dictation (12/34). On the remaining 22 items there were 16 totally unsuccessful attempts of writing and six whole word errors.

3. The two (function) words which were "not understood at all" yielded one success and one omission in writing from dictation.[3]

To resume: Michel's success in writing words from dictation seems to be related to the degree of auditory comprehension of the same words on *another* occasion.

However, since many of these words were rather long (e.g., *chenille, citation*) and, moreover, of *low* frequency of occurrence, we agree with Shallice (1981) that such a subset may be near the limit of the patient's vocabulary and thus constitute difficulties for both writing and understanding that obscure the particular mechanisms of processes underlying writing.

Repetition, Comprehension and Writing to Dictation of Same Words on Same Occasion

Because of the foregoing arguments the patient was once more presented with the list of *high* frequency monosyllabic content words (30 concrete and

---

[3]With regard to the stimulus properties of the items administered for writing to dictation, note that the patient wrote 16/20 concrete words, 7/20 abstract words, and 7/20 function words correctly. The writing of nonsense syllables (n = 60) yielded three correct realisations, 41 omissions, and 16 unsuccessful attempts of writing, only four of them resulting in real word productions, e.g., CHON→chant ; LIVER→livre.

30 abstract nouns) and asked to first repeat them, then indicate simultaneously auditory comprehension (by YES = + / NO = − decisions) and finally write the word. The patient's performances on these three tasks are represented in Table 14.8.

It is clear from Table 14.8A that the patient correctly wrote from dictation an almost equal number of words with and without simultaneous semantic comprehension (21 vs 22). Comparison of comprehension and writing from

TABLE 14.8
Pairwise Comparison of Oral Repetition, Judgements on Semantic
Comprehension, and Writing from Dictation
(Same Words/Same Occasion)

A

Comprehension Writing	YES	NO
Correct	22	21
Incorrect	4	13

(n = 60)

B

Comprehension Repetition	YES	NO
Correct	25	26
Incorrect	1	8

(n = 60)

C

Writing Writing	Correct	Incorrect
Correct	40	11
Incorrect	3	6

(n = 60)

dictation of the auditorily presented stimuli furthermore shows that the patient's writing performance is better than his comprehension of the dictated words (p < .01). A test of the difference between proportions also yielded a significant difference between comprehension and oral repetition of the target words: the patient repeated the words more easily than he understood them (p < .01). Table 14.8C shows that the patient moreover repeated the words more easily than he wrote them (.01 < p < .05).

At this juncture I only want to refer to the patient's repetition performance and would like to emphasise that an apparent relation between word production and semantic knowledge may indeed be rather fortuitous. The point we ought to make may be not so much that words that are comprehended are well reproduced, but rather that words are correctly reproduced although they are not comprehended: cf. Funnell's (1983) argument for a lexical non-semantic route (for *reading* aloud).

Our patient's oral repetition performance seems to require a similar interpretation. Indeed, the patient never produced a semantic error while repeating words, and there was no word-class effect. Note also that Michel scored only 70% correct on the auditory version of the synonym comprehension test (chance level being 50%) and that he judged himself to have no semantic comprehension for approximately half of the words he had repeated correctly (see Table 14.8B). That at least a considerable proportion of the patient's oral repetition of words is, however, achieved by a lexical strategy (in spite of preserved acoustic-to-phoneme conversion!) is documented by the observed influence of the frequency of the presented target words which we mentioned earlier (see Table 14.1).

The patient's oral repetition of real words thus seems to be mediated by direct connections from the auditory input logogen to the phonological output logogen. The existence of such lexical but non-semantic pathway for the oral reproduction of auditorily presented stimuli is predicted theoretically by Morton's logogen model and has also received some experimental confirmation. On the one hand, a case study of a patient with an auditory parallel to phonological dyslexia has been presented (Beauvois, Derouesné & Bastard, 1980): J.L. was able to repeat *all* kinds of words without producing semantic errors in spite of a disturbance of acoustic-phonemic conversion. On the other hand, patients with an auditory analogue of deep dyslexia have also been described (Goldblum, 1979; Michel, 1979; Michel & Andreewsky, 1983; Morton, 1980b).

However, because of the scarcity of the published data it cannot be determined whether J.L. (Beauvois et al., 1980) obtained lexical phonology by use of the direct or of the semantic pathway. Our patient's superior performance in oral repetition, compared to his impaired semantic knowledge of auditorily presented words, is, however, incompatible with a production strategy dependent upon semantic processing. The observed pattern of performance rather suggests that Michel obtains lexical phonology (for repetition of auditorily presented isolated words) by use of direct input/output connections.

Writing to Dictation and Oral Repetition

Comparison of task performances (see Table 14.8) may also suggest that there is a possible relation between success in repetition and success in writing the same words from dictation. Such a correspondence, however, is unexpected for a patient with deep dysgraphia (and should definitely be fortuitous) as this syndrome is taken to reflect "writing through semantics." Even for P.R., a patient with so-called phonological agraphia, it is explicitly argued "that in order for him to write the word merely dictating it to him was insufficient: he needed to access its meaning (Shallice, 1981, p. 421)." Our patient, in contrast, did not seem to solely rely, for writing from dictation, on simultaneous auditory comprehension. It therefore seemed legitimate to study more closely a possible relation between repetition and writing.

Since Michel's oral output in repetition, as well as in reading aloud, so crucially depended on the length of the stimuli—only short items could more or less successfully be orally reproduced by the patient—it did not seem useful to study the patient's repetition performance on longer words (for comparison with writing from dictation). We decided instead to inhibit the patient's oral repetition by bandaging his mouth. This somewhat brutal method seemed to be the only way to prevent the patient from making numerous *spontaneous attempts* at repetition while writing from dictation. Note that this strategy was *always* used by the patient while writing function words, and it became more general for content words also in the "second" stage of writing from dictation we mentioned above. The relevance of this manipulation is that if deep and/or phonological dysgraphics do accomplish writing by the graphemic output logogen system *solely* by access from the cognitive system, then the inhibition of oral repetition should not have any influence on writing words from dictation, at least not with regard to their total score (success/failure).

It remains open to question however whether (overt?) production of a phonological code has any influence on the pattern of errors obtained while writing words from dictation. It seems plausible indeed that "very minimal phonological re-coding can block the overt expression of semantic errors." This was indeed the early suggestion of Newcombe and Marshall (1980, p. 185) to deal with the wide range in the number of semantic reading errors produced by different deep dyslexic patients. In line with this reasoning one may expect to find a qualitative (but not quantitative) change in the error

TABLE 14.9
Writing Items From Dictation With and Without Permission to Repeat Them

(Score correct)	Oral repetition required		Oral repetition prevented	
Content words	70%	(56/80)	45%	(38/80)
Function words	23.3%	(14/60)	5%	(1/20)[a]
Nonsense syllables	0%	(0/10)	0%	(0/10)

[a]Only 20 items tested since the patient refused to continue under this condition.

pattern (of one and the same patient) along with the production/inhibition of an overt phonological code.

The patient was thus presented with a list of short content words (which included the 60 monosyllabic content words of high frequency given previously) and a list of short function words (which included the 30 monosyllabic function of words high frequency mentioned earlier). The short nonsense syllables were also presented. The patient's writing from dictation of these stimuli, *with and without previous oral repetition of the target item* is summarised in Table 14.9. It is clear from Table 14.9 that the patient's writing from dictation was facilitated by previously repeating the stimulus. The overt production of a phonological code indeed facilitated the writing of both content words (p = .003) and function words (p = .028). The interaction effect between content words/function words and with/without oral repetition is non-significant. Note that oral repetition was helpful only for the writing of words and not for the writing of nonsense syllables. This state of affairs should preclude the possibility that more success in writing, due to repetition, reflects residual use of peripheral mechanisms (phoneme-grapheme conversion) since simple rules have no notion of wordness.

With regard to the hypothesised possibility of a qualitative change in the error pattern, it should be emphasised that the presence/absence of oral repetition did not have any influence on the number of semantic paragraphias. The only mixed error, "feuille" (leaf)→*fleur* (flower), occurred in fact with (and in spite of) correct oral repetition. More close inspection of the patient's writing performances under both experimental conditions (see Appendix) reveals however another, unpredicted, qualitative change in the error pattern of writing the same words from dictation: with previous repetition omissions constitute only 8.3% of total errors (2/24) on content words, whereas omissions constitute 64.2% of total errors (27/42) when repetition is inhibited.

Discussion

From the published literature there is compelling experimental evidence for the existence of independent lexical and non-lexical pathways for writing. On the one hand cases of "surface dysgraphia" document the functioning of the non-lexical route which bypasses conventional orthography by applying grapheme-phoneme conversion procedures (Beauvois & Derouesné, 1981; Hatfield, 1982a; Hatfield & Patterson, 1983; Kremin, 1985; Newcombe & Marshall, 1985; Roeltgen & Heilman, 1984). On the other hand patients have been described who provided evidence that (some) lexical spelling can be preserved in spite of a disturbance of non-word spelling (Assal, Buttet, & Jolivet, 1981; Bub & Kertesz, 1982, a,b; Hatfield, 1982a; Nolan & Caramazza, 1982, 1983; Patterson, this volume; Roeltgen & Heilman, 1984; Roeltgen, Sevush & Heilman, 1983; Shallice, 1981).

It has also been theoretically argued that the orthographic code may be accessed by two different pathways, through semantics or by direct lexical connections which bypass semantics (see Ellis, 1982; Morton, 1980a). Such an independent lexical (non-semantic) pathway for writing from dictation has, however, received little experimental confirmation. In fact, most authors have considered only two routes for the production of written output (see, however, Shallice, 1981). Even from the writing of words from dictation by M.H. (Bub & Kertesz, 1982b)—which showed no effects of part-of-speech and concreteness—it cannot be deduced *which* of the possible two *lexical* processes supported her performance since "near perfect scores were obtained for all comprehension tests on the Western Aphasia Battery, including comprehension of written words and sentences (Bub & Kertesz, 1982b, p. 702)." A dissociation between (impaired) comprehension and (preserved) reproduction of the target words was, however, the crucial pattern which lent support to the notion of a distinct lexical non-semantic pathway in reading (Funnell, 1983; Schwartz et al., 1980).

Our patient's writing performance was investigated in more detail in order to circumscribe the relative contribution of both lexical pathways. The data we obtained will be discussed with respect to theoretical assumptions from the published literature.

Writing Through Semantics.   The general pattern of the patient's performance is compatible indeed with a lexical strategy for writing. One aspect of the patient's writing from dictation is the non-availability of phoneme-to-grapheme conversion. In addition, the writing of isolated words shows an effect of grammatical class and concreteness. The standard position is that the effect of such lexical dimensions reflects the patient's reliance on a semantic strategy for writing (see, for example, Nolan & Caramazza, 1982, 1983; Shallice, 1981).

With regard to the patient's writing, it is noteworthy that Michel always produced only a small number of orthographic errors. In this respect our case is similar to patient P.R. reported by Shallice (1981). As both patients can make little or no use at all of the phoneme-grapheme conversion system it seems plausible that the accessing of the orthographic code of a word does not depend on the phoneme-grapheme conversion process. This view is at variance with a model proposed by Nolan and Caramazza (1983) in which phoneme-grapheme conversion constitutes an important component of the writing process. According to Nolan and Caramazza (1983) "we are normally dependent on the phoneme-grapheme conversion process to maintain graphemic representations for output (p. 324)," since orthographic representations are more rapidly decaying than the phonological form placed into the response buffer where it can be rehearsed.

Ellis (1982) also opts for an intervening phonological code in writing. In contrast to Nolan and Caramazza, however, who assume the use of the phoneme-grapheme conversion system, Ellis proposes that the phonemic code which is recycled is lexical in nature: "Words whose spelling is familiar have entries in the graphemic output logogen system. Each logogen within that system makes available its grapheme string in response to a unique combination of semantic and phonemic specifications. The semantic code originates in the cognitive system where it simultaneously activates the appropriate logogen unit in the speech output logogen system, releasing the phonological form (p. 117)" which is recycled as inner speech. "In addition to being recycled as inner speech, the phonemic code combines with the semantic code to release the graphemic code from the graphemic output logogen system (p. 118)."

But let us go back and look at Michel's case again. Remember that it was necessary to postulate a disruption between the cognitive system and the phonological output logogen system in order to explain the presented *oral* performances in our patient, whose only spontaneous output is a recurrent utterance. This assumption is indeed compatible with the patient's performances discussed so far. Why, then, should it not hold for writing? This would mean that for writing Michel can activate the graphemic output directly from the cognitive system, but he cannot simultaneously activate a phonological code originating from semantics: neither for the purpose of recycling as inner speech (as proposed by Ellis, 1982) nor for the purpose of an input to the phoneme-grapheme conversion system (as postulated by Nolan & Caramazza, 1983). Michel's writing words from dictation (with inhibited oral repetition) should therefore most truly reflect a patient's writing solely relying on orthographic codes originating from semantics; in the frame of dual pathway approaches there would indeed be no other possibility left to Michel for obtaining a phonological code. However, our patient's writing under this condition (that is, *without* oral repetition) does not show the pattern predicted by Nolan and Caramazza (1983): "If normal subjects are prevented from using phonological rehearsal during writing their errors should resemble those produced by this patient (p. 324)"—that is V.S., whose writing is deep dysgraphic with the presence of semantic paragraphias and an important number of orthographic errors. However, Michel did not produce any semantic error, nor did the number of orthographic errors increase. In fact, there were no true orthographic errors. Instead, omissions were the characteristic feature of Michel's writing from dictation when he was prevented from oral repetition at the same time. Indeed, 27/42 (64.3%) of his writing errors were omissions. On only 5/42 (11.9%) occasions the patient produced another word of the language. These errors had, however, no semantic relation to the target; almost all the other errors ought to be classified as miscellaneous.

We are thus confronted with the fact that a patient who, according to the cited dual pathway approaches, *cannot* rely on an intervening phonological code for writing (because of the postulated disruption between the cognitive system and the phonological output logogen system) but nevertheless did not produce semantic errors, although the patient's comprehension of words, when formally tested, was far from perfect and remained *unchanged* throughout the testing period. Semantic errors are, however, the defining characteristic of deep dysgraphia which is supposed to result from a "central disruption of the lexicon" (Nolan & Caramazza, 1983).

However, Michel's writing was deep dysgraphic only in the initial stage of his illness. In a later stage it rather resembled phonological agraphia. This qualitative (but *not* quantitative) change in the patient's error pattern between March and October 1983 was observed only in writing from dictation but not in the oral production tasks (reading and repetition).

With respect to dual pathway models and more specifically in the framework of the semantic attainment theory (Shallice & Coughlan, 1980) Michel's lexical writing to dictation ought to be interpreted in the following way.

Writing words from dictation relies on the verbal comprehension of the stimuli. Michel has a problem with the comprehension of all sorts of words (concrete, abstract, and function words). Consequently his writing from dictation shows the effects of word-class and of concreteness as well as the presence of semantic errors in an initial stage of the illness. Minimal phonological coding, derived from the oral repetition of the stimuli, blocks the overt expression of semantic errors (due to problems of precise semantic knowledge) in the second stage of the patient's writing disturbance.

The patient's quantitative gain from simultaneous oral repetition for writing words to dictation (compared with prevented repetition of the target words) is due to multiple auditory input to *semantics*: by the patient's own repetition the cognitive system receives the input a second time. Reinforcement through repetition may indeed constitute a sort of checking procedure for the semantic system that is somewhat, but not sufficiently, activated by previous input.

Writing words to dictation, in the initial stage, yields many more semantic paragraphias than written naming of objects and pictures because of the patient's specific problem with *auditory* as compared to visual input.

The interpretation of the patient's writing from dictation by means of impaired semantics is, however, at variance with the following data: the patient correctly wrote from dictation an almost equal number of words with and without simultaneous semantic comprehension (21 vs 22), that is, approximately half of the words of the list presented in October 1983 (see Table 14.8) were correctly written, although the patient claimed that he did not know the precise meaning of the target word.

Because of the patient's specific problems in accessing *auditory* semantic information we administered the previously described synonym comprehension test another time with auditory input only (March 1984). This time the patient was allowed to ask for the experimentor's *repetition* of a given triad *as often as he wanted.* The 30 different triads were administered three times each, resulting in a total of 90 trials. The patient spontaneously asked to have 32 triads repeated (16 concrete and 16 abstract items). On the 32 triads that were repeated (at least once) on the patient's own request Michel committed nevertheless eight errors. This constitutes 25% errors on repeated word triads as compared to 20.7% errors (12/58) on triads where he responded immediately without demanding repetition. Although this pattern of performance does not necessarily preclude the possibility that multiple auditory input did facilitate Michel's semantic comprehension of the target words, it should however be underlined that even with *multiple* auditory input the patient's semantic understanding of words remained almost as impaired (25% errors—March 1984) as with just one auditory presentation of the triads (30% errors—October 1983). The patient's request for repetition may indeed reflect a problem with semantic comprehension. Uncertainty with regard to semantic knowledge does not however seem to be substantially reduced by multiple auditory input to the cognitive system.

It has been shown that the patient has specific problems of attaining semantic access given auditory input. His general problems of semantic knowledge are, however, severe and stayed unchanged through the end of the testing period (see Table 14.7). With respect to the standard position that naming is necessarily mediated by semantics (see Morton, 1984) it is difficult to conceive how Michel was able to perform written naming so successfully—18/20 and 17/20 correct on different occasions with no semantic error—in spite of rather impaired semantic knowledge of even concrete words.[4]

Note also that the standard interpretation of deep dysgraphia in terms of writing through *impaired* semantics (see Nolan & Caramazza, 1982; Shallice, 1981) seems to be in conflict with some observations from the literature. Bub and Kertesz's (1982a) study of J.C., a patient with deep agraphia, suggests indeed that at least some of the problems in writing may arise at the level of the graphemic output only and are not due to a central disturbance. Bub and Kertesz (1982a) explicitly state: "Evidence tends to support the first alternative since (J.C.'s) reading comprehension was relatively good compared to the writing of even the most elementary abstract nouns. In addition, comments supplied by J.C. during writing suggest that she understood the word but could not generate a graphemic representation for the stimulus. For example, when asked to write "mind," J.C. commented "Mind over matter, but I can't write it (p. 60)." Thus "superior performance of concrete nouns compared to abstract nouns, function words, and verbs is due to the fact that translation of semantic information into graphemes is impaired for certain items *or* that the semantic representations themselves are compromised (Bub and Kertesz, 1982a, p. 160)."

Lexical Non-Semantic Writing.   Successful writing from dictation of words which are *not* understood is of course the main argument for Michel's progressive use of lexical (but non-semantic) connections.

With regard to the relationship between writing from dictation and semantic comprehension, it should also be mentioned that Michel ingeniously pointed out himself that he can access the meaning of a spoken word—after having written it without auditory comprehension—by use of a *visual* code. Once he had omitted to indicate his (required) judgement on

---

[4]Note that a similar dissociation, but in the reverse direction, may be supposed for B.L., a case with deep dyslexia. Nolan and Caramazza (1982) explicitly state that B.L.'s naming performance was very poor and that 42% and 52% of his errors (on two different lists) were semantically related to the target word. B.L.'s writing to dictation was "strikingly similar to oral reading" with the effect of word-class and concreteness. "*Many errors were visually similar* to the stimulus word and *some were semantically related*" (Nolan & Caramazza, 1982, p. 250—my emphasis. If "deep dyslexia is not simply a reading deficit but a more general language deficit" (Nolan & Caramazza, 1982, p. 257) that should result in semantic errors not only in reading but in repetition, writing, and naming as well, then it is astonishing that approximately half of the failures in naming result in semantic errors as compared to only "some" semantic errors in writing from dictation. In the light of the assumption that "graphemic and phonemic representations for words will be available simultaneously" from the central lexicon (Nolan & Caramazza, 1983, p. 322)—which in B.L.'s case suffers from a supramodal deficit—it is difficult to conceive of a unitary account for the cited dissociation between confrontation naming and writing words from dictation. We will come back to this point later.

auditory semantic comprehension and immediately started to write the target word (correctly). When I asked him thereafter for his comprehension of the stimulus word, the patient became puzzled. From his wordless but agitated way of explaining the situation, it appeared that comprehension had been achieved visually, and that it was based on the graphic output. For the following words Michel spontaneously indicated the "place" of his comprehension by writing "oreille" (ear) or "vue" (vision) while writing words from dictation. We were thus able to collect the following statements of the patient: out of 26 words judged in this way, Michel claimed to have understood only eight by "ear" as compared to fourteen by "vision" subsequent to writing. (4/26 words were understood neither by ear nor by vision.) Similar, although more exclusive, use of a *visual* code to access the meaning of a spoken word has been observed with Gail, a patient reported by Morton (1980) who suggests that "she cannot get from the auditory input logogen to the cognitive system directly but has to go via a graphemic code (p. 130)."

In contrast to Gail, however, our patient could not use the conversion from an acoustic code to a graphemic one (by rules via the response buffer). Michel's writing from dictation relied on the use of the auditory input logogen system. This system produces a code relevant to the word as a whole which can "flow" via the phonological output logogen system *or* via the cognitive system and then to the graphemic output system. "By conventions to date, passing through the cognitive system would involve accessing some at least of the semantics (Morton, 1980a, p. 131)." Remember, however, that Michel wrote a considerable number of words without any comprehension and repeated even more so.

Michel's correct writing to dictation of many words which were not simultaneously understood is indeed compatible with a lexical but non semantic strategy. From the perspective of direct lexical writing (via the phonological output logogen to the graphemic output logogen) the qualitative change in the patient's writing pattern (i.e., the absence of semantic errors in the later stage of his illness) would not result from "response blocking" of semantic errors (originating from the cognitive system) by means of phonological checking procedures (from overt oral repetition). Rather, the absence of semantic errors would reflect the patient's acquired strategy of direct lexical writing which bypasses semantics. I think indeed that it is because of the progressive use of a phonological code—obtained from *lexical repetition* and not from semantics—that Michel's initially deep dysgraphic writing shifted to lexical phonological writing.

Remember that the patient spontaneously discovered this procedure. Remember also that when he was not allowed to repeat the target words his writing from diction deteriorated as compared to his significantly better performance when obliged to first produce the corresponding phonological form by oral repetition of the stimulus (Table 14.9). The patient produced indeed only 8.3% omissions (on total errors) with oral repetition as compared to 64.3% without previous repetition (when writing 80 content words from dictation); he produced 75% whole word errors, mostly structurally similar, at first attempts of writing with repetition, as compared to 11.9% whole word errors without oral repetition. (Miscellaneous and gap errors amount to 16.6% and 23.8% respectively. There was no unambiguous semantic paragraphia in either condition—see Appendix.)

It is evident, however, that in spite of the increasing use of a "phonological writing" process (which no longer seems to depend on verbal semantic comprehension) Michel's writing from dictation *cannot*—even in the later stage of his illness—*solely* be accounted for by direct lexical writing: the input/output logogen system has only a notion of "wordness" and the phonological code is used as a unit to access the letter code for all sorts of words. However, besides the statistically significant effect of frequency (see Table 14.3) which might be a reflection of the direct route, "lexical" variables such as part-of-speech and concreteness continue to remain important for the patient's writing of words from dictation. Effects of part-of-speech and concreteness do not have a ready explanation at the level of output logogens. Indeed, it has been standard to date that the influence of such variables originates as a consequence of effects in the cognitive system. The apparent contradiction between the patient's progressive use of lexical phonological writing and the effect of "lexical" variables on his writing words to dictation will be discussed in the next section.

Direct Writing by Means of Visual Images.   With regard to oral *reading* it has been noted that the effects of part-of-speech and concreteness cannot be considered as unitary. Sartori, Barry and Job's (1984) review of the published cases of phonological dyslexia showed that an effect of part-of-speech is not necessarily associated with an effect of concreteness. For some patients the dimension of abstractness (of content words) was irrelevant in spite of a problem with reading functors (Patterson, 1982, see Sartori et al., 1984, for review). Patterson (1981) indeed argued that such dissociations support "the notion of separated semantic and syntactic processes in reading single lexical items (p. 165)" and it is clear that the status of grammatical lexical items is far from being settled (see also Patterson, this volume). Moreover, even considering semantic processes alone it may well be premature to comment on *general* issues with regard to semantic treatment of "words." Indeed discussions are just beginning concerning the possible existence of *several* semantic systems (see Beauvois, 1982; Shallice, this volume) that may differentially be activated with regard to functional and/or sensory attributes of "words" and thus may have different patterns of associative links (Warrington & Shallice, 1984).

It seems evident, however, that the specificity of selective deficits cannot be accounted for simply by differential degrees of difficulty in information processing of words *per se*. Some patients indeed read abstract words more easily than concrete ones (Warrington, 1975; Warrington & Shallice, 1984). Also many head-injured patients show a significant deficit in their recall of concrete as compared to abstract words (Richardson, 1979, 1984). According to Richardson (1984), among other authors, "semantic information can be represented either in abstract propositional terms or in the form of mental imagery (p. 414)". Individual case studies may thus help to define *which of several systems* is addressed to in a specific task and/or by a specific patient.

Following this line of reasoning it may be tentatively proposed that Michel (when writing from dictation with oral repetition prevented) may have rather relied on a process like imagery. The 80 presented content words were rated for imageability by six independent judges on a four point scale: 0 = definitely no image; 1 = hardly imageable; 2 = imageable (medium); 3 = image is there immediately. Comparison of stimuli that were rated with a mean of 2 or more yielded 63.3% correct writings (28/44), whereas stimuli with an average rating of less than 2 yielded only 27.7% correct writings (10/36). (None of the stimuli rated zero elicited correct writing). Functors were not rated for imageability, but it is known that they obtain low imageability ratings (see, for example, Funnell, 1983). Michel's writing from dictation, with suppressed articulation, may thus have solely relied on the image-evoking quality of the dictated stimuli for both content and function words. Some of the case studies reported in the literature seem to lend support to such a view. Roeltgen et al. (1983) found that their (four) patients with a disturbance of non-lexical phonological writing reproduced nouns of high imagery better than nouns of low imagery. (The two groups of words were matched for length and frequency.)

If Michel relied on such a strategy of obtaining an orthographic code in writing from dictation it should closely resemble that used by the patient in written naming of objects and/or images. The apparent discrepancy, in the initial stage of the patient's illness only, between a high incidence of semantic paragraphias while writing concrete words from *dictation* and the virtual absence of frank semantic errors in *written naming* of objects may also receive an explanation in terms of this hypothesis. In the initial (deep dysgraphic) stage the patient's writing from dictation may well have depended on his comprehension of the target words; but comprehension was perturbated for all kinds of words given auditory input and indeed continued to be so. This comprehension problem may well have stimulated the switch, at a later stage of his illness, from "writing through comprehension" to "writing by naming visual representations." Note that the patient's oral naming was character-ised by steady (although unsuccessful) attempts of sounding out the target word and never resulted in a clear semantic error. The patient's oral as well as written naming may thus have relied—in *all* stages of his illness (see also footnote[2])—on connections which bypass verbal semantics.

That the function of naming does not necessarily rely on concomitant semantic comprehension of the stimuli has been suggested elsewhere through experimental investigation (see Heilman, Tucker, & Valenstein, 1976; Kremin, 1984), and also is suggested by some rare observations from the literature. On the one hand, Nolan and Caramazza (1983) explicitly stated that "One of these semantic errors in written naming was accompanied by the pronunciation of the correct word (p. 314)." On the other hand, Roeltgen, Sevush and Heilman (1983) observed (with their patient n°1): "When writing names to confrontation he often says 'no' or 'I don't know' while writing the correct response (p. 756)"; also, "he occasionally wrote one word and said another (p. 756)." Such dissociations between oral and written naming cannot easily be accounted for by current models of naming (Morton, 1984; Warren & Morton, 1982) which assume that naming relies solely on semantic access (which should be the same for both output modalities oral and written).

The interpretation that is tentatively proposed with respect to the change in the patient's error patterns is that it is due to a change in the *strategy* he uses for writing words from dictation. Whereas his rather good naming performance may always have relied on connections which bypass the semantic system, dictation performance may well have relied on (impaired) verbal comprehension, but only in the initial stage. At a later stage the patient supposedly resorted to using the same non-semantic lexical pathway for writing words to dictation as for naming. This may also account for the benefit he obtained at the later stage from previous oral repetition of the target word for writing from dictation. Oral repetition may operate as a sort of self-prompt, not so much for semantic comprehension (as pointed out before) but, rather, in order to match an internally generated image and/or its corresponding orthographic code with a spoken word (rehearsed for the ease of the working memory). A connection between phonological and "visual object" codes may indeed reconcile the apparent contradiction at a later stage of Michel's illness between the effect of "lexical" variables such as part-of-speech and concreteness on the one hand and, on the other hand, the patient's progressive use of "phonological writing" which no longer seems to be mediated by verbal semantic comprehension. Rather, the phonological code (from oral repetition) serves for the purpose of "deblocking" the visual/ orthographic code.

Note that a process like imagery does not require that a memory image be consciously experienced. But note also that patients may occasionally report such images. Thus Gail, who "cannot get from the auditory input logogen to the cognitive system directly" (Morton, 1980 a, p. 130), was asked to define the spoken word *plough*. "She had no idea of its meaning but then wrote it down correctly—not as "plow," which would have been the obvious result of a simple phoneme-grapheme conversion. She still seemed to have no idea of what it meant and then said "I've forgotten what it is—(pause) see it in a field—using some sort of machine—something to do with soil ..." (Morton, 1980a, p. 131).

Far more complexities may indeed be lying beneath the performance of patients who write lexically than is touched upon by current accounts of this form of dysgraphia. The proposed direct connection between "name" (spoken)→*image*→*name* (written) certainly is only one of several possible ways to obtain a written output when writing lexically from dictation.

ACKNOWLEDGEMENTS

I am thankful and indebted to Tim Shallice for helpful criticism at various stages of this work. I would also like to thank Jean-Marc Bernard, who conducted the statistical analyses.

APPENDIX

Target words	Patient's writing from dictation		Target words	Patient's writing from dictation	
	With oral repetition	*Without repetition*		*With oral repetition*	*Without repetition*
(a) *content words*					
VIE	+	+	SEAU	+	OMISSION
FOIS	*fort*	a	PAUL	*peau?*	om
SOIR	+	spar	TEMPS	*ta ton tant dans*	+
FORCE	F | V |	OMISSION	OEIL	+	+
			MOT	*nous* mat	0
EAU	+	0	MOIS	+(*mais*) *mois*	OMISSION
DIEU	+	+	CORPS	+[*cor; corps*]	OMISSION
VILLE	+	+	NOM	(1.) *on*	OMISSION
FEUILLE	*fleur*	OMISSION	PEINE	+	è
FIN	F	+ [*faim*]	SUITE	*scène?*	i
RUE	+	+	MERE	+	+ [*mer*]
PIED	+	+	LOI	+	+
FORT	*haut*	OMISSION	FRANC	+	+
MER	+	+ [*mère*]	TARD	(*derri*)	*sa ta*
RIRE	+	+	ROI	+	+
GRACE	+	+	CHEF	+	+
CLEF	+	+	MASSE	OMISSION	*masque*
SOL	+	+	SCIE	+	OMISSION
CAS	*car*	ca	FER	+	+

APPENDIX—contd

Target words	Patient's writing from dictation With oral repetition	Without repetition	Target words	Patient's writing from dictation With oral repetition	Without repetition
VUE	+	(d)...on	(b) *function words*		
MAL	*malade*	OMISSION	PEU	+	p...
CAEN	+*[Caen, quand]*	OMISSION	TEL	*de*	OMISSION
CHOSE	+	OMISSION	DONT	...on (*ton*)	c u
GUERRE	+	+	NI	é	*nid*
LIEN	*lieu*	OMISSION	QUELQUE	*delà*	OMISSION
NUIT	+	+	PUIS	*peu*	p...
FORME	OMISSION	*force*	MEME	m e l	B | P ⟩ ?
COEUR	+	+			
PERE	+(*peine*) *père*	+	EUX	eu	*oeuf*
CAUSE	(*chose*) (o)	OMISSION	CELUI	*sel*	OMISSION
SORTE	+	OMISSION	LEUR	*le*	OMISSION
AME	+	+	ENTRE	+	OMISSION
GOUT	*eau*	OMISSION	LORSQUE	OMISSION	v/c/(c)v
FRANCE	+	+	CONTRE	+*[contre=561234]*	*donc*
AGE	+	+			
SCENE	+*[Seine]*	+*[Seine]*	DEVANT	+(..f..v) devant	..f..
BOL	+	+	MALGRE	m e re	*mais*
MOU	+	+	CHEZ	+	+
FARD	+*[phare]*	(ar)(dess)farc+	POURTANT	....t	... ourant
LOURD	+	OMISSION	JUSQUE	OMISSION	OMISSION
BOUT	(*peau*) b...	o in	PLUSIEURS	OMISSION	OMISSION
MARC	+*[marre]*	OMISSION	AINSI	cesi *ceci* cesi?	...e..
FEMME	+	(m)+	DEPUIS	pi	NT
MAIN	(*mère*) (*mai*)+	OMISSION	AUTRE	o auvant	
COUP	+	*couteau*		*autant*	NT
PART	*pas*	OMISSION	ASSEZ	ainsé *ainsi*	NT
TERRE	+	+	LES	+	NT
DOUTE	*donc*	OMISSION	TOI	+*[toi; toit]*	NT
PORTE	+	OMISSION	SI	+	NT
VOIX	+	OMISSION	AUCUN	(aussez) *au co*	NT
DROIT	*doigt*	OMISSION	MOINS	*mon*	NT
FOND	*jonc*	OMISSION	AVANT	...v	NT
JEU	(jon) (jo)	OMISSION	DONC	OMISSION	NT
PAS	+	OMISSION	PRES	+	NT
DAME	+*[dame=1324]*	OMISSION	CHAQUE	*j'ai*	NT
GESTE	+	*gêne*	LAQUELLE	OMISSION	NT
VERRE	+	+	PARFOIS	(de pui)	NT
CHOU	+	+	ICI	(issi) ci	NT
TAS	+	+	AILLEURS	OMISSION	NT
OS	+	+	CELLE	*sel*	NT
FEU	+	+	DESSUS	OMISSION	NT
PORC	+	+*[porc=2134]*	TON	+	NT

APPENDIX—contd

	Patient's writing from dictation			Patient's writing from dictation	
Target words	*With oral* repetition	*Without* repetition	Target words	*With oral* repetition	*Without* repetition
EST	*à*	NT	CHACUN	*chaque*	NT
AUSSI	+	NT	TROP	o (*tout*) r...	NT
BEAUCOUP	pro	NT	PARMI	pe.. *n*	NT
TE	+	NT	PUISQUE	OMISSION	NT
PARCE QUE	(pr c pes)	NT			
QUAND	+[Caen; quand]	NT	(c) *nonsense syllables*		
QUOI	(...oi)	NT	RON	o rum	OMISSION
VOTRE	OMISSION	NT	CUME	com	ceum
Y	*qui*	NT	NAN	e	OMISSION
ALORS	(ar ors o)	NT	VASSE	v(s)ase	OMISSION
PRESQUE	*près*	NT	PALGRE	po	OMISSION
APRES	+	NT	CHOCON	suri ch	OMISSION
ETRE	*était été?*	NT		j c	
POURQUOI	p...	NT	REU	re	OMISSION
SOUS	*où*	NT	CHAVEL	chajé	OMISSION
LEQUEL	*lesquels*	NT	SILAN	*ceylan**	OMISSION
QUEL	...e../	NT	BIEU	*pion**	OMISSION

Note: +   Correct writing
         *   Writing errors resulting in real words are in italics
         ( ) Round brackets indicate that the patient knew these realisations were
              not correct
         [ ] Square brackets indicate legal transcriptions of the auditorily presented
              target word
         NT   Item was not tested

REFERENCES

Alajouanine, T. (1956) Verbal realisation in aphasia. *Brain, 79*, 1–28.

Allport, D. A., & Funnell, E. (1981) Components of the mental lexicon. *Philosophical Transactions of the Royal Society of London, B295*, 397–410.

Assal, G., Buttet, J., & Jolivet, R. (1981) Dissociations in aphasia: A case report. *Brain and Language, 13*, 223–240.

Balota, D. A., & Chumbley, J. I. (1984) Are lexical decisions a good measure of lexical access? The role of word frequency in the neglected decision stage. *Journal of Experimental Psychology: Human Perception and Performance, 10*, 340–357.

Beauvois, M. F. (1982) Optic aphasia: A process of interaction between vision and language. *Philosophical Transactions of the Royal Society of London, B298*, 35–47.

Beauvois, M. F., & Derouesné, J. (1981) Lexical or orthographic agraphia. *Brain, 104*, 21–49.

Beauvois, M. F., Derouesné, J., & Bastard, V. (1980) *Auditory parallel to phonological alexia.* Paper presented at the Third European Conference of the International Neuropsychological Society, Chianciano, Italy, June.

Boller, F., & Hécaen, H. (1979) L'évaluation des fonctions neuropsychologiques. Examen standard de l'Unité de Recherches Neuropsychologiques et Neurolinguistiques (U- 111) de l'INSERM. *Revue de Psychologie Appliquée, 29*, 247–266.

Broca, P. (1861) Remarques sur le siège de la faculté du langage articulé suivies d'une observation d'aphémie (perte de la parole). *Bulletin de la Société d'Anthropologie, 2ème série, t. VI*, 330–357. (Cited from H. Hécaen & J. Dubois (1969) (Eds.), *La naissance de la neuropsychologie de langage 1825–1865*. Paris: Flammarion.

Broca, P. (1865) Sur le siège de la faculté du langage articulé. *Bulletin de la Société d'Anthropologie, t. VI*, 337–393. (Cited from H. Hécaen & J. Dubois (1969) (Eds.), *La naissance de la neuropsychologie du langage, 1825–1865*. Paris: Flammarion.

Bub, D., & Kertesz, A. (1982a) Deep agraphia. *Brain and Language, 17*, 146–165.

Bub, D., & Kertesz, A. (1982b) Evidence for lexicographic processing in a patient with preserved written over oral single word naming. *Brain, 105*, 697–717.

Coltheart, M., Patterson, K. E., & Marshall, J. C. (1980) *Deep dyslexia*. London: Routledge & Kegan Paul.

Derouesné, J., Beauvois, M. F., & Ranty, C. (1977) Deux composantes dans l'articulation du langage oral: preuve expérimentale de leur indépendance. *Neuropsychologia, 15*, 143–153.

Ellis, A. W. (1982) Spelling and writing (and reading and speaking). In A. W. Ellis (Ed.), *Normality and pathology in cognitive functions*. London: Academic Press.

Ellis, A. W., Miller, D., & Sin, G. (1983) Wernicke's aphasia and normal language processing: A case study in cognitive neuropsychology. *Cognition, 15*, 111–144.

Funnell, E. (1983) Phonological processes in reading: New evidence from acquired dyslexia. *British Journal of Psychology, 74*, 159–180.

Goldblum, M. C. (1979) Auditory analogue of deep dyslexia. In H. Scheich & C. Schreiner (Eds.), *Experimental brain research supplementum II: Hearing mechanisms and speech*. Berlin: Springer Verlag.

Hatfield, M. F. (1982a) Diverses formes de désintégration du langage écrit et implications pour la rééducation. In X. Seron & C. Laterre (Eds.), *Rééduquer le cerveau. Logopédie, psychologie, neurologie*. Bruxelles: Mardaga.

Hatfield, F. M. (1982b) *Visual factors in acquired dysgraphia*. Paper presented at the Meeting of the International Neuropsychological Society, Deauville, France, June 15–18.

Hatfield, F. M., & Patterson, K. E. (1983) Phonological spelling. *Quarterly Journal of Experimental Psychology, 35A*, 451–468.

Hécaen, H., & Kremin, H. (1976) Neurolinguistic research on reading disorders resulting from left hemisphere lesions: Aphasic and "pure" alexias. In H. Whitaker & H. A. Whitaker (Eds.), *Studies in neurolinguistics (vol.2)*. New York: Academic Press.

Heilman, K. M., Tucker, D. M., & Valenstein, E. (1976) A case of mixed transcortical aphasia with intact naming. *Brain, 99*, 415–426.

Hier, D. B., & Mohr, J. P. (1977) Incongruous oral and written naming. Evidence for a subdivision of the syndrome of Wernicke's aphasia. *Brain and Language, 4*, 115–126.

Jackson, J. H. (1879–1880) On affections of speech from disease of the brain. *Brain, 2*, 203–222.

Juilland, A., Brodin, D. & Davidivitch, C. (1970) *Frequency dictionary of French words*. The Hague: Mouton.

Kremin, H. (1984) *Spared naming without comprehension*. Paper presented at the 7th European Conference of the International Neuropsychological Society. Aachen, West Germany, June 13–15.

Kremin, H. (1985) Routes and strategies. Data on acquired surface dyslexia and surface dysgraphia. In K. E. Patterson, J. C. Marshall, & M. Coltheart, (Eds.), *Surface dyslexia: neuropsychological and cognitive studies of phonological reading*. London: Lawrence Erlbaum Associates.

L'Hermitte, F., & Derouesné, J. (1974) Paraphasies et jargonaphasie dans le langage oral avec conversation du langage écrit. Génèse des néalogismes. *Revue Neurologique, 130*, 21–38.

Michel, F. (1979) Préservation du langage écrit malgré un déficit majeur du langage oral. *Lyon-Médical, 241,* 141–149.

Michel, F., & Andreewsky, E. (1983) Deep dysphasia: an analog of deep dyslexia in the auditory modality. *Brain and Language, 18,* 212–223.

Morton, J. (1980a) The logogen model and orthographic structure. In U. Frith (Ed.), *Cognitive processes in spelling.* London: Academic Press.

Morton, J. (1980b) Two auditory parallels to deep dyslexia. In M. Coltheart, K. E. Patterson, & J. C. Marshall (Eds.), *Deep dyslexia.* London: Routledge & Kegan Paul.

Morton, J. (1984) Naming. In S. Newman & R. Epstein (Eds.), *Dysphasia.* Edinburgh: Churchill Livingston.

Morton, J., & Patterson, K. E. (1980) A new attempt at an interpretation or an attempt at a new interpretation. In M. Coltheart, K. E. Patterson, & J. C. Marshall (Eds.), *Deep dyslexia.* London: Routledge & Kegan Paul.

Newcombe, F., & Marshall, J. C. (1980) Transcoding and lexical stabilisation in deep dyslexia. In M. Coltheart, K. E. Patterson, & J. C. Marshall (Eds.), *Deep dyslexia.* London: Routledge & Kegan Paul.

Newcombe, F., & Marshall, J. C. (1985) Sound-by-sound reading and writing. In K. E. Patterson, J. C. Marshall, & M. Coltheart, (Eds.), *Surface dyslexia: Neuropsychological and cognitive studies of phonological reading.* London: Lawrence Erlbaum Associates.

Nolan, K. A., & Caramazza, A. (1982) Modality—independent impairments in word processing in a deep dyslexic patient. *Brain and Language, 16,* 232–264.

Nolan, K. A., & Caramazza, A. (1983) An analysis of writing in a case of deep dyslexia. *Brain and Language, 20,* 305–328.

Patterson, K. E. (1981) Neuropsychological approaches to the study of reading. *British Journal of Psychology, 72,* 151–174.

Patterson, K. E. (1982) The relation between reading and phonological coding: Further neuropsychological observations. In A. W. Ellis (Ed.), *Normality and pathology in cognitive functioning.* London: Academic Press.

Poeck, K., De Bleser, R., & Keyserlinck, D. Graf von (1984) Neurolinguistic status and localisation of lesion in aphasic patients with exclusively consonant-vowel recurring utterances. *Brain, 107,* 199–217.

Richardson, J. T. E. (1979) Mental imagery, human memory and the effect of closed head injury. *British Journal of the Society of Clinical Pathology, 18,* 319–327.

Richardson, J. T. E. (1984) The effects of closed head injury upon intrusions and confusions in free recall. *Cortex, 20,* 413–420.

Roeltgen, D. P., & Heilman, K. M. (1984) Lexical agraphia. Further support for the two-system hypothesis of linguistic agraphia. *Brain, 107,* 811–827.

Roeltgen, D. P., Sevush, S., & Heilman, K. M. (1983) Phonological agraphia: Writing by the lexical-semantic route. *Neurology, 33,* 755–765.

Sartori, G., Barry, C., & Job, R. (1984) Phonological dyslexia: A review. In R. N. Malatesha & H. A. Whitaker (Eds.), *Dyslexia: a global issue.* The Hague: Martinus Nijhoff Publishers.

Schwartz, M. F., Saffran, E. M., & Marin, O. S. M. (1980) Fractioning the reading process in dementia: Evidence for word-specific print-to-sound associations. In M. Coltheart, K. E. Patterson, & J. C. Marshall (Eds.), *Deep dyslexia.* London. Routledge & Kegan Paul.

Shallice, T. (1981) Phonological agraphia and the lexical route in writing. *Brain, 104,* 413–429.

Shallice, T., & Coughlan, A. K. (1980) Modality specific word comprehension deficits in deep dyslexia. *Journal of Neurology, Neurosurgery and Psychiatry, 43,* 866–872.

Warren, C., & Morton, J. (1982) The effects of priming on picture recognition. *British Journal of Psychology, 73,* 117–129.

Warrington, E. K. (1975) The selective impairment of semantic memory. *Quarterly Journal of Experimental Psychology, 27,* 635–658.

Warrington, E. K., & Shallice, T. (1984) Category specific semantic impairments. *Brain, 107,* 829–854.

Yamadori, A., & Ikumura, G. (1975) Central (or conduction) aphasia in a Japanese patient. *Cortex, 11,* 73–82.

15 Phonemic Deafness in Infancy and Acquisition of Written Language

Gianfranco Denes, Sandra Balliello, and Andrea Pellegrini
*Clinica Neurologica, Università di Padova, Via Giustiniani 5,
35128 Padova, Italy*

Virginia Volterra
*Istituto di Psicologia del C.N.R., Via dei Monti Tibertini 509,
00100 Roma, Italy*

INTRODUCTION

In 1957 Landau and Kleffner described an acquired language disorder in children consisting of severe aphasia and epileptic seizures. Behavioural disturbances are sometimes reported. In all cases severe paroxysmal EEG abnormalities, usually diffuse, are present.

From the analysis of the some 80 cases reported (for a review see Toso et al., 1981; Van de Sandt-Koenderman et al., 1984) it appears that both sexes are equally affected; the onset of aphasic disorder varies from 18 months to 13 years; and in contrast to acquired aphasia in children due to left hemispheric damage (Alajouanine & Lhermitte, 1965) disturbances of comprehension up to a total disappearance of verbal comprehension are most common, while isolated deficits of language production are rare. Other symbolic functions and intelligence are in general normal. The behavioural changes, not always present, range from simple distractability to marked instability with considerable lack of concentration. Prognosis of aphasia is always poor, one third of the cases being unchanged, even after a number of years. The only laboratory datum being constantly altered is EEG showing bilaterally syncroneous high-amplitude spike wave discharges.

CT scan is reported normal. From the few histological examinations

337

performed, no specific abnormalities were found and the aetiology is therefore obscure.

The object of this study is an 11-year-old boy, affected by such a syndrome, who, despite an almost complete word deafness and lack of oral production, showed a striking ability in processing written language.

A number of studies was therefore performed in order to investigate: (1) the nature of auditory comprehension deficit; (2) how syntactic and semantic abilities might develop in absence of auditory comprehension; (3) how STM for verbal material might develop in absence of phonological coding.

CASE REPORT

S.C. is an 11-year-old, right-handed, boy referred to our clinic for evaluation of speech and language disturbances. This boy was born in July 1972 after an unremarkable pregnancy and birth history. He walked between the ages of eight and 10 months, used single words before one year, and put words together at the age of two. At age three (at that time his language development was, according to his parents, normal) he became gradually less responsive to oral speech and his expressive language began to deteriorate. At the same time behavioural changes consisting mainly of aggressive and oppositional traits were noted. Medical evaluation included skull X-ray and brain scan that were considered normal. EEG showed the presence of an epileptic focus in the right posterior temporal region. Despite anti-epileptic treatment, six months later he developed an epileptic seizure. At that time he had essentially no oral language and could understand only few words.

At the age of four, following the onset of myoclonic jerks and absences, he was admitted to the neurological department of another hospital. EEG showed presence of bilateral paroxysmal discharges, maximal in the left hemispheric region.

S.C. was continent, able to feed and dress himself, and able to handle and play with toys. He was able to recognise and use common objects, and showed no difficulty in orienting in familiar surroundings. Recognition of faces was normal.

His behaviour was characterised mainly by a certain degree of indifference to the external milieu, interrupted from time to time by mimic reactions or smiles when his gaze crossed that of familiar people. He showed no interest toward words uttered to him. Sometimes he had startle reactions to sudden noises. His oral production consisted only of unarticulated sounds. In the following years, despite speech therapy, he showed no substantial changes in auditory comprehension and oral production, apart from some lip-reading ability. In contrast, according to his parents, the patient showed an increase in his non-verbal abilities proportional with his age.

In her effort to communicate with him, his mother taught him to match the picture of a common object with the corresponding written word. In the following months and years S.C. developed a striking ability to handle written language, in such a way that he was able to successfully attend primary school.

At the time of admission to our department, the patient was 10 years old. Neurological examination was normal, apart from his language disturbances. Laboratory exams were within normal limits, including CT scan, EEG and pure tone audiometry.

Neuropsychological examination, apart from language disturbances (discussed later) and some elements of oral apraxia, was normal. He was oriented in time and place, and recognition and use of objects was normal. His drawing ability was remarkably good for his age. No prosopagnosia was noted. His ability in written calculation was well within limits for his age. He scored 34 out of 36 on the R.C.P.M. 47.

On the Corsi tapping test (quoted by Milner, 1971) his span was four.

During the many testing sessions his collaboration and interest were excellent, except in the tasks where auditory comprehension was specifically tested: in these tasks the patient often showed signs of irritability and refused to collaborate.

Language Examination

The most striking aspect of S.C.'s language performance as clinically assessed was a modality dependent dissociation in language production and comprehension. He appeared to be almost totally incapable of producing and understanding oral speech, but performed almost normally with written language.

Oral Production. This was extremely poor, being limited to only a few frequent bisyllabic words that he uttered in a dyslalic way, without intonation. Singing was absent. Repetition of orally presented items was very poor.

Auditory Comprehension Tasks

Auditory Agnosia Test. Twelve familiar environmental non speech (ringing of a telephone) sounds were presented and the patient had to match the sound with the corresponding picture. He scored 10/12 correct.

Auditory Evoked Potentials. Absolute and interpeaks latencies of brain stem auditory evoked potentials following stimulation of either right or left ear were within normal limits. Similarly, using trains of non-verbal synthe-

CNL-L

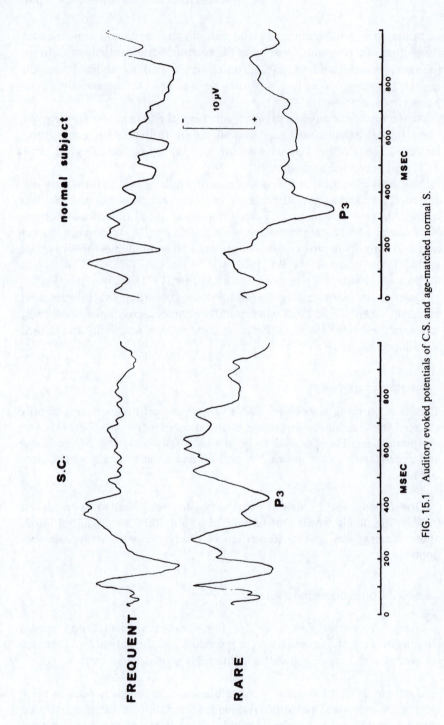

FIG. 15.1   Auditory evoked potentials of C.S. and age-matched normal S.

tised auditory stimuli, the primary response at cortical level was normal. When, however, an analysis of the stimuli on the basis of their frequency was required, as for event related potentials, the response (P3) was abnormally long in latency and of reduced amplitude. These data are consistent with the presence of a normal conduction of the acoustic stimulus at peripheral and brain stem level up to the cortex, while a selective difficulty appears when the stimulus has to be processed on the basis of frequency at a cortical level. Figure 15.1 illustrates this.

Discrimination of Natural Speech Vowels and Consonants.   Naturally produced pairs of syllables varying either in the initial consonant or final vowel were used. Stimuli were presented through a stereo headset in a quiet but not soundproof room.

In the vowel discrimination task, 65 pairs of syllables were presented, and the patient's task was to indicate if the two syllables were "same" or "different." Forty couples were composed of the same syllables, while in the remaining 25 the two members of the pair were different.

The vowels tested were: /a/, /i/, /u/, /o/, /e/, always coupled with the letter /p/ in initial position.

In the consonant discrimination task the consonants tested were: /p/, /b/, /s/, /k/, /f/, /g/, /m/, /d/, /n/, always coupled with the vowel /a/ in final position, featuring a total of 117 couples.

Forty-five pairs were composed of the same syllable, while in the remaining 72 the two members of the couple were different.

Members of a pair were separated by one second silence. S.C.'s performance was at chance in both the vowel and consonant discrimination tasks.

Identification of Vowels and Consonants.   Fifty syllables varying in the final vowel and 50 in the initial consonant were presented; the patient's task was to write what he had previously heard. The same vowels and consonants were used as in the discrimination task. He scored 33/50 correctly in the vowel identification task when the examiner uttered the stimuli in front of him, but his performance was at chance when the stimuli were presented from the back. In the consonant identification task, the patient's performance was at chance on both cases.

Word Processing Tasks

From the previous experiments it was evident that the patient, despite having normal hearing, had an almost total inability to discriminate and identify single phonemes.

Since recent data obtained with adult aphasics (Baker, Blumstein, & Goodglass, 1980) have shown that there is an intimate interaction between the phonological and semantic components for word processing, our patient was submitted to a series of experiments assessing the contributions of phonemic and semantic factors in single word perception and comprehension.

Lexical Decision.   In this task the patient had to decide if a given auditory stimulus, presented by examiner in front of him, was or was not a real word. Eighty stimuli were used. Forty were frequent bisyllabic words (mean frequency = 64.71), while non-words were obtained by changing a single phoneme from the test words. All non-words were legal. The patient's performance was at chance.

Word Discrimination.   One hundred pairs of bisyllabic words were auditorily presented to the patient (uttered by the examiner in front of him). The patient's task was to indicate if the two words were "same" or "different." In half of the cases the two words were the same, while in the remaining half they were different, each word differing from the other of the pair in the initial syllable. Half of the target words were frequent (mean frequency = 58.53), while the others were not (mean frequency = 8.42). The speaker produced the words as naturally as possible, taking care they were uttered at approximately equal intensity. Order of presentation was counterbalanced. The patient's performance was at chance.

Word Identification

First Experiment.   In this task the patient had to decide if an auditory presented stimulus (uttered by the examiner in front of him) matched or did not match a drawing. Fifty stimuli were used (mean frequency of words = 53.01). In half of them the word corresponded to the name of the drawing, while the other half were non-words obtained by changing a syllable of a common word. The patient's score was 85% correct.

Second Experiment.   Fifty target words (all bisyllabic with a mean frequency of 43.51) were auditorily presented to the patient (uttered by the examiner in front of him), and his task was to select the corresponding drawing from a set of four. One figure was a drawing of the word just presented auditorily (correct choice); one was of an object semantically related to the target (semantic foil); one was of an object whose name was auditorily similar to the target word (phonemic foil); and the last picture was of an object unrelated to the target word.

The patient's performance was well above chance, his score being 34/50 (68%) correct, the errors consisting only in phonemic confusions.

Written Modality

Naming.   Written naming of common objects, geometrical figures, colours, drawings of familiar objects, and geometrical figures was flawless. On the naming subtest of the BDAE (Goodglass & Kaplan, 1972) his score was 100%. Similarly in category naming (e.g., animals, fruits, etc.) his performance was excellent.

Syntactic and Grammatical Production.   In these tests we tapped S.C.'s ability in handling the grammatical and syntactic components of language production. Specifically we tested his ability to produce articles (number and gender); prepositions (locatives, simple, articulated); verbs (persons, tense, use of auxiliaries, active/passive); gender and number of adjectives and nouns. The task was a sentence completion test: the patient was presented with an incomplete sentence written on an index card that he had to complete in such a way that the sentence could correctly describe a picture in front of him. A hundred and two sentences were constructed. His score was 75% correct. A rank order of difficulty was obtained, from which it seems that the most difficult syntactic aspects were the use of passive, followed by locative prepositions and auxiliary verbs (see Table 15.1).

Reading Tests

Cross-Case Matching.   One hundred and fifty-four pairs of letter strings were presented written on an index card. In every case, one member of the pair was written in upper case, while the other was written in lower case. Fifty percent of the pairs were composed of the same letters, while in the remaining 50% one member of the pair differed from the other by changing one letter. Half of the "same" pairs were composed of real words (mean frequency = 217.37), while the remaining half was composed of non-words obtained by changing one letter of frequent words.

The patient task was to sort out the "same" pairs. His performance was 100% correct.

TABLE 15.1
Errors in Sentence Production

Passive sentences	100%
Use of simple prepositions	62.3%
Use of auxiliary verbs	50%
Use of locative prepositions	47.8%
Use of articles	12.5%

Lexical Decision.   A list of 40 familiar words (mean frequency = 52.5) and 40 legal non-words of approximately the same length, obtained by changing a single letter from a familiar word, were presented on index cards to the patient, whose task was to sort out the words. His performance was 95% correct.

Word Identification.   The same material used in the auditory word identification tests was used in the word visual modality. His performance was 100% correct.

Sentence Comprehension.   S.C.'s comprehension of visually presented sentences was assessed by using a sentence-picture matching task in which he was presented with written sentences and was required to choose from four pictures the one that correctly depicted the meaning of the sentence. Thirty-two sentences requiring successful syntactic analysis for correct performance were used. The sentences were constructed to focus different aspects of syntactic comprehension.

1. Eight sentences tapping comprehension of locative prepositions (in, out, under, on, in front, behind).
2. Eight sentences exploring comprehension of nouns (gender and number).
3. Eight sentences focusing on word order, using reversible sentences (e.g., the boy kisses the girl).
4. Eight sentences exploring his knowledge of passive.

The four picture contrasts from which the patient was required to choose included the correct choice, one syntactic foil, one lexical foil, and an unrelated item.

S.C. correctly understood 70% of the sentences. He showed consistent difficulties in handling passive sentences (e.g., the sentence "the girl is kissed by the mother" was interpreted as "the girl kisses the mother") and locatives (e.g., the sentence "the dog is behind the girl" was interpreted as "the dog is in front of the girl").

No errors were made on nouns and word order comprehension.

TABLE 15.2
Errors in Sentence Comprehension

Comprehension of passive sentences	87.5%
Comprehension of locative prepositions	62.5%
Comprehension of reversible sentences	37.5%
Comprehension of nouns	12.5%

Memory Tasks

Single Letter Recall.   In order to assess S.C.'s ability to remember single letters we used a test procedure developed by Posner and Keele (1967). In this procedure the subject is shown for one second a single letter written on an index card in either upper or lower case. The patient was asked to remember either the name and the case of the letter (physical match) or the name only (name match). In the "physical" match the patient's task was to find the same letter in an array of five; while in the "name" match he was asked to sort out from a set of five the letter that shared with the test letter the same name, but it was written in different case.

The test was composed of 54 letters, half in upper and half in lower case, covering the entire alphabet. S.C.'s performance was 100% correct.

Recall of Homophonic vs Non-Homophonic Pictures.   Conrad (1964) found that lists of letters comprising acoustically similar items were less well remembered than those which were acoustically distinctive. This effect was present even when the stimuli were presented visually. In a further study Conrad (1971) pursued the problem of covert verbal mediation of visually presented stimuli, using pictures rather than letters. Conrad required his subjects to match sets of pictures with homophonic names in an immediate visual memory experiment and compared the results with memory for non-homophonic pictures. In spite of the fact that no verbalisation was required or even suggested, the performance on sound-like words was significantly worse than on the acoustically distinctive words.

In order to test if our patient used verbal mediation in STM memory tasks, we used Conrad's paradigm, submitting S.C. to a series of STM tests using homophonic, non-homophonic, and nonsense pictures. The material was constructed following the Goodglass et al. (1974) study which showed that aphasics could not use verbal mediation in STM tests.

Three subtests requiring matching from visual memory were designed. The first consisted of nonsense figures; the second of similar-sounding pictures divided into two groups of eight each (*cane, cono, case, nani, mani, pane, rane, canne, gallo, molla, bolla, bollo, collo, poppo, palla, pialla*); and the third of pictures whose name was not similar in sound (*nave, rosa, pipa, topo, dado, peso, sole, mela, barca, fiore, sacco, sedia, penna, fuoco, ferro, gatto*).

Previous tests on normal subjects had shown uniformity in naming the meaningful pictures across the subjects.

Two sets of eight individual cards were made up for presentation to the subject as stimuli to be remembered. The same eight stimuli were assembled on a double sheet of cardboard that could be opened to reveal the eight stimuli or folded over to conceal them. Three such sets were made for each of the subtests, with the pictures or designs arranged in different locations, to prevent the subject from remembering their positions from trial to trial.

Each subtest began with memory for two stimuli. Two of the eight cards were selected and placed face up in front of the subject, who was given five seconds to remember what the stimuli were. During this exposure one of the cardboard display folders lay closed before the subject. At the end of five seconds the two stimulus cards were turned face down, the display folder was flipped open, and the subject was required to place the two stimulus cards, still face down, over the figures to which they corresponded.

Six trials of two stimuli for 12 possible points were used, followed by four presentations of three stimulus cards at a time, and three presentations of four stimulus cards at a time. The maximum score for any subtest was thus 36 points.

No difference was found in recalling nonsense figures, homophonic, and non-homophonic pictures, S.C.'s scores being, respectively, 32/36 correct in the three subtests.

Memory for Sentences. In order to explore our patient's ability to recall written sentences, we used an Italian version of the Newcombe and Marshall Test (1967). They found that left brain damaged patients showed a selective deficit in recalling sentences whose normal linguistic contrasts were either not present or were insufficient to permit the unique reconstruction of the material. They interpreted this result as due to a tendency to normalise the "structure" (either syntactic, or syntactic and semantic) when the material was deviant.

Thirty-five sentences, between five and six words long, were constructed. They included the following type of sentences:

1. Fully grammatical and meaningful structures that varied in syntactic complexity (e.g., "the boy is eating some ice-cream").
2. Grammatically well-formed sentences that were semantically deviant (e.g., "Mario's bicycle has three wheels").
3. Reversible and irreversible sentences (e.g., "the mother greets the boy; the little girl strokes the cat").
4. Sentences containing modifier strings in correct and incorrect order (e.g., "in the garden there are many nice flowers; I ate good cakes two").
5. Random word strings (e.g., "with yellow jumps hand eight").

Sentences were written on index cards and presented for about 10 seconds to the patient, then turned face down. Immediately afterwards the patient was asked to write the sentence that he had just seen. S.C. correctly recalled 24 sentences. The errors were mainly omission of articles, substitutions of prepositions, insertions of articles or prepositions not present in the target sentences.

TABLE 15.3
Errors in Memory for Sentences

Reversible and irreversible sentences	30%
Sentences containing modifier strings in correct and incorrect order	30%
Random word strings	20%
Grammatically well-formed sentences which were semantically deviant	10%

DISCUSSION

S.C. showed an almost complete absence of oral language, coupled with a severe auditory comprehension deficit that could not be accounted for by a peripheral deficit, since pure tone audiometry and brain ´stem auditory evoked potentials were within normal limits.

At the cortical level, while primary responses to non-verbal stimuli were of normal latency and amplitude, late responses were abnormally long and of reduced amplitude. This fact suggests some residual cortical activity in processing auditory stimuli. Further evidence for this processing is offered by S.C.'s almost normal performance in identifying meaningful non-verbal sounds.

We may reasonably assume that this abnormal auditory processing will also apply to speech stimuli as there are no reports of patients with abnormal cortical auditory potentials for non-speech stimuli where the evoked potentials to speech stimuli were normal (Auerbach et al., 1982).

This cortical auditory activity is, however, clearly insufficient for normal processing of linguistic stimuli, as our patient showed a total inability in discrimination and identification tasks with single phonemes. He scored above chance only in vowel identification tasks. It is possible to postulate that this residual activity could find an explanation in the physical character-istics of the stimuli. While natural vowels usually average 100 to 150 ms in duration, consonants are characterised by rapid frequency changes within the first 40 ms of onset of the stimulus.

These data suggest that his auditory processing system is functioning almost normally except at the phonetic level. The phonetic deficit hypothesis is, however, insufficient to explain his residual ability in word identification tasks, as he performed well above chance in word to picture matching tasks. This result contrasts with lexical decision tasks, where the patient had to discriminate words from legal non-words differing from the former only by a single phoneme. In this test, S.C.'s performance was at chance. Similarly in auditory word discrimination tasks his performance was very poor.

CNL–L*

These data probably reflect the fact that in audio-visual word discrimination and word-picture matching tasks, where semantic mediation is available, the role of phonological analysis is less crucial, the patient being able to profit from contextual semantic clues. (Caplan, 1978; Saffran, Marin, & Yeni-Komshan, 1976).

As far as his inability to produce oral language is concerned, we might assume that a total deprivation of phonemic input occurring at the age when the language is not fully established can reasonably block the development of the ability to produce phonemic output.

On linguistic tasks not requiring the use of the oral-auditory channel S.C.'s performance was markedly superior. Both in production and comprehension, his lexical-semantic ability was within normal limits. His score in lexical decision tasks and memory was flawless. Equally good was his performance in matching letter strings differing only in case (upper or lower) suggesting the use of an abstract graphemic code, rather than using a visual code that demands an identity match.

Correct written production of single words can be explained according to models such as that of Shallice (1981) postulating that the specification of the overall orthography of a word can be accessed directly from the semantic representation, bypassing phonological operations.

Similarly comprehension of written words can be performed through direct access from the written material to the cognitive system by passing phonological mediation.

Tests of reading and writing at the sentence level, however, revealed a variety of deficits in syntactic reception and production. Such deficits would be expected if one took the view that there is an intimate relationship between syntax and phonology, a view often taken with respect to syntactic disturbances in acquired aphasia (see, e.g., Caramazza, Berndt, Basili, & Koller, 1981). However, current work (see, e.g., Chapters 6, 7, 9, 10, 12, and 17 of this volume) strongly suggest that this view is much too global. Various dissociations between different types of syntactic disturbances can be found, as can various dissociations between different types of phonological disturbance, and various dissociations between particular syntactic impairments and particular phonological impairments. Thus S.C.'s syntactic difficulties may not be related to his very severe phonological impairment. What is clear in his case, however, is that very competent single-word reading and spelling can be acquired without the benefits of phonological mediation. This observation may not be easy to reconcile with theories of spelling such as the one advanced in Chapter 11 by Miceli, Silveri, and Caramazza, in which phonological support plays a crucial role in normal skilled spelling. The results we report are also relevant to theories about learning to read and spell, theories of the kind discussed by Seymour in the following chapter.

REFERENCES

Alajouanine, T. H., & L'hermitte, F. (1965) Acquired aphasia in children. *Brain, 88,* 653–662.

Auerbach, S. H., Sanford, H., Allard, T., Naeser, M., Alexander, M. P., & Albert, M. L. (1982) Pure word deafness: Analysis of a case with bilateral lesions and a defect at the prephonemic level. *Brain, 105,* 271–300.

Baker, S., Blumstein, S. E., & Goodglass, H. (1980) Interaction between phonological and semantic factors in auditory comprehension. *Neuropsychologia, 19,* 1–15.

Caplan, L. R. (1978) Variability of perceptual function: The sensory cortex as a "categoriser" and "deducer". *Brain and Language, 6,* 1–13.

Caramazza, A., Berndt, R. S., Basili, A. G., & Koller, J. J. (1981) Syntactic processing deficits in aphasia. *Cortex, 17,* 333–348.

Conrad, R. (1964) Acoustic confusion in immediate memory. *British Journal of Psychology, 55,* 75–84.

Conrad, R. (1971) The chronology of the development of covert speech in children. *Developmental Psychology, 24,* 505–514.

Goodglass, H., & Kaplan, E. (1972) *The assessment of aphasia and related disorders.* Philadelphia, USA: Lea & Febiger.

Goodglass, H., Denes, G., & Calderon, M. (1974) The absence of covert verbal mediation in aphasia. *Cortex, 10,* 264–269.

Landau, W. M., & Kleffner, F. R. (1957) Syndrome of acquired aphasia with convulsive disorder in children. *Neurology, 7,* 523–530.

Milner, B. (1971) Interhemispheric differences in the localisation of psychological processes in man. *British Medical Bulletin, 27,* 272–277.

Newcombe, F., & Marshall, J. C. (1967) Immediate recall of "sentences" by subjects with unilateral cerebral lesions. *Neuropsychologia, 5,* 329–334.

Posner, M., & Keele, S. (1967) Decay of visual information from a single letter. *Science, 158,* 137–139.

Saffran, E. M., Marin, O., & Yeni-Komshan, G. (1976) An analysis of speech perception in word deafness. *Brain and Language, 3,* 209–228.

Shallice, T. (1981) Phonological agraphia and the lexical route in writing. *Brain, 104,* 413–429.

Toso, V., Moschini, M., Cagnini, G., & Antoni, D. (1981) Aphasie acquise de l'enfant avec épilepsie. *Revue Neurologique, 137,* 425–434.

Van de Sandt-Koenderman, W. M. E., Smit, I. A. C., Van Dongen, H. R., & Van Hest, J. B. C. (1984) A case of acquired aphasia and convulsive disorder: some linguistic aspects of recovery and breakdown. *Brain and Language, 21,* 174–183.

16

Developmental Dyslexia: A Cognitive Experimental Analysis

Philip H. K. Seymour
Department of Psychology, The University, Dundee DD1 4HN, Scotland

INTRODUCTION

A main objective of this paper is to put forward some ideas concerning the disturbance of basic reading and spelling functions that occurs in childhood dyslexia. The approach adopted is not dissimilar to that which has been followed in the analysis of "acquired dyslexia," although it will be argued that the acquired and developmental dyslexias require slightly different theoretical approaches, and slightly different methods of investigation.

When used in relation to adult neurological patients, "dyslexia" is a general label for disturbances of basic reading functions which may be analysed into various sub-types or syndromes. A more confused situation exists with regard to childhood dyslexia. One reason for this is that attempts have been made to stipulate that "dyslexia" should be used in a restrictive, rather than a general sense. The motivation has been the belief that inferior intelligence or adverse educational or social circumstances constitute a sufficient explanation for impaired reading development. It is considered that the term "dyslexia" should be applied only in those cases where such explanations appear not to be applicable. An analogous situation would arise in adult neuropsychology if it was maintained that reading problems inevitably occurred in aphasia, and that the term "dyslexia" should not be applied unless it could be shown that the patient was not aphasic. In practice, in adult neuropsychology, the preference has been to apply a descriptive label where an observable deficit exists irrespective of what other impairments may be present. Following the same logic, it would be appropriate to refer to a child as "dyslexic" if basic reading functions were impaired (impairment being operationally defined using information processing indicators of the kind to be discussed later in this paper).

In the study of acquired dyslexia, the contribution of neuropsychological research has been to establish detailed descriptions of the preserved and impaired capabilities of individual subjects. These descriptions are typically based on the assumption that the information processing system underlying a complex cognitive function is modular in structure. Proposals regarding the components that are impaired or preserved constitute the theoretical basis for specification of a sub-type, and the naming of the sub-type may make reference to the impaired component or to the component that is preserved or relatively less impaired (Marshall & Newcombe, 1973; Shallice, 1981).

It is natural to ask whether a similar analysis may be made for developmental dyslexia. In a sense, the restrictive definition of dyslexia incorporates a sub-type proposal. However, one cannot at present differentiate between high and low IQ dyslexics in the way that one can specify differences between, say, deep dyslexics and word-form dyslexics. Thus, the question is whether childhood dyslexia, considered irrespective of intelligence, is analysable into sub-types or syndromes and whether it would be reasonable to anticipate that the sub-types, if discovered, would correspond to those identified in the analysis of acquired dyslexia.

A correspondence between acquired and developmental sub-types might be expected on the basis of a neurological theory that asserted that specific brain areas were necessarily involved in the construction of processing systems essential for basic competence in reading. If these areas were degraded, as a consequence either of a genetic anomaly or of adverse pre- or peri-natal conditions, then a disturbance of reading development would follow. In order to obtain patterns corresponding to the acquired syndromes, it would be necessary (1) that the brain regions affected contained functionally specialised modules; (2) that, on a proportion of occasions, the degradation was localised in areas corresponding to those affected in the adult cases; and (3) that the observable effects of damage inflicted in adulthood might be comparable to those obtained when a system was constructed on a defective neural substrate. If dissolution and construction were converse processes extending over time, it would be possible for a partially disintegrated system to produce effects that were similar to those of a partially constructed system.

Nonetheless, in an acquired disorder a disturbance of a particular system would not alter the established capabilities of other systems, whereas, in a developmental disorder, a specifically localised disturbance might distort the development of other systems that relied on transmission of data from the impaired system. Because of this specifically developmental aspect, it seems likely that the relationship between acquired and developmental dyslexic sub-types will be one of general similarity rather than of exact correspondence.

Various procedures for investigation of developmental sub-types have been tried, including experimental comparisons of dyslexic and control groups, psychometric and factor analytic studies, and clinical case-oriented approaches (cf. Boder's (1973) dyseidetic/dysphonetic distinction).

More recently, Temple and Marshall (1983) have provided a detailed case description of a 17 year-old developmental dyslexic, H.M., who demonstrated a reading pattern consisting of (1) non-word reading markedly more impaired than word reading; (2) a tendency towards lexicalisation in non-word reading; (3) homophony effect on non-word reading; (4) visual and derivational paralexias in word reading, but no effects of spelling-to-sound regularity, and few regularisation errors or neologistic responses. Semantic paralexias were not observed but reading of function words in text was impaired. The case is in various respects similar to adult phonological dyslexia, and was viewed by Temple and Marshall as a developmental analogue of the adult syndrome. Evidence for a developmental form of surface dyslexia has been presented by Holmes (1973), and more recently by Coltheart et al. (1983). Coltheart described the case of a 15 year-old dyslexic girl, C.D., who showed a strong effect of spelling-to-sound regularity on accuracy of word reading. In a homophone matching test performance was worse with lists containing irregular words than with lists containing only regular words or non-words. Further, C.D. produced the regularisation errors and stress errors that had been viewed by Marshall and Newcombe (1973) as characteristic of surface dyslexia. C.D.'s comprehension of words depended on her capacity to form an adequate phonological representation. Her performance in non-word reading was also seriously impaired, and showed a slight bias towards production of words as error responses.

These two case studies reinforce the conclusion that developmental versions of phonological and surface dyslexic sub-types can be found. However, it is not clear that the type of classification would have been the same in the absence of prior analyses of acquired cases. If the theoretical significance of derivational errors and phonetic regularisation errors had not been apparent, then both H.M. and C.D. might have been categorised as poor readers who had a particular problem in phonological assembly (non-word reading).

It is possible to supplement the psycholinguistic and competence descriptions of a developmental dyslexic by a *processing description* derived from a systematic application of the cognitive experimental method. Using techniques of this kind, Seymour and MacGregor (1984) reported a cognitive experimental analysis of four adolescent developmentally dyslexic subjects who were considered to illustrate a phonological pattern, a morphemic (surface dyslexic) pattern, a visual/analytic (attentional dyslexic) pattern, and a combined phonological-morphemic impairment.

READING AND SPELLING DEVELOPMENT

The cognitive experimental analysis of developmental dyslexia depends on assumptions regarding (1) the normal course of reading/spelling development; and (2) the structure of an information processing model of basic reading and spelling functions.

An account of reading and spelling development, deriving from proposals by Frith (1985), Marsh et al. (1981), Bryant and Bradley (1980), and from observations of early reading made by Leona Elder at Dundee (see Seymour & Elder, 1986) was set out by Seymour and MacGregor (1984). It was assumed that development involves a number of "stages," although these need not be strictly successive or independent. The scheme can be diagrammatically represented, as in Fig. 16.1.

Reading begins with the establishment of visual discriminations between words selected from a limited vocabulary. A rudimentary word recognition system is set up. This is referred to as a *logographic lexicon*, and is assumed to

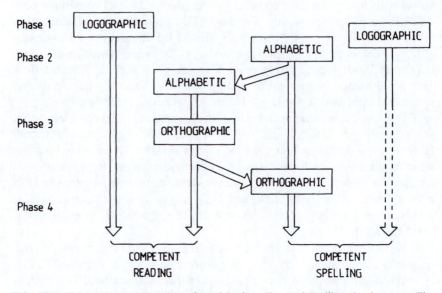

FIG. 16.1 Schematic representation of model of reading and spelling development. The formulation differs from that of Frith (1985) in suggesting that logographic development may co-exist with alphabetic/orthographic development.

recognise words on the basis of whatever features may be functional for discrimination, and to interface directly with a semantic/episodic memory in which pointers to the word name may be stored. The results obtained by Seymour and Elder (1986) indicate that beginning logographic readers (1) cannot assemble phonology from print; (2) produce visual, semantic, and episodic paralexias; and (3) are able to read known words despite spatial distortion (e.g., zigzag or vertical arrangement of letters). Thus, logographic recognition is probably not strictly ideographic, but may depend on identification of features (e.g., salient letters or letter groups, letter position, word length) that can survive spatial distortion. It is assumed that the range of vocabulary discriminated by the logographic lexicon expands progressively with advancing age, and that the lexicon becomes capable of handling different typefaces and handwritings.

The structure initiated at the logographic stage may be represented in the form of a simple information processing diagram (Fig. 16.2). Visual feature information (salient letters, letter position, word length) is sampled from the display and passed to the logographic lexicon. It is assumed that sampling typically operates on the whole display, but that some segmentation or focus is possible. Discrimination within the lexicon is imperfect, and misclassification due to sharing of features or inadequately precise features specification will occur. Recognition gives direct access to semantic information, including episodic records of the contexts in which a word has been encountered. The subset of items from his vocabulary that constitute his "reading words" are specified in the child's episodic memory (referred to as the "response set" in Fig. 16.2). If the data retrieved include a pointer to one of these it will be

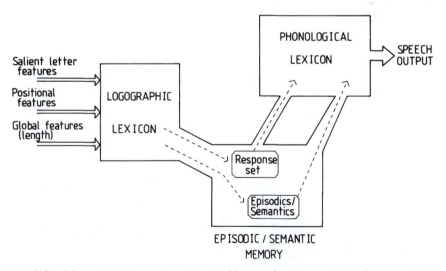

FIG. 16.2 Diagrammatic representation of logographic/semantic system for reading.

possible for it to be produced as a vocal response. Thus, access to phonology is assumed to be semantically mediated, and it is proposed that the logographic lexicon remains primarily a system specialised for direct access to semantics.

A second stage, referred to as the *alphabetic stage* by Frith (1985), may initially be introduced by copying and writing exercises. The children learn to isolate the individual letters within words and to copy their shapes. Letter-sound relationships may be pointed out by the teacher, often with emphasis on sound→letter (phoneme-grapheme) associations. This learning will give rise to the triangular associative structure which may, at first, be oriented more towards writing then reading. The two tasks may appear episodically distinct to the children. As phoneme-grapheme relations are established it becomes possible for children to write some simple words to dictation, although they will not be able to read these words unless they have been established in the logographic lexicon. Progress from an alphabetic stage in writing to an alphabetic stage in reading depends on a realisation that grapheme-phoneme associations may be helpful in word identification. The resulting information processing model (Fig. 16.3) includes a second and functionally distinct visual recognition system, initially specialised for identification of individual graphemes, that will be referred to as the *alphabetic lexicon*. The visual information passed to the lexicon must be segregated into individual graphemes (referred to as "selection" in the diagram), and transfer should be systematically ordered on a left-to-right basis. It is assumed that the lexicon is interfaced directly with a system for production of graphemes in writing (the orthographic processor), and with a phonemic representational level of the phonological processor. Access to semantics occurs via phonology.

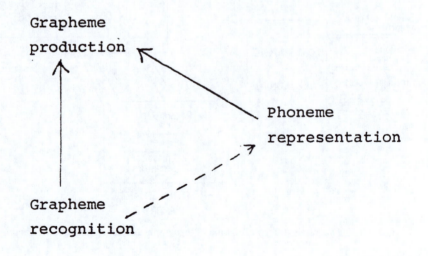

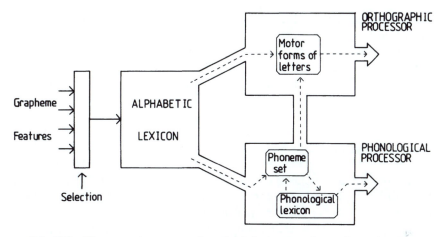

FIG. 16.3   Diagrammatic representation of alphabetic system for reading and spelling.

Many current models of reading assume that there is no significant development beyond the logographic and alphabetic stages, and maintain the idea of separate and non-interacting alphabetic (grapheme→phoneme) and logographic (visual word recognition) systems. In some cases it is argued that episodic connections between visual words and their phonology become isolated from semantics as a set of direct associations between the logographic lexicon and speech production. For example, in the version of the logogen model described by Morton and Patterson (1980) there is a distinct grapheme-phoneme translation channel (alphabetic system) and a visual input logogen system (logographic lexicon) that interfaces directly with semantics and phonology—i.e., a standard three-route model. A difficulty with this type of model is that it does not indicate the manner in which word recognition development may be assisted by a grasp of grapheme-phoneme relationships, or explain how a spelling production system based on phoneme-grapheme associations comes to be lexicalised—i.e., modified to take account of the idiosyncracies present in the spellings of individual words.

Both Frith and Marsh et al. have discussed the possibility of a third stage during which an increasingly sophisticated knowledge of orthographic regularities is acquired, and in which lexically based information (analogies) may be consulted when considering how to read or spell new words. This can be referred to as the *orthographic stage*. Frith has argued that a distinction may be made between an orthographic stage for reading and an orthographic stage for spelling. This is because it is possible to find children who develop a full (orthographic) competence in reading but who remain poor (alphabetic) spellers, lacking word-specific knowledge and tending towards production of phonetically regularised spelling errors (Frith, 1980). Hence, in the developmental diagram in Fig. 16.1 the orthographic stage for reading is shown as preceding and leading to the orthographic stage for spelling.

Seymour and MacGregor argued that the orthographic stage might most naturally be seen as an expansion of the capabilities of the alphabetic lexicon. It was noted that Gibson et al. (1962) had demonstrated that reading development includes a growth in sensitivity to spelling patterns, i.e., single or multi-grapheme clusters corresponding to vowel and consonant groups occupying a particular position in a word. The main proposal was that the alphabetic lexicon might be progressively transformed from a system for recognition of isolated graphemes to a system which recognised vowel and consonant grapheme clusters in their appropriate positions. This idea has been further explored in relation to the mono- and disyllabic words listed in the *Phonetic Lexicon* published by Rockey (1973). In Rockey's lexicon words are analysed into (1) an initial consonant cluster; (2) a terminal consonant cluster; and (3) a vowel cluster. The lexicon is phonetically organised, and thus defines the phonemic groupings that occur in the initial, medial, and terminal positions of English monosyllables and disyllables as well as detailing the orthographic structures which are used to represent those sounds. According to Rockey, the phonetic lexicon is a three-dimensional structure having an ordered array of initial consonants on one dimension (the x-axis), an ordered array of terminal consonants on a second dimension (the y-axis), and an ordered array of vowels on the third dimension (the z-axis). Seymour and MacGregor proposed that an *orthographic lexicon* might be constructed that was aligned with the phonetic lexicon. This means that the orthographic lexicon should also be a three-dimensional structure, having initial consonant groups on its x-axis, terminal consonant groups on its y-axis, and vowel groups on its z-axis. The orthographic and phonetic spaces could be aligned with one another if the principle for ordering elements on the dimensions of the phonetic space was also followed in ordering elements on the dimensions of the orthographic space.

It appeared to Seymour and MacGregor that a development of this kind could result in the establishment of a sophisticated system for translation from print to pronunciation. Associations between an element on a given dimension of the orthographic space and the corresponding element on the equivalent dimension of the phonetic space could be used for grapheme-phoneme translation. Alternatively, recognition of the initial, terminal, and medial components of a letter array would give access to a point in orthographic space, and this could in turn be used to access the correspond-ing point in phonetic space, from which the marginal x, y and z elements could be synthesised as a syllabic production. In this way it would be possible for an orthographically regular letter array directly to address its standard pronunciation. Such a system would be effective for pronunciation of regular words or non-words, but would make errors on those words which incorporate non-standard spelling-to-sound relationships. Seymour and MacGregor suggested that this difficulty could be met by a procedure of *address modification*. The assumption here is that an alteration to a phonological address may be written at any point in orthographic space. In practice, these alterations relate primarily to vowel pronunciation, and so the alteration would consist of an indication that the z-axis value for the item was not the one given by the correspondence and alignment of the two lexicons.

So that this possibility might be explored further, Dave Maccabe at Dundee University made a search of Rockey's lists, and identified the initial consonant, terminal consonant, and medial vowel groups that occurred in the word sample. After rejection of clusters that occurred in only a very small number of items, a set consisting of 56 initial clusters and 75 terminal clusters was assembled. A computer program, based on the Apple II microprocessor, was written, which generated all possible combinations of the initial and terminal clusters with a medial vowel. The program was initially run using the five single vowels, A, E, I, O and U, thus simulating an orthographic lexical space containing $56 \times 75 \times 5 = 21,000$ locations. The items successively generated were classified as (1) known English words (i.e., rare words which could only be verified by resort to a dictionary were not accepted); or (2) non-words. The words were classified as being standard in pronunciation, which meant that the consonants received their expected values and the vowels were pronounced short (as in "c<u>a</u>t," "p<u>e</u>t," "p<u>o</u>t," "p<u>i</u>t," "c<u>u</u>t"); or as exceptional, which meant that there had been a change in the value of a consonant (e.g., "h<u>a</u>s"); or a vowel (e.g., "t<u>a</u>lk," "f<u>i</u>nd," "p<u>u</u>t," "h<u>o</u>st"). In addition, the non-words generated were categorised as homophones of known words, word stems (BOSSes, in the sense of Taft (1979), or fragments recognisable as part of words), or as non-words. The progam printed out a listing of the matrix for a particular vowel. A fragment of the words section of the matrix for the vowel 'a' is shown in Table 16.1. This is based on the full set of 56 initial consonants, but on only seven of 75 terminal consonant groups.

The sample matrix illustrates the types of columns which may be produced. An example of a column containing only items which are regular in pronunciation is given by the endings -CK and -G. These are referred to as *consistent regular* columns. The column for -LK is an example of a *consistent irregular* column. For all of the items, vowel pronunciation must be modified from /æ/ to /ɔː/.

The other columns are inconsistent. Column -LL is inconsistent but with a bias in favour of irregular pronunciation, i.e., in most of the items 'a' must be modified from /æ/ to /ɔː/ but a standard pronunciation is retained in such entries as "shall" and "mall." -SH is an inconsistent column with a bias towards regular pronunciation. The irregularity is caused by an initial consonant effect due to a /w/ sound, present in the initial groups (w, sw, qu, squ, wh). In this environment "a" is modified from /æ/ to /ɒ/ for the items

TABLE 16.1
Fragment of Matrix for Vowel "a" Words With Non-Standard Pronunciation are Marked With an Asterisk

Initial consonant group	T	CK	SK	LK	G	SH	LL	Total
ø	øAT		*øASK			øASH	*øALL	4
P	PAT	PACK					*PALL	3
PL								0
PR								0
B	BAT	BACK	*BASK		BAG	BASH	*BALL	6
BL		BLACK						1
BR	BRAT				BRAG	BRASH		3
T	TAT	TACK	*TASK	*TALK	TAG	TRASH	*TALL	6
TR		TRACK						2
TW								0
D						DASH		1
DR	DRAT				DRAG			2
C	CAT		*CASK			CASH	*CALL	4
K								0
CL		CLACK				CLASH		2
CR		CRACK			CRAG	CRASH		3
QU		QUACK				*QUASH		2
G						GASH	*GALL	2
GL								0
GR								0
F	FAT				FAG		*FALL	3
PH								0
FL	FLAT		*FLASK		FLAG	FLASH	*FALL	4
FR								0
V	VAT							1
TH	*THAT							1

Terminal consonant group

Initial consonant group

360

Initial consonant group								Total
THR	*THRALL	THRASH						2
S		SASH	SAG			SACK	SAT	4
SP							SPAT	1
SPL		SPLASH						1
SPR							SPRAT	1
ST	*STALL	STASH	STAG	*STALK		STACK		5
STR								0
SC								0
SK								0
SCR			SCRAG					1
SQU	*SQUALL	*SQUASH					*SQUAT	3
SM	*SMALL	SMASH				SMACK		3
SN			SNAG			SNACK		2
SL		SLASH	SLAG			SLACK	SLAT	4
SW			SWAG				*SWAT	2
Z			ZAG					1
SH	SMALL		SHAG			SNACK		3
SHR								0
H	*HALL	HASH	HAG			HACK	HAT	5
CH				*CHALK			CHAT	2
J			JAG			JACK		2
M	MALL	MASH			*MASK	MACK	MAT	5
N			NAG					1
KN						KNACK		1
L		LASH	LAG			LACK		3
R		RASH	RAG			RACK	RAT	4
WR						WRACK		1
W	*WALL	*WASH	WAG	*WALK				4
WH						WHACK	*WHAT	2
Y								0
Total	15	23	21	4	6	22	22	113

Initial consonant group

361

"quash," "squash," and "wash." Inspection of the matrix indicates that this W- influence does not operate when the terminal groups is a velar, as in -CK, or -G, and may be over-ridden by the terminal consonant group, as in "walk" and "wall." In some instances, the classification of a column depends on considerations of regional pronunciation differences. For example, the -SK column is consistent irregular in my (southern English) dialect, but consistent and regular in Dave Maccabe's Yorkshire dialect.

The sample of the matrix indicates the types of modification that would have to be written into an orthographic lexicon that was built up on the principles of positionally constrained vowel and consonant letter groups and alignment with the dimensions of the phonological lexicon. An input lexicon set up in this way, i.e., with *address modifications* written in whenever the pronunciation of a vowel or consonant departed from what was standard for the matrix, would be capable of translating both words and non-words of standard spelling structure to their correct pronunciation. The model allows for three distinct procedures of print-to-pronunciation translation:

1. Marginal Associations.   If null values are assigned for two of the three dimensions, translation of the value assigned to the remaining dimension will yield a pronunciation for an isolated vowel or consonant group. If the groups were handled successively in this way this would be equivalent to looking up a series of grapheme-phoneme associations. These could be ordered and blended for pronunciation. The process would operate serially, segment by segment, and would always generate standard pronunciations. The procedure can be viewed as the operation of a traditional grapheme-phoneme translation channel, although it is envisaged as using letter-sound associations, but not conditional rules.

2 Point-to-point Correspondence.   This procedure involves access to a point in the orthographic space followed by access to a homologous point in phonological space. Orthographic access depends on prior marking of vowel and consonant segments in the letter array. It is assumed that activation at a point in phonological space is equivalent to an instruction to produce a synthesised syllabic form composed of the phonetic elements that define the accessed location. This could approximate a parallel process, and would generate a standard pronunciation unless an address modification had been written in at the relevant point in the orthographic lexicon. Taking account of an address modification might involve some cost in processing time.

3. Analogy or Lexical Pooling.   In this procedure access to a point in orthographic space is accompanied by activation of locations that are adjacent on the x-, y- or z-axes of the lexicon. This results in activation of homologous points in the phonological lexicon, and of points indicated by address modifications. If this information is taken into account when pronunciation is synthesised, the effect will be for pronunciation to reflect the existence of non-standard associations represented in the lexicon (cf. Henderson, 1982).

In order to assess the degree to which an analogies and pooling influence was apparent in adult readers, Dave Maccabe assembled a list of non-words which were drawn from columns of the $56 \times 75 \times 5$ matrix which exemplified (1) consistent regular pronunciation; (2) consistent irregular pronunciation; (3) inconsistent pronunciation with a regular bias; and (4) inconsistent pronunciation with bias equal or favouring irregular pronunciation. A preliminary study was conducted in which 10 adult subjects read the non-words under conditions of vocal reaction time measurement. The pronunciation of the vowel in correct responses was classified as (1) a regular vowel pronunciation (RVP); or (2) an acceptable (i.e., lexicalised) irregular vowel pronunciation (AIVP). The proportions of these responses are shown in Table 16.2 (taken from Maccabe, 1984).

These figures provide clear evidence for an influence of column content on non-word pronunciation. Thus, non-words are not read solely by processes 1 or 2 above (marginal associations or point-to-point correspondence) and pooling or analogy procedures are sometimes involved. On the other hand, these procedures are either only intermittently applied, or else do not have an overriding influence. Lexicalisation occurs only about half the time for columns with consistent irregular pronunciations, and only about a quarter of the time for inconsistent columns that are not biased towards regular pronunciation. Dave MacCabe's study also tested for an influence operating across the rows of the matrix by including items in which the vowel "a" was preceded by a consonant cluster containing a /w/. Lexicalisation occurred on about 70% of occasions.

TABLE 16.2
Incidence of Regular Vowel Pronunciations (RVP) and Acceptable
Irregular Vowel Pronunciations (AIVP) in Naming Non-Words from
Consistent and Inconsistent Columns

	Consistent		*Inconsistent*	
	Regular	*Irregular*	*Regular bias*	*No regular bias*
RVP	333	179	136	116
AIVP	—	166	3	43
Percent AIVP	—	48.12	2.16	21.72

Source: Maccabe, 1984.

The *orthographic lexicon* therefore provides the basis of a model of a system for accessing phonology from print. Obviously the model is restricted in its scope, since it has been discussed only in relation to the Consonant-Vowel-Consonant (C-V-C) structures considered in Rockey's lexicon, and with only a limited sub-set of vowels.

The vocabulary covered by the lexicon can be extended by enlarging the set of vowels and by adding rarely occurring consonant clusters. Seymour and MacGregor (1984) considered that a further extension to handle polysyllabic words could be achieved if the lexicon was expanded by addition of a prefix recognition system and a suffix recognition system. The orthographic lexicon would then be seen as a mechanism for identification of syllabic word stems, analogous to the Basic Orthographic Syllabic Structures (BOSSes) discussed by Taft (1979). The information contained in the slots of the central component of the lexicon would then have to take account of the possibility of combination with a prefix or suffix. A possible mechanism for this might be one in which identification of a prefix or suffix was flagged as an event and reported to all locations in the orthographic lexicon where it was allowable. Semantic and phonological addressing could be differentiated to reflect distinctions of affixation.

Developmentally, the establishment of an orthographic lexicon and its interfacing with phonology and semantics, combined with the continued expansion of the range of vocabulary discriminated within the logographic lexicon, constitutes the achievement of a basic level of competence in reading. It will be argued later that the reading disturbances observed in cases of developmental dyslexia reflect a disruption of the development of these two types of lexicon. Possible causes of disruption, and their effects on reading processes will be discussed subsequently.

The developmental diagram in Fig. 16.1 follows the proposals made by Frith by allowing that establishment of an orthographic lexicon for spelling production depends both on the availability of a foundation of simple phoneme-grapheme associations and on the availability of an orthographic lexicon for reading. In the discussion of the alphabetic stage it was suggested that a triangular associative structure might be built up that links the visual and written forms of graphemes with a phonemic level of speech representation. Progress towards an orthographic input lexicon involved a move towards an orthographic organisation (the three-dimensional structure) that was consistent with the organisation of the phonological lexicon (i.e., alignment of the elements on the orthographic and phonological dimensions). A first step towards establishment of an orthographic output lexicon for spelling production could be achieved if the dimensions and categories of the input lexicon were copied into an orthographic output lexicon. The output lexicon would then consist of a three-dimensional space with categories defining the written forms of initial consonant letter groups on its x-axis, terminal consonant letter groups on its y-axis, and vowels on its z-axis. The ordering of elements on these dimensions would duplicate the ordering established for the input lexicon, and would, consequently, be aligned with the structure of the phonological lexicon. The output lexicon would then provide a basis for spelling knowledge that was informed with respect to the orthographic conventions of English while incorporating an organisation which was compatible with speech categorisation in the phonological system.

A system of this kind would mediate efficient copying (marginal or point-to-point correspondences between the orthographic input lexicon and the output lexicon) and would also function as a general purpose system for translation from speech to writing. Two procedures for phoneme-grapheme conversion might be distinguished.

1. Marginal Associations. In this procedure elements on the dimensions of the phonological space are serially converted to elements on the equivalent dimension of the orthographic output space. Phonetically acceptable spellings of consonant and vowel groupings would be generated.

2. Point-to-Point Correspondences. Because of the alignment of the orthographic space with the phonological space, access to a point in phonological space followed by activation of a homologous point in orthographic space would result in production of an orthographically acceptable spelling of a syllable without the necessity for consideration of isolated vowels or consonants.

Either of these processes could be used to generate a plausible spelling of a non-word. Writing of words would be subject to numerous errors on account of the one-to-many mapping between phonology and orthography. In order that the system could become lexically informed it would be necessary to write orthographic *address modifications* into the phonological lexicon. Once this had been done, access to a point in phonological space would allow addressing of the appropriate point in orthographic space. Obviously, different modifications would be required for spellings of homophones, which would require distinct semantically selectable slots at the appropriate location in the phonological lexicon. In this theory, the orthographic output lexicon does not itself contain lexical information or "word images." The output lexicon is simply a device for generation, at an abstract level, of spelling codes. The lexical information is stored, as address modifications, in the phonological lexicon, and it is these that determine which point in the orthographic lexicon is accessed. It would be quite possible for a pooling or analogies procedure of the kind discussed in relation to reading to be involved in spelling production. This would require that access to a point in phonological space resulted in an expansion of influence along the x-, y- and z-dimensions of the lexicon, thus activating points for words of similar phonology. If address modifications written at these points were considered, and the corresponding points in the orthographic lexicon were activated, lexical influences on non-word spelling would be apparent.

One implication of the developmental theory is that failure to develop a proper orthographic input lexicon will result in a disturbance of spelling. This follows from the assumption that the orthographic output lexicon is a copy of the input lexicon. It is additionally possible that the copying process itself could fail, even though an adequate input lexicon had been established. Even if copying was successful, spelling competence would still require that a large number of address modifications should be written into the phonological lexicon. If this did not go ahead successfully, the result would be a tendency to produce phonetically acceptable misspellings on irregular words and regular words for which some component sounds admitted alternative spellings. Thus, a spelling impairment is expected in those cases of developmental dyslexia where an impairment of the orthographic input lexicon is implicated (phonological and morphemic dyslexias). Seymour and MacGregor (1984) considered the additional possibility that visual (analytic) dyslexia, which involves a disorder of analytic visual processing, might be associated with the good reader/poor speller pattern described by Frith (1980) on account of disruption of the copying or address modification processes, both of which might require focussed attention on individual graphemes during reading.

The end point of the developmental process discussed in this section may be summarised in the form of an information processing diagram. This is shown in Fig. 16.4, and has been reproduced from Seymour and MacGregor (1984). The model postulates four major processors (or modules) which are concerned respectively with: (1) visual analysis of print (the visual graphemic processor); (2) comprehension and expression of intentions (the semantic processor); (3) representation and production of speech (the phonological processor); and (4) representation and production of spelling and writing (the orthographic processor). The semantic and phonological systems incorporate bi-directional addressing procedures, and pre-date reading and spelling acquisition. With regard to word recognition, the model incorporates the *dual lexicon* assumption that derived from the developmental analysis, i.e., the existence of two recognition systems, one specialised for direct access to semantics (the logographic lexicon) and the other for access to phonology (the orthographic lexicon). Logographic recognition is based on visual features that may be unrelated to phonology. Orthographic recognition requires a pre-processed graphemic code in which letter identities, letter positions, and consonant and vowel groupings are specified. This is indicated in the diagram by distinct visual inputs to the two lexicons, consisting of visual features for the logographic lexicon, but of features converted to

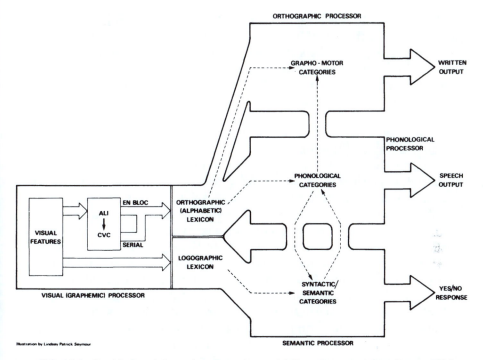

FIG. 16.4   Dual lexicon information processing model (from Seymour & MacGregor, 1984)

"abstract letter identities" (ALI) and thence to consonant-vowel-consonant (CVC) groupings for the orthographic lexicon. Strong evidence for the existence of these two types of early visual word-processing (one based on abstract letter identities and the other not) is provided by Howard in Chapter 2. Assumptions regarding information transfer within the visual processor are outlined in Seymour and MacGregor (1984), and will be discussed further in connection with the dyslexic sub-types.

DYSLEXIC SUB-TYPES

The combined developmental/information processing model provides a framework that may be used to identify and interpret the disordered reading processes of developmental dyslexics. This is done by setting up a structure of experimental task and factor manipulations that may be individually administered by means of a microprocessor, and that provide precise reaction time (RT) data in addition to error frequencies and classifications. An account of the procedure, and a listing of the tasks and factors is given by Seymour and MacGregor (1984).

The set of tasks was designed to analyse reading processes in teenage or adult developmental dyslexics. In particular, the aim was to test the efficiency of the processes of (1) access to phonology; and (2) access to semantics, and to assess the functioning of the visual (graphemic) processor. Access to phonology was tested in vocalisation of tasks in which a voice-switch was used to record vocal reaction times (VRTs). Lexical and semantic decision tasks were used to test access to semantics. Visual processor functions were tested by means of matching tasks, and by assessments of the effects of word length and format distortions.

Using this procedure, it was possible to formulate two types of description of each dyslexic subject. These may be referred to as: (1) a psycholinguistic description; and (2) a processing description. The *psycholinguistic description* specified the influence of lexical variables (word frequency, lexicality, syntactic class, concreteness of meaning, typicality and semantic relatedness, spelling-to-sound regularity, non-word homophony, orthographic regularity, orthographic complexity) on reaction time and error levels in different tasks, and provided the main basis for description of a dyslexic individual's word recognition system, and hence his assignment to a dyslexic sub-type. The *processing description* dealt with the effects of structural and procedural variables (word length, position of difference, format distortion) on reaction time. This provided an indication of degree and types of dysfunction in the visual processor, and thus allowed an assessment of the possibility that a visual processor disorder was responsible for defective development of a word recognition system. It will be proposed that in phonological dyslexia a visual processing disturbance is *not* implicated, but that in morphemic (surface) dyslexia a disturbance of wholistic visual processing may constitute a primary cause of the disorder.

A. Phonological Dyslexia

The term "phonological dyslexia" can be applied to cases for whom a difficulty with phonological assembly appears to be a major characteristic. This is indicated by a large discrepancy in performance on word and non-word reading tasks. To illustrate, Table 16.3 gives a summary of vocal reaction times (VRTs) and error percentages for high frequency words, low frequency words, and non-words for three developmentally dyslexic subjects: L.T., an 18 year-old student discussed by Seymour and MacGregor; S.B., a 13 year-old boy (IQ = 122; RA = 10 years; SA = 9–2 years); and J.B., a 12 year-old girl (IQ = 97; RA = 9–4; SA = 8–2). These three subjects all show large and significant differences between high frequency words and non-words both for reaction time and for error levels. The VRT differences between low frequency words and non-words are also significant in each

TABLE 16.3

Summary of Results for Reading of Words of High and Low Frequency and Non–Words by L.T., S.B., and J.B. (VRTs and standard deviations are given in milliseconds).

| | | Words | | Non–words |
		HF	LF	
L.T.	VRT	1247	1750	3858
	sd	1362	1719	2467
	E%	7.7	16.7	31.1
S.B.	VRT	1031	2008	3055
	sd	648	2093	3107
	E%	16.7	32.5	44.1
J.B.	VRT	1612	3685	5298
	sd	874	3706	3027
	E%	14.9	36.5	41.9

case, and the error differences are significant for L.T. and S.B., but not for J.B.

Inspection of the distributions of VRTs produced by these subjects demonstrates a clear and consistent pattern, which is shown in Fig. 16.5. High frequency words produce a distribution of fast responses. For low frequency words, the distribution is less peaked, and there is a larger tail of slow responses. The non-words distribution does not contain a preponderance of fast responses, but forms an approximately rectangular distribution extending over the range 1000–5000 ms and beyond. This collapsed appearance of the non-word distribution recurs from case to case, and seems almost to constitute a "signature" for phonological dyslexia. S.B.'s distributions are very similar to L.T.'s. In J.B.'s case, the distribution for low frequency words shows the same depression as the distribution for non-words.

The differentiation between word and non-word reading is also reflected in the reaction times for incorrect responses. Overall, VRTs for error responses to words were faster than error responses to non-words for L.T., but not for S.B. and J.B. However, a contrast between word responses to word targets and non-word responses to non-word targets shows an advantage for the word→word case, detailed in Table 16.4. These differences are significant in each case. Temple and Marshall (1983) reported that their subject showed a tendency toward lexicalisation in error responses (i.e., a bias towards production of words). Contingency tables relating target and

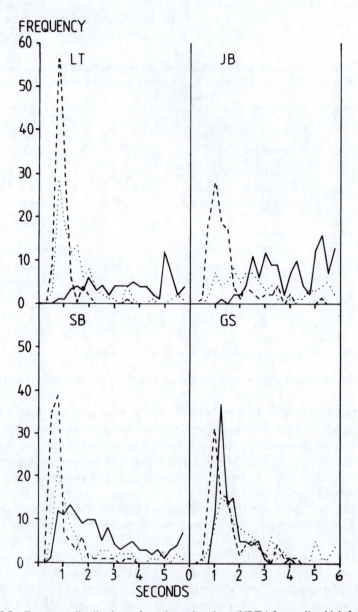

FIG. 16.5 Frequency distributions of vocal reaction times (VRTs) for reading high frequency words (‑‑‑‑), low frequency words (.....), and non-words (———) by the phonological dyslexics L.T., S.B. and J.B. and the morphemic dyslexic, G.S. Data are plotted in 250 ms intervals.

TABLE 16.4
Latencies of Incorrect Word Responses to Words
and Non-Word Responses to Non-Words for
L.T., S.B. and J.B. (in Milliseconds)

	Word→Word	Non-word→Non-word
L.T.	1879	5620
S.B.	1971	4124
J.B.	5559	7114

response lexicality are given in Table 16.5. L.T. and S.B. do not show a lexicalising bias, but rather a tendency for error responses to be from the same category as the target. This is significant by a chi-square test. The same tendency is evident in J.B., but is offset by a bias toward word responses. These results were obtained from five experiments, using two word lists, one non-word list, one mixed list, and one non-word list incorporating non-word homophones. It is evident from the table that non-word responses are frequently produced by these subjects.

An alternative way of examining the possibility of a lexical involvement in non-word reading is to consider (1) the effects of homophony on non-word reading; and (2) whether or not an advantage in VRT is obtained when a word is produced as an error response to a non-word. Results relevant to these questions are shown in Table 16.6. The homophone results are taken from one experiment in which homophones and non-homophones were contrasted. The word and non-word error results come from each subject's full error set. The homophony effect is significant for reaction time for L.T. and J.B., and for error rate for S.B. and J.B. Word errors do not differ from non-word errors for L.T. or J.B., but there is a significant effect for S.B. These non-word→word errors have a slower latency than word→word errors for L.T. and S.B. but not for J.B. Thus, each subject gains some

TABLE 16.5
Relationship Between Target Lexicality and Response Lexicality for
Errors by L.T., S.B. and J.B.

		L.T.		S.B.		J.B.	
Response		W	NW	W	NW	W	NW
Target	W	28	7	42	27	56	15
	NW	24	48	40	64	55	44

TABLE 16.6

Effects of Non–Word Homophony on VRT and Error Rate, and VRTs for
Incorrect Word and Non–Word Responses to Non–Words for L.T., S.B.
and J.B. (VRTs in Milliseconds)

	L.T.	*S.B.*	*J.B.*
Homophone	2832	2413	4205
E%	23.3	28.3	30
Non-homophone	4082	2185	6941
E%	37.3	48.3	48.3
Word response	4204	2786	6526
NW response	5620	4124	7114

advantage in non-word reading from a relation of homophony between
target and response. Non-word→word errors appear not to involve the same
process as word→word errors for L.T., and lexicalisation of the response
does not confer an advantage. For S.B., word responses to non-words do
give some advantage, though a differentiation relative to word→word
responses is maintained.

Errors almost invariably involved production of a response that was
structurally related to the target. L.T. never refused a response, S.B. refused
on three irregular verbs (aisle, ought, muscle), and J.B. on one regular word
(lid). Structural correspondence was quantified by analysing the target and
response into vowel and consonant letter groups, and making a cluster by
cluster comparison, scoring 1 for a match, 0.5 for a partial match, and 0 for a
mismatch. Examples, taken from S.B.'s error corpus, are shown in Table
16.7. Similarity was expressed by taking the total match score as a percentage
of the number of vowel and consonant clusters located in the larger of the
two arrays. The arrays were considered to be structurally similar if the match

TABLE 16.7

Examples of Cluster by Cluster Assessment of Similarity Between Targets
and Error Responses

Flaunt --- *"fault"*			*Frosk* --- *"forisk"*			*Sheam* --- *scream*		
FL	F	.5	FR	F	.5	SH	SCR	.5
AU	AU	1.0	0	0	1.0	EA	EA	1.0
NT	LT	.5	*	R	—	M	M	1.0
			*	I	—			
			SK	SK	1.0			
Score:		66%		50%			83%	

TABLE 16.8
Percentage of Matching (+), Partially Matching (?), and Mismatching
(−) Clusters in Error Corpora of L.T., and J.B.

	L.T.			S.B.			J.B.		
	+	?	−	+	?	−	+	?	−
Vowels									
Simple	64	16	18	54	13	32	47	17	35
Complex	32	60	7	16	74	9	22	62	15
Consonants									
Simple	63	14	21	74	16	8	62	8	28
Complex	53	42	4	47	45	6	55	31	13

score equalled or exceeded 50%. On this criterion, the percentages of structurally similar errors were: 91% for L.T., 86% for S.B., and 89% for J.B.

The cluster analysis procedure made it possible to consider which fragments of the words and non-words producing errors were most likely to be mis-read. Clusters were categorised as vowels or consonants, and as simple (containing only one grapheme) or complex (containing more than one grapheme). The percentages of match, partial match, and mismatch correspondences obtained for each type of cluster were calculated. The results for the three subjects are given in Table 16.8. Chi-square tests on the frequencies of observations in each category indicated that the three subjects were significantly affected by complexity for both vowels and consonants. All three subjects showed better reading of complex consonants than of complex vowels. For S.B. and J.B. there is also a difference between simple vowels and consonants. Thus, errors are generally in structural correspondence with the target, and misreadings are likely to occur on complex grapheme structures, especially vowels.

Error responses to word targets were also examined in order to determine whether the errors fell into the categories observed in cases of acquired dyslexia. This classification, which was subordinate to the judgement of structural similarity, identified three sub-classes: (1) semantic errors, in which the response was meaningfully associated with the target; (2) derivational errors, in which target and response shared the same stem; and (3) phonetic errors, in which the response was a reasonably exact phonetic rendering of the target. The frequencies of errors falling into these three categories are given in Table 16.9.

L.T.'s two possible semantic errors (rhyme→"rhythm," quest→"question") may simply be visual errors. The derivational errors are reasonably clear, and include variety→"vary," crept→"creep," hunger→"hungry,"

TABLE 16.9

Frequencies of Semantic, Derivational and Phonetic
Regularisation Errors by L.T., S.B. and J.B.

	Semantic	Derivational	Phonetic
L.T.	2	4	1
S.B.	0	3	2
J.B.	0	7	1

and beauty→"beautiful" for L.T.; these→"this," know→"known," and eighth→"eighty" for S.B.; and heroism→"hero," loyalty→"loyal," greed →"greedy," these→"those," variety→"vary," drunk→"drink," and won→ "win" for J.B. Possible phonetic errors were ought→"out" by L.T., isle→ "is-le" by J.B., and heir→"hair," and ache→"arch" by S.B. These classifiable errors form a small proportion of the total, but confirm Temple and Marshall's observation that phonological dyslexics tend to make some derivational errors.

The experiments also provide an indication of the influence of the psycholinguistic factors on the latency and accuracy of reading. The variables of interest are: (1) spelling-to-sound regularity, which is not expected to influence the reading of phonological dyslexics; (2) abstract/concrete meaning; and (3) form class (function versus content), which are expected to produce effects. The results given in Table 16.10 indicate that regularity was not an important variable for these subjects. No effects on error rates or reaction times were significant, except for S.B.'s error rate on low frequency words. Nonetheless, this indicates that a regularity effect may be found in an individual who would, on other criteria, be classified as a phonological dyslexic. The concreteness dimension was effective in that: (1) L.T. had some very slow responses to low frequency abstract words; (2) S.B. showed reaction time delays for both high and low frequency abstract words; and (3) J.B. showed an effect on error rate for high and low frequency words, and a reaction time effect for low frequency words. The function/content dimension was not effective for S.B. or J.B., but was associated with a significant reaction time delay for L.T.

These results form the basis of a *psycholinguistic description* of developmental phonological dyslexia: (1) non-words are read less accurately than words, and are associated with a radically different (rectangular) reaction time distribution; (2) responses to non-words may be words or neologisms, and are generally structurally related to the target. Mis-readings cluster on the complex letter structures, especially the vowels. If the non-word is a homophone of a known word this confers some advantage. (3) Word reading, though markedly more efficient than non-word reading, is impaired both with regard to accuracy and response time. Responses are structurally

TABLE 16.10
Reaction Times (ms) and Error Rates for Vocalisation of High and Low
Frequency Words by L.T., S.B. and J.B., with Variations in
Spelling–to–Sound Regularity, Concreteness, and Form Class

	L.T.		S.B.		J.B.	
	HF	LF	HF	LF	HF	LF
Regular	1014	1494	976	2093	1586	2297
E%	10.7	28.6	17.9	14.3	10.7	35.7
Irregular	928	1625	1063	2314	1542	3287
E%	21.4	25	14.3	46.4	14.3	28.6
Concrete	1032	1274	823	1040	1511	3226
E%	0	4.8	14.3	28.6	4.8	28.6
Abstract	1149	2285	1239	2062	1834	8630
E%	9.5	4.8	23.8	33.3	28.6	57.1
Function	1799		955		1644	
E%	2.4		9.5		11.9	
Content	1088		1018		1650	
E%	4.8		19.1		16.7	

related to the target, and may be words or non-words. Some derivational errors occur. Concrete/abstract meaning may affect performance, especially for lower frequency words. An effect on function word reading may occasionally be observed.

Seymour and MacGregor argued that this pattern was consistent with a two process model in which reading was routed preferentially via the logographic-semantic system in Fig. 16.4, but with support from a slow and inefficient grapheme-phoneme translation channel. Logographic recognition is assumed to be somewhat imprecise, giving rise to visual and derivational paralexias. Semantic mediation of response retrieval is suggested by the occurrence of effects of abstractness of meaning, and the function word effect shown by L.T. According to the two-process account, logographic-semantic processing may be exclusively used in semantic access tasks. These tasks are performed relatively efficiently, and processing appears to be wholistic (i.e., relatively unaffected by variations in word length). Effects, on both accuracy and reaction time, of zigzag or vertical distortion of words, are either absent or very slight. The one exception to this pattern, shown in the lexical decision data for L.T. reported by Seymour and MacGregor, is that negative responses to regular non-words are made slowly, and with evidence of a large influence of word length. This suggests that the logographic-semantic route does not incorporate procedures for deciding whether or not an unfamiliar but orthographically well-structured letter array is a word. The large length effect, which is illustrated in Fig. 16.6, could then reflect an attempt to process the non-word through the defective grapheme-phoneme channel, so that the decision could be based on a phonological code. A suggestion that dual (logographic and grapheme-phoneme) processing is involved in phonological access is made by differences in word length effects between the decision and vocalisation tasks. Length effects tend to be minimal or absent in the decision tasks but larger, and linearly related to word length, in vocalisation tasks. L.T.'s data from experiments involving format distortions (zigzag or vertical presentation) may be taken as an illustration of this point. In the lexical and semantic decision tasks length and format effects were slight. This implies a form of wholistic recognition which is not disrupted by spatial distortion (i.e., is not ideographic). In the word vocalisation task, VRT increased at a rate of more than 200 ms/letter for normal and vertical displays, and at over 400 ms/letter for zigzag displays. The interpretation proposed is that some serial grapheme-phoneme processing is often needed to assist logographic-semantic access to phonology, and it is this process which introduces the length effect.

Developmentally, the phonological dyslexic pattern can be interpreted as reflecting the long-term effects of a disruption of progress at the alphabetic

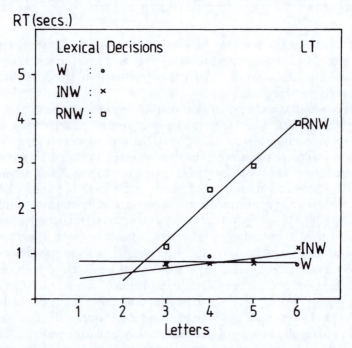

FIG. 16.6   Yes and no reaction times (ms) plotted as a function of word or non-word length from a lexical decision task by subject L.T. Data are shown for words, illegal non-words and regular non-words.

and orthographic stages postulated previously. This results in a reliance on logographic semantic reading. Although some form of alphabetic (grapheme-phoneme) processing is established, perhaps as a consequence of phonics-oriented remedial instruction, an orthographic lexicon has not been constructed as an efficient general purpose procedure for accessing phonology. The experiments do not provide evidence of a visual processing disturbance that could give an explanation for the failure to establish an orthographic lexicon. A more central origin, located in the phonological processor, is probably indicated. Seymour and MacGregor suggested that this might be a matter of categorisation of sub-syllabic speech elements, or of working memory or associative functions. Temple and Marshall discuss some phonological tasks which might be used to verify this hypothesis. Also particularly relevant here are observations provided by Denes, Balliello, Volterra, and Pellegrini, in Chapter 15. They provide some data describing the levels of spelling and silent reading performance that can be attained when phonological processing ability is almost completely absent in a child.

B. Morphemic Dyslexia

Morphemic dyslexia will be discussed only briefly, mainly with the objective of pointing out some contrasts with phonological dyslexia. The position adopted by Seymour and MacGregor was that morphemic dyslexia derived from a primary disturbance of the *wholistic* function of the visual (graphemic) processor. This was considered to impair the development of a logographic lexicon and of an orthographic lexicon by favouring serial letter-by-letter processing at the expense of whole words or multi-letter segments. Developmentally, this would involve disruption throughout the logographic stage, and at the transition from alphabetic to orthographic reading. Seymour and MacGregor proposed a single process account of morphemic dyslexia in which access to phonology and semantics was mediated by an *alphabetic lexicon*.

This account predicts an impairment of both word and non-word reading, but not the word/non-word differences that were found in the cases of phonological dyslexia. These contrasts are given in Table 16.11 for G.S., the subject discussed by Seymour and MacGregor; S.M., a 13 year-old boy (IQ = 105; RA = 11–2; SA = 9–6); and L.H., an 11 year-old girl of low general intelligence (IQ = 74, RA = 8–10, SA = 8–5). In the cases of G.S. and L.H. the error rates for non-words do not differ from the rates for high frequency words, and are significantly better than the rates for low frequency words. For S.M., there is no difference between low frequency words and non-words. VRTs for all three subjects are similar for low frequency words and non-words. In addition, VRT distributions for non-words are similar in shape to the distribution for words. This is shown for G.S. in Fig. 16.5. Thus,

TABLE 16.11
VRTs (ms) and Error Rates for Vocalisation of Words and Non-Words by
G.S., S.M. and L.H.

		Words		Non–words
		HF	LF	
G.S.	VRT	1695	2562	2292
	sd	782	1817	1063
	E%	9.5	24.6	13.1
S.M.	VRT	1490	1906	2023
	sd	775	975	819
	E%	5.9	23.8	27.1
L.H.	VRT	2205	2761	2566
	sd	2206	2093	1411
	E%	21.4	44.9	25.4

these subjects do not show the clear word/non-word discrepancies that are the characteristic feature of phonological dyslexia.

A second point of differentiation concerns the relative impact of spelling-to-sound regularity and semantic/syntactic variables on reading accuracy and latency. The relevant results are displayed in Table 16.12 and indicate that all three subjects showed large and significant effects of regularity on error rate for low frequency words. For L.H., the effect was also significant for high frequency words. S.M. has a significant effect on VRT for low frequency words. The form class variation had no influence on VRT or accuracy for any of the subjects. The concrete-abstract dimension had a small effect on error rate for G.S., and an effect on VRT for L.H., both limited to high frequency words.

The three morphemic dyslexics appear similar to the phonological dyslex-ics in general aspects of their errors; (1) word and non-word responses were about equally frequent for word and non-word targets for S.M. and L.H., though G.S. showed a tendency for response lexicality to vary with target lexicality; (2) the majority of errors were structurally close to the target, with scores of 50% or greater on 94% of items for G.S., 88% of items for S.M., and 86% for L.H. Refusals to respond did not occur. Mis-readings again clustered on the complex grapheme-clusters, especially vowels. However, G.S. and L.H. did not show the latency difference between word→word and non-word→non-word errors that was characteristic of the phonological dyslexics. What is more evident is a tendency for non-word responses to words to appear particularly slow, as shown in Table 16.13. These effects were significant in each case, and were also shown by subject S.E., a

TABLE 16.12
VRTs (ms) Error Rates for Vocalisation of High and Low Frequency
Words Varying in Regularity, Concreteness of Meaning and Form Class
by G.S., S.M. and L.H.

	G.S.		S.M.		L.H.	
	HF	LF	HF	LF	HF	LF
Regular	1539	2542	1402	1919	2025	2206
E%	0	10.7	3.6	7.1	10.7	28.8
Irregular	1744	2043	1553	2813	3053	2212
E%	7.1	67.9	14.3	53.6	35.7	67.9
Concrete	1902	3057	1304	1584	1835	3683
E%	0	0	0	9.5	14.3	38.1
Abstract	1794	3457	1684	1920	3545	4278
E%	19.1	9.5	9.5	28.5	38.1	38.1
Function	1861		1444		2555	
E%	16.7		4.8		16.7	
Content	1853		1479		2552	
E%	9.5		4.8		26.2	

morphemic/phonological dyslexic described by Seymour and MacGregor. This suggests that non-word responses may occur as a last resort after lexical search has failed. G.S. showed an effect of homophony in non-word reading on both errors and VRT, but S.M. and L.H. did not.

A characteristic feature of morphemic (surface) dyslexia is the production of regularisation errors. Frequencies of semantic, derivational, and regularisation errors have been tabulated in Table 16.14. S.M.'s semantic error (debt→"debit") may well be a visual error. The derivational errors were eight→"eighth" for G.S., loyalty→"loyally" and eight→"eighth" for S.M., and several→"severally" and sign→"signer" for L.H. Thus, occasional derivational errors may occur, although these are clearly outnumbered by phonetic regularisation errors. Examples are: canoe→"kano" (/kænoɷ/),

TABLE 16.13
Mean VRTs (ms) for Word and Non-Word Error Responses to
Word Targets by G.S., S.M. and L.H.

	G.S.	S.M.	L.H.
Word → word	3187	2113	3093
Word → non-word	6336	4555	5331

TABLE 16.14
Frequencies of Semantic, Derivational and Phonetic
Regularisation Errors for G.S., S.M. and L.H.

	Semantic	Derivational	Phonetic
G.S.	0	1	10
S.M.	1	2	12
L.H.	0	2	23

plough→"plo" (/ploɷ/) and muscle→"muskel" (/mʌskɛl/") for G.S.; heir →"hair," corps→"corpse," bomb→"boom," ache→"ach" (/ætʃ/) for S.M.; and heir→"here," ski→"sky," sew→"sue," tongue→"tong," anger→ "anjer" (/aendzə:/), blood→"blude" (/blu:d/) for L.H.

The morphemic impairment shown by these subjects extends to performance on lexical and semantic decision tasks where reaction times are slow and dispersed and discrimination between low frequency words and nonwords is poor. If the relationship between reaction time and word length is calculated it is found that processing is consistently slow and serial with a rate in excess of 200 ms/letter. This is illustrated for vocalisation of high and low frequency words and non-words in Fig. 16.7. The same linear relationship between RT and number of letters is found when data for semantic decisions and lexical decisions are plotted. In addition, in a comparison task when"different" displays differ in only one position, the No RT increases as a slow linear function of the left-to-right position of the difference. Comparable evidence for slow serial processing was presented for the subjects G.S. and S.E. by Seymour and MacGregor. L.H. has extremely slow processing rates, averaging 400–500 ms/letter.

It seems, therefore, that morphemic dyslexics may be differentiated from phonological dyslexics with respect to visual processor functions. Phonological dyslexics preferentially adopt a wholistic mode (supported by some serial processing in vocalisation tasks), whereas morphemic dyslexics appear to be restricted to serial letter-by-letter processing in vocalisation and decision tasks. Format distortion, which tends to force normal readers to switch from wholistic to analytic processing, generally does not alter the rate of processing in a morphemic dyslexic (since processing is already in a serial mode). It is only in cases of visual analytic dyslexia, such as the subject R.O. described by Seymour and MacGregor, that a major alteration in processing rate is produced by the imposition of distortion. Thus, in a semantic decision task, the three types produce results of the kind shown in idealised form in Fig. 16.8. On the basis of such findings, Seymour and MacGregor proposed that disturbed wholistic processing was a primary cause of impairment in morphemic dyslexia, whereas defective analytic processing was primary in visual (analytic) dyslexia.

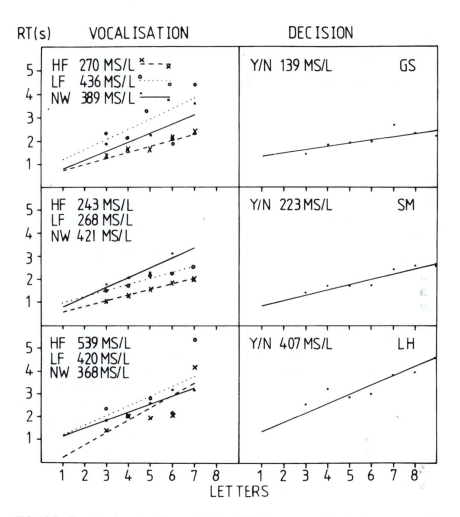

FIG. 16.7 Reaction times (ms) for vocalisation of high frequency words, low frequency words and non-words, and for yes/no decisions about category membership for G.S., S.M. and L.H., plotted as a function of word length. Slopes of lines of best fit are shown in the panels.

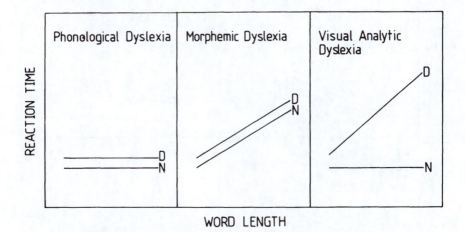

FIG. 16.8   Idealised data to illustrate effects of word length and format distortion on R.T. for different dyslexic sub-types. (N = normal, D = distorted.)

Morphemic dyslexia, like phonological dyslexia, involves a disruption of development of an orthographic lexicon, although a moderately efficient alphabetic organisation may be achieved. In a single process interpretation it is assumed that access to both semantics and phonology is mediated by an alphabetic lexicon operating on the basis of serial recognition of individual graphemes. This interpretation is consistent with (1) a lack of differentiation between words and non-words; (2) slow processing in semantic and vocalisation tasks; and (3) the evidence for serial letter-by-letter processing. In this account, the wholistic impairment is assumed to have blocked the development of a logographic lexicon. This leaves open the question of how the address modifications necessary for pronunciation of words of non-standard spelling-to-sound association are established. It is evident that this lexicalisation is possible, since high frequency words that are irregular are generally correctly read. Seymour and MacGregor proposed that lexical addresses might be written, with difficulty, into an alphabetic lexicon. The alternative possibility is that these associations are mediated by a rudimentary logographic lexicon (i.e., a dual process interpretation).

SPELLING AND WRITING

In the section on reading and spelling development it was argued that a *developmental* dependency exists between the establishment of an effective spelling production system (orthographic output lexicon) and the prior achievement of an efficient orthographic input lexicon. On these grounds, it would be anticipated that phonological and morphemic dyslexics should also be dysgraphic, as both groups are characterised by a failure to develop an orthographically organised recognition system. However, the types should differ in the degree to which the spelling output system incorporates regularities of sound-letter association. In phonological dyslexia, a primary disturbance of phonemic segmentation and manipulation would be expected adversely to affect the establishment of alphabetic spelling as well as alphabetic reading. In morphemic dyslexia, by contrast, alphabetic phoneme-grapheme associations should be quite successfully established. What would be lacking would be the higher order correspondences relating speech to vowel or consonant clusters and syllabic or sub-syllabic letter groupings. It can be argued that an alphabetic organisation is inefficient as a general purpose representation of the relationships between phonology and orthography, and thus provides a framework that is less useful than an orthographic organisation for storage of word-specific information. From this it follows that morphemic dyslexics will have difficulty in writing words of non-standard sound-spelling structure (irregular words), although, at an alphabetic (phoneme-grapheme) level their mis-spellings may be phonetically well-formed.

The tendency to produce phonetically accurate efforts is not expected to be strong in cases of phonological dyslexia on account of the absence of an adequate alphabetic base of phoneme-grapheme associations. It seems likely that a phonological dyslexic will be forced to resort to a *logographic* mode of spelling organisation, that is the formation of a set of associations between whole word forms in the phonological lexicon and grapheme lists in the orthographic output lexicon. In a system of this kind, spelling regularity should not be a factor affecting performance, and errors might be expected to be phonetically inaccurate, to include orthographic illegalities, and, on occasion, to give evidence of a partial knowledge of the letters making up a word. If logographic spelling is, to some degree, a copy of logographic reading, then it seems possible that spelling knowledge will be focussed on the word stems, and that the derivational errors observed in reading may also occur in spelling.

In order to investigate these issues, an analysis was carried out on spelling errors produced when writing to dictation isolated words and non-words from various lists. The analysis included an assessment of structural correspondence, based on the same cluster by cluster matching procedure as was used for reading errors, and a classification of each error as: phonetically accurate/inaccurate, legal/illegal orthography, containing evidence of partial lexical knowledge, derivationally or semantically related to the target, and as involving or not involving a homophone confusion.

Two of the lists, one containing non-words of varying length, and the other words that varied in frequency, regularity, and length, were presented under conditions that allowed precise timing of writing functions. The items were written to dictation on the surface of an Apple graphics tablet interfaced with the computer. Vocal presentation of the target by the experimenter triggered a timing routine that measured the delay before first contact of the pen with the tablet and thereafter recorded the values of successive intervals in which the pen was pressed down or lifted. The position of the pen was sampled at 13 ms intervals, and this allowed for a measurement of the distance traversed during writing, and the speed of pen movement.

A. Phonological Dysgraphia

Table 16.15 shows the proportions of errors categorised as being phonetically accurate or inaccurate for the phonologically dyslexic subjects, L.T., J.B. and S.B. It can be seen that the results for L.T. and J.B. are in line with expectation, as a substantial majority of errors may be classified as being phonetically inaccurate. However, this is not true of S.B., whose phonetic and non-phonetic errors are in approximately equal proportions. It will be recalled that S.B. was also differentiated from L.T. and J.B. by showing a regularity effect on accuracy of reading words of lower frequency (see Table 16.10). One possibility is that S.B. has received more effective phonics-oriented instruction than L.T. or J.B., and that this has resulted in the establishment of a better alphabetic basis for spelling, and a readiness to attempt to use an alphabetic strategy when reading unknown words.

The spelling errors were also analysed to assess the contrast between regular and irregular words and between words and non-words. A phonological disturbance, combined with a logographically-based spelling system, should result in better spelling of words than non-words, and in an absence of regularity effects. The relevant results for the three subjects have been summarised in Table 16.16. This table shows the error levels for high

TABLE 16.15

Frequencies of Errors in Spelling Words to Dictation Classified as
Phonetically Accurate or Inaccurate for L.T., S.B. and J.B.

		L.T.	S.B.	J.B.
Phonetically accurate	N	36	85	34
	Percent	28.57	52.47	16.04
Phonetically inaccurate	N	90	77	178
	Percent	71.43	47.53	83.96
Total		126	162	212

TABLE 16.16
Percentages of Errors in Writing Regular and Irregular Words of High
and Low Frequency and Non-Words to Dictation by L.T., S.B. and J.B.

	High frequency words			Low frequency words			Non-words
	Regular	Irregular	All	Regular	Irregular	All	
L.T.	5.26	30	17.9	20	35	27.5	40
S.B.	5	20	12.5	40	75	57.5	37.5
J.B.	25	35	30	39	63	51.4	71.8

frequency words, low frequency words, and non-words. L.T. and J.B. both had significantly higher error rates on non-words than on high or low frequency words, but this was not true of S.B., who had an elevated error rate on low frequency words. Regularity did not affect J.B.'s performance but influenced error rates on high frequency words for L.T., and on low frequency words for S.B.

Errors in writing words to dictation were also classified on the basis of presence or absence of a semantic/syntactic relation between target and response, and the occurrence of orthographic illegalities and demonstrations of partial lexical knowledge. The frequencies of these types of error have been summarised in Table 16.17. J.B.'s data included some semantic paragraphias, "freeze"→fresh, "wing"→wind, "rag"→rug, "life"→live, "edge"→ echo, though the responses are structurally fairly similar to the targets and may represent phonological rather than semantic confusions. Derivational errors occurred with appreciable frequencies in the results of L.T. and J.B., but not of S.B. These included "various"→varies, "resource"→source, "prematurely"→premiture, for L.T.; and "entered"→entry, "pay"→paid, "come"→came, "liquid"→liquer, and "proposal"→porposely, for J.B. All three subjects made some errors which included orthographically illegal

TABLE 16.17
Frequencies of Semantic and Derivational Errors, and of Errors
Containing Orthographic Illegalities or Giving Evidence of Partial Lexical
Knowledge in Spelling to Dictation by L.T., S.B. and J.B.

	Semantic	Derivational	Orthographically illegal	Partial lexical knowledge
L.T.	0	14	4	14
S.B.	1	1	5	13
J.B.	5	14	4	7

sequences, e.g., "signature"→sengnchr and "anxious"→annouous, for L.T.; "capacity"→dpastil, "prevailing"→prvaling, and "protection"→prtesion, for J.B.; and "persecution"→persiqution, for S.B. Errors were coded as demonstrating partial lexical knowledge if they contained phonetically implausible letters deriving from the correct spelling of the word, e.g., "colonel"→coleonel, "people"→pepeol, "hymn"→hynm, for L.T.; "beauty"→beauit, "laugh"→launge, for J.B.; and "yacht"→yath, "answer"-→anweser, "tongue"→tounge, and "onion"→oinon, for S.B.

The results for L.T. and J.B. suggest that phonological dyslexia may be associated with a parallel spelling impairment, reflected by inaccuracies in non-word writing, the production of phonetically poorly formed errors, derivational paragraphias, illegal letter sequences, and indications of incomplete lexical storage. S.B. shows large effects of lexicality on reaction time in both reading and spelling, but his spelling is phonetically fairly well-formed, and he does not have a high error rate on non-word writing or a tendency to produce derivational errors, and shows effects of regularity in both reading and writing lower frequency words. It seems likely that S.B. is a "taught dyslexic" in the sense described by Frith (1985), that is a phonological dyslexic who has responded to phonics-oriented remedial instruction, and who consequently shows some "surface dyslexic" features.

B. Morphemic Dysgraphia

The spelling errors and writing of the three morphemic dyslexics, G.S., S.M. and L.H. were analysed in a similar way. It was anticipated that these subjects should produce phonetically well-formed errors, and that they should be affected by irregularity of spelling more strongly than by lexicality. The results for the assessment of phonetic accuracy, summarised in Table 16.18, are in line with expectation for G.S. and S.M. For both subjects, over 70% of errors in word writing can be classed as being phonetically well-

TABLE 16.18
Frequencies of Errors in Spelling Words to Dictation Classified as
Phonetically Accurate or Inaccurate for G.S., S.M. and L.H.

		G.S.	S.M.	L.H.
Phonetically accurate	N	154	95	103
	Percent	71.6	71.4	44.8
Phonetically inaccurate	N	61	38	127
	Percent	28.4	28.6	55.2
Total		215	133	230

TABLE 16.19
Percentages of Errors in Writing Regular and Irregular Words of High
and Low Frequency and Non-Words to Dictation by G.S., S.M. and L.H.

	High frequency words			Low frequency words			Non–words
	Regular	Irregular	All	Regular	Irregular	All	
G.S.	5	35	20	26.3	85	55.7	30.8
S.M.	5	45	25	40	65	52.5	41.03
L.H.	15	42	28.5	45	80	62.5	43.6

formed, and this pattern is in direct contrast with the results for L.T. and J.B. shown in Table 16.15. L.H. does not show a preponderance of phonetically correct errors. As was noted earlier, this girl has quite a low general intelligence level and may be disadvantaged in other respects. These factors may have contributed to a lower level of alphabetic learning than is evident in the other subjects.

Table 16.19 shows the effects of lexicality and regularity on error frequencies for the three subjects. All three show a pattern in which error rates on low frequency words are higher than on non-words. They also show very large effects of spelling regularity, especially with lower frequency words, few of which are spelled correctly.

As was noted in the discussion of reading processes, the observation that a morphemic dyslexic is able to deal successfully with irregular words of higher frequency implies that some lexicalisation of the reading and spelling systems is possible. This could be achieved within an alphabetic lexicon by modification of addresses, or by the establishment of a limited number of logographic (word-specific) associations. Either of these accounts could allow that morphemic dyslexics might produce some errors which appeared indicative of partial lexical knowledge. Errors containing orthographic illegalities would also be expected on account of the absence of a well-formed orthographic input lexicon to serve as a model. On the other hand, if derivational errors are a feature of a logographically-based process, these should not occur unless word-specific knowledge in morphemic dyslexia is based on a logographic system.

Table 16.20 reports frequencies of errors of these types for the three subjects. S.M. and L.H. produced no semantic or derivational errors, but both made an appreciable number of errors which are suggestive of partial lexical knowledge. These included: "onion"→onine, "hymn"→hym, "monkey"→monky, "laugh"→laght, "hawk"→hack, "plough"→plougt, and "machine"→michien for L.H.; and "cough"→coulf, "daughter"→doughter, "listen"→liston, "laugh"→laught, "answer"→answer, for S.M. S.M.'s

TABLE 16.20

Frequencies of Semantic and Derivational Errors, and of Errors
Containing Orthographic Illegalities or Giving Evidence of Partial Lexical
Knowledge by G.S., S.M. and L.H.

	Semantic	Derivational	Orthographically illegal	Partial lexical knowledge
G.S.	0	3	1	6
S.M.	0	0	5	11
L.H.	0	0	12	16

illegalities mainly involved confusion over the use of "qu-", which was
written either without the "u" or as "qw," but also included "colonel"→
curnl, and "genuine"→jueniuin. L.H.'s illegalities reflected a lack of orthographic knowledge, e.g., "quartz"→cwots, "affixed"→aficst, "encamped"
→incampt, as well as use of partial lexical information, as in "laugh"
→laghf. G.S. was slightly different, in that his spellings generally did not
contain illegalities, although occasional derivational errors were made
("aunt"→antie, "contextual"→contexture, "bananas"→banana). He also
made errors showing partial lexical knowledge, "worry"→wory, "laugh"→
laufe, "tongue"→tong, "monkey"→monky.

This analysis illustrates the difficulty of discriminating dyslexic types
simply on the basis of error classifications or word class effects. Morphemic
dyslexics cannot be distinguished from phonological dyslexics on the basis of
liability to produce orthographically illegal letter sequences or tendency to
produce errors which are indicative of partial lexical knowledge. Production
of derivational errors distinguishes L.T. and J.B. from S.M. and L.H., but
not S.B. from G.S. Phonetic accuracy of misspelling differentiates L.T. and
J.B. from G.S. and S.M., but not S.B. from L.H. The lexicality and regularity
effects appear to be the strongest basis for discrimination, but S.B. remains
out of line, given that his error distribution on these dimensions resembles
the morphemic pattern rather than the phonological pattern.

C. Writing Functions

Another possible basis of discrimination is given by the processing measures
of writing production. These include the time to initiate writing (the start
RT), the speed of pen movement during contact with the tablet surface, and
the average duration of pauses during production. The factor of regularity
exerted only slight and inconsistent effects on these measures. Lexicality had
much more consistent and stronger effects. All six subjects were significantly
slower to initiate non-word writing than word writing. These effects,

TABLE 16.21

Start RT (ms), Pen Speeds (mm/s) and Mean Pause Duration (ms) in Writing to Dictation High and Low Frequency Words and Non-Words by the Phonological Dyslexic Subjects, L.T., S.B. and J.B., and the Morphemic Dyslexic Subjects, G.S., S.M. and L.H.

	High frequency words			Low frequency			Non-words		
	Start RT (ms)	Pen speed (mm/s)	Mean pause (ms)	Start RT (ms)	Pen speed (mm/s)	Mean pause (ms)	Start RT (ms)	Pen speed (mm/m)	Mean pause (ms)
L.T.	1218	16	434	1500	16	499	2292	15	537
S.B.	932	16	263	1114	15	259	2417	10	415
J.B.	2140	13	476	2135	11	508	2824	10	826
G.S.	924	11	—	987	9	—	1747	11	—
S.M.	686	17	250	686	16	258	921	18	241
L.H.	842	17	287	905	16	275	1135	18	225

summarised in Table 16.21, were relatively larger for L.T., J.B., S.B. and G.S. than for S.M. and L.H. G.S. and S.M. did not show effects of lexicality on pause time during writing, and the effect was reversed in the case of L.H. J.B. and S.B., on the other hand, showed a significant increase in mean pause duration of 336 ms for J.B. and 154 ms for S.B. There was also a significant effect of 103 ms for the comparison between high frequency words and non-words in L.T.'s data. An analogous result holds for speed of pen movement. The phonological dyslexics, L.T., J.B. and S.B., all showed a reduction in pen speed when writing non-words, amounting to 1 mm/s for L.T., 2 mm/s for J.B., and 5 mm/s for S.B. The effects were in the reverse direction for the morphemic dyslexics, G.S., S.M. and L.H., involving an increase of speed in non-word writing of 1–2 mm/s.

These comparisons are somewhat complicated by differences in writing competence that cut across the sub-type divisions. S.B. and S.M. were both quite rapid and efficient writers, producing legible, well-formed script, with writing speeds of 15 mm/s and 16mm/s respectively, and an average letter size of 7 mm/letter and 6 mm/letter. A plot of their start RTs, accumulated contact time, and accumulated pause time against the number of letters written is shown in Fig. 16.9. This illustrates well the enhanced effects of lexicality on the writing processes of the phonological dyslexic, S.B. The other subjects all appeared to be to some degree dysgraphic at the level of response execution. G.S. wrote a large, connected well-formed script very slowly, with an average speed of 10 mm/s, and an average letter size of 17 mm/letter. L.T. and J.B. both produced rather poorly-formed writing, at

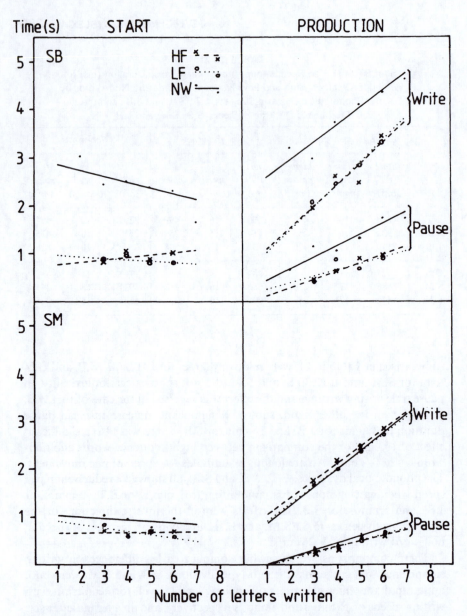

FIG. 16.9 Start RTs, accumulated contact time, and accumulated pause time for writing to dictation of high frequency words, low frequency words, and non-words, by S.B. and S.M., plotted as a function of the number of letters written.

speeds of 16 mm/s and 12 mm/s, and average letter sizes of 12 mm/letter and 13 mm/letter. L.H. had a fast writing speed of 17 mm/s and an average letter size of 10 mm/letter.

CONCLUSIONS

The intention of this chapter has been to discuss the concept of "childhood dyslexia," to outline a theory of development of information processing capabilities for reading and spelling that might provide a framework for discussion of dyslexic disorders, and to describe a method of investigation supported by some illustrative data from individual cases. The following general conclusions are proposed:

1. The term "dyslexia" may be applied, without resort to exclusionary criteria, to all children beyond an agreed age (say 7+ years) whose basic reading functions are impaired. Impairment might be operationally defined by means of information processing indicators, such as the statistics of reaction time distributions for reading words and non-words, as well as by the more usual accuracy measures.

2. Childhood dyslexia, like acquired dyslexia, may be analysed into a number of sub-types or syndromes. The developmental sub-types may correspond, at a rather general and qualitative level, to previously identified acquired sub-types.

3. A theoretical interpretation of developmental dyslexic sub-types can be built up on the basis of: (1) a distinction between a primary *source* of disturbance (such as disordered phonemic representation or disordered visual analytic or wholistic processing) and its *effects* on the development of a word recognition and spelling production system; (2) a developmental model which distinguishes overlapping stages for (a) logographic recognition and spelling, (b) alphabetic phoneme-grapheme and grapheme-phoneme associations, (c) orthographic reading, and (d) orthographic spelling; and (3) information processing analyses of the functions involved at each stage. Dyslexia is interpreted as a disruption, due to the source of impairment, arising at entry to a stage or combination of stages. Sub-types constitute descriptions of the effects of the impairment on lexical information processing achievements normally associated with each stage.

4. A useful methodology for analysing developmental sub-types combines: (1) an individual case approach; (2) a psycho-linguistic analysis of reading and spelling performance; and (3) a cognitive experimental analysis, based on reaction time measurement and factorial experimental designs, of reading and writing processes. The key features of this approach consist in the application to *individuals* of cognitive experimental procedures more

usually used with groups of subjects, and in the focus of the investigation on the analysis of the reading and spelling disturbances which are central to the definition of dyslexia. A more detailed account of the application of the procedure to the analysis of reading disorders has been given by Seymour and MacGregor (1984).

Dyslexic Sub-Types

The approach to the definition of dyslexic sub-types that has been adopted has involved the formation of a detailed information processing description of each of a series of individual cases. The objective is to derive theoretically coherent descriptions of individuals. Each of these may stand as a sub-type proposal, although, evidently, wherever descriptions are judged to be sufficiently similar, individuals are liable to be grouped together under the same sub-type heading.

The data reported in summary form in the chapter were intended to contribute to the definition of two broadly-defined contrasting types, corresponding approximately to the distinction between "phonological dyslexia" and "surface dyslexia" in the analysis of acquired types, and between "dysphonetic dyslexia" and "dyseidetic dyslexia" in the analysis of developmental types.

Phonological Dyslexia.   The source of phonological dyslexia was considered to be a disturbance of the phonemic categorising, assembly or associative functions of the phonological processor. This was seen as impairing the development of alphabetic systems of grapheme-phoneme and phoneme-grapheme associations for reading and spelling. The absence of a properly formed alphabetic base then blocks progress to the orthographic levels in reading and spelling. In consequence, reading tends to be preferentially mediated by a logographic-semantic process based on discrimination of features of words which are uncorrelated with phonology. Logographic recognition is not an ideographic process, as distorted words are well read, but is somewhat imprecise, giving rise to visual paralexias, and may focus on word stems, resulting in derivational errors. A slow and inaccurate alphabetic grapheme-phoneme conversion process is used to assist phonological access. A major and defining characteristic is a marked differentiation between word and non-word reading that is reflected in the distributions of vocal reaction times as well as in liability to error. This lexicality effect is also evident in spelling. Non-words will be written less accurately than words, and processing delays may be evident in the time to initiate writing, as well as in the process of production itself. Spelling errors are often phonetically poorly formed, and may include derivational paragraphias and errors giving evidence of partial lexical knowledge. An effect of systematic remedial instruction should be to improve the adequacy of the support provided by the grapheme-phoneme channel, and also of the alphabetic basis of the spelling system.

Morphemic Dyslexia.   The source of this disorder was considered by Seymour and MacGregor to be located in the wholistic function of the visual processor. This was seen as impairing the early development of a logographic lexicon, which may require parallel uptake of salient feature and position information, and the processing of global features, such as word length. The developmental model would then predict normal establishment of an alphabetic system for spelling (phoneme-grapheme correspondences) and a transfer to alphabetic reading (grapheme-phoneme correspondences). Reading will then be preferentially mediated by an alphabetic lexicon, specialised for serial identification of individual graphemes, using a letter-based addressing mode for both phonological and semantic access. Defining characteristics will be serial letter-by-letter reading (indexed by the slope of the regression of reaction time against word length), slow access to semantics, errors in reading irregular words, and a tendency to produce phonetic regularisation errors. It is assumed that orthographic development depends on a capability for processing multi-letter segments as units, and that this development is blocked by the primary impairment of wholistic visual functioning. The result will then be that reading remains alphabetic, and this will, in its turn, block progress to an orthographic level in spelling. Reliance on an alphabetic output lexicon results in spellings that are often well-formed phonetically, although some orthographically illegal letter sequences may occur. Since the alphabetic system is inefficient as an organisation for storage of word specific information (orthographic address modifications), words of lower frequency that are irregular in spelling will tend to be incorrectly written. Some impairment of non-word reading and writing is expected, since an alphabetic system is less efficient than an orthographic system.

The way in which these dyslexias present in individual cases will depend on the exact balance of impairments in the different processing systems, and, doubtless, on such factors as the age of the subject, his general abilities, and the nature and extent of standard or remedial educational input. It is probable that multiple-component developmental dyslexias are possible (see the case of S.E. described by Seymour & MacGregor, 1984). In addition, Seymour and MacGregor (1984) described a subject, R.O., who demonstrated an impairment of analytic visual processing that appeared, in the long run, to be compatible with the development of an orthographic input lexicon, but to have impaired the entry of word specific information in an orthographic output lexicon.

The concept of an *orthographic lexicon* is an important element in the theoretical approach adopted here. Dyslexia has been analysed as a failure to develop an orthographic input lexicon consequent on the presence of primary impairments of phonemic representation or visual processing, and in terms of the consequence of this failure for development of an effective spelling system. The analysis also has implications for models of normal competent reading, especially the proposal in favour of a dual lexicon system for word recognition contained in the processing diagram in Fig. 16.4.

ACKNOWLEDGEMENTS

This research was carried out with the support of a grant from the Medical Research Council of the UK. I am grateful to the subjects for their participation, and to Jane MacGregor and Penny Balfour for their assistance with data collection and analysis.

REFERENCES

Boder, E. (1973) Developmental dyslexia: A diagnostic approach based on three atypical reading-spelling patterns. *Developmental Medicine and Child Neurology, 21*, 504–514.

Bryant, P. E., & Bradley, L. (1980) Why children sometimes write words which they do not read. In U. Frith (Ed.), *Cognitive processes in spelling*. London: Academic Press.

Coltheart, M., Masterson, J., Byng, S., Prior, M., & Riddoch, J. (1983) Surface dyslexia. *Quarterly Journal of Experimental Psychology, 35A*, 469–495.

Frith, U. (1980) Unexpected spelling problems. In U. Frith (Ed.), *Cognitive processes in spelling*. London: Academic Press.

Frith, U. (1985) Beneath the surface of developmental dyslexia. In K. E. Patterson, J. C. Marshall, & M. Coltheart (Eds.), *Surface dyslexia*. London: Lawrence Erlbaum Associates.

Gibson, E. J., Pick, A., Osser, H., & Hammond, M. (1962) The role of grapheme-phoneme correspondence in the perception of words. *American Journal of Psychology, 75*, 554–570.

Henderson, L. (1982) *Orthography and word recognition in reading*. London: Academic Press.

Holmes, J. M. (1978) "Regression" and reading breakdown. In A. Caramazza & E. B. Zurif (Eds.), *Language acquisition and language breakdown; parallels and divergences*. Baltimore: Johns Hopkins Press.

Maccabe, D. (1984) *Phonography: Data and speculations*. Paper presented at meeting of the Experimental Psychology Society, London.

Marsh, C., Friedman, M. I., Welch, V., & Desberg, P. (1981) A cognitive-developmental approach to reading acquisition. In T. Waller & G. E. MacKinnon, (Eds.), *Reading research: Advances in theory and practice (vol. 2)*. New York: Academic Press.

Marshall, J. C., & Newcombe, F. (1973) Patterns of paralexia: A psycholinguistic approach. *Journal of Psycholinguistic Research, 2*, 175–199.

Morton, J., & Patterson, K. E. (1980) A new attempt at an interpretation, or, an attempt at a new interpretation. In M. Coltheart, K. E. Patterson, & J. C. Marshall (Eds.), *Deep dyslexia*. London: Routledge & Kegan Paul.

Rockey, D. (1973) *Phonetic lexicon: Of monosyllabic and some disyllabic words with homophones, arranged according to their phonetic structures*. London: Heyden.

Seymour, P. H. K., & Elder, L. (1986) Beginning reading without phonology. *Cognitive Neuropsychology, 3*, 1–36.

Seymour, P. H. K., & MacGregor, C. J. (1984) Developmental dyslexia: A cognitive experimental analysis of phonological, morphemic and visual impairments. *Cognitive Neuropsychology, 1,* 43–82.

Shallice, T. (1981) Neurological impairment of cognitive processes. *British Medical Bulletin, 27,* 187–192.

Taft, M. (1979) Lexical access via an orthographic code: The Basic Orthographic Syllabic Structure (BOSS). *Journal of Verbal Learning and Verbal Behaviour, 18,* 21–39.

Temple, C., & Marshall, J. C. (1983) A case study of developmental phonological dyslexia. *British Journal of Psychology, 74,* 517–533.

17 Intimations of Modularity, or, the Modelarity of Mind: Doing Cognitive Neuropsychology Without Syndromes

Andrew W. Ellis
Department of Psychology, University of Lancaster, Lancaster LA1 4 YF, England

Present-day interest in cognitive neuropsychology is perhaps best regarded as the renaissance of an approach to the mind and brain that had an earlier flowering from about 1870 to 1910 and that included among its exponents such names as Wernicke, Bastian, Lichtheim, Dejerine, Liepmann and, for a time, a certain Sigmund Freud. To be sure, there are important differences between the old and the new cognitive neuropsychology, most notably in the growing acceptance of the logical independence and complementarity of psychological and physiological levels of explanation of the structure and behaviour of that complex system that is the mind and brain (Clark, 1980; Marr, 1982; Mehler, Morton, & Jusczyk, 1984; Oatley, 1978). I write this chapter, however, in the knowledge that what has vanished once can disappear again. In particular, I wish to draw attention to certain trends that I think could bring about the second demise of cognitive neuropsychology if allowed to continue unchecked. What follows is a personal view. I do not expect everyone engaged in the field to agree with everything I say, but I believe that a calm airing of the issues can only be of benefit in the long term.

THE DIAGRAM MAKERS STRIKE BACK

I shall begin by inviting the reader to inspect briefly Fig. 17.1. Doubtless many readers will dismiss it at a glance as just another Gothic outpouring of a cognitive psychologist's fevered imagination. They would be wrong to do so, however, because Fig. 17.1 is the diagram used by Dennis Klatt (1979) to illustrate his successful *working* computer simulation of auditory word (and

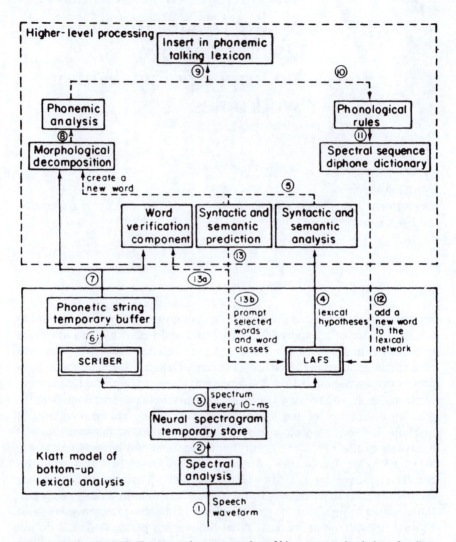

FIG. 17.1   Klatt's (1979) diagrammatic representation of his computer simulation of auditory word recognition.

non-word) recognition. Klatt's system lends itself to diagrammatic representation because it is *modular* in design; that is, it is built up from many separate but interconnected sub-systems. Each of the boxes represents a different sub-system or module with a different role to play in the total architecture; arrows represent the flow of information between modules.

Marr (1976; 1982) argued that as *any* system becomes more complex it will tend to evolve towards a modular design. A major advantage of modularity noted by Marr is that it is possible to improve a particular module without needing to redesign the entire system as long as the revamped module accepts the same input and gives the same output as the old one (N.B. if the inputs or outputs do change then some lexical local alterations of adjacent modules will also be needed, but more distant ones will still not require attention). To the advantages that Marr listed we may add the observation that with a modular system it is easier to create new modules and interface them onto pre-existing ones. Only a tiny minority of humans have ever learned to read and write with an alphabetic script, but becoming literate appears to establish within the brain cognitive modules that behave just like those that are either given genetically or developed early in life, in that they can be selectively impaired by brain injury to produce a wide variety of different forms of reading and writing disorder (Coltheart, 1981; Ellis, 1982, 1984a; Patterson, 1981).

Arguments for the modularity of the mind and brain are greatly strengthened by the array of different selective impairments documented by cognitive neuropsychologists (Ellis & Young, in preparation), but modularity can also be argued for with reference to experimental data from normal subjects. Thus Allport (1980a, b) makes a case for regarding the mind as a composite of independent processing components, arguing from the results of so-called "dual task" experiments. If normal subjects can simultaneously perform two complex demanding tasks without detriment to either then, Allport argues, the two tasks must be subserved by distinct and separate sets of cognitive modules (see also Fodor, 1983; Schwartz & Schwartz, 1984).

Wherever modular systems are used—whether in hi-fis, chemical processing plants, or minds—diagrams are a popular illustrative device. With a diagram one can simultaneously display all the separate components and their interconnections, and one can also work out more easily the consequences of damage to a component or to an element (Morton, 1981). For this reason diagrams have always been popular among cognitive neuropsychologists of whatever generation. For them the mind shows modelarity as well as modularity. That said, there is nothing in a diagram that could not also be expressed in words. A diagram is simply a device for imaging a theory. It may have certain advantages over verbal exposition, but it may also have its disadvantages. It is perhaps too easy to draw a rectangle, label it "grapheme-phoneme conversion," "semantic system," or whatever, and think that in so doing one has actually explained something. When an electronic engineer draws a box labelled "graphic equaliser" that is just a shorthand notation for a component whose internal workings can readily be described and explained. One of the problems for the 19th-century diagram makers was that they had few ideas about how their postulated "centres" (modules) might work (Marshall, 1974). If cognitive neuropsychology is to remain viable this time around, its exponents must show the same willingness to unpack the contents of the boxes as they now show in elucidating the overall cognitive architecture. This volume comtains numerous examples of such unpacking—for example, in the chapter by Bub, Black, Howell, and Kertesz, the box often labelled "grapheme-phoneme conversion" is described as consisting of several subcomponents such as a graphemic parser, a set of correspondence rules, and a phoneme assembler.

SYNDROMES OR SYMPTOMS?

It is possible for the components of a system that is modular at one level of description to be inextricably intermingled in their physical realisation. However, as Shallice (1981) noted, cognitive neuropsychology is only viable if modules that are distinct cognitively are also spatially separated in the brain. Only that way can local damage to the brain selectively impair cognitive modules (cf. Lashley's, 1941, remark that, "The discovery that the various capacities which independently contribute to intellectual performance correspond to the spatial distribution of cerebral mechanisms represents a step toward the recognition of similar organisation in neurological and mental events").

Modules can malfunction as a result of brain injury such as a stroke or missile wound, or possibly through developmental misfortune. We must acknowledge, however, that such injuries are unlikely to be respectors of the theories or diagrams of cognitive neuropsychologists. It will be a rare injury indeed that impairs only one module leaving the rest intact and functioning normally. Cognitive neuropsychologists *could* decide to base a new set of "syndromes" on the modules of a best-bet model of the functional architecture. A putative syndrome would be identified when a patients' symptoms seemed explicable in terms of impairment to one module alone. This approach might create a new, theoretically motivated set of syndrome categories that could, in principle, overcome some of the current dissatisfaction with traditional neurological categories (see Caramazza, 1984; Coltheart, 1984; Marshall, 1982; Saffran, 1984). I would argue, however, that such a research program is neither necessary nor wise: indeed, I think it would be a recipe for disaster.[1]

---

[1]Should this attempt to scupper syndrome-based cognitive neuropsychology fail, let me at least try to reverse a recent trend in the *naming* of syndromes. It is becoming a widespread practice to name a new "syndrome" after the module thought to be impaired. To pick but one example out of the hat, Warrington and Shallice (1980) believe that patients who read in a letter-by-letter manner, naming each letter of a word before identifying it, have suffered impairment to the system for identifying familiar words as wholes. Warrington and Shallice call that system the "word-form system" and so dub the syndrome "word-form dyslexia."

As Shallice (1979a) observed, cognitive neuropsychology is "inherently progressive." A syndrome thought at time t to be due to damage to a single, unitary module is bound to have fractionated by time $t+2$ years into a host of awkward subtypes. Further, although modularity is a banner that many cognitive neuropsychologists are happy to congregate beneath, we would be deluding ourselves if we thought that any *actual* set of modules we were to propose today might bear anything more than a passing resemblance to the ultimate "true" set (assuming they are discoverable). Klatt (1979) could provide a complete diagram for his system because he designed it. We are as yet a long way from being able to provide an equally complete account of the cognitive system bestowed upon us by millions of years of evolution.

If cognitive neuropsychologists elect to adopt a revamped syndrome-based approach they must anticipate that the set of recognised syndromes will inevitably be prone to multiply and change at an alarming rate. We can already see this happening around us in areas where syndromes have been sought. Among the acquired dyslexias, the "syndrome" of "surface dyslexia" is dissolving before our eyes (Patterson, Marshall, & Coltheart, 1985). The same is happening to phonological dyslexia (Bub et al., this volume); Broca's aphasia (Berndt, this volume); Wernicke's aphasia (Ellis, Miller, & Sin, 1983); and promises to happen to amnesia (Moscovitch, 1982; Squire, 1982). In such a kaleidoscopic world textbooks will be hard to write and will have half-lives measurable in months rather than years once they do appear. Anyone not constantly reading and researching within the field will find it impossible to keep up with the shifts of fashion, and we will be in danger of

---

There are several reasons for thinking that this naming procedure might be misguided. First of all, even if a theorist's model is broadly correct, a particular syndrome may be misconstrued within it. Normally this would be no particular problem and the error could be rectified by new data, but if the original misconstrual has been incorporated into a syndrome label which has caught on and been widely adopted, then we are in trouble. For example, Patterson and Kay (1982) gave an alternative explanation of letter-by-letter reading in terms of some sort of reduction in channel capacity of the visual system prior to the word-form system. Should this, or indeed *any* other proposal prove superior to Warrington and Shallice's, then "word-form dyslexia" will be utterly unsuitable as a label. Secondly, it is a fact that a theoretical concept in modern-day cognitive psychology does well if it lasts 10 years without seeming either quaint or ridiculous. There is nothing inherently wrong with that fact, which could even be interpreted as indicating the vigour and rapid progress of the subject. Warrington and Shallice's "word-form system" will have acquitted itself more than creditably if it is still being found useful by theorists (including its originators) in the mid-1990s. But it is in the nature of a progressing scientific approach that its constructs are sooner or later superseded and replaced by newer and (hopefully) better ones. Syndrome labels like "transcortical motor aphasia," "apperceptive agnosia," and "ideational apraxia" illustrate what happens when temporary, evolving theoretical concepts get incorporated into semi-permanent syndrome labels: they create living fossils, relics of a bygone era that only serve to confuse and deter those coming new to the subject. Do we *really* want to be responsible for a new generation of such terms?

losing the sympathy and support of those upon whose co-operation we depend (neurologists, clinical psychologists, speech therapists, and so on).

Further, as single-module syndromes multiply and fractionate, pure cases of each sub-type will become progressively harder to find. The vast majority of patients will not fit into a single syndrome category (though they should, in principle, be explicable as combinations of the deficits of the theoretically pure types). The cognitive neuropsychologist will pass over 999 patients to find the one thousandth who comes close to being a pure case of "word meaning deafness" or whatever[2] (surely another source of antagonism to speech therapists and others), and the temptation will become ever stronger to report impure cases as approximations to the Platonic ideal. That, I would submit, is a prospect to be avoided at all costs. And it *can* be avoided.

DOING COGNITIVE NEUROPSYCHOLOGY WITHOUT SYNDROMES

We can characterise the research program adopted in much of present-day cognitive neuropsychology as follows:

Step One: Study a patient (or set of patients) in order to give as precise a description as possible of their symptoms.

Step Two: Assign the patient(s) to a syndrome category on the basis of the symptoms discovered in Step One.

Step Three: Try to explain the *syndrome* in terms of impairment to one or more of the components of a theory of normal cognitive functioning.

Step Two is where all (or many) of cognitive neuropsychology's problems lie, yet I believe that the solution is both simple and straightforward—do away with it!

Strokes, tumours, missile wounds, and the like are essentially experiments, albeit sad, crude and regrettable ones, performed upon the structure and functions of the mind and brain.[3] Good case studies collate and analyse the

---

[2]"Word meaning deafness" is a particularly suitable example here, since it is a Platonic "syndrome" of considerable potential theoretical importance for which a clear prototypical case has *never* been reported (see Ellis, 1984b).

[3]Many, though by no means all, neuropsychological cases resemble those "dual task" experiments in which a normal subject is given a subsidiary task designed to occupy certain cognitive components while the rest of his or her cognitive system tries to carry out the primary task. In a patient the lesion may have taken some components out of operation, leaving the remainder to perform the cognitive tasks demanded of the patient by everyday life or a psychologist. Note that only a modular architecture permits some components to continue to perform normally when others may have been totally eliminated. There can be no argument with the fact of modularity, only about its nature and extent.

results of such experiments. From there the *cognitive* neuropsychologist is free to do just what he or she would do when presented with the results of a laboratory experiment, which is to pass immediately to the level of cognitive theory, that is, to ask "Is this pattern of data (deficits *and* intact skills) interpretable within the framework provided by existing theories, or are modifications called for?"

Let us briefly consider a few examples. Patient K.F. of Shallice and Warrington (1970) showed normal long-term memory function but was impaired on tasks thought to tap verbal short-term memory (though unimpaired on tests of nonverbal short-term memory). This pattern *alone* is sufficient to cause a reconsideration of the nature of short-term memory and its relationship to long-term memory (Shallice, 1979b). Patients like R.G. of Beauvois and Derouesné (1979), A.M. of Patterson (1982), and W.B. of Funnell (1983) are very poor at reading unfamiliar words and invented non-words but relatively good at reading familiar real words. This pattern is *sufficient* to disprove any theory that asserts that the identification of familiar written words necessarily involves an early stage in which the spoken form of the word is assembled piecemeal from its written form by the application of sublexical grapheme-phoneme conversion rules. The speech of patients like K.C. of Butterworth (1979), J.S. of Caramazza, Berndt, and Basili (1983), and R.D. of Ellis, Miller, and Sin (1983; Miller & Ellis, this volume) is littered with "target-related neologisms"—recognisable but incorrect attempts at particular words. The occurrence of such neologisms implies that retrieval of the phonological forms of words from the internal speech output lexicon is not all-or-nothing but can show states of partial retrieval or activation. Patients E.B. of Levine, Calvanio, and Popovics (1982), and M.H. of Bub and Kertesz (1982) could write correctly words that they could not even begin to say and whose phonological forms they seemed to have no access to at all. This implies that availability of the phonological forms of words is not a necessary prerequisite of being able to spell them. Patient T.M. (Howard, this volume) could read a fair proportion of words even though his ability to assign abstract identities to letters (as indexed by cross case matching tasks) was virtually absent. Having demonstrated this, Howard's next step was not to define the syndrome represented by these novel observations, but instead to proceed immediately to a consideration of the implications of T.M.'s performance for current models of visual word recognition.

And that is all that matters. Questions as to whether R.G., A.M., and W.B. fit into one category called "phonological dyslexia," or whether K.C., J.S., and R.D. are Wernicke's aphasics, neologistic jargonaphasics, cases of pure word deafness or whatever, or what to call T.M.'s new syndrome, are (or should be) complete and utter irrelevancies to the *cognitive* neuropsychologist. It is similarly a waste of time and energy asking how M.H. (Bub & Kertesz, 1982) should be classified. All that matters is the compatibility or otherwise between symptoms patterns and cognitive theories; whether theory

A satisfactorily explains the symptoms of patient X.Y. or must yield to those symptoms.

One can, of course, see why syndrome thinking held such an appeal for a while. If valid, it offered the promise of considerable potential simplification of explanation. Instead of having to explain (and remember) separately the symptoms of large numbers of patients we might have got away with explaining and remembering just a few syndromes. This seductive program has not, however, delivered the goods. It has *not* proved possible to give a unified account of *any* of the putative syndromes thus far identified. Wernicke's aphasia, Broca's aphasia, surface dyslexia, deep dyslexia, amnesia ... all have proved heterogeneous rather than homogeneous. In every case theorists wishing to hold onto the essence of syndromes have been forced to postulate subtypes in the hope that they will prove homogeneous when the parent category didn't. They won't.

Not all research avenues live up to their initial promise. The art lies in spotting early on when an avenue isn't leading anywhere. If you are going nowhere, all you can do is retreat, remembering to take with you such useful snippets of information as you may have gathered en route. In the case of the syndrome cul-de-sac, those snippets are the valuable details of individual patients that have emerged from the many excellent case studies conducted during the past decade.

Grouping patients into classes may, for all I know, be useful for other people with other aims. A neurologist may be able to classify patients in ways that predict lesion sites (cf. Poeck, 1983), or a speech therapist may be able to group patients in terms of their responsiveness to different therapeutic regimes. All well and good, but the cognitive neuropsychologist needs only patients and theories (and rules for bridging between the two).

Cognitive neuropsychologists must learn (or relearn) to *treat single patients like single experiments*. Rather than saying "Syndrome X implies Z," we must say "Patient X.Y. of Smith and Jones (1990) implies Z," just as we would say "Experiment 2 of Smith and Jones implies Z." It may be that in everyday conversation we might want to summarise a patient as an "anomic" or a "deep dyslexic," just as we might refer to an experiment as a "semantic priming experiment" or a "concurrent vocalisation experiment," but such talk must never be more than a loose, if expedient, shorthand. Our public theoretical pronouncements must always be from particular patients to theories and vice-versa.

Where syndrome thinking has already crept into cognitive neuropsychology, as in the unhappy taxonomies of the acquired dyslexias, then it should be allowed to quietly creep out again. The way to a progressive, cumulative, *cognitive* neuropsychology lies in a two-step methodology:

Step One: Study a patient in order to give as precise a description as possible of that patient's symptoms. (This should include an analysis of preserved as well as impaired abilities.)

Step Two: Treat the results of the case study as one would the results of a laboratory experiment, evaluating the implications of the results obtained for theoretical understanding of the cognitive domain under investigation.

Note that I am most emphatically *not* advocating a return to the bad old days of comparing twenty "aphasics" with twenty "controls." The individual patient remains the unit of investigation. Indeed, by advocating the elimination of the syndrome level of analysis I am assigning *more* power to the case study. Those patients with relatively pure, circumscribed deficits who would most have interested the syndrome-oriented researcher are still likely to be especially worthy of scrutiny in a non-syndromic(?) cognitive neuropsychology. However, patients with mixed, unclassifiable symptoms may also yield valuable insights, patient M.H. of Bub and Kertesz (1982) being a good example, and also patients G.A. (Patterson, this volume) and Michel (Kremin, this volume).

Let all the recent hoo-ha over how to define "surface dyslexia," "Wernicke's aphasia," "prosopagnosia," and the like slip into history. We don't need it. The effect of ceasing to try to force square pegs into round holes should be exhilarating.

AGAINST COGNITIVE NEUROPSYCHOLOGY

Having argued against a syndrome-centred approach to cognitive neuropsychology I should like to close by arguing against cognitive neuropsychology *per se*; or, more exactly, by arguing against any tendency for cognitive neuropsychology to become a distinct sub-discipline within psychology. While cognitive neuropsychologists should be actively engaged in trying to fractionate the mind into components and elucidate the nature of the intercommunications between them, psychology itself is already fractionated into too many specialisms, communication between which ranges from sparse to non-existent. The last thing psychology needs is yet another set of specialists speaking their own language and communicating only in their own private journals and at their own select conferences.

Cognitive neuropsychology, like all scientific approaches, has its own strengths and its own weaknesses (Caramazza, 1984; Saffran, 1982; Shallice, 1979a). One weakness which threatens the program I have just outlined is the impossibility of replicating a case study. In contrast, one of the attractions of syndromes has obviously been the fact that if patients did come in neat, homogeneous syndrome packages then it should have been possible to replicate and extend results from one exemplar of the category on another. It is now apparent that this ambition, though laudable, was misguided. Patients do *not* fall into syndrome categories and it is no use pretending any longer that they do. It seems to me that opportunities for anything like substantive replication in cognitive neuropsychology will always be severely limited, a fact which makes it all the more vital that cognitive neuropsychologists should heed Shallice's (1979a) advice and replicate crucial findings on more than one occasion with the *same* patient. If we are to regard case studies as analogous to experiments as I propose, then we should do what we can to conduct those studies with the same rigour we expect of a standard laboratory experiment (and that includes showing that the effects we intend to build upon are statistically significant and reliable).

Cognitive neuropsychology has both weaknesses and strengths. So has experimental psychology. The point is that they are in large measure *different* strengths and *different* weaknesses. Psychologists should be looking wherever possible for theoretical conclusions supported by converging evidence from different sources, experimental *and* neuropsychological. Sometimes this may not be possible: some questions may only be answerable by a particular constellation of neuropsychological symptoms, others only by a particular experimental manipulation with normal subjects. However, a model of the mind that evolves in response to data from multiple sources will be far more trustworthy than one erected on the fallible foundations of a single approach (cf. Garner, Hake & Eriksen, 1956).

Much of the vigour of cognitive neuropsychology over the past decade is attributable to the incursion into the field of experimental psychologists conversant with findings and theories derived from work on normals. Many have tried to keep at least a toe in that camp. This seems to be a highly desirable state of affairs. If cognitive neuropsychologists ever lose track of developments in experimental psychology, if they ever stop taking every opportunity to bring their findings to the attention of researchers working elsewhere in the behavioural and brain sciences, then the field will become in-bred and its hybrid vigour will be lost.

Cognitive neuropsychology stands at the intersection of many different disciplines—that is what makes it so exciting and so important. It must avoid the temptation to become a discipline in its own right. By drawing on, and feeding into cognitive psychology, linguistics, clinical medicine, philosophy, physiology, and other cognate disciplines, cognitive neuropsychology will gain the maximum benefit, make the maximum impact, and possibly—just possibly—outlive its current set of practitioners.

ACKNOWLEDGEMENTS

This paper is based on an earlier version presented and discussed at the Venice conference. I should like to thank my fellow participants for many comments that helped shape this final version (though I am sure they will still find much to disagree with), and Max Coltheart for helpful comments on an earlier draft. The preparation of this paper was assisted by grant number G8305511N from the Medical Research Council, and by a grant from the University of Lancaster Research Fund.

REFERENCES

Allport, D. A. (1980a) Patterns and actions: Cognitive mechanisms are content-specific. In G. Claxton (Ed.), *Cognitive psychology: New directions*. London: Routledge & Kegan Paul.

Allport, D. A. (1980b) Attention and performance. In G. Glaxton (Ed.), *Cognitive psychology: New directions*. London: Routledge & Kegan Paul.

Beauvois, M. F., & Derouesné, J. (1979) Phonological alexia: Three dissociations. *Journal of Neurology, Neurosurgery and Psychiatry, 42*, 1115–1124.

Bub, D., & Kertesz, A. (1982) Evidence for lexicographic processing in a patient with preserved written over oral single word naming. *Brain, 105*, 697–717.

Butterworth, B. (1979) Hesitations and the production of verbal paraphasias and neologisms in jargon aphasia. *Brain and Language, 8*, 133–161.

Caramazza, A. (1984) The logic of neuropsychological research and the problem of patient classification in aphasia. *Brain and Language, 21*, 9–20.

Caramazza, A., Berndt, R. S., & Basili, A. G. (1983) The selective impairment of phonological processing: A case study. *Brain and Language, 18*, 128–174.

Clark, A. (1980) *Psychological models and neural mechanisms*. Oxford: Clarendon Press.

Coltheart, M. (1981) Disorders of reading and their implications for models of normal reading. *Visible Language, 15*, 245–286.

Coltheart, M. (1984) Acquired dyslexias and normal reading. In R. N. Malatesha & H. A. Whitaker (Eds.), *Dyslexia: A global issue*. The Hague: Martinus Nijhoff.

Ellis, A. W. (1982) Spelling and writing (and reading and speaking). In A. W. Ellis (Ed.), *Normality and pathology in cognitive functions*. London: Academic Press.

Ellis, A. W. (1984a) *Reading, writing and dyslexia: A cognitive analysis*. London: Lawrence Erlbaum Associates.

Ellis, A. W. (1984b) Introduction to Bramwell's (1897) case of "word meaning deafness." *Cognitive Neuropsychology, 1*, 245–258.

Ellis, A. W., Miller, D., & Sin, G. (1983) Wernicke's aphasia and normal language processing: A case study in cognitive neuropsychology. *Cognition, 15*, 111–144.

Ellis, A. W., & Young, A. W. (in preparation) *Human cognitive neuropsychology*. London: Lawrence Erlbaum Associates.

Fodor, J. A. (1983) *The modularity of mind*. Cambridge, Mass.: MIT Press.

Funnell, E. (1983) Phonological processes in reading: New evidence from acquired dyslexia. *British Journal of Psychology, 74*, 159–180.

Garner, W. R., Hake, H. W., & Eriksen, C. W. (1956) Operationalism and the concept of perception. *Psychological Review, 63*, 149–159.

Klatt, D. H. (1979) Speech perception: A model of acoustic-phonetic analysis and lexical access. *Journal of Phonetics, 7*, 279–312.

Lashley, K. S. (1941) Coalescence of neurology and psychology. *Proceedings of the American Philosophical Society, 84*, 461–470.

Levine, D. N., Calvanio, R., & Popovics, A. (1982) Language in the absence of inner speech. *Neuropsychologia, 20*, 391–409.

Marr, D. (1976) Early processing of visual information. *Philosophical Transactions of the Royal Society of London, B, 275*, 483–524.

Marr, D. (1982) *Vision.* San Francisco: W. H. Freeman.

Marshall, J. C. (1974) Freud's psychology of language. In R. Wollheim (Ed.), *Freud: A collection of critical essays.* New York: Anchor Books.

Marshall, J. C. (1982) What is a symptom-complex? In M. Arbib, D. Caplan, & J. C. Marshall (Eds.), *Neural models of language processes.* New York: Academic Press.

Mehler, J., Morton, J., & Jusczyk, P. (1984) On reducing language to biology. *Cognitive Neuropsychology, 1*, 83–116.

Morton, J. (1981) The status of information processing models of language. *Philosophical Transactions of the Royal Society of London B, 295*, 387–396. (Also published as H. C. Longuet-Higgins, J. Lyons, & D. E. Broadbent (Eds.), *The psychological mechanisms of language.* London: The Royal Society and the British Academy, 1981.)

Moscovitch, M. (1982) Multiple dissociations of function in amnesia. In L. S. Cermak (Ed.), *Human memory and amnesia.* Hillsdale, N.J.: Lawrence Erlbaum Associates.

Oatley, K. (1978) *Perceptions and representations: The theoretical bases of brain research and psychology.* London: Methuen.

Patterson, K. E. (1981) Neuropsychological approaches to the study of reading. *British Journal of Psychology, 72*, 151–174.

Patterson, K. E. (1982) The relation between reading and phonological coding: Further neuropsychological observations. In A. W. Ellis (Ed.), *Normality and pathology in cognitive functions.* London: Academic Press.

Patterson, K. E., Marshall, J. C., & Coltheart, M. (Eds.) (1985) *Surface dyslexia.* London: Lawrence Erlbaum Associates.

Poeck, K. (1983) What do we mean by "aphasic syndromes?": A neurologist's view. *Brain and Language, 20*, 79–89.

Saffran, E. M. (1982) Neuropsychological approaches to the study of language. *British Journal of Psychology, 73*, 317–337.

Saffran, E. M. (1984) What the classical aphasia categories can't do for us, and why. *Brain and Language, 21*, 3–8.

Schwartz, M. F., & Schwartz, B. (1984) In defence of organology. *Cognitive Neuropsychology, 1*, 25–42.

Shallice, T. (1979a) Case study approach in neuropsychological research. *Journal of Clinical Neuropsychology, 1*, 183–211.

Shallice, T. (1979b) Neuropsychological research and the fractionation of memory systems. In L. G. Nilsson (Ed.), *Perspectives on memory research.* Hillsdale, N.J.: Lawrence Erlbaum Associates.

Shallice, T. (1981) Neurological impairment of cognitive processes. *British Medical Bulletin, 37*, 187–192.

Shallice, T., & Warrington, E. K. (1970) Independent functioning of verbal memory stores: A neuropsychological study. *Quarterly Journal of Experimental Psychology, 22*, 261–273.

Squire, L. R. (1982) The neuropsychology of human memory. *Annual Review of Neuroscience, 5*, 241–273.

Warrington, E. K., & Shallice, T. (1980) Word-form dyslexia. *Brain, 30*, 99–112.

Author Index

Subject Index